HIDE, WOOD, AND WILLOW

THE CIVILIZATION OF THE AMERICAN INDIAN SERIES

HIDE WOOD *and* WILLOW

CRADLES OF THE GREAT PLAINS INDIANS

Deanna Tidwell Broughton

UNIVERSITY OF OKLAHOMA PRESS : NORMAN

Publication of this book is made possible through the generosity of Edith Kinney Gaylord.

Library of Congress Cataloging-in-Publication Data

Names: Broughton, Deanna Tidwell, author.
Title: Hide, wood, and willow : cradles of the Great Plains Indians / Deanna Tidwell Broughton.
Other titles: Civilization of the American Indian series ; v. 278.
Description: Norman : University of Oklahoma Press, [2019] | Series: Civilization of the American Indian series ; volume 278 | Includes bibliographical references.
Identifiers: LCCN 2018036255 | ISBN 978-0-8061-6227-0 (hardcover : alk. paper)
Subjects: LCSH: Cradleboards—Great Plains. | Indian infants—Care—Great Plains. | Indians of North America—Great Plains—Social life and customs.
Classification: LCC E78.G73 B697 2019 | DDC 978.004/97—dc23
LC record available at https://lccn.loc.gov/2018036255

Hide, Wood, and Willow: Cradles of the Great Plains Indians is Volume 278 in The Civilization of the American Indian Series.

The paper in this book meets the guidelines for permanence and durability of the Committee on Production Guidelines for Book Longevity of the Council on Library Resources, Inc. ∞

1 2 3 4 5 6 7 8 9 10

To Joe, my husband of fifty-seven years,
and to Molinda Jean Barker Good,
Mary and Quintus Herron, Mark Awakuni-Swetland,
and John Sipe Jr. and his family

CONTENTS

List of Illustrations **ix**

Preface **xi**

Acknowledgments **xiii**

Introduction **3**

PART ONE CRADLES ON THE GREAT PLAINS AND THE WOMEN WHO USED THEM **9**

"A Cradle for This Child," by N. Scott Momaday **10**

1. The Woman's Place **11**
2. Plains Cradles **21**

PART TWO NORTHEASTERN CRADLEBOARDS **25**

3. Santee Dakota **27**
4. Yankton and Yanktonai **37**
5. Ioway **41**
6. Plains Cree **44**
7. Plains Ojibwa **50**

PART THREE PRAIRIE CRADLEBOARDS **57**

8. Otoe-Missouria **59**
9. Osage **62**
10. Kaw **69**
11. Omaha **73**
12. Ponca **79**
13. Pawnee **82**

PART FOUR NORTHERN PLAINS FLAT BOARDS **89**

14. Crow **91**
15. Blackfoot **97**

PART FIVE HURDLE CRADLES **105**

16. Arapaho **107**
17. Wichita **119**
18. Lipan Apache **124**

PART SIX LATTICE FRAMES AND SOFT HOODS **129**
"Pahn-t ope" (Cradle), by Ray C. Doyah **130**
19. Comanche **131**
20. Kiowa **139**
21. Apache Tribe of Oklahoma **163**
22. Cheyenne **167**
23. Tonkawa **178**
24. Lakota **181**
25. Assiniboine **192**

PART SEVEN HIDE BABY BAGS, SWINGS, AND HAMMOCKS **195**
26. Hidatsa **197**
27. Mandan **200**
28. Arikara **202**
29. Gros Ventre **205**
30. Sarcee **209**
31. Stoney **212**
32. Plains Métis **214**
33. Quapaw **217**

Conclusion: Leather Shall Breathe and Wood Shall Sing Again **219**

Appendix A. Tribes Historically on the Plains **223**
Appendix B. Plains Indian Terms for Cradles **224**
Appendix C. List of Museums **226**

Notes **231**

Glossary **245**

Bibliography **249**

ILLUSTRATIONS

FIGURES

Plains woman with dog travois 11
Santee Dakota cradleboard 35
Dakota (Yankton) baby in cradleboard 38
Sioux (Yanktonai) soft cradle 39
Plains Cree family with child in cradleboard 44
Ojibwa (Chippewa) cradleboard 53
Osage child LeeAnn Yarbrough on cradleboard 63
Osage cradleboard 67
Three Kaw cradleboards 70
Ponca woman with child in cradleboard 79
Pawnee family with child in cradleboard 82
Crow cradleboard 96
Blood woman holding cradleboard 97
Blackfoot cradleboard 103
Three Northern Arapaho cradles 107
Northern Arapaho cradleboard and detail 117
Wichita baby in a cradle 119
Wichita cradleboard 121
Lipan Apache cradleboard 126
Two Comanche boys in cradleboards 131
Comanche skin bed (night cradle) 136
Comanche cradleboard 138
Ray Doyah with grandchild in cradleboard 140
Kiowa beaded cradleboard 144
Emma Walters, Cheyenne, with baby on cradleboard 167
Cheyenne soft cradle 175
Oglála lattice cradle 190
Hidatsa baby swing used as cradle 198
Sarcee baby Elsie Bull in moss bag 209
Stoney mother with child in moss bag 212

PLATES

1. Santee Dakota cradleboard **147**
2. Dakota baby cradle **148**
3. Eastern Cree cradleboard **148**
4. Plains Cree moss bag **149**
5. Sioux (Yanktonai) soft cradle **149**
6. Plains Ojibwa cradleboard **150**
7. Ioway cradleboard **150**
8. Otoe grandmother, Hilda Harris, with baby in cradleboard **151**
9. Osage carved, painted panel **151**
10. Omaha cradleboard **152**
11. Kaw prairie cradleboard **152**
12. Pawnee cradleboard **153**
13. Blackfeet carrier **154**
14. Crow babies in beaded cradleboards **154**
15. Arapaho cradleboard **155**
16. Arapaho soft hood **155**
17. Wichita cradleboard **156**
18. Northern Cheyenne cradleboard **156**
19. Cheyenne beaded soft hood cradle **157**
20. Kiowa cradleboard **157**
21. Comanche hide cradleboard and beaded cradleboard **158**
22. Lakota soft cradle **159**
23. Oglála lattice cradleboard **159**
24. Tonkawa beaded baby canopy **160**
25. Assiniboine cradleboard **160**
26. Sarcee baby wrapper **161**
27. Sahnish (Arikara) baby carrier **161**
28. Plains Métis moss bag **162**

PREFACE

Hide, Wood, and Willow: Cradles of the Great Plains Indians is a reference book of American Indian baby carriers, including their forms and function. One of the main events among the tribes that hunted buffalo on the plains was the birth of a child, and the cradles they made and used reflected both the importance of children and the varied customs surrounding their birth and first years of life.

I am not a historian, an anthropologist, or an ethnologist. I write this book as a retired educator, an enrolled member of the Oklahoma Cherokee Nation, and a sister, wife, mother, grandmother, and great-grandmother. My husband, Joe, and I have two fine sons, Andy and Dusty, and five wonderful granddaughters, Amanda, Ashley, Tera, Samantha, and Brianna; two grandsons, Razvan and Liam; and five great-grandchildren, Ryder, Dylan, Isla, Daphne, and Genevieve. We live near the small community of Spruce Pine, North Carolina.

This book began with my interest in American Indian cradles, which in turn led me to sculpt my own miniature cradles. On retirement from education, my thoughts turned to children, and I began sculpting Native cradles and the babies they held. To make the cradles as authentic as possible, I started researching cradle construction, materials, color, and details. I collected photographs of cradles and of American Indian babies. I went on fact-finding jaunts to storage areas and small out-of-the-way museums, including six wonderful weeks spent in the depths of the anthropology archives of the Smithsonian National Museum of Natural History in Suitland, Maryland, through a grant from the Smithsonian Institution. Because of the time I spent there, the idea crystallized to compile a resource book on cradles.

I examined actual baby carriers, read about them in literature, read oral histories of people who actually made or used cradles, and interviewed people who reproduce them. I met people with their own passions for cradles, including people still making them today, many of which are sold in the tourist trade. For example, Vanessa Paukeigope Jennings, in Oklahoma, makes Kiowa cradleboards for her family and for museums. She has dedicated her life to continuing the artistic traditions of her cradle-making family.

After my successful art show at Red Earth in June 2003, my cousin Jean Good and I hurriedly planned a trip to Cody, Wyoming. In three weeks, we sorted the accumulated information in seven plastic file boxes and developed a plan for a book. *A* for Arapaho was a good place to start. So I dictated, and Jeannie typed. The next morning, we pored over the map to find Browning, Montana. We had heard that a museum there had a Blackfoot cradleboard. But we did not make it to Montana that year. We were called home because of my mother's health.

Two weeks after I arrived home, I had a stroke. Not long after the first, on July 17, 2003, I had a massive stroke. As a result, I now have partial hearing as well as aphasia, which is a total or partial loss of the ability to use or understand words. My speech therapist, Julie Owens Norris (who, by the way, was a student in my fourth-grade classroom at Franklin Elementary School in Ardmore, Oklahoma), helped me to work up from simple words to simple sentences, to a paragraph, and finally to a page. She encouraged me to begin working on my book again. Although the stroke was severe and caused some damage, with the encouragement and prayers of many people, including my husband, other family members, doctors, therapist, and friends, I began to walk in the world again. The book became a journey back to who I was. My passion for cradles has endured.

My fascination with the beauty of cradles led me to explore who created the cradles and how. Rather than simply describing the cradle, I include birth customs, such as the amulet; how to distinguish the sex of a baby based on the type of cradle used; and the symbolism associated with particular cradles. I have attempted to compile in a straightforward way all the information I have gathered. The resulting book is a collection of ethnological, historical, and anthropological studies of Plains Indian birth customs and cradles, carriers, and cradleboards.

ACKNOWLEDGMENTS

This book would not have been possible without the research of other scholars and the expertise of many friends. A book like this is a patchwork of knowledge and life experiences, firsthand accounts from years ago, documents, and many books. I would like to thank the following people and institutions for their assistance in the research and production of this volume. I recognize the wonderful help I have received from staffs in obtaining records and photographs at the Smithsonian National Anthropological Archives, National Museum of the American Indian, and National Museum of Natural History; the American Museum of Natural History; the North Dakota Heritage Center and State Museum; the Buffalo Bill Center of the West; Milwaukee Public Museum; the Wheelwright Museum of the American Indian; the Peabody Museum of Archaeology and Ethnology at Harvard; Yale's Beinecke Rare Book and Manuscript Library; the Canadian Museum of History (formerly Canadian Museum of Civilization); the Glenbow Museum; the McCord Museum; and several Oklahoma museums: Southern Plains Indian Museum, Sam Noble Oklahoma Museum of Natural History, Museum of the Great Plains, Marland Grand Home, Philbrook Museum of Art, Ataloa Lodge Museum, Gilcrease Museum, and the Museum of the Red River.

JoAllyn Archambault, director of the Smithsonian's American Indian Program at the National Museum of Natural History, sponsored my research grant and spent many hours traveling to and from her office in Washington, D.C., to the National Anthropological Archives in Suitland, Maryland, to assist me. I am grateful for the time and knowledge of North American Indian ethnology that she graciously shared. My thanks also go to Candace Greene, specialist in North American ethnology research in the Smithsonian Institution's Department of Anthropology, who shared her research on soft cradles.

I am also grateful to cradle collectors Don and Doris Smithee, Harrah, Oklahoma; Quintus H. and Mary Herron, former director emeritus and senior curator, Museum of the Red River, Idabel, Oklahoma; and John Koontz, Hartwell Francis, and David Roods, linguists, Department of Linguistics, University of Colorado Boulder.

Acknowledgment with much appreciation goes to the new American Indian friends I have met in person and online, who shared some of their life experiences, tribal knowledge, and personal photographs: N. Scott Momaday, Pulitzer Prize–winning Kiowa author, who graciously allowed publication of his poem "A Cradle for This Child"; John Sipe Jr., Northern Cheyenne chief, Cheyenne historian and consultant, Norman, Oklahoma; Jimm GoodTracks, Ioway and Otoe language specialist, who shared much information; Don

Patterson, former tribal historian and chief of the Tonkawas; Rachel Red Corn, Osage; Daniel Castro Romero Jr., general council chairman of the Lipan Apache Tribe of Texas, Sanger, California; and John L. Elder, writer, historian, and publisher, Edmond, Oklahoma. I owe much to Ray C. Doyah, Kiowa historian, writer, and poet, Oklahoma; and Lance M. Foster, Ioway, who shared his knowledge of the Ioway language. My gratitude also goes to Mark Awakuni-Swetland, Omaha historian and assistant professor of anthropology, geography, and ethnic studies at the University of Nebraska, who was not Omaha by birth but was Native in his heart and in the eyes of the Omaha tribe. Each person named above furnished much valuable information.

Warmest thanks to Julie Owens Norris, speech-language pathologist, Norman, Oklahoma. I am also grateful for friends, relatives, and others who provided their time, support, and involvement with this endeavor: Pam Vetch, typist, Lexington, Oklahoma; Diane Caudle, proofreader, sometime computer researcher, and expert tea brewer when I needed a tea break; Peggy Sanders Shelden, friend and copyeditor; my sister Dorothy, book illustrator and supporter, who planted the seed of creating miniature clay cradles and started this quest to research cradles; and Ronald Good and Molinda Jean, Little Sis, who encouraged me to begin the journey, in June 2003, to Cody, Wyoming. Jean lived through all the rewrites long distance. Using her computer and scanner, we put together the first manuscript draft. Alessandra Jacobi Tamulevich believed my first manuscript had merit in 2007. My interest then turned to making miniatures and selling them at art shows, while researching the rest of the Great Plains Indians until I had made miniatures representing all thirty-four tribes. I was then able to submit a suitable manuscript. Many thanks, Alessandra.

Christopher R. Shove pulled all the pieces together into this manuscript with his meticulous copyediting, computer knowledge, and overall expertise.

Last of all, I thank my husband, Joe, my companion, chauffeur, interpreter, telephone operator, and appointment secretary; without his support and encouragement, this book would not have been written.

Wado ("thank you" in Cherokee).

HIDE, WOOD, AND WILLOW

INTRODUCTION

Pretty-shield and Plainly-painted, two Crow women, were reminiscing about losing a baby in their care when they were girls. Their village had been on the move, and Pretty-shield, Plainly-painted, and other girls had stopped to swim in a creek after racing their ponies. A busy mother stopped to water her horse, on which a baby was riding, bundled in what was likely a skin pouch cradleboard. The mother was clearly in a rush to catch up with the village, so Pretty-shield said, "Let us girls take care of your baby. We will be kind to it, and bring it safely to your lodge when the people make camp."

To the girls' surprise, the mother agreed, leaving behind the pack horse, with baby, and riding quickly away to catch up with the travois. "Of course we quarreled over it a little," Pretty-shield recalled. "Each of us wanted to mother it first; and we all did, in turn, feeling very happy with the little child until we happened to remember that all this playing was letting the moving village get farther and farther away." The sun was setting as the girls bundled the baby back into the cradle on the pack horse, which Pretty-shield led behind her as she rode. "At first I kept looking back, until my neck ached, to see if the baby was there, and all right," but at some point, the girls started racing their ponies, and Pretty-shield soon got caught up in the race, forgetting to check the baby. After a while, when she remembered to look back, the baby was gone.

"Stop! Stop!" Pretty-shield called to her friends. "We have lost the baby!"

The girls began riding back the way they'd come, "dizzy with fear. Buffalo were coming. A great herd, headed so that it would cross over the very tracks our horses had made, was sweeping toward us. We ourselves were in danger. But what of the little baby?" As they retraced their tracks, scanning the ground for the baby, they encountered a small party of young men out buffalo hunting and enlisted their help.

> Their horses were fast. When the dust they had made blew away I saw the young men on a hillside, all of them sitting on their horses, in a circle. *None got down*. My heart smothered me. They must have found the little child. It must be dead, or one of those young men would have got down from his horse!
>
> I whipped my horse, that seemed to be standing still and not to feel my quirt. The hillside seemed to be moving away from us. But at last we reached it, our eyes sweeping the dry grass inside the circle of young men, who were . . . laughing. And there, face upward, and sound asleep, lay the baby, unharmed.

Being tied to the stout board, with soft padding inside the hide pouch, had prevented injury.

"We were off our horses before they stopped running. The child, awakened, began to cry." Pretty-shield was just so glad the baby was alive, and frightened of how the mother would react. When they caught up to the village, Pretty-shield recalled, "We were scolded, of course, as we ought to have been. The baby's mother said sharp things to us, especially to me, things that smarted for a long time afterward. For more than a whole snow I was afraid of that woman. Whenever I saw her coming toward me in the village I hid myself. . . . The baby's name was Turtle."[1]

Cradleboards, recognized as the universal symbol of infancy in Indigenous North America, were devised as the most effective way to care for precious babies like Turtle during their vulnerable years. Nearly every tribe in North America had some type of rigid cradle. Many of these carriers are some of the finest examples of North American Indian craftsmanship and decorative art, particularly in basketry and beadwork. The cradle was a familiar article that had many names: cradleboard, baby carrier, baby board, baby bag, baby bundle, sitting basket, and so forth. No one word was used to refer to a baby cradle. Each particular tribe has its own term or terms for the kinds of cradles its people used. The word *cradle* in this book refers to a small bed for a baby, a device in which an infant was bound during the first months of life. The term *carrier* refers to a device for transporting a child. I at times use the terms interchangeably because many cradles were used as carriers, although some were not. A flat framework or board to which American Indians historically bound, and sometimes still today bind, a baby is called a *cradleboard.*

Traditional Uses of Cradles

According to some Native beliefs, a child had many nurturing influences. The first was Mother Earth, who gave life to all beings; the second was the woman who gave birth to the child; and the third was the father, who made life possible. Finally, there was the cradle, which nurtured and protected the infant in the earliest years.[2] Linda Poolaw, a Kiowa from Oklahoma, describes a cradleboard as "a house for the beginning of life."[3] The birth of a child was a special blessing as well as a mysterious and potentially dangerous event. Some tribes had elaborate ceremonials and complex events for the first year of infant care. Cradles were imbued with symbolic ritual content to ensure the child's spiritual and physical well-being. The Pawnees, for instance, adorned their cradleboards with the morning star; the symbol united the infant with the power of the universe and provided protection during the vulnerable first year.[4]

In early times, prior to and for a time after European contact, the cradle carrier was vital to the Indian infant's first months of life, providing warmth, security, and portability, as well as firm, protective support for the baby's spine. The cradle carrier was the key to a baby's well-being and survival. The primary purpose was to transport the infant. A mother would carry the cradle on her back, strapped to her shoulders or suspended from her forehead using a beautifully woven tumpline, also known as a burden strap. In the carrier, the baby was secure, safe, and near the mother. The devices used to contain and carry infants also needed to allow mothers to move their hands and arms freely. Women spent long hours gathering, preparing, and storing food or dressing skins. Young infants were kept close to their mothers so they could be fed and watched while their mothers worked. Mothers also needed a way to provide protection for an infant from the weather, insects, and falls. As Mary Jane Schneider wrote, "A common solution would be for babies to be tied or bound to their mother's body in some way. Another practice, swaddling, tightly wrapping the infant in cloth, occurred throughout North America and Europe. In the Americas and northernmost parts of the Old World, the swaddled infant was lashed to a rigid frame or strapped into basketry or a wood boxlike cradle."[5]

Newborn babies were wrapped or swaddled completely before being placed in a cradle. After three months, when infants began to grasp and play with objects, their arms were left free for intervals during the day, depending on the weather. Swaddling the baby greatly reduced involuntary movements that would cause a baby to awaken. Research has indicated that swaddled infants tend to sleep more than those not wrapped. Cradleboards also restrict movement, providing security and support, as well as protecting the baby from changes in temperature, similar to the conditions in the womb. Today, Comanche mothers who are culturally connected continue to swaddle their infants shortly after they are born.[6]

Great Plains tribes used light, compact designs for cradles, making them easy to handle and move. When the mother worked in her dwelling, village, or field, she could often stand the cradle nearby. Cradleboards could be placed in a vertical or a horizontal position, hung from a tipi pole or a tree branch, propped against the lodge wall, or carried on the mother's back. Frequently, cradleboards were used to safely carry babies on horseback, making them the forerunners of car seats as well as of backpacks. A cradle was also a baby-tending device; in a sense, it served as a baby carriage, a playpen, and a bed. Another function of the cradle was to hold absorbent diapering material, such as moss. A cradle was the first major object in an infant's life.

Cradle carriers were part of the everyday lives of Plains peoples, as utilitarian items, objects of beauty, and personal expressions of the makers. Styles were as diverse as the artist who created them; yet, cradles were so distinctively connected to their tribe and region that you can almost read some carriers to see who made them and which tribe they came from. Crow women were famous for the fine, detailed beadwork on the top of their cradleboards. The variety of cradle designs stemmed from, and depended on, the availability of materials and tribal customs regarding the manufacture of cultural articles. There were dugout cradles, board cradles, bark cradles, skin cradles, and basket cradles, each one the best possible type and material for its particular area. Some were simple, little more than a shallow trough, but they all served the same basic purpose of carrying and providing protection for the baby. Most cradles were made with loving care.

Whether plain or fancy, carved of wood and decoratively painted or woven of willow, dogwood, or yucca, cradleboards generally had a firm, wide, flat back; a small footrest; and a broad, rounded headpiece that bowed above the infant's head to provide shade and protection. Suspended from the top of the protective headpiece, sacred amulets (such as protective herbs, beaded umbilical cord cases, dream catchers, or medicine wheels) would catch the baby's attention and train its eyes to focus. The baby was amused by small toys, brightly colored feathers, bells, and beads attached to the cradle.

Cradleboards were also used for socialization. Many American Indians believe that the upright position of cradles, worn on mothers' backs at eye level with adults, helped socialize babies and develop their sense of belonging to the tribal community. Babies were always included and not left alone. Children's constant association with their mothers resulted in close relationships.

The baby's back and head were well supported when laced securely into the carrier with soft leather or, later, with cloth. Babies went into their cradle generously padded with fresh, dried sphagnum moss, cattail fluff, shredded bark, or powdered buffalo dung, which functioned as diapers. Infants were usually left in the cradle during the day and removed at night and, occasionally, for bathing and changing. Some carriers were designed to solve the problem of soiled diapering materials, allowing the mother to untie the lacing from the bottom enough to remove the soiled material and add fresh moss or cattail fluff, without having to take the baby out of the carrier. The Comanches and Utes used a urine shield for boys. A rectangular piece of rawhide, usually harness leather, was attached to the lower half of the cradle, and the boy's penis was placed on the leather shield so that he could urinate outside the cradle and not stain the interior. Often, mothers would nurse their babies while the infants were still on the board. Babies usually stayed in their carriers for a year or until they were walking.

Many tribes used the rigid carrier to intentionally mold or reshape the infant's head by applying some type of pressure to the skull. It was not a painful process, being done while the bones of the head were still soft, and it produced no harmful effects. Tribes of the far Northwest and some tribes of the Southeast practiced a form of head shaping. The Choctaws used small sandbags to flatten boys' foreheads; the Flathead tribe in the Northwest used a slanted board to apply pressure to the forehead. A southeastern tribe bound the baby's head with soft hides to form a cone shape.

Another common use for cradles was as learning toys for young girls. Miniature cradleboards were often as elaborately made as the full-sized ones. Play and playthings in general were used as a form of education, providing children with miniatures of the tools they would use in adult life and encouraging imitation of the tools' proper use. A girl could practice lacing her doll in the cradle, singing lullabies, and rocking the doll to sleep. Thus, for girls especially, the cradle was engrained in everyday life in different ways from infancy through their adult lives as women.

Structure of This Book

This book is a journey through the use of cradles by Indigenous peoples living on the Great Plains during the end of the nineteenth and the first half of the twentieth century. It is a compilation of information from primary and secondary sources, including my own review of specific cradles.

The Plains culture area is defined as the region of tall-grass prairies and short-grass high plains extending west from the upper Mississippi River valley to the Rocky

Mountains and the Saskatchewan River south to the Rio Grande.[7] Plains societies were units of extended families organized in nomadic bands or semisedentary villages, each independent but related to others through shared language and culture. Plains cultures depended on the buffalo for subsistence, integrating the animal into all aspects of life. Differentiation of work according to male and female roles was a universal feature. Material culture shared a basic commonality of style with regional and tribal variations, such as in the type of cradle used by Plains mothers.

Part 1 of this book provides additional background on cradles of the plains and the women who used them. Chapter 1 is devoted to women's roles in Plains Indian cultures, and chapter 2 illuminates the types of cradles used and how they were adapted as necessary to the harsh environment on the Great Plains.

The next thirty-two chapters are grouped in parts 2–7 by the major type of cradle used: northeastern cradleboards, prairie cradleboards, northern plains flat boards, hurdle cradles, lattice cradleboards and soft cradles, and hide bags, swings, and hammocks. Some of the tribes used more than one type; for example, Santees used the northeastern cradleboard and later adopted the soft cradle. Each chapter focuses on an individual tribe or tribal grouping, including ethnographic information, how the tribe used cradles, and detailed descriptions of characteristic examples. The Kitsas and various Northern Caddoan–speaking tribes are grouped with the Wichitas. I devote a chapter to the Plains Métis because of the significant role they played in Plains history.

Each tribal chapter begins with a summary of background information on the tribe, including language, subsistence, original home, and reservations. Next, I describe the types of cradles used by the tribe, followed by specific birth customs, including the use of amulets. Where relevant, I describe differences in cradle design for boys versus girls and any symbolism associated with the tribe's cradle design and decoration. Finally, each chapter ends with details on the specific cradles I studied. Each tribal chapter, chapters 3 through 33, follows this preliminary plan whenever documents and facts are available.

Part 2 focuses on tribes that primarily used the northeastern cradleboard, including the Santee Dakotas, Yanktons and Yanktonais, Ioways, Plains Crees, and Plains Ojibwas. Dakota tribes also made soft cradles, and Plains Crees and Plains Ojibwas used the hide bag, often attaching it to a northeastern cradleboard.

Prairie tribes—Kaw, Omaha, Osage, Otoe-Missouria, Pawnee, and Ponca—made a distinct cradle called a prairie cradleboard, the focus of part 3. Part 4 includes chapters on two tribes, Crow and Blackfoot, that used a northern plains flat board, a cradleboard commonly found among Plateau tribes. This cradleboard was covered in hide, with a pocket to hold the infant.

Part 5 focuses on the unusual cradle called the hurdle, a name given it by Otis T. Mason, ethnologist and Smithsonian curator. It consists of an oblong hoop attached to rods or small canes held together with lashing. Leslie Spier, in "Havasupai Ethnography," wrote that the Western Apache used an elliptical hoop, crossed with closely spaced transverse bars, and that the Arapaho cradle was the same shape, with a framework of sticks.

Lipan Apaches and Plains Apaches (now known as the Apache Tribe of Oklahoma) used a similar cradle before they adopted the lattice frame. Spier further stated that the elliptical type was very old. Several prehistoric cradles were found in Arkansas in 1936 by Samuel C. Dellinger. The cradles were made by the Ozark Bluff Dwellers, who lived in rock shelters. The Ozarks were home to several cultures. Pottery found in several of the rock shelters resembles that of the Caddoan, an Eastern Woodlands–Plains culture who originally lived in Arkansas, Louisiana, Texas, and Oklahoma.

One type of hurdle cradle was formed by folding a mat of wild sunflower stems around a hickory stick bent and lashed together to form an elliptical frame. The Wichitas, who spoke the Northern Caddoan language, used a cradle frame of willow sticks lashed to an elliptical hoop.

Part 6 focuses on tribes that used lattice cradleboards, soft hoods, or both. Comanches, Cheyennes, Kiowas, Plains Apaches, Tonkawas, and Lakotas made the lattice frame in a V shape. Cheyennes and Lakotas also used the soft cradle. Comanche mothers used a hide bag laced up the front for infants.

The chapters in part 7 focus on tribes that primarily used hide baby bags, swings, hammocks, or some combination: Hidatsas, Mandans, Arikaras, Gros Ventres, Sarcees, Stoneys, Plains Métis, and Quapaws.

The cradle carrier is almost completely out of use among American Indian mothers today. For Native North American people in the past, however, the "third mother" was a source of comfort to babies and an ingenious solution to the problem of childcare, especially in societies where women were always on the move, in their daily work and lifeways and during the seasonal and subsistence travel of their villages.

PART ONE

CRADLES ON THE GREAT PLAINS AND THE WOMEN WHO USED THEM

A Cradle for This Child

This child who draws so near,
Who has no name, who cannot see,
Into an empty world,
I make a cradle for the child.

This child whose trust we keep,
Who knows nothing but our love,
Whose hands will guide our
destiny
I make a cradle for this child.

This child who will enter
Among us in our empty world
And stands before us in our need
And promises us the dawn,
I make a cradle for this child.

N. Scott Momaday

CHAPTER 1

THE WOMAN'S PLACE

In Native societies on the Great Plains, women occupied positions of respect and often had a great deal of power and authority over their lives. A woman's traditional social role was as the owner and guardian of the home. She was revered as one of the mothers of the people. The ultimate achievement for a woman in pre- and postcontact indigenous societies was being a mother and rearing a healthy family, but she also gained social prestige for her family through her contributions. While men had responsibilities in hunting and warfare, women were expected to be fine housekeepers, to keep parfleches (rawhide bags) filled with dried meat and provisions, and to be skillful in making and decorating clothing and gear for people, horses, and dogs. Women who attained distinction as religious practitioners, medicine workers, and skilled artisans in craftwork fulfilled their tasks by also bearing and raising children. The roles of men and women were both valued and necessary for the survival of the tribe. Life revolved around basic survival.

Most Indian women carried out their unceasing tasks with a sense of pride and satisfaction. They raised their children, cooked meals, built houses, nursed the ill, had sex (with

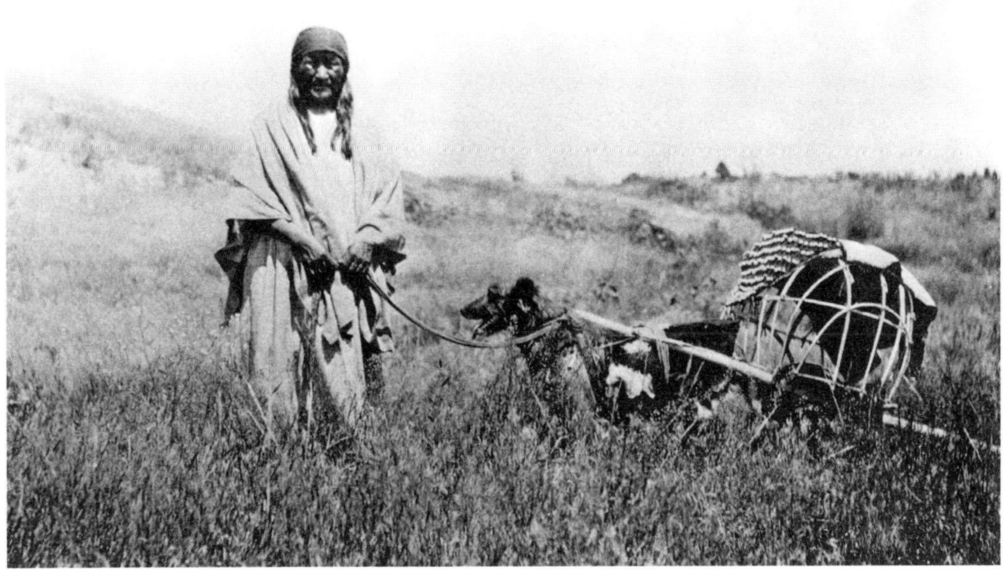

Women on the plains used dog travois long before they had the horse. Babies were placed in small cages on the travois. Courtesy of Western History Collections, University of Oklahoma Libraries, Norman, Oklahoma, Campbell 26.

their husbands or sometimes with others), prayed to their gods, and mourned the dead. All the numerous tasks women did promoted tribal welfare. A woman's place in Plains Indian culture was as an indispensable part of tribal life.

When nomadic people of the Plains moved their campsites, the women took down the tipis and packed their possessions in parfleche to be carried by dogs, horses, or travois. Before horses were introduced to North America in the sixteenth century, Native camps were often moved by large dogs. Mothers placed babies and young children into small enclosures of sticks with a covering for shade. Small babies were swaddled and laced onto cradleboards, which were hung on the mother's saddle horn or strapped on her back. At the next campsite, women would unpack, erect the tipis, and set up housekeeping. Daily duties included gathering firewood, cooking food, fetching water, and making and repairing clothing and tipis.

Tanning Skins and Preparing Food

Preparing skins was also a woman's job, and Plains women were fine craftspeople in the art of dressing hides. Being an expert tanner was one of the most prized accomplishments among women. The process involved staking a hide to the ground, then preparing and smoking it. Elk, antelope, and deer skins were used for clothing, and furs were used in bedding, bags, and decorative items. Women used chalk, porous bone, native clay, or porous rock to clean skins; for example, they would rub wet clay on the skin, then brush it off after it dried. "The Blackfeet Indians," according to Thomas E. Mails, "cleaned tanned skins with a piece of sponge-like fungus. Lice on clothing were removed by leaving the articles on an anthill for a day or so."[1]

The buffalo was the commissary of the Plains Indians, providing food, lodging, clothing, and utensils; no part of the animal was wasted. Harvesting buffalo was a man's job, but once the animal was killed, it became the woman's property. Women spent most of their time dealing with the enormous amount of meat and hides the men harvested. Even the most industrious woman could not keep up with her daily tasks along with all the work of butchering a buffalo. One cow could yield fifty-five pounds of pemmican and forty-five pounds of dried meat. The labor of two women was required to keep up with one hunter. A woman of average skill would take about three days to dress a hide, but a skilled woman could process three buffalo a day.[2]

Plains tribes lived primarily on buffalo and what plants they could forage. The annual cycle of migration for food gathering began in early spring. The semisedentary Prairie tribes, like the Pawnee, Kaw, Osage, Omaha, Quapaw, and Wichita, farmed maize, beans, squashes, pumpkins, and sunflowers. Women did most of the cultivating. After gardens were established, some tribes packed up and traveled throughout the summer, hunting and gathering. When they returned to their lodges, they harvested the garden and stored the produce for the winter. In early spring, Dakota women collected sap, which they boiled, strained, and shaped into loaves. As the soon as the ice began breaking, some of the women accompanied men on muskrat hunts. Men would spear the animals, and women would butcher the rats and process the pelts. At the end of summer, Dakota men and women harvested wild rice.[3]

Gathering was a necessary task for Plains tribes to supplement their food. Women continually gathered and prepared seeds, berries, and edible roots. Berry and root-gathering expeditions often turned into forays of joyous camaraderie. Wild berries were an essential ingredient in making pemmican, dried food made from jerked meat, pounded to powder, and mixed with melted fat and crushed berries. Pemmican could be preserved for several years when stored in parfleche bags and kept dry.

Social standing in a community depended on the family's food supply, which women completely controlled. Women obtained honor and clout through their close relations to food, such as by how they distributed their reserve of provisions. Generosity and hospitality were highly valued. In Plains Indian culture, when a visitor entered the home, women offered food, and they usually provided a gift of food for the guest to take home.

Women also took pride in preparing feasts, which were social events for the whole tribe. They made many nutritious dishes with various vegetables, such as onions, turnips, and carrots, as well as assorted berries and nuts. In addition to cooking buffalo, elk, deer, antelope, and mountain sheep, women served small game, such as jackrabbits, sage hens, and pheasants. The meat was added to soups and stews, roasted over an open fire, or served in dried strips. Some meals were cooked in pits lined with a hide and filled with water, into which women dropped heated stones along with meat and vegetables wrapped in pieces of hide. Semisedentary tribes made crude earthenware pots for boiling. Meat was also broiled over flame, with the chunks skewered on roasting sticks and covered with moistened rawhide strips to prevent burning.

Decorative Crafts

Women gained prestige through their crafts as well as through their skill and generosity with food. Achievements in a decorative craft were deemed as valuable as men's war deeds. Productivity and proficiency in crafts, quillwork, and beadwork established the rank of a woman in some tribes, such as in the Northern Cheyenne, Arapaho, and Blackfeet quill guilds. "Women produced objects for their own use a well as making clothing, housing and furnishing that were used by the entire family. Beadwork and quillwork were exclusively women's art as were hide processing, pottery making, and basketry."[4] Many women also engaged in hide painting with geometric design.

Quillwork was a major decorative skill on the northern and central plains for a long period; many Plains people believed it to be an ancient art.[5] (Southern tribes, such as the Comanche and Kiowa, did not produce quillwork.) Craftswomen used the hollow quills of the porcupine (*Erethizon dorsatus*) or the shafts of bird feathers, which they dyed, flattened, and sewed to leather with sinew. Quillwork was widespread in northern North America, where porcupines were abundant. Men hunted porcupines, sometimes throwing a robe or blanket over a living animal to entice it to release its quills. The largest quills were found in the tail, with decreasing sizes found on the back, neck, and belly. Quills were also obtained by trade.

Hidatsa people gathered molded feathers from gulls. A craftswoman would strip a feather to the shaft, split it into four quarters, and remove most of the pith, the white spongy center, leaving just enough to absorb color from dyes. Quills were then sorted by size, cleaned, and dyed before being sewn to leather from bison, elk, or deer. The hide was prepared by removing the flesh and hair, then stretching the skin to separate fibers. To tan the hide, women worked water-soaked animal brains into the fiber of the hide until it was soft and pliable. Smoking the hide over a bed of coals made it waterproof and gave it a brown color. Women soaked quills briefly in a bowl of water or in the mouth to soften them before beginning to sew. Using an awl or needle, they then secured the quills to buckskin by weaving them into a series of sinew threads. One to three threads could secure one to four quills. When the design was completed, the artist flattened and polished the quillwork with a quill flattener made of bone or metal. Southern Cheyenne and Arapaho women, after their removal to present-day Oklahoma, incorporated prepared plant fibers into their quillwork. Southern tribes such as Comanches and Kiowas did not produce quillwork.

Beadwork was a direct outgrowth of quillwork, adapting its techniques, forms, and designs.[6] All Native peoples on the plains produced beadwork, using a variety of local materials until small glass beads became widely available during the second half of the nineteenth century. The art tradition of beadwork on the plains has continued into the twenty-first century.

Bearing and Raising Children

Child rearing was the primary and dominant role of the Plains Indian woman. She had to rear mannerly children, teach them to respect the elders, and train them in the tribal way of life. "She was the spiritual teacher of the child as well as its tender nurse and brought its developing soul before the 'Great Mystery' as soon as she was aware of its coming."[7]

When Plains babies uttered their first cries of life and opened their dark eyes on the world, they faced an ordered pattern of human relationships, institutions, and values shaped to ensure the preservation of the tribe from babyhood to old age. Most Native women were in vigorous good health and well equipped to manage their pregnancies. They relied on herbal medicine, help from relatives and specialists, and rituals to guide them during birthing. An expecting mother was usually assisted by female relatives, midwives, or elderly women knowledgeable about birthing. During labor, assistants encouraged the mother, supported her as she knelt or squatted, rubbed her back, and sometimes pressed her abdomen to force the child out. After the delivery, they helped care for the newborn.

In many tribes, midwives received their skills through a vision or a calling. Mandan medicine women and men bought the right to their profession and sacred bundles from others who already owned the profession and sacred bundles. In most Plains tribes, a woman was not allowed to practice medicine alone until she reached middle age or older. A medicine woman was considered to have a special connection to the spirit world, and that link empowered her to heal others. Plains Indians believed that physical and emotional illnesses reflect an imbalance between the natural world and the spirit world. To restore balance and harmony was a healer's task, using herbs, poultices, or spoken formulas. Some women who acquired supernatural abilities became shamans, who were believed to possess the power to influence good and evil in the spirit world. An older shaman would usually choose a younger successor to inherit her power. The new shaman would use her own creations—songs and formulas—as well as those she inherited. Plains women gained respect and prestige by practicing medicine, one of the most powerful roles for women in Plains Indians culture.

Some midwives were very skilled at their profession, often able to turn a baby in the womb to ensure an easier delivery. An Arikara midwife shared how a malposition of the child was corrected: "The helpers lift the woman and gently sway her from side to side while her abdomen is gently manipulated in order to change the child's position."[8] One Crow midwife, Muskrat, rubbed the laboring woman's back with a horned toad combined with special roots to hasten delivery. Muskrat had received her knowledge in dreams after the deaths of her husband and a brother: "On the first occasion, a supernatural came up to her in her sleep and said. 'Chew that weed (*batse'kice*; literally, man-imitation), and you will give birth without suffering.' She boiled the leaves and made the infusion, but she was not supposed to pull up the plant except for doctoring. The second time she was granted a plant called *bice'-waru'ci-se* (literally, buffalo-don't-eat-it) and told that it was even more effective than the first. Whenever anyone touched Muskrat's face or body with it, she went in a trance from which she recovered by chewing the weed."[9]

Louise Plenty Holes, an Oglala Lakota elder medicine woman, or *pejuta win*, delivered many "new travelers." She and her mother were "stronghearted" ones who delivered babies in their community before doctors were available. Louise said, "We haven't lost one yet," delivering "even six sets of twins."[10] The first thing she did before a birth was put water to heat. Then she examined the expecting woman. If the baby was not in position, assistants helped the woman walk. Sometimes Louise had to turn the baby. "When the baby doesn't come, we reach up inside and get the baby, or we would turn them around. If one has its feet come first, we could take the feet and push it back in. If the [woman's] belly is way up there, they haven't turned yet. If you rub and push while she holds her breath, the babies turn, and the belly goes down right away. Then they start hurting really bad. They start contracting."[11] Louise would tell the mother to lie still so that the baby would "come good" and the baby's head would be round. If the mother did not breathe properly, or if she talked too much, the baby's head would be elongated. Louise used no medicine or Vaseline, only buffalo grease, to ease the delivery. She would also pray that nothing bad would happen to the baby, asking the Great Spirit for help.[12]

An Indian woman would predict her delivery date by the moons. If the woman ceased menstruation during a new moon, she would mark a piece of wood with charcoal or notch a stick each successive time the moon was in that phase. She would usually estimate it right.

Plains Indian people believed that menstrual blood was the manifestation of the female capacity for creation and the powers that mystery contains. Countless stories explain the origin of the menarche in ways that give power and respect to that phase of life. There was an obvious harmony between the moon's monthly twenty-eight-day cycle and a woman's monthly cycle. Most Plains tribes had menstrual tipis, moon lodges, or brush arbors where women of the tribe could seclude themselves. Isolation was to show respect for a woman's power and keep it contained. Among the Lakotas, a young woman had a special ceremony when she began her first moon, or monthly cycle. A well-respected older woman would instruct the girl in how she should conduct herself as a Lakota woman. Assiniboine women were not permitted near the sacred bundles during their monthly cycles, but instead of women leaving their lodges, the husbands moved out with their bundles. It was believed that if a menstruating woman entered a lodge containing a medicine bundle, she would continue to menstruate indefinitely.

The late Joseph Rocky Boy, a revered Yankton/Sicangu Sioux elder, explained the woman's role:

> A woman is the only one who can bring a child into the world. It is the most sacred and powerful of all mysteries. Certainly the man must be there to plant the seed, but his part is simple and relatively unimportant.
>
> Some people focus on the Sun Dance as the male power of the sky, but it is to bless Mother Earth with new life that the dance is held. When we pray in the sweat lodge in our ceremonies, we remember *Maka Ina*, Mother Earth. We get our health from Mother Earth and the herbs that grow from her. We use some for food and others for doctoring.
>
> When a woman is having her time, her blood is flowing, and this blood is full of the mysterious powers that relate to childbearing. At this time she is particularly powerful. To bring a child into this world is the most powerful thing in creation. A man's power is nothing compared to this, and he can do nothing compared to it. We respect that power.
>
> If a woman should come in contact with the things that a man prays with [pipe, rattle, and medicine objects] during this time it will drain all the male powers away from them. You see, a woman's power and a man's are opposites—not in a bad way, but in a good way. Because of the power a woman has during this time it is best that, out of respect for her men and their medicine things, she stay away from them. In the past they would build a little lodge for her, and their other female relatives would serve on her needs. She would get a rest from all her chores. It was not a negative thing like people think now. So you see, we did this out of our respect for the great mystery, out of respect for the special powers of women.[13]

Many reports document Native women who had to face the birth process alone. John C. Ewers wrote that "sometimes an expectant mother's labor pains came while she was riding with a moving camp. She dropped out of the line of march and two or three hours later she returned to the caravan with a newborn babe in her arms."[14] If the Arikara village was traveling on a hunt, and a woman gave birth along the trail, the woman would wrap the newborn infant in a piece of buffalo robe, tie it to a small board about three feet long, and catch up with the rest of the party when the camp stopped.[15]

Buffalo Bird Woman, a Hidatsa, gave birth to her son in 1869 while the tribe was camped for the night on a sandbar, during a buffalo hunt. She delivered the baby in her mother's tipi at sunrise. Later that morning, she and the tribe crossed the ice-clogged Missouri River in a bullboat. During the cold November journey, when riding on a horse-pulled travois, Buffalo Bird Woman and the baby were both wrapped in buffalo robes, partly tied with a thong like a large sack. When she rode a horse, she belted her robe and thrust the baby on her left side, with his feet downward within the robe.[16]

Pretty-Shield, a Crow woman, related how new mothers managed during campsite moves. She said that after the birth, for about a month, she took short steps when walking, and when she rode, she sat on flat packs, with her legs tied together just above the knees and sticking out in front, on either side of the horse's neck. With her legs tied together and holding her infant in her arms, she had to be helped off the horse.[17]

Following childbirth in many American Indian cultures, both mother and newborn remained in seclusion for a period ranging from a few days to several weeks. This was no doubt a welcome time to recuperate before returning to strenuous daily duties.

Turtle Lung Woman, a Lakota medicine woman, said that mothers rested four days after childbirth, keeping their babies near. "On the fourth day after giving birth, the mother was purified. She was cleaned with water mixed and boiled with leaves from a sage plant. An older woman relative helped her bathing by gently [washing] with a soft deerskin cloth dipped in the sage water that was cooled to lukewarm. She was then wiped clean. Once she was purified, she was free to resume her life as before."[18]

NURSING

Plains women nursed their children for up to four or five years as long they had milk and did not become pregnant again during that time. Nursing mothers often abstained from conjugal relations while nursing, making it a form of birth control that helped parents space out their children. Following Cheyenne custom, a woman did not have her second child until her first was about ten years old, and Cheyenne parents were praised for their self-control. Similarly among the Sioux, getting pregnant while breastfeeding was considered shameful for the woman's husband.[19] This careful family planning and high infant mortality rates meant the number of children in a family was usually small.

Many tribes had an herbal remedy to help a new mother's milk come in. Cheyenne women used "*Actaea arguta* . . . sweet medicine, *mŏstsī' īŭn*," the dried roots and stems of which were "pounded up to make an infusion to be given a woman after childbirth, to make her first secretion pass off quickly."[20] Most of the people on the plains felt that colostrum, the yellowish fluid that precedes the appearance of milk, was not good for the baby, causing such ailments as diarrhea, so the mother would not breastfeed her newborn immediately. Among Cheyennes and Arapahos, another nursing mother would feed the newborn for those first few days, or longer if the newborn's mother had died.[21] In other instances, the infant was fed berry juices and soups from a bladder with a shaped nipple or was simply not fed until the mother's milk came in.

Usually someone else helped draw out the colostrum, or "first milk," and spit it out. According to Royal B. Hassrick, the Lakotas often used an old woman, called a "sucking woman," or a ten-year-old girl to remove this initial milk. Delphine Red Shirt wrote, however, that the mother was encouraged to let the infant "suck at the breast" immediately after birth.[22] Some Crow women used a two-week-old puppy to suck out the colostrum or to suck first-time mother's nipples that were not large enough or not properly formed to get a good flow of milk going. One Gros Ventre woman who could not feed her infant well supplemented her breastmilk with meat broth. Arapaho mothers sometimes applied thick pads to the breast to protect the milk. Lakota women made pacifiers for babies after six months to help mothers who were too busy to nurse. "The pacifier was made from the ligament of the buffalo. It was a tough piece of meat from the muscle or tendon that the mother had boiled and used . . . as a pacifier."[23] It was thought that this type of pacifier, combined with breastfeeding for a long time, was good for children's teeth and helped them grow straight and strong.

DIAPERS

Plains mothers made their own disposable diapers from materials in their environments: sphagnum and other leafy mosses, cattail down, shredded bark, and buffalo chips. Aged buffalo chips were pounded to a fine powder and sifted into an even finer delicate powder of high absorbency. Blackfeet mothers mixed sage leaves with the powdered buffalo dung. Babies in colder climates, like Plains Cree and Assiniboine environs, were kept in moss bags stuffed with dried moss. Plains Cree women mixed in rotten and crumbled wood, as well as pulverized dried buffalo chips mixed with cattail down. When the child soiled the moss bag, the mother would shake out the contents and add a fresh supply of absorbent material.

Comanches and Cheyennes wrapped dried moss around the baby's lower body and later used soft pieces of buckskin and flour sacks for diapers. Sphagnum was naturally antiseptic and absorbent; women dried the moss and used it again. Arapaho mothers also practiced an early form of recycling. They cleaned and dried the padding in the sun, and then reused it. Not only were all these materials naturally antiseptic, they also insulated and protected the baby's skin. Agnes Deernose, born in 1909 on the Crow Reservation, shared what her mother used for diapering materials: "My family was still using powdered dust from rotting wood and red paint powder to keep me dry and free from chafing and itching. Pieces of cloth soaked up my soil in place of soft hide, or my mother slipped a kind of pillow made of hide and stuffed with pine needles under me."[24]

Lakota, Assiniboine, Omaha, Ponca, and Hidatsa mothers used cattail down (*Typha latifolia* L.) for their newborn babies' diapers. If a birth was expected, the women collected a great quantity of down to lay the newborn on. Cattail down was also used in pillows, padding on cradleboards, and quilting in baby wrappings. It was soft and fluffy, prevented chafing, and could be renewed as necessary.[25]

Hidatsa men gathered cattail down to use as insulation on cold weather journeys, as well as for diapers, which women made by stuffing a sack with the whole heads of cattails. "Changing" a child's diaper simply involved pulling out the soiled down as needed. For a single diaper, ten cattails lasted two or three days, as Buffalo Bird Woman explained:

> I would apply, say, ten cattails in the morning as we started on a journey. At noon or evening the child would cry and I knew he was uncomfortable. I would open his bundle and remove the wetted part which would make a kind of ball, for the down would ball up with the wetting. But I would not put in down.
>
> But at the end of two or three days I had taken out so much of the down that I had now to replace with some more of the down.[26]

A skin diaper was placed between the baby's legs, with the ends drawn up on the stomach and back. A wide leather band, lined with fur on the side next to the baby's skin, held the diaper in place by wrapping under the arms and around the body. Well protected, the baby was then dropped in its sack.

Apache and Lakota mothers used pieces of soft skin for diapers. Lipan Apache women used rabbit skin pads, with shredded bark packed around and between the legs of the baby. In the summertime, the Lakotas used pieces of fawn skin lined with cattail down and powdered buffalo chips. Both substances absorbed urine and kept the baby dry. Mothers would remove the feces and add more absorbent materials as needed.[27] Blackfeet used cottonwood tree punk like talcum powder to prevent chafing, and the Cheyennes dusted the inner surfaces of the baby's legs with powder from the prairie puffball.

Arapahos used finely ground buffalo or horse manure as talcum powder for diapers, grinding it between the palms of their hands before sifting it. Mothers rubbed infants with buffalo tallow before spreading the fine powdered manure between the babies' legs and over the rest of their bodies from the waist down. The diaper was held in place by the way the cradle was covered and laced. A mother would check the diaper when taking the baby from the cradle. If the diaper did not contain feces, it was dried, powdered, and used again. If chafing occurred, the mother used ointment made from dried red clay mixed with grease or tallow. The natural forms of throwaway diapers lessened the task of keeping the baby clean and protected against diaper rash.

ABORTION AND INFANTICIDE

Infanticide and abortion were known to occur among the Plains tribes. Abortion was practiced by forceful blows on the abdomen, sometimes with stones. Assiniboine women followed this custom if they were left without a provider, such as being deserted by the father of the child. An infant with marked physical defects obvious at birth was sometimes left to die. The fate of an imperfect Comanche infant was decided by the medicine women attending the birth. A newborn judged unfit to live was left on the prairie to die. The attitude about twins was mixed. Often the mother could not care for two babies, in which case a girl twin would be killed. Some tribes considered having twins to be a disgrace. The Sioux saw twins as special or holy and believed that a female twin would be a good quillworker.

A Woman's Place in the Cosmos

Anna Lee Walters, a Pawnee and Otoe-Missouria writer, explained that the power and presence of the female element was an essential companion to the male to make the cosmos whole: "My mother called me before I was born! She searched for me in her dreams and prayed to the spirits that her call would be heard. After I was conceived, lying curled in her belly, the older women came forth to sit at my mother's side. Learned in child-rearing, they advised her about the nation's children—ancient knowledge and taboos to keep the cycle going. My mother listened, taking to heart everything they said and did, because it was for her and me that the nations lived! So I was given life, an iridescent rush first in my mind and heart, and later, her child was born!" Walters continues to tell about her birth: "One of my grandmothers helped me into this physical world. She cut my umbilical cord . . . and wiped my face and body until my skin was rosy and warm. My tiny hand caught and clutched firmly at her finger." This was the young Anna Lee's first realization of "what it meant to enter the circle of these dwellings and to be one with the nations."[28]

Walters describes being given a name, by which she "would be forever known to the cosmos," and moccasins, which "symbolized the path I would follow in this physical world. Afterward, I was lifted up and introduced to the dawn. My first view of this world was from my mother's back as I was carried about, laced onto a board." That view was of women—making clothing and crafts, gathering food, and cooking.

Her early tactile memories are of "hands, soft and warm, reaching for me, . . . feeding me from wooden bowls and buffalo-horn spoons." She also remembered the sounds: "women's voices, lullabies crooned softly into my ears and laughter that fell into each woman's lap as she cared for the nations." Ultimately, she saw herself in the "dancing black eyes" of the women around her: "Eyes spoke to me more eloquently than words of who I am—a daughter of the ancient nation."[29]

CHAPTER 2

PLAINS CRADLES

Thirty-three tribes, who roamed and lived in the territory between the extremes of the frigid northern plains and the searing heat of south Texas, adopted styles of cradle that best suited their climates and lifestyles. The Great Plains area encompassed the grasslands of North America, bounded on the west by the foothills of the Rocky Mountains and merging on the east into the prairie woodland fringe of the Mississippi River. Since before European contact, all Indian tribes of the Great Plains had shared an economy based on buffalo as their major source of food and material for clothing, shelter, and tools, but the arrival of the horse in 1519, brought to the Americas by Spanish conquistador Hernán Cortés, gave the tribes better means to exploit the buffalo. Initially, Plains Indians had access only to those horses that had escaped or could be stolen from the Cortés expedition, but eventually the Spanish horse spread throughout western North America. Many tribes quickly adopted the animal as a primary means of transportation and greatly improved success in battles, trade, and bison hunts, and the Plains Indian culture flourished from the late seventeenth century to the nineteenth. That culture included later arrivals to the region, such as the Sioux and the Crows, former Woodland tribes that had been pushed out of their lands by European expansion on the American continent, as well as buffalo-hunting tribes that were not nomadic: Mandan, Hidatsa, and Prairie tribes like the Pawnee and Otoe, for example, who supplemented their hunting with horticulture. They lived in earth lodges within fortified villages.[1]

Babies are universal among all peoples, of course, and represent the survival of the human race. In light of the fragility and helplessness of a newborn, the very existence of Plains Indians was a tribute to Native parents' ability to subsist in the harsh environment of the plains and to solve the problems involved in protecting and caring for their offspring. Tribes developed various customs and procedures to keep babies comfortable, fed, and safe, including different styles of carriers and cradles to protect and transport their babies. Plains Indian mothers used wood, hide, and willow, or similar sticks, to craft any of seven types common in the region: northeastern cradleboard, prairie board, flat board, hurdle frame cradle, lattice frame, soft hood, and hide bag cradle.

The Santee Dakotas, Yanktons and Yanktonais, Ioways, Plains Crees, and Plains Ojibwas used the northeastern cradleboard. In this type of cradle, three or four pieces of wood form a flat, almost rectangular, solid board frame, equipped with a deeply bent U-shaped footrest, or a small footboard, and a narrow projecting face guard, also bent in a U shape. Some northeastern cradleboards have a brace across the back to secure the face guard.

A mother would swaddle her baby in blankets and secure the infant to the board with broad bands, which were often elaborately decorated. The top panel of the board, above the baby's head, is another common site for decoration, usually with carvings and paint. Plains Cree and Ojibwa mothers frequently attached a hide bag cradle to northeastern cradleboards designed without the footrest.

The horticultural people who lived in villages between the Mississippi River and the high plains—the Otoe-Missourias, Osages, Kaws, Omahas, Poncas, and Pawnees—used a prairie board cradle: a long rectangular board without a footrest to which a bent face guard is attached using rawhide thongs. Some of the boards have stairsteps at the bottom of each side to help hold the decorated bands or finger-woven sashes used to secure the baby to the board. The upper-third panel of the backboard, which extends above the baby's head, is decorated with paint and carved geometric designs, often outlined with brass tacks.

Crow and Blackfoot tribes, and the adjoining mountain people, used a distinctive type of flat board cradle: the northern plains flat board, sometimes called a plateau cradleboard. The flat board cradle is a large oval-shaped board, completely flat, including at the bottom, with a covering of skin attached so that it blouses out in the front, forming a sack to hold the baby. The rest of the skin fits smoothly over the board, and the top panel is decorated with beadwork or quillwork. The Crow version of the cradle tapers almost to a point at the bottom. Crow mothers would strap the baby to the board with three decorative beaded bands.

Arapahos, Wichitas, Plains Apaches, and Lipan Apaches made cradles using frames of willow sticks. A "hurdle cradle," according to Otis Mason, "consists of a number of rods or small canes or sticks arranged in a plane on an oblong hoop and held in place by lashing with splints or cords."[2] The Northern Arapaho frame is an elliptical hoop with long, nearly parallel sides, usually of willow, and one transverse stick at the bottom. This type of frame was found in the Southwest, but the Arapahos used a distinctive soft buckskin cover decorated with quillwork, in which the baby was wrapped and tied in the cradle. Apaches also made an elliptical hoop of willow covered with buckskin, but to this frame they added a hood of wickerwork, often covered with buckskin, that was lashed to the oval rod with thongs. The Wichita version is an elliptical hoop with transverse bars spaced along the back, within a rectangular rod frame twined together with sinew. Three curved willow sticks make a cradle hood bow, and the baby is bound to the frame with colorful woven sashes. Cradles of this type have been found in ancient archaeological sites in the Southwest.[3]

The nomadic tribes of the southern and central Great Plains—Comanche, Kiowa, Apache Kiowa, Cheyenne, and Sioux—spent much of their time on horseback, so the cradles were worn on mothers' backs, hung from their saddles, or packed on a travois. According to Barbara A. Hail, the lattice, or slat, frame cradle was developed by the Kiowas and spread to other tribes.[4] Otis Mason described "cradles made of dressed skins [which] were lashed to the lattice of flat sticks. . . . In these are to be seen the perfection of this device."[5] The cradle's wooden frame is a modified V-shape framework of two long upright slats with two flat crosspieces. A skin bag attached to the framework forms the baby's bed, and the long pointed slats extend more than a foot beyond the top of the bag. The skin bag is laced up the front, and a curved, stiff piece of rawhide across the top of the cradle protects the baby's head and face. The Apache Kiowas and the Plains Apaches used a hurdle cradle before the lattice was made.

Cheyennes and Lakotas used a soft hood cradle,. A heavy skin, decorated with quillwork or beads, forms a protective hood, and the skin, or sometimes a cloth, hangs down as a wrapping for the infant's body. The hood cradles are useful when mothers needed to carry children in their arms. The Cheyennes made triangular hoods, and the Lakotas made square, with tabs on top of both types. The Lakota cradle was often mounted on a lattice frame.

Hide bag cradles were used by the Plains Crees, Plains Ojibwas, Plains Métis, Stoneys, Assiniboines, Hidatsas, Mandans, Arikaras, Sarcees, and Gros Ventres of the northern plains. The carriers were also referred to as skin bag, sack, or moss bag cradles and were originally made of hide until mothers started using trade cloth, such as velvet. The hide bag is made from a rectangular piece of hide or cloth folded in half lengthwise and sewn at one end, with eyelets laced up the front. The infant would be packed with absorbent material, wrapped in blankets or furs, and tightly laced in the bag. These carriers, along with swings and hammocks, kept the baby warm and safe. Mothers also carried babies on their backs using tumplines or by attaching the hide bag to a northeastern cradleboard.

PART TWO

NORTHEASTERN CRADLEBOARDS

Santee Dakota

Yankton and Yanktonai

Ioway

Plains Cree

Plains Ojibwa

CHAPTER 3

SANTEE DAKOTA

Santee (Isanti) Dakotas are members of the Eastern Dakota, a cultural and dialectal grouping of four of the seven major tribes (Seven Council Fires) of the Great Sioux Nation. The other two groupings are the Middle Dakota, which includes the Yankton and Yanktonai bands, and the Western Dakota, better known as the Lakota. Santee Dakotas speak a Dakota dialect of the Siouan language and were historically a Woodland culture, although some bands migrated to the western prairies to hunt buffalo. Four Council Fires are Eastern Dakota tribes: (1) the Mdewakanton (or Mdewakantonwan, which translates to Spirit Lake Village); (2) the Sisseton (or Sissitowan, Fishysmell Village); (3) the Wahpeton (or Wahpetowan, Leaf Village); and (4) the Wahpekute (Shooters among the Leaves).

All Dakotas lived in north-central Minnesota when Europeans first mentioned them in the late seventeenth century. The tribe organized around extended family units rather than clans. When the Dakotas began separating, some moving southwestward, the Santees remained, and others occupied North and South Dakota. The Santees evolved a diverse lifestyle that mixed Plains and Woodland culture, refocusing subsistence efforts on hunting, fishing, foraging, and limited horticulture of beans, squash, pumpkins, and corn instead of wild rice. Although all Santees, regardless of location, were involved with the fur and hide trade, the ecological diversity of the lands they occupied varied markedly. They had permanent villages of square bark lodges near rivers and lakes, but they also used tipis at times. The more eastern groups adapted to using wood and plant fibers in the clothing they made and in decorative crafts, like floral beadwork, which reflected their Woodland culture. The more westerly group relied on the buffalo and adopted the Plains lifestyle.

During the middle decades of the nineteenth century, the Santees gradually moved from self-sufficiency and autonomy to destitution and dependency by ceding their lands. The tribe was assigned a reservation in Minnesota, but reservation living failed to provide an adequate means for survival, which resulted in the Dakota Uprising of 1862. The tribe was divided and widely scattered. Some Dakotas went to Canada and others to reservations farther west in the United States, but a few were able to return to Minnesota.[1] Some of the Santee people still reside on Nebraska's Santee Sioux Reservation; the Flandreau Santee Sioux Reservation, in South Dakota; the Devil's Lake (now Spirit Lake) Reservation, in North Dakota; the Sisseton Wahpeton Sioux Reservation, straddling the border between South and North Dakota; the Fort Peck Reservation, in Montana; and various reservations in Canada.

Cradleboards

The Santee cradleboard, or *iyoḳopa* (which means "the board to which the child is bound"), was a flat board with a bent wooden face guard and footrest that curved around the bottom.[2] In missionary and linguist Stephen R. Riggs's Dakota dictionary, he notes that sometimes "'hokśi' is added to 'iyoḳopa,' . . . and we have the long descriptive name for '*baby*,' 'hokśiyoḳopa.'" Riggs admired one such cradleboard: "This board is shaved out nicely, and often ornamented in various ways, with beads and quills, having a stay board around the foot, and a strap board or handle standing out over the head of the child, which serves both for protection and to tie the mother's strap to."[3]

One Santee northeastern cradleboard that I studied had two pieces of stretched hide tacked around the edges of the curved footrest and laced together in the middle to form the baby bag. The board, often carved and painted, was usually about two and half feet long and about a foot wide. The bent U-shaped bow was lashed to a wooden crosspiece with rounded ends or diamond shapes as well as secured to the back with leather cords. The head bow was notched on each end to enable the two pieces to slip together.

The head bow was often wrapped with buckskin or cloth and decorated with quillwork, metal dangles, and hawk bells. Elaborately decorated vertical bands, attached at the bow and tied to the bottom of the board, held the bow in place. Samuel W. Pond, a missionary among the Dakota people, described "a veil or curtain . . . fastened to the top of the cradleboard and hung down to the foot, being kept from the child's face by a wooden bow. The veil protected the child's face from wind, cold, sunshine, dust, insects, etc. The bow also served to protect the child in case of an accidental fall."[4]

The infant would be placed on a soft bed, well padded with dried moss, and secured to the board with wool cloth wrapped around both baby and board. The Santee cradleboard I studied, originally collected by George Catlin, had eleven holes that could have also been used to secure the bedding to the board. Two broad bands, covered with embroidery quillwork, laced in the back, providing additional cover to the baby. The mother carried the baby on her back, and a wide burden strap, or tumpline, went across her forehead to balance the cradleboard. When the mother traveled on horseback, the board was strapped to her back. When not traveling, the mother would lean the cradle against the lodge or a tree. The baby was fed on the board and slept on the board until outgrowing the cradle, at which point, the mother would carry the child in her robe or blanket.[5]

Pond commented on the woodworking tools Dakotas used to manufacture cradleboards—axes, adzes, hatchets, and knives—and noted that everything they made themselves was well made. "The Dakota had to get his board out of a tree with a hatchet and finish it with a knife, yet it was as well made as though from a cabinet maker shop." He described the cradle as "carved and painted," and "highly ornamented," noting that a mother might spend weeks "embroidering the wrappings of her child."[6]

I focus on five Santee cradleboards in this study: one collected by George Catlin in 1832 and acquired July 1884 by the Smithsonian National Museum of Natural History (plate 1); the Peabody Essex Museum (PEM) cradleboard (cat. no. E27984), a twentieth-century restoration of a board from circa 1840; two miniature cradleboards, one at the Brooklyn Museum (accession no. 50.67.44), and one in Berlin, Germany, at the Staatliche Museen zu Berlin in the Ludwig von Rönne collection (ca. 1830); and a watercolor done by Duke Paul von Württemberg (ca. 1830–1850) of a cradleboard originally identified as Chippewa. Three of the cradles have two large disks on the board across the back that attaches the head bow to the cradleboard; in Catlin's sketch of the mourning cradle, the backboard ends are diamond shaped.[7] Three of the boards are carved on the interior. One is completely incised with lines in a diamond pattern. Two have incised lines in various geometric shapes. The cradleboard in Württemberg's watercolor is elaborately carved in various patterns of horizontal stripes, and three identical floral designs fill the area where the baby's head would rest.

The Brooklyn Museum identified its miniature model cradleboard as a Sioux (Dakota) baby carrier made at Fort Snelling, Minnesota, using wood, hide, porcupine and bird quills, tin cones, glass beads, and woolen cloth. The backboard for the cradle is missing. The two quilled ornaments, wrapped around the cradle, are made of smoked skin adorned with orange, white, red, brown, light blue, and yellow porcupine quills. Two ornamental straps are decorated with quill-wrapped thongs, tin cones, and blue and white pony beads.

The cradleboard in PEM beautifully illustrates Dakota quillwork. Karen Kramer, a curator at the museum, noted the significance of the materials and design: "Given the quantity of metal cones used on this carrier, the tremendous feat involved in processing the thousands of porcupine quills, and the weaving of such an elaborate and meaningful design, it is likely that it was made for a family of very high rank." The tumpline and the tinklers depict the spirit being known as the thunderbird. The backboard may have been decorated with carving.[8]

All the boards are decorated with elaborate quill embroidery and metal cone dangles; the dangles' cords are also wrapped with quillwork. The two bands for securing the baby to the board are all completely quilled; the two vertical bands used to hold the head bow in place are decorated with quillwork and dangles. The quill embroidery is in natural and dyed black or dark red and orange colors, and the quillwork is sewn with sinew, with both geometric and figurative designs depicting deer and thunderbird.

In *Letters and Notes on the Manners, Customs, and Conditions of the North American Indians*, George Catlin described the cradle he had purchased from a Santee Dakota mother as she was carrying her infant in it.

> The child in its earliest infancy, has its back lashed to a straight board, being fastened to it by bandages, which pass around it in front, and on the back of the board they are tightened to the necessary degree by lacing strings, which hold it in a straight and healthy position, with its feet resting on a broad hoop, which passes around the foot of the cradle, and the child's position (as it rides about on its mother's back, supported by a broad strap that passes across her forehead), that of standing erect. . . .
>
> [T]he bandages that pass around the cradle, holding the child in, are all the way covered with a beautiful embroidery of porcupine quills, with ingenious figures of

horses, men, etc. A broad hoop of elastic wood passes around in front of the child's face, to protect it in case of a fall, from the front of which is suspended a little toy of exquisite embroidery, for the child to handle and amuse itself with. To this and other little trinkets hanging in front of it, there are attached many little tinselled and tinkling things, of the brightest colours, to amuse both the eyes and the ears of the child.[9]

In 1839, Thomas L. McKenney wrote about a Santee cradle from a museum collection in Berlin, Germany:

> In this the little fellows are placed almost as soon as [they are] born—with their backs to the board which command. It is not always they use a padding, or bed—but a little moss is used—during their tender age—after which the board & back of the boy or girl are in close fellowship. At the foot is a little projection of wood. On this the heels rest—a little moss being placed between, for comfort. The bow, or projection in front is intended to guard the face, & head when by accident the cradle falls. The arms and hands being laced down the sides, never project, and are never injured. Thus ensconced, the mother when on a journey slips the cradle over her shoulders, and rests it against her back, a strap of deer skin being brought around her forehead by which sustains its weight.[10]

In *Letters and Notes*, Catlin drew two Dakota cradleboards and described the practice of using a mourning cradle, which the mother carried if her baby died and was buried during the time of cradle use. According to Pond, the Santees did not use a mourning cradle, but the custom was well known among the Ojibwas. Dakota mothers frequently deposited the cradle on a scaffold or in a grave when the baby died. Samuel Pond and his brother, Gideon, started working with the Dakotas in 1834. Samuel wrote his ethnography most likely in 1870–71.[11] David I. Bushnell's report on burial practices of the Algonquian, Siouan, and Caddoan tribes told of the Dakota custom of relatives cutting a lock of hair from the deceased—from the top of a warrior's head (a scalp lock) or from the left side of a woman's—preserving it in a "spirit bundle," and hanging it in their lodge. Primary sources on the Dakotas note that mourning might last over a year for a widow, but none (except for Catlin) mentions a mother wearing a mourning cradle.[12]

Soft Cradles

In the early eighteenth century, when the Eastern Dakota bands were separating, the wide northeastern cradleboard was replaced with lightweight leather wraps or containers for swaddled babies, which were carried in the mothers' arms. During Prince Maximilian of Wied's visit to the West in 1830, he commented on the beautifully worked baby bags of the Dakotas and the Assiniboines. Early decorative material must have been either paint, quills, or pony beads.[13]

Soft carriers gained shape only when wrapped around a baby. "The bottom of the wrapper folded up over on the baby's lower body, the sides folded in to overlap in front and a separate thong or strip of cloth was used to tie the carrier snuggly around the child."[14] Many had linings for additional comfort. The Dakota soft cradle was a rectangular piece of hide folded in half, with another piece of hide cut to fill the space between the two sides and a rectangular tab extending from the top of the back. Most soft carriers had a separate panel in the back, but some had a central seam instead.

Dakota women were skilled quillworkers. Quills were the major decorative material used by Plains tribes before the introduction of trade beads in the mid-seventeenth century. The highest attainment for Santee women was proficiency in quilling, which demands delicate dexterity. Those famous for their ability to do porcupine quillwork had dreamed of the Double Woman, or Deer Woman. The first woman who dreamed of the Double Woman was taught the art of quilling. After her vision, she set up a tipi and asked that a porcupine be brought to her. She sorted and dyed the quills and chose a helper to aid her in quilling a robe.[15] From the realm of spirits, the Double Woman appears in dreams to bestow talents from the realm of the *wakan*, which translates as "sacred." Many Dakotas believe that the work itself is wakan. Creating and beautifying an object to honor the spirit of a relative require special attention and focus, which makes the work a sacred spiritual practice.

In Dakota quillworking societies, new members were taught the skill, techniques, and rituals necessary to master the craft. The quills were sorted by size, dyed, and stored until needed. Dakotas used natural vegetable dyes until after the 1880s, when traders brought aniline dyes to the plains. Roots, berries, seeds, flowers, nuts, and various parts of trees produced specific colors. The women would boil dye materials together until they achieved the desired color. Black dye was obtained from wild grapes, hickory nuts, walnuts, or oak burs. Nuts of either sort were used only when grapes were not obtainable, because they produced a brownish color rather than deep black. Reds were obtained from the bark of the alder mixed with bloodroot or wild plum. Fresh bloodroot made an orange yellow or yellow dye, which could also be made from wild sunflowers and yellow coneflowers. Green was obtained from lamb's-quarter. The Eastern Dakotas plaited, sewed, wrapped, and wove quills. Santees and Sissetons preferred floral patterns.[16]

An exhibit curated by Mark J. Halvorson, *Sacred Beauty: Quillwork of the Plains Women*, featured four Dakota quilled soft cradles made between 1880 and 1910. Two cradles were quilled using a simple line technique (see, for example, plate 2), and two had floral designs.[17]

Birth Customs

The birth of a child was a momentous event to a Dakota mother and her relatives. Delivery was in a separate lodge from the family, where a new fire was kindled after the old ashes had been thrown out. The new mother would not return for seven or eight days. During a difficult or unduly delayed birth, a medicine man would be called in "to ascertain the cause of the delay. He sings and so frightens the infant that it soon effects an exit."[18] If this did not work, he might then give the mother a potion made of powdered rattle from a rattlesnake. Not every delivery was difficult, however; Stephen Riggs once traveled with a woman who delivered her baby unaided on the journey. As he recounted, the party went ashore after the woman said she was sick, and "an hour later she came back with her newborn infant to resume paddling the canoe."[19]

Usually, a midwife skilled in birthing, along with her assistants, would help deliver the baby. After the umbilical cord was cut, they tied the stub with soft buffalo sinew then wrapped a broad band of soft hide around the infant to cover the navel. According to Melvin R. Gilmore, "the Dakota used the prairie mushroom or puffball as a styptic for any wounds and especially . . . on newborn infants. In Dakota language, *hokshi chekpa* means 'baby's navel'" (*hokshi*, baby; *chekpa*, navel).[20] The afterbirth was buried outside the camp. The midwife and her assistants washed the newborn with water heated by hot stone in a birch bark container. For this ceremony, a special stone, called a "wakan stone," was used to ensure the baby would grow healthy and strong. The newborn would then be wrapped in rabbit skins, lined with soft feathers or down, and laced up in an outer layer of rawhide.[21]

Dietary taboos affected Dakota women after giving birth as well as while pregnant. While expecting, they were not to eat eggs, liver, fowl, salt, or the female or young of any animal. Eating young animals would cause the child to be weak. Eating rabbit meat could cause the rabbit curse—cleft lip. For about a week after giving birth, a mother refrained from eating hot food and remained in cooled air. When the infant seemed strong and healthy, she could then eat anything she wished.[22]

The naming of a Dakota child was an important event. A given name was believed to help a child grow and become strong. A boy was often considered "the future defender of his people," and a girl, "the future mother of a noble race." At birth, the first five boys and the first five girls of a family would receive one of ten traditional Dakota names, which they inherited as a birthright. The names indicated the sex and birth order of the children. For example, the firstborn son was called Chaska (or Ćaské), and the first daughter was called Winona (or Winóne). Parents with more than five girls or more than five boys gave the younger children other names. A medicine man publicly announced the newborn's name at a feast given by the parents.[23]

Amulets

Relatives created special gifts to honor a new baby, such as a cradleboard cover or an amulet. The Santee amulet was a small buckskin bag, decorated with beads and quills, which hung by a buckskin string on the head bow of the cradleboard. The dried umbilical cord was sewn into the center of the bag with cotton or moss. Catlin described the amulet as "the carefully and superstitiously preserved umbilicus, which is always secured at the time of its birth. . . . [B]eing rolled up into a wad of the size of the pea, and dried, it is enclosed in the centre of this little bag, and placed before the child's face, as its protector and its security for 'good luck' and a long life." He was able to purchase several amulets after the women had cut them open and removed the "little sacred medicine, which to part with would be to 'endanger the health of the child'—a thing that no consideration would have induced them in any instance to have done."[24]

In Colette Hyman's *Dakota Women's Work: Creativity, Culture, and Exile*, she tells how the gifts for a new baby honor the women who made them as well as the baby, becoming part of a spiritual tradition of honoring relatives while celebrating life cycle events. The spiritual and sacred nature was shown in items made for Newborn infants were considered *wakanyeza* (sacred beings). In making a cradleboard cover or a pouch for a baby's *cekpa* (umbilical cord), a Dakota woman was performing work to honor the wakan in that young being. According to Hyman, the amulet was often made in the shape of a turtle, which represented longevity, and it became the baby's first toy.[25] When the child reached puberty, the amulet was attached to ceremonial clothing.

One of the Dakota amulets in the Canadian Museum of History (formerly Canadian Museum of Civilization) is a twelve-by-two-inch diamond-shaped leather bag covered with quills, decorated with dangling metal cones, or tinklers, on rawhide thongs (object no. V-E-323c). Another amulet, a hide pouch shaped like a turtle and decorated with quills, is housed in the Bern Historical Museum, donated from the collection of the Swiss count Albert Alexander von Pourtalès, who traveled in the United States in 1835–36.

Sex-Specific Cradle Design

Santee boys' cradles were equipped with a shield of leather or bark laced to the lower half, which deflected the baby's urine. McKenney described the bark shield in 1839: "To ease trouble, there is with the males, & for their accomation [*sic*] a small aperture, or opening through which his little contrivance is let out—& thence he sends his urine, over a little piece of bark which is put there to carry [it] off."[26]

Santee Cradle Symbolism

The Great Lakes people revered the deer as other Plains tribes revered the buffalo. Santee baby carriers often have a zoomorphic deer motif, an angular style with four legs, neck, head, and rectangular body. Floral patterns in dyed quillwork and, later, beadwork on Santee cradles represented the medicinal plants used by Dakota women. Another common subject of Eastern Dakota art is the thunderbird, a powerful spirit being who creates thunder by beating its wings, wielding lightning "to keep dangerous Underworld creatures at bay." Aside from explaining some forces of nature, "Thunderbird can . . . bestow blessings on humans, and the depiction on [a] cradleboard can be understood as a request to protect the baby and deflect harm."[27]

The four cardinal directions were another important concept for Dakotas. Their art sometimes symbolizes this concept using a square or rectangle, sides straight or concave, often with a line extending from each corner. As John Fire Lame Deer explained, the number four is most wakan and stands for the four quarters of the earth. Lines projecting from each corner of this motif represent the unused earth force and the four winds, whose symbol is the cross. On a baby carrier, this design was a powerful protective symbol for the infant. The Santee cradle that Catlin collected (plate 1) has a row of the four-direction motifs on the upper band of the cover panel, among other symbols, making it an illustrative cradle to examine in more detail.

Santee Dakota Cradleboard

I identified the Santee Dakota cradleboard collected by George Catlin based on the resemblance to his written description and sketch in *Letters and Notes*, an accurate drawing of the Santee Dakota style, and a cradleboard example of that style I found in a German museum. Catlin collected this cradle near the Falls of St. Anthony, on the upper Missouri River, in 1832, but it was not among the Catlin collection donated by Sarah Harrison to the Smithsonian Institution on May 15, 1879. In September 1881, a second lot of Catlin's collection was discovered in a Philadelphia warehouse. This lot contained the Santee Dakota cradle.

The cradleboard is of undetermined wood about a tenth of an inch thick, measuring 31.1 inches long, 17.5 inches wide, and 9.8 inches high. Other materials include leather; iron sheet and nails; sinew thread; red and brown paint; orange, brown, and green wool; and orange, brown, green, and white porcupine quills. The carved wooden frame is a flat board with slightly rounded edges.[28] Eleven holes were drilled into the board—four in the center, one at the top, three at the bottom, and six along the sides. Two of the holes on each side were used to attach the headboard and to secure the carrying strap; two of the holes on each side were for the footrest and the baby bag. Fabric is attached underneath two holes, perhaps from padding or exhibition display. The bottom edge has three small nails, and four rusted nails are embedded at the top.

The head bow consists of two pieces: the bent bow and the crosspiece. The wooden bow is 16.5 inches long and 2 inches wide, bent in a U shape to fit the width of the back brace, from which it projects 9 inches. The ends of the bent bow are notched and lashed to the wooden crosspiece, 17 inches long, which projects 4 inches from the board on each side, with carved wooden disks, 3 inches in diameter, on each end. The crosspiece is carved in an elongated diamond shape, tapering to 1 inch wide at the ends. The head bow is wrapped with two leather pieces, stitched together with black wool thread and decorated with quills. The head bow (including bent bow and crosspiece) is lashed to the backboard 9.5 inches from the top. Two wide, vertical quilled bands that held the head bow in place are broken in several spots. The bands are tied to the bottom of the board with braided leather strips.

A wooden strip, 1.75 inches wide, bent next to the bottom edge is attached to the wooden board with a leather cord on each end. Four holes just below the head bow are for attaching the footrest, along with the two side holes mentioned above. Two pieces of leather stretched over the curved wooden strip form the baby bag.

The frame pieces, head bow, footrest, and back brace to hold the head bow are bound together with leather thongs that tie through the holes drilled in the board. The two wide pieces of leather that hold the baby to the cradle are stitched together in the back with wool and secured with iron nails.

The decorated heavy leather carrying strap, called a tumpline, is lashed with leather strings to the horizontal back brace, although one of the strings is missing. The strap is 21 inches long and 3 inches at the widest part, tapering to 1 inch. Designed to fit across the mother's forehead, the tumpline distributes the weight against her back, which frees her hands. It could also be used to hang the cradle from a branch or pole.

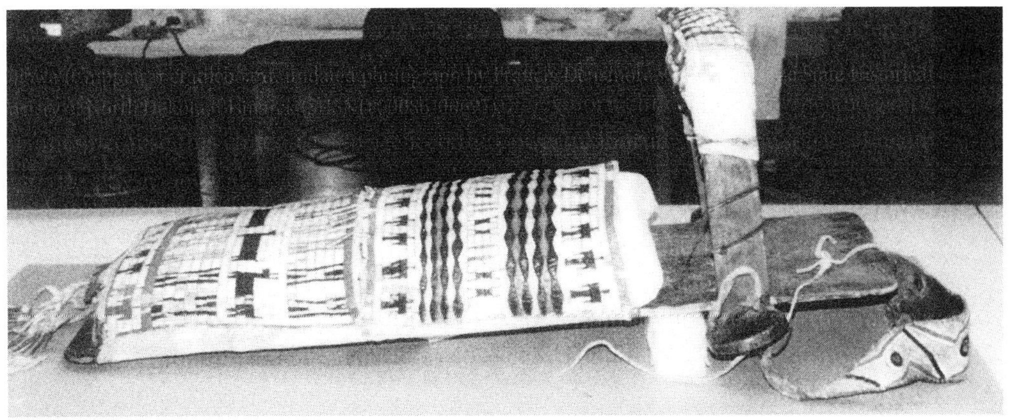

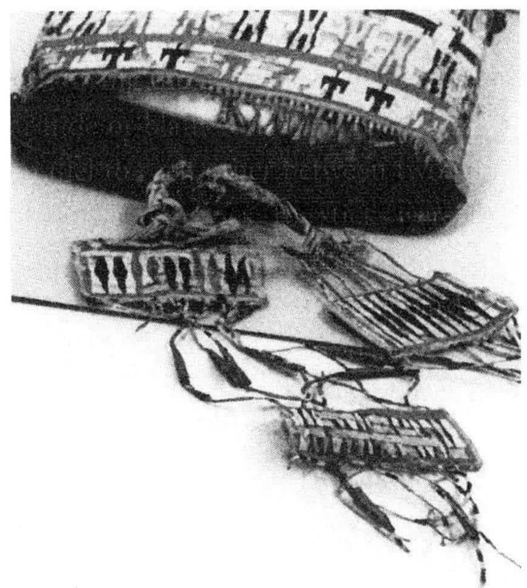

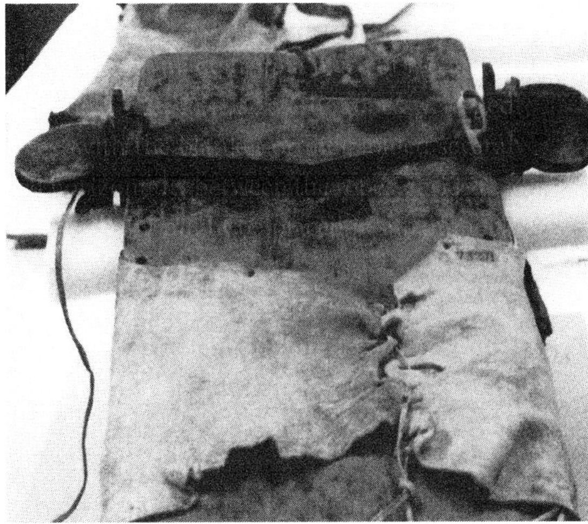

Santee Dakota cradleboard, 1832, 31.1 × 17.5 × 9.8 inches. (*top*) View of the carved, painted, padded headboard, with wooden disk on side and quilled covering; (*left*) decorated ends of cradleboard; and (*right*) back of cradleboard. Courtesy of the Department of Anthropology, Smithsonian Institution, Suitland, Maryland (E73311-0).

The upper interior of the board is painted red and brown and carved with rows of varying geometric designs, evoking spiritual protection: Xs enclosed in circles, triangles, large Xs, half circles, and small triangles enclosed in rectangles. The paint is faded and hard to see.

Elaborate quillwork in horizontal rows on the two baby-holding bands is sewn with sinew on natural color buckskin. The quill embroidery completely covers the front of the bands in brown, orange, green, and white geometric and figurative designs of deer and thunderbirds. The top band is a solid orange stripe, followed by five white stripes with brown thunderbirds; nine wavy stripes in a pattern of white, brown, and orange, repeating the design but changing the color pattern; four white bands with elongated orange diamonds and brown rectangles with long bars on each corner; nine bands with wavy stripes in a brown, orange, and white design with changing color pattern; and another band of thunderbirds against five white stripes, followed with an orange stripe. The top band has a total of thirty-four horizontal rows.

The bottom band is similar, with different motifs: one stripe of orange; six rows of white with elongated Xs, in alternating pairs of orange and green outlined in brown; one row of white; six rows of white with brown deer figures; one white row; six rows of white with elongated Xs identical to the first set; one row of orange; four rows of white with alternating pairs of brown and orange thunderbirds; and a final zigzag line in orange. This lower band has a total of twenty-seven horizontal rows of quillwork.

The green quills are mostly faded, and the coloring is hard to see. The two leather panels have large areas of lost quillwork. The wool thread stitching the two panels together is mostly broken or missing and is not original, probably resewn for display, which is also the likely purpose of the added tacks and nails securing the panel to the edges of the board.

The bottom edge of the leather band is decorated with iron sheet dangles, supported by cords wrapped with quills. Most dangles at the bottom are missing, however, and the quillwork wrapping is loose on the remaining cords.

The head bow is wrapped with buckskin, decorated with quills in a pattern and design that echoes the front bands: horizontal rows of white, with elongated Xs in green and orange outlined in brown, followed by a stripe of brown squares on white and one orange stripe. Some sinew thread is loose, and much quillwork is loose or missing.

Straps used to keep the head bow in place consist of quilled patches joined by ten quill-wrapped leather cords, with metal dangles, braided together at the bottom and tied through a hole in the board. The straps are fragmented, with many distorted and missing cords. The original sketch of the cradle shows how the straps were attached and how extensive the decoration was.

The carrying strap is decorated with two narrow orange and white quillwork horizontal lines in a large zigzag pattern, connected with repeating diagonal vertical lines in brown and white. Rosettes in white, brown, green, and orange appear in the center of the space created by each set of zigzag and diagonal lines. Eastern Dakota women practiced single-thread sewing, in which a single quill is wrapped around a single thread, enabling flexible, curvilinear quillwork.[29]

Almost two hundred years after Catlin collected this Santee Dakota cradleboard, it now has another chapter in its story. Through Colette Hyman's research for her book *Dakota Women's Work*, we now know who made the beautiful cover for this ornately carved cradleboard: a twenty-three-year-old woman named Wicacaka. "The beauty of this cradle embodies the care and nurturing showered on children, but it also tells many stories about the work of Wicacaka and other Dakota women. The cradleboard reflects the hours spent on creating and decorating implements of daily life in the midst of many other responsibilities and the hours of work that women spent together creating and beautifying these items for each other's families."[30] Wicacaka was the woman carrying her baby on her back when Catlin purchased her beautiful cradleboard.

CHAPTER 4

YANKTON AND YANKTONAI

Yankton (Ihanktonwan, or End Village) and Yanktonai (Ihanktonwanna, or Little End Village) are names for the Middle Dakota people and their council fires (two of the Seven Council Fires of the Great Sioux Nation). The Middle Dakotas lived in the upper Mississippi region and spoke the same Dakota dialect of the Siouan language, similar to the Nakota dialect of the Siouan spoken by Assiniboines and Stoneys. In the late seventeenth century, Middle Dakota people began moving westward, separating into two distinct groups. The Yanktons moved southwest into parts of present-day Iowa, southwestern Minnesota, and southeastern South Dakota. The Yanktonais also traveled west but farther north of the Yanktons, into present-day southern North Dakota and eastern South Dakota. Both tribes jointly claimed the prairies east of the Missouri River from the Painted Woods on the north to the mouth of the Big Sioux River extending northeast, beyond Devils Lake to the Red River.

Middle Dakota culture was a mix of the Eastern (Santee) and Western (Lakota, or Teton) Dakota divisions, with variations. Both Yanktons and Yanktonais were organized into extended family bands, not clans. Yankton culture was influenced by the tribe's close association with the Tetons and other Plains cultures. The Yanktonais shared more traits with the Woodland culture (i.e., Santees, Plains Crees, and Plains Ojibwas). Both Middle Dakota tribes were influenced by the Mandans, Hidatsas, and Arikaras. Yanktons and Yanktonais lived in tipis and built permanent villages, which they abandoned during the summer communal buffalo hunts, when they ranged far into the plains on horseback. Fishing was also an important activity for both tribes. In addition to hunting, the Yanktons and some Yanktonais practiced horticulture.

The Middle Dakota tribes would eventually be widely dispersed geographically on reservations in North Dakota, South Dakota, and Montana: Standing Rock, Devils Lake, Crow Creek, Fort Peck, Rosebud, and Yankton. Some Yanktonai people moved to Canada with the Santees.

Cradles and Cradleboards

Of all the Sioux tribes, Yankton and Yanktonai cradle information was the most challenging to research. I failed to find information specific to these tribes on the soft cradle, cradleboard, birth customs, symbols, and diapering materials. Both tribes absorbed some beliefs and adopted many practices common to the tribes that preceded them on the northern plains. Yankton culture resembled that of the Tetons, while the Yanktonais shared more traits with the Santees. F. Dennis Lessard, in a preliminary investigation of art styles among

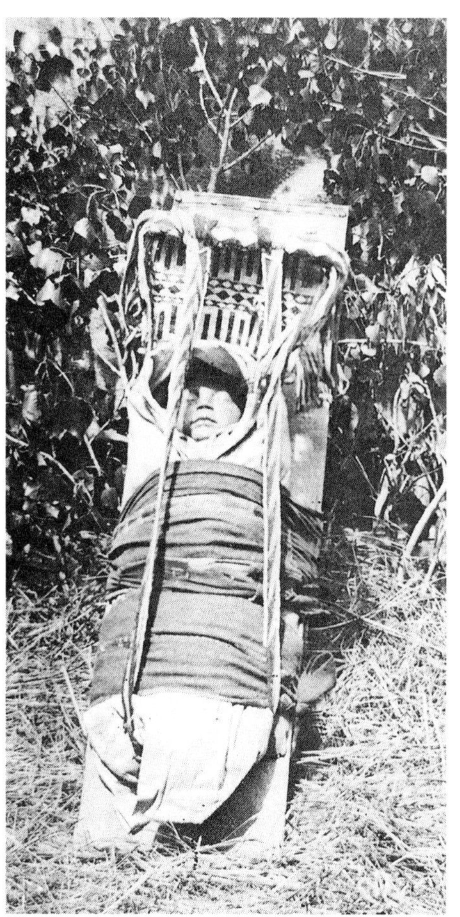

Dakota (Yankton) Indian baby in cradleboard, date unknown. Stereograph by Stanley J. Morrow, Yankton, South Dakota. Courtesy of the National Anthropological Archives, Smithsonian Institution (NAA INV 09860900).

the tribes of the central plains, found signs of a developing tribal style among Yanktonais. Nonetheless, a comprehensive study of their arts has yet to be done. Northern Sioux groups were known by their broad color palette and use of full-color backgrounds, usually blue, and Yankton and Yanktonai tribes both used floral designs and geometric patterns in their quillwork and beadwork. Lessard identified a fully beaded soft cradle as Yanktonai at the Fort Peck Reservation in Montana. The cradle hood had a "blue background, soft buckskin beaded tab, stacked triangles, design layout, bead colors, and designs typical of this tribe's style."[1]

At the Smithsonian, I examined a cradle, identified as Sioux and collected on the Standing Rock Sioux Reservation, that was similar to one in a photograph from F. D. Lessard's article. I examined another similar cradle at the Museum of the Red River.

In the Smithsonian's National Anthropological Archives, I found a stereoscopic photograph taken in Yankton, Dakota Territory, of a Dakota baby in a cradleboard. The stereograph was undated, but the Dakota Territory only existed between 1861 and 1889. The cradle is a Woodland type of flat board cradle: a rectangular board, bent bow, and decoratively carved or painted headboard. The head bow is held in position by decorative beaded straps, and the baby is tied to the board with bands of cloth. A footrest is not visible because of the swaddling wrap.

When the Yanktons and Tetons moved farther west and south onto the plains, they lost the ancestral Dakota-style cradleboard. European and American observers of the Dakotas in the nineteenth century described in writing and depicted in drawing cradles of the ancient Siouan type. The baby was swaddled and wrapped in a hide bag then bound with two wide bands to a rectangular board, with a narrow U-shaped board fastened to the main board at a right angle, protruding forward, and a U-shaped footrest. During the time the Eastern and Middle Dakota groups separated, starting in the late seventeenth century, the wide cradleboards began to disappear from use.[2] This disappearance of styles coupled with the lack of information on Yankton and Yanktonai cradles specifically means looking more closely at items with vague attributions, such as "Sioux," for possible Yankton or Yanktonai fingerprints.

Yankton Soft Cradle

On May 21, 1888, the Smithsonian Institution acquired a box of various ethnological specimens, including a soft cradle (or soft hood) labeled "Lone Wolf" and identified as Sioux (plate 5). The donor, Lieutenant Herbert M. Creel, had collected the cradle (or "pappoose [*sic*] bonnet," as he called it) at the Standing Rock Sioux Reservation, suggesting the possibility that a Yanktonai woman created it. Furthermore, the quilled soft hood is similar to the beaded hood that F. D. Lessard identifies as Yanktonai in "Defining the Central Plains Art Area."

The soft cradle is 36 inches long and 25 inches wide; its tab is 6 inches long and 3 inches wide at the bottom, 2 inches wide at the top. The material used in this cradle includes red woolen cloth, Native-tanned animal hide, faded porcupine quills (originally dyed red, orange, or green, or left natural), seed beads (sky blue, pink, rose, red, white, green, and dark blue), red and brown flannel, multicolored yarn, and tin cones.

The hood was constructed in three pieces: hood, wrap, and lining. To form the hood, rawhide was cut into rectangles, 20 inches by 18 inches, and folded in half. Undecorated

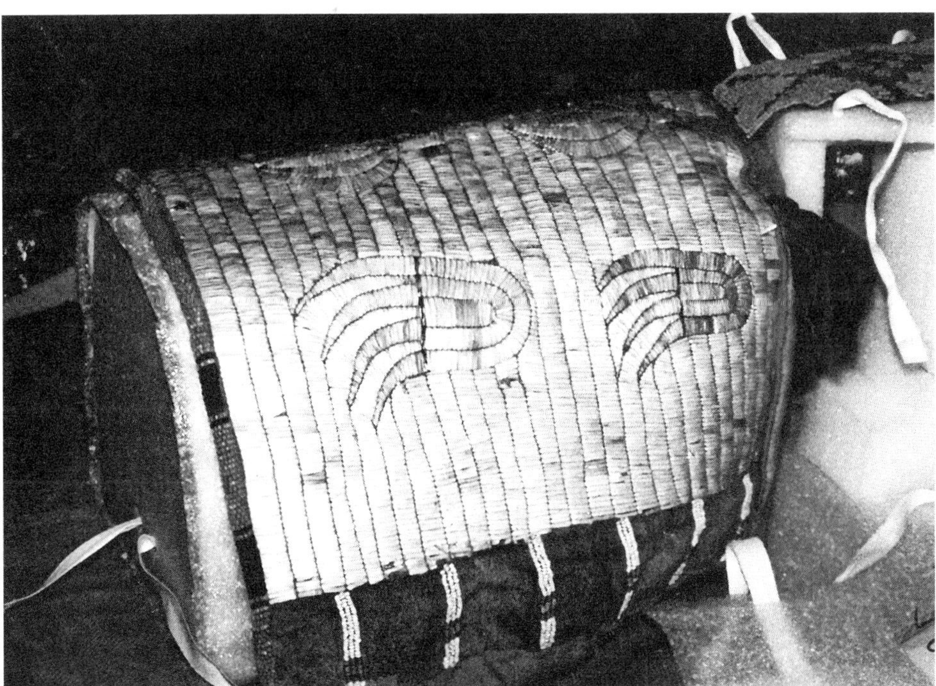

Sioux (Yanktonai) soft cradle, showing quillwork on top of the "Lone Wolf" bonnet, 36 × 25 inches; tab: 6 × 3 inches. Donated by Lt. H. M. Creel, May 21, 1888. Courtesy of the Department of Anthropology, Smithsonian Institution (E129885-0).

rawhide, 7 inches square, was then sewn to the back. A rectangle of red wool cloth, 18 inches by 25 inches, was sewn along the rawhide edge, and a strip of that wool was also sewn to the back piece, forming a 2.5-inch red band along the back edge. Then the hide was lined with red and brown flannel cotton. The tab is triangular, narrow at the base, and sewn to the middle edge of the hood, with no interior extension.

Twenty-six parallel rows of quillwork run across the top part of the hood, with five designs in the rows of quills, two on each side and one on top, including bear claws and flower designs with curved lines. Faded dye on the quills makes it difficult to discern the designs. One side appears to have a row of four chunky crosses, but little color can be made out in the quills on the other side.

The Sioux woman used a simple band quill technique, which enabled her to use two lines of stitching and more than one quill simultaneously, although the simplest method is to fold one quill from a line of stitching to the next. The quill rows are interrupted by the curving lines of the claws and flowers. The quillworker worked the tips of the claws into rows of quills, adjusting some rows wide as necessary. She used a simple line technique on the flower designs, which interrupt the rows of quill embroidery. Like the rest of the cradle, the dye is faded on the flower. The only identifiable colors are green and red. The flower has five curved, closed petals with a thick stem and a leaf on each side.

Three lanes of white beads with narrow bands of sky blue and red stripe the sides of the heavy hide. Six white lanes run vertically, connecting to the quillwork and the red cloth wrapper. The cradle has a rolled edge in rose beads, with bands of sky blue and dark green beads. The tab background is sky blue with designs in rose, red, dark green, and dark blue, and at its wide edge, the tab is decorated with fourteen small tin cones attached with buckskin strings. Two multicolored yarn tassels are attached at the bottom of the tab with ten-inch strings.

CHAPTER 5

IOWAY

At one time, the Ioways (or Iowas), Otoes, Missourias, and Winnebagos were one united people residing in the Great Lakes region. They spoke a mutual dialect of the Chiwere language, a subdivision of the Siouan family. When the ancestors of the Otoes, Missourias, and Ioways separated from the Winnebagos and migrated southwest, the Ioways (who call themselves Báxoje, or Bah Kho-je, which means People of the Gray Snow, or Gray Heads) settled at the mouth of the present-day Iowa River, where it branches off from the Mississippi.[1] Their original lands spanned the present states of Iowa, Minnesota, and Missouri. Archaeological research has shown that ancestral Ioways were part of the Oneota culture, developing from Woodland people to Upper Mississippian people starting around A.D. 1000.

The Ioways have always stayed close to the Mississippi River. In 1686 the French established trading agreements with the tribe, followed by the Spanish, then the British in 1785. The Ioways were involved in the War of 1812, which caused a split in the tribe. By 1827, most Ioways were on the Little Platte River in northern Missouri until 1837, when they moved to a reservation in Kansas and Nebraska Territories. The tribe members who opposed the allotment system on that reservation moved to a different reservation in Indian Territory (present-day Perkins, Oklahoma), which split the tribe again. One group is identified as the Iowa Tribe of Kansas and Nebraska, and the other is the Iowa Tribe of Oklahoma.

Ioways integrated cultural elements from a horticultural society, Woodland neighbors, and Plains peoples into their tribe's lifestyle. They integrated elements of the Algonquian social system, including patrilineal descent and clans. From Plains culture, they adopted the biannual bison hunt, living in tipis, and some material items, although men also continued to fish and trap furbearers. In Ioway permanent villages, they built lodges with pole frameworks, covered with slabs of bark or woven mats. Women grew corn, beans, and squash in gardens, while men raised tobacco and maize for ceremonial use. Formal rituals marked the Ioway's life cycle, as with other Siouan Plains peoples, although research information on such practices is sparse, including for Ioway birth customs beyond what know of cradleboard design and use.

Cradleboard

The Ioway cradleboard, *hoxwawe*, was similar to the Woodland and Central Algonquian types—a flat board with a curved head bow and moveable footrest. Ioway Lance M. Foster explained that the term is a slight variation on *hoqwawe*, the spelling on an exhibit label for a toy cradleboard on display at the Iowa, Sac and Fox Mission museum in Highland,

Kansas, in the 1980s. Foster photographed the label and wrote the word down.[2] Jimm GoodTracks, an Ioway linguist, emailed me the words for cradleboard from his online Ioway, Otoe-Missouria dictionary: "I have the following: *hoháwe* (I.), *hokwáwe* (I.), *hokúwe* (O.), *hóxuwe* (IB), *uk^íwe* (LWR), *oyáⁿ rihú^dhe/uyáⁿ rihúdhe.* Uyáⁿ rihúdhe (uyáⁿ—lie in; rihúdhe—to shake or rock) was the hammock that hung in the corner of a bedroom or over the parents' bed. The word cradleboard was broken down to mean: há (skin; cover) + uwé (wrapped in covers) and the 'kwá' indicated a possession 'gra-' (one's own) thus wrapped in one's own covers." According to GoodTracks, the word *uk^íwe* would be a contemporary version of the other term, *uk^íwe^iñe*, for a newborn infant, or "little one carried around on," implying the infant is carried around on a cradleboard.[3]

During George Catlin's visit to Fort Leavenworth, Kansas, in 1834, he noted an Ioway "cradleboard decorated with porcupine quills and small trinkets that dangled from the handle to catch the child's attention. . . . [W]ith the child on her back, the mother's hands were free for other activities." Catlin apparently did not see mourning cradles among the Ioways, although he did witness grief over the loss of a child: "Infants and children were deeply mourned at death, and offerings were placed at their graves periodically."[4] In 1841–45, Catlin accompanied White Cloud, Ioway chief; thirteen tribal representatives; a promoter; and an interpreter on a journey to Europe, where White Cloud hoped they could earn money for the tribe. Among White Cloud's entourage was an infant, Corsair, who appears in a sketch Catlin made of the group, possibly the only picture of an Ioway baby in a cradleboard.[5]

The two Ioway cradles I studied were collected in 1922 by Alanson Skinner from Four-Winds-Woman, or Tadjeto'wime, an Ioway woman who resided near Perkins, Oklahoma. One board was a Central Algonquian–type cradleboard like those used by Sauks, Menominees, and Potawatomis. This undecorated flat board measures 27 inches long and 10 inches wide, with bent bow and a moveable footrest in a squared U shape (plate 7). The wide head bow is bent in two curves across the front, with a strip of wood notched on each end and slipped through a slit cut into the backboard. The bow and foot support are attached to the board with leather thongs that thread through multiple drilled holes: above each notch, on each side of the backboard, through the middle of the head bow, in the support, and through the middle of the backboard in two places.

The mother would use this cradleboard, along with leather tumplines (head straps), to carry the baby on her back, or when traveling by horse. The baby would have been swaddled, placed on a pad on the board, and then secured with wide bands wrapped around both infant and cradle. When crossing the prairies, Ioway mothers placed older babies and young children on a travois in brightly painted rawhide boxes or trunks, "with their heads sticking out."[6]

The other cradle Skinner collected in Perkins was larger than the Algonquian type, measuring 34.5 inches long and about 12 inches wide. He described this Siouan-type prairie board as "the regulation every day Ioway cradle," with a plain bow and no foot support.[7] The head panel had two distinct design areas, each carved and painted (in red, yellow, and green) with triangles enclosed in an X-shaped figure. Brass brads added further embellishment. Skinner commented on seeing "similar examples, both as to form and decoration, even to the brass tacks, among the Kansa, Osage and Oto."[8]

Ioways decorated with quillwork, including plaiting; beadwork; and ribbons. Rosettes on the cradleboard wrapper in Catlin's sketch were concentric circles of quilled bands. Plaiting, which was characteristic of the Ioways, involved intertwining two quills between two parallel sinew threads. A six-point star was a common beadwork design among Ioway women, who were also noted for their beautiful ribbon appliqué, which they used on many surfaces, in addition to attaching ribbons as streamers.[9] Bulky three- and four-ply commercial yarns were available after the 1860s in a great variety of colors, which Ioways used to make finger-woven sashes, a craft they continue to this day.

CHAPTER 6

PLAINS CREE

The Plains Crees (Paskwâwiyiniwak) speak a dialect of the Algonquian language family and are closely related to the Ojibwas. Crees (Nêhiyawak) were a large Indigenous nation, originally subarctic boreal forest hunters, who would branch out into multiple tribes and bands across the prairies and plains of present-day Canada and the northern United States. In the early seventeenth century, Crees began working with the Hudson's Bay Company (HBC) as intermediaries in the fur trade, expanding westward in the process. When the HBC followed the fur trade south, many Crees were right behind the company, eventually migrating to the northern plains, a region that straddled what would become the border between the United States and Canada. When the HBC headed north again, in the mid-eighteenth century, some Crees chose to remain on the plains, adopting a lifestyle dependent on the buffalo. The fledgling Plains Cree tribe, which had assimilated some

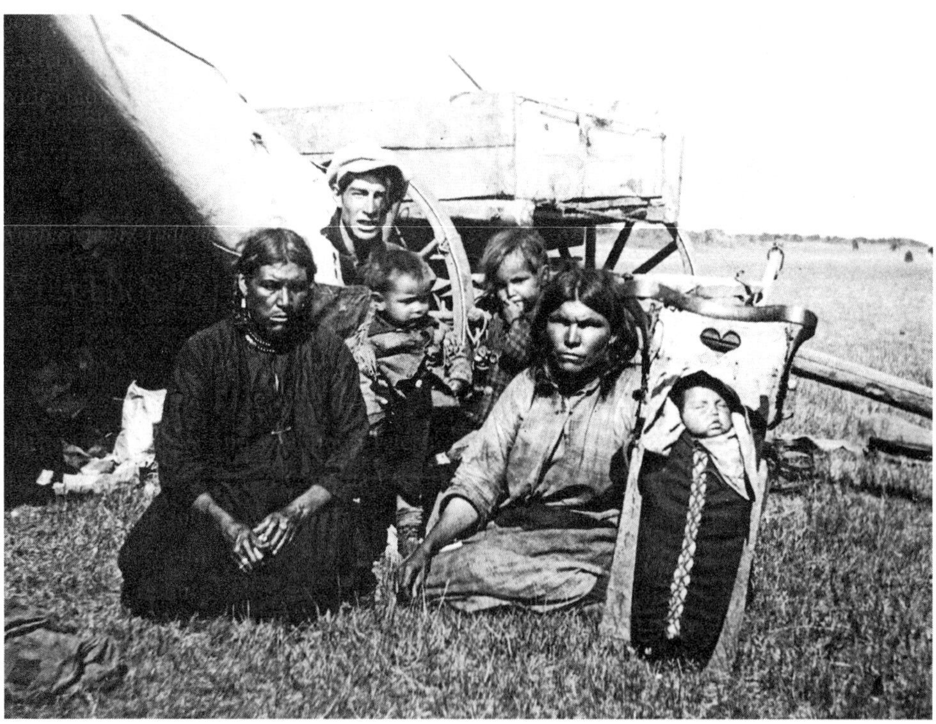

Plains Cree family with child in cradleboard on File Hills reserve, Saskatchewan, undated. Courtesy of the Glenbow Museum, Calgary, Alberta (NA-3454-48).

cultural elements from European fur traders, now incorporated useful traits and practices from neighboring tribes, such as the Assiniboine and the Ojibwa. Plains Crees relied on hunting, fishing, and gathering for subsistence, and they lived in the tanned leather tipis common among Plains peoples, who frequently moved camp to follow the buffalo.

By the second half of the nineteenth century, the Plains Cree tribe had divided into eight major bands, each with at least one prominent chief. The bands all gathered once a year, in the summer, for their sacred ceremonies. This was also a time of increasing conflict, however, exacerbated by the decline and then disappearance of the buffalo from their land. Tribes clashed with other tribes, with white settlers, and with the Canadian and U.S. governments. By the 1870s, most Plains Crees had moved to reserves (reservations) in Alberta and Saskatchewan, although in 1885, a group of Plains Crees crossed the border into Montana, ultimately joining up with a Chippewa band, with whom they would settle, about twenty years later, on the Rocky Boy's Indian Reservation in Montana.

Carriers

Cree mothers used two kinds of carriers, a wooden cradleboard, *tihkinâkan*, and a baby bag or moss bag, *wâspison*.[1] Plains Cree mothers believed that the moss bag helped the baby make a smooth transition from the womb into the world, and that the baby bag helped the infant feel calm and more secure.[2] The main purpose of the moss (sphagnum) was to absorb urine. When the moss was soiled by urine or feces, the mother would replace it in the bag with freshly gathered and dried moss from a supply she replenished daily. Moss bags were used for infants until they began crawling.

Both types of bags are made by first folding a rectangular piece of tanned skin or cloth lengthwise, then cutting small slits along each side of the long opening (similar to the placement of eyelets in a lace-up shoe), tucking in the bottom or folding the bottom up, and sewing that end closed. The sides are then laced together by threading a thong through slits, alternating sides to crisscross the opening, then tying the thong at the top. If cloth is used to make the bag, a strip of leather is usually sewn on to each side of the long opening, with slits in the leather aligned with those in the cloth. In the wintertime, baby bags, including moss bags, were lined with rabbit fur.

Baby bags were often decorated with quillwork, moose hair embroidery, or beadwork. I examined five Cree moss bags of similar construction but different dimensions and various materials, such as leather, velvet, and cotton cloth. The American Museum of Natural History has two Cree baby bags: an Eastern Cree plain cotton bag, 31.5 inches long, collected by Skinner at Moose Factory, Ontario; and a red velvet cloth bag, about 19 inches long and 10 inches wide, with an 11-inch-long bonnet to match. The cap is decorated with small white beads, rabbit fur, and leather. A beaded blue velvet bag I viewed at the Thomas Gilcrease Museum is 28 inches wide and 50 inches long. The Canadian Museum of History has a beaded black velvet bag 20.5 inches long and 8 inches wide. Finally, the fifth baby bag I examined—at the Colter Bay Visitor Center Indian Art Museum, at Grand Teton National Park—was leather, decorated with beaded black front panels, and measuring 11 inches long and 26 inches wide. (See plate 4 for an example of a Plains Cree moss bag, from the collections of the McCord Museum in Montreal.)

Cradleboards

Anthropologist David Mandelbaum speculated in 1940 that Crees might not have used cradleboards until European traders started selling them. The oldest Plains Cree informants at the time of his research told him that mothers bought cradleboards from the Hudson's Bay Company, and Amelia M. Paget, daughter of an HBC trader and a Métis mother, who had lived among the Crees in the late eighteenth century, recalled that Cree women saw cradleboards as a luxury item.[3] Fur trader Edwin T. Denig noted that some Cree men made cradleboards, which were "often handsomely carved, painted and otherwise adorned."[4]

Plains Crees did have their own term for the cradleboard, tihkinâkan, spelled phonetically as *te'-ke-na'cun* in Victor F. Lotrich's "Indian Terms for the Cradle and the Cradleboard," published in 1941. Citing E. E. McNeilly, the superintendent of the Rocky Boy's Indian Reservation in Montana, Lotrich wrote, "The word means 'protection basket.' The Indians explain the term thus: Sometimes when the basket was leaned against a tree or post it might fall over and the hooded part, which covered the head and face of the child, protected its face from coming in contact with the ground. This also applied if the basket was left hanging by a string and the string broke."[5]

The typical Plains Cree cradleboard was a nearly square flat board with a U-shaped wooden bow, or hoop, which was attached with thongs to a brace on the back of the board, one foot down from the top. The brace was a narrow strip of wood designed to extend the same length from each side of the board. Like the bow, the brace was attached with thongs. As Lotrich described, the hoop was designed to prevent injury if the cradleboard fell forward. Carrying straps could be worn across the mother's chest or forehead. The Eastern Cree cradleboard differed from the Plains Cree cradleboard in that the bag was laced to the board instead of being detachable.[6] A Cree cradleboard collected by Skinner, for example, has a bag that laces up the front, similar to a Plains Cree moss bag, but the bag is in two pieces that are also laced to the board (plate 3). The cradleboard is painted blue and scalloped across the top, with a heart-like shape cut into the top panel. The projecting bow is straight across the top instead of curved, which is unusual for an Eastern Cree board.

Quillwork and Beadwork

The floral quillwork and beadwork designs of the Plains Crees and the Plains Ojibwas spread across the northern plains as the tribes migrated westward. Denig described the garments crafted by Plains Crees as "neatly wrought both on skin and cloth with silk, beads, porcupine quills, feathers and moose hair."[7] Symmetry and realistic depictions of a wide variety of plants were characteristic of Plains Cree embroidery, as was a rounded, fontal look to the flowers. Barbara Hail describes the beadwork in *Hau, Kóla!*: against a solid backdrop of beaded lines in a single color, usually blue or white, "forms were outlined with single or double rows of beads and had gradual color shading. An overlay bead stitch was used, with interior beading following the shape of a form."[8]

As the Crees moved onto the plains, they brought other artistic traditions as well. Most of the women's work was perishable material, such as quillwork and moose hair embroidery. Quillwork diminished as small beads became widely available. According to Candace Greene, stylistic diversity increased on the plains after 1860, as seed beads arrived, enabling easier identification of regional and tribal style traditions.[9] Edward S. Curtis described some of ways in which Cree women made dyes. They "obtained a scarlet dye from the roots of bedstraw (*Galium tinctorium* and *G. boreal*). The roots, after being carefully washed, are boiled gently in a clean copper kettle, and a quantity of the juice of the moose-berry (*Viburnum edule*), strawberry, cranberry, or arctic raspberry, is added together with a few red tufts of pistils of the larch." Porcupine quills were tinted scarlet. Black was made from dried and pounded elder bark and bog iron ore. Yellow was made from lichens.[10]

Birth Customs

Plains Cree children, called "little travelers," were viewed as sacred bundles, gifts from the spiritual realm. During childbirth, a Plains Cree woman was assisted by three women, at least one of them an experienced older woman, usually a grandmother. One focused on supporting the mother through labor and delivery; one cared for the newborn; and the third assisted with whatever was needed. Curtis described the area where the woman would labor: "A pole with its base resting on the ground near the door is lashed at its other end to one of the tipi-poles at such a height that she can conveniently rest her arms on it while kneeling," the position in which she would give birth.[11]

Mandelbaum noted that instead of a bath after birth, newborns were "dried with dry rotted wood or moss. Leather from the top of an old tipi cover, soft and well smoked, was used to wrap infants. Mother's milk was squeezed on the child's eyes. The baby was not nursed until two days after birth." After the umbilical cord was cut, "the down inside the prairie puffball . . . was packed over infant's navel and held in place by a bandage" of soft buckskin.[12] The cord would become part of an amulet, wrapped in a bit of hide and tied at the side of the baby bag, while the knife used to cut the cord could not be employed again for any purpose until the baby's navel healed. The care of the umbilical cord and disposal of the placenta and afterbirth were part of the ceremony surrounding the birth of a new baby. All ceremonial responsibilities were handled by grandmothers, who also taught new mothers the sacred offering of newborn hair and teeth to the holy fire. The afterbirth was wrapped in a piece of hide and hung in a tree in the woods. The new mother or a grandmother would sing to the baby, welcoming the infant to the world.[13] A few days later, the baby would be placed in a moss bag.[14] As Leah Marie Dorion writes, "All new born children are spiritually pure. Parents were taught to treat all newborn children in a loving and gentle manner because this child just experienced the powerful journey from the spiritual realm into this physical world."[15]

An expecting Cree woman followed certain taboos and rituals during her pregnancy. She prayed every day to Ki-sei-men'-to and petitioned for good luck in the delivery of her baby. She also asked that the baby would be healthy and grow to be a good person. A pregnant woman was also supposed to turn over in bed a certain way, to be sure that the cord would not twist around the baby's neck. Sitting too close to a hot stove could cause the afterbirth to grow to the pregnant woman's stomach and give her a great deal of trouble.

Cree children were named soon after birth by an older member of the band, and a feast was held for the special occasion.

Amulet

According to Mandelbaum, the dried umbilicus was preserved in a small ornamented buckskin bag and tied to the baby's moss bag: the little bag, about four inches long, was decorated with beads and quills and had two compartments. The navel cord was wrapped and stored in one compartment, and the other was filled with tobacco. As soon as the child was able to run about, the little bag was tied around the his or her neck and hung down the back.[16] According to Curtis,

> An old person could give a child a blessing from his spirit helper by taking a pipe-full of tobacco from a child's bag. Before the old person smoked the pipe, he would ask his helpers to grant good fortune to the child. The parents were assured a continual round of supplications for their child. Not all the children wore the bags, for only the wealthy could afford to keep the bags filled with tobacco. Ceremonial elements common to all Cree were offerings of tobacco to the supernatural, particular spirit powers, vision songs, and prayers.[17]

Children discarded the amulet after puberty.

In addition to the amulet tied to moss bags, boys often had a pair of fetal caribou legs tied to their cradle to bring luck in hunting caribou in later life.

Cree Baby Bag

The baby bag or moss bag in the Gilcrease Museum (cat. no. 84.742) was identified as Cree or Ojibwa. No history was available on the specimen.

The bag, 25 inches long and 38 inches wide, is a U-shaped cover made of faded blue velvet with a cotton lining. The construction pattern was a rectangle, folded in half vertically, with a seam across the top. A small V shape, twelve inches long, was cut out of the center of the narrow side of the material. Two small Vs were cut out horizontally across the point of the larger V. The three edges of the Vs were then drawn together to make a T-shaped seam, forming the hood. The material was doubled under along the edge the entire length of the velvet. Holes were punched along the folded material. One long rawhide thong was threaded through the first hole, and then tied to the material. The thong was then threaded through all holes from one side to the other. Enough of the thong was left before tying to the hole to form a loop three inches long. There are nine loops along each side. At the ninth loop, the thong was pulled tight, making a decorative leather lacing around the hood. The loops were continued along the other side and tied at the edge of the material. Lacing was tied to the bottom loop or eyelets. The cloth was tucked in at the bottom and folded over at the side, and the edges were then laced together with the lacing thong.

The moss bag was used for a covering, protection from the elements, and to transport a small child. The mother was free to go about her daily chores with the swaddled baby close by, securely fastened to her back. After the baby was crawling, sometimes a larger moss bag was attached to a cradleboard.

Realistic floral designs were contour embroidered with glass seed beads, placed on the velvet on each side on the bag. The beads are white, yellow, red, light and dark green, light and dark blue, and orange, some translucent, some opaque. The design is symmetrical, with four separate floral designs on each side—bilateral symmetrical units of rounded forms, narrowly pointed leaves, and buds with color outlining. The Cree were known for the tradition of ornate delicate floral beadwork.

CHAPTER 7

PLAINS OJIBWA

The names Ojibwa and Chippewa refer to the same people, although the Plains Ojibwa (Nahkawininiwak), an Algonquian-speaking group from the woodland area around Lakes Superior and Huron, migrated farther west than did most Chippewas (Anishnaabe). On the western and northern plains, the Plains Ojibwas (also called Bungis, Bungays, or Salteaux) were buffalo hunters. After moving out of the woodland regions of present-day Michigan, Wisconsin, Minnesota, and Ontario in the late eighteenth century, they were able to establish a territory for their descendants in Ontario, North Dakota, and South Dakota. They evolved a cultural identity, similar to that of the Crees and Assiniboines, based on an equestrian buffalo-hunting lifestyle. The early emergence on the plains of the Ojibwas combined buffalo hunting with big game and fur trapping, fishing, and gathering. In the mid-nineteenth century, the Plains Ojibwa became fully dependent on the buffalo.

During the annual buffalo hunt in summer and early fall, they lived in hide tipis, using horse and travois and the Red River cart to move from place to place. They made parfleche and birch bark containers and wove baskets from willow. Their embroidery remained mainly Eastern Woodland with detailed geometric and floral motifs.

The Plains Ojibwa people were eventually scattered on various reservations and reserves in Montana, North Dakota, and Canada. In 1971, the Rocky Boy's reservation was established for a segment of the remaining Plains Ojibwa, Cree, and Plains Métis in Montana.

Cradles

Plains Ojibwa infants were swaddled in a baby bag and laced into a soft skin or cloth bag. Mothers carried the bags on their backs by passing a thong across their chest. In the wintertime, the bag was placed under the mother's loose parka, where the baby was kept warm and nursed if needed. The bag was lined with soft sphagnum moss or powdered buffalo dung and, in winter, a rabbit skin blanket or squirrel or weasel fur. Caribou skin cured with the fur on was often used as bag material because the skin was easy to obtain, warm, and light. To make a baby bag, women folded a rectangular piece of soft leather or cloth lengthwise and sewed it at one end. Similar to a lace-up shoe, perforations were made along each side of the edges, with a thong threaded through and tied at each hole, forming a loop about three inches from the thong. Baby bags of cloth were usually edged with leather and laced with leather lacing. The baby was swaddled with layers of cloth; placed in the bag, which was often packed with absorbent material (such as moss or buffalo dung); and then tightly laced with a leather thong. Every night, the baby was cleaned, and more absorbent material was added. Mothers would decorate the sides of the moss bag with beadwork embroidery, which a boy sometimes saved from his moss bag to decorate his Grass Dance regalia when he was older. Infants in moss bags were often placed in a basketry bassinet.[1]

A Plains Ojibwa baby wrapper in the American Museum of Natural History was collected on the Little Pine Reservation, Saskatchewan, in 1911. The plain blue velvet carrier, 27 inches long and lined in tan cotton, was laced with a leather thong along one edge to form hoops for lacing the baby in the bag.

Sometimes a mother placed her baby in a large oblong basketry bassinet woven with alternating brown and white willow withes. The rim is reinforced with a wood hoop. Rectangular openings at the center of the rim on both sides serve as handles. A Ojibwa baby basket can be seen in the Minnesota Historical Society (MNHS) Collections Online.[2] The basket is 9 inches high, 28.5 inches long, and 18 inches wide.

The MNHS also has a fawn hide Ojibwa cradleboard blanket with spot-stitched beadwork (access. no. 10000.92).[3] The hide is lined with blue-gray cotton and edged with olive-green cloth. The hide side is decorated with the beadwork pieces in the center and at two corners.

Cradleboards

Cradleboard in the Obijwa (or Chippewa) language is "*a'dikina'gûn* (*adikina*, cradle; *gûn*, article or object)—'cradle board.'"[4] Victor F. Lotrich writes that the board was used "to fulfill the desire that children should be straight and vigorous. . . . The language of the Chippewa [Ojibwa] differed in pronunciation . . . in different localities. . . . Great Lakes—*di ki na gon*, cradleboard. The word means 'to tie or wrap.' . . . Lake Superior—*dĭ kĭ nä'gän*, cradleboard. Diki means 'something solid or hard'; nagan means 'something you can handle, like a lively child or a hard body.'"[5] The Little Shell Chippewa use the word "*tikinagan*, cradleboard, and *tchitchibakonagan*, cradle."[6]

Peter Rindisbacher, a Swiss American artist, painted an untitled watercolor in 1821–1823 depicting a Plains Ojibwa family. His painting shows an Ojibwa mother with a baby in a cradleboard strapped to her back. Edwin T. Denig, a trader in the upper Missouri River area, noted that Plains Crees and Assiniboines traded cradleboards with the Ojibwas.

Robert E. Ritzenthaler and Pat Ritzenthaler describe the typical Ojibwa cradleboard as a "cedar board about two feet in length, ten inches wide, three eighths of an inch thick. A foot brace was fastened at one end, and a hickory hoop, which served to protect the head, was fastened near the other. Sphagnum moss in a shallow birch bark tray did double duty as both cushion and diaper when necessary, the entire tray with its moss was discarded and a fresh one installed."[7] A light rod was fastened loosely to one side of the cradleboard, attached to the binding bands and pinned or tied over the baby. James H. Howard notes that the moss bag was fastened to a cradleboard and that several of his informants had been raised in cradleboards, a fact attested to by the occipital flattening of their skulls. Howard describes a cradleboard found in the collections at the North Dakota Heritage Center and State Museum (plate 6) as a rectangular board "with its top highly carved and decorated with brass tacks. A forward projecting arc of wood is provided in the area of the child's head to protect the child if the cradle is dropped or tipped over. The moss bag part of this particular cradleboard is beautifully decorated in beaded openwork designs. A U-shaped wooden piece is set at the bottom of the cradleboard as a rest for the infant's feet."[8]

Another cradleboard identified as Plains Ojibwa, in the collections of the Canadian Museum of History (V-F-203), is similar to the board Howard describes, with carved notches along the top of the board and a heart cut-out where the baby's head would lie. The cradleboard from the Canadian Museum of History, however, is painted red instead of blue and measures 29.9 inches long and 17 inches wide, with the bent bow, or hoop, height at 15.5 inches. A line of metal tacks below the notched carving provide decoration. The bow is notched, slipped over a narrow board fastened to the back of the main board, and tied to the sides with rawhide thongs.

George Catlin celebrated the Fourth of July in 1835 among the Chippewas and Dakotas at Fort Snelling, in Minnesota Territory, where he painted several Chippewa portraits. One, *Ojibwa/Chippewa Woman with Baby in Cradle* (1835), depicted Ju-ah-kis-gaw with her baby in a cradleboard on her lap. He mentioned the Sioux's (Dakotas') similar custom of cradling infants and of "the ni-ahkust-ahg (or umbilicus) hanging before the child's face for its supernatural protector."[9] The cradleboard in Catlin's painting is similar to the traditional Ojibwa cradleboards found in museums; the baby is laid on a pad and bound to the board with two wide bands.

According to Frances Densmore, the principal woodworking tools Ojibwas used for making a cradleboard were an ax and carving knife. The bow was bent by placing the wood in hot water or holding it near the fire. Bows provided babies protection not only from falls but also from the weather and insects, providing a place to fasten a blanket (in winter) or a thin cloth. Small objects were also hung from the bow for the baby to look at and sometimes play with (when arms were free). Carrying straps, or tumplines, fastened to the bow at each end, enabling the mother to carry the baby on her back. She would cross the strap over her chest or forehead, and the tumpline would support and balance the load on her back. The flat straps were usually about 3 inches wide and 12 inches long.[10]

Plains Ojibwa babies were not always fastened to the cradleboard with wide decorated bands; often a baby bag was tied to the board at the height of the head bow. Two leather loops were threaded through two holes drilled in each side of the board, about two inches from the edge, and were then tied together with leather lacing. Before being confined to the cradleboard, the baby would be wrapped securely, wearing little or no clothing. Mothers let their babies off the board to play, and then put them back on their boards to sleep or nurse. If a mother was traveling, the board was strapped to her back. Sometimes a mother placed the board upright so that the baby could be entertained nearby as she worked or while the family ate meals. When babies were able to control their arm movements, their arms were released above the cradleboard's binding bands for a little while at a time. The cradleboard afforded warmth, protection, and security. Densmore's informants told him that "children cried to be put back in the cradle board after being out of it for a time."[11]

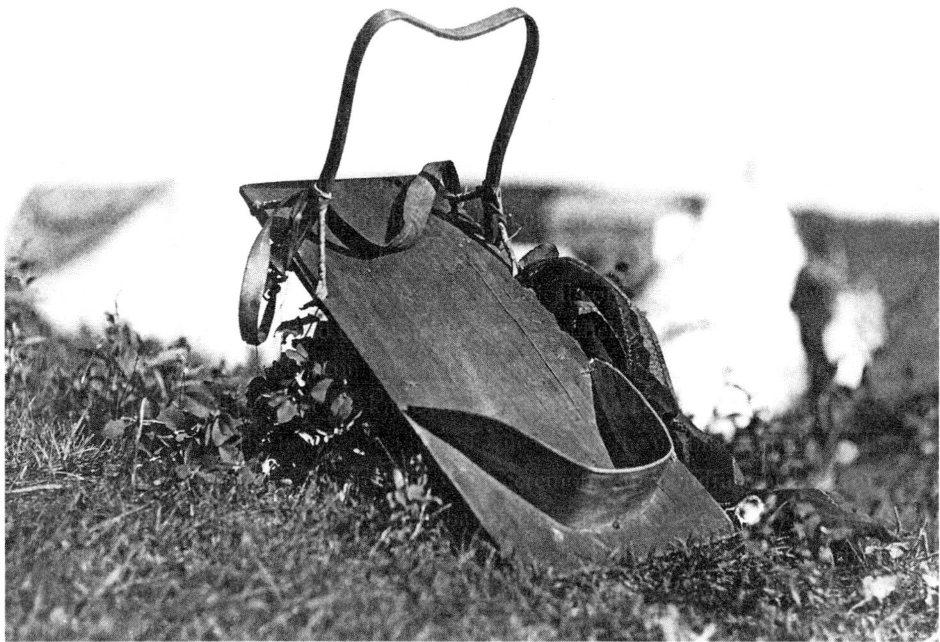

Ojibwa (Chippewa) cradleboard, undated photograph by Francis Densmore. Courtesy of the State Historical Society of North Dakota, Bismarck (SHSND 00086-00697).

Another purpose for cradleboards was to ensure that children had straight arms, legs, and backs—the arms of newborns were fastened straight against their sides at all times. In addition to the cradleboard, Ojibwa mothers employed the custom of "pinning up the baby" as a means of physically training their children's limbs and posture starting in early infancy. Tightly pinning the child in cloth, a form of swaddling, confined the arms and legs as closely as in the cradleboard. In warmer weather, the fingers and toes were uncovered. This was also how mothers prepared children for sleeping in a blanket at night or on the mother's back.[12]

During the day, Plains Ojibwas also used hammocks, made from a piece of rectangular hide or blanket, two pieces of rope, and two sticks the same size. The ropes were tied parallel to each other between two posts or trees, with the blanket or hide folded several times over the ropes. The sticks were then placed horizontally between the ropes, inside the blanket, to keep the blanket from the baby's face. A baby might be placed in a hammock while swaddled and in a cradleboard.

Cradleboards also played a role in Plains Ojibwa mourning practices. It was customary to wear outward signs of grief for about a year after a death, including keeping a "spirit bundle." Some mothers who lost a child placed the child's clothing in the cradle instead of carrying a spirit bundle.

Quillwork and Beadwork

Early contact with Euro-Americans well before their move onto the northern plains led to changes in Ojibwa lifestyle and material culture. Porcupine quill decorative work was more common than beadwork because all available material was perishable: birch bark, reeds, and hides. The custom of burying a person's possessions at death has limited the examples available of early Ojibwa art. For materials, Plains Ojibwas used grasses, porcupine quills, decorated birch bark, and leather. "Grasses were the more primitive, as they required less preparations," explains Densmore, "and it is also said that they were used prior to porcupine quills by the Chippewa."[15] The earliest use of decorative materials was in geometric and simple line patterns. Later designs included solid patterns representing leaves and flowers dyed red, yellow, and sometimes purple. When traders began to bring in cloth and ribbons, Ojibwas used decorative appliqués on clothing and on baby binding bands for cradleboards.

Glass beads from Italy and Czechoslovakia became plentiful in overland traders' inventories in the mid- to late nineteenth century. The early forms of beadwork, like early Ojibwa quillwork, were geometric and line patterns. Densmore identified six simple line patterns used by the Ojibwas along with "a border 3 or 4 inches wide on each edge, entirely covering the cloth except for a narrow space where the woven braid was tied around the cradle board."[16] Geometric patterns were especially suited for loom beadwork. After the advent of seed beads, Ojibwa women frequently used them when weaving on a small loom panel to adorn clothing and other items. The black wool baby bag on the cradleboard shown in plate 6 is covered with alternating ottertail and diamond patterns of beadwork in blue, white, red, and green. The ottertail pattern was developed before contact with Europeans. Patterns from nature stemmed from the Ojibwa philosophy to live in harmony with the natural world. Applied design beadwork was older than woven work. The embroidery was done with the overlaid, or spot, stitch, in which a string of beads is laid along a line or pattern and another thread is passed over the string every two or three beads. This is substantially the same stitch used in Ojibwa quillwork.

The spot stitch gives artisans flexibility in creating floral patterns and tight beadwork that follows the curving lines and motifs; the design is executed, and then the background is filled in. Ojibwas developed beadwork designs in imitation of nature, including many of the plants around them. Old floral beadwork depicts the wild rose motif, which appears as buds and petals. The wild rose was considered a representative flower of the Ojibwas, and it grows in profusion throughout their country. The old floral patterns are conventional and truthful depictions of nature.

Beadworkers had their own patterns, which they seldom exchanged, cut from birch bark or paper. They used the patterns in units and combined in designs on all decorative work. Units comprised types of patterns that could be outlined, like flowers, leaves, and double curves. Before women obtained scissors, they cut the outline of patterns by perforating the birch bark with a sharp fishbone, then cutting along the perforated lines with a knife.[17]

Birth Customs

Plains Ojibwa babies were delivered in a special hut away from the main camp. Women experienced with birth assisted the expecting mother, who also relied on a delivery rack—a pole set horizontally in the Y of two vertical posts, about two feet off the ground. The woman, her chest against the pole, delivered the baby while kneeling on a mat or blanket. The midwife then severed the umbilical cord and tied it. When dried, the cord was sewn into a small leather bag. The newborn was then bathed in warm water containing herbs, dried with soft moss, dusted with powdered bison dung, and wrapped in a piece of soft buckskin or cloth.[18]

Names were bestowed on infants at birth, based on various inspirations, such as an unusual event at the time, the war exploit of a relative, or a distinguishing personal characteristic.

Amulet

The small leather pouch, sewn with sinew, in which the umbilical cord was preserved hung on the cradleboard. This amulet was the child's first toy, but it was expected to be kept for a lifetime. A mother who lost a child kept and treasured the little amulet. Ritzenthaler described the charm as a small buckskin pouch the shape of a diamond, decorated with dyed quills, beads, and dyed moose hair embroidery. Two amulets collected by Alanson Skinner on the Long Plain First Nation reserve in Canada were identified as Plains Ojibwa at the American Museum of Natural History. The amulets are irregular hexagons, completely beaded with different patterns on each side: one embroidered with flowers, and the other with geometrical shapes. Each measured 5.5 inches long, 3 to 3.5 inches wide, and 1.2 inches thick. The reasons for preserving the navel cord, according to Densmore, were "securing wisdom for the child" so that he or she "would not be foolish"; if the cord wasn't kept, "the child would always be searching for something."[19]

PART THREE

PRAIRIE CRADLEBOARDS

Otoe-Missouria

Osage

Kaw

Omaha

Ponca

Pawnee

CHAPTER 8

OTOE-MISSOURIA

The Otoe-Missouria (Jiwere-Nut'achi) and the closely related Ioway tribe spoke mutually intelligible dialects of Chiwere, of the Siouan language family. Otoe-Missourias once lived in the Great Lakes region as Winnebago (Ho-Chunk) people until the 1600s, when the Otoes, Missourias, and Ioways split off and migrated separately to the south and the west.

The Otoes, who call themselves Jiwere (People of This Place), settled south of the Platte River in what is now southeastern Nebraska. The Missourias, who call themselves Nut'achi (Dwellers on the River), remained on the Missouri River. During the eighteenth century, the Missouria tribe was decimated by wars and smallpox. Survivors joined the Otoe and lived together as a social, political, and economic unit, merging the two cultures.

Otoes and Missourias were sedentary village horticulturalists, dependent on gathering and bison hunting. They built earth lodges covered with sod and lived in skin tipis when traveling during the hunting season. Their society was organized into clans and by rank. Each clan had its own sacred origins, legends, rituals, privileges, rights, and duties. Today the Otoe-Missouria tribe has seven clans.

Otoe-Missouria lands were ceded to the United States by treaty in 1854, when the tribe accepted a reservation along the Big Blue River, on the current border between Nebraska and Kansas. Ideological factions split the tribe during the 1870s. In 1881, the Otoe-Missourias sold the reservation along the Big Blue River and migrated south to the Cherokee Outlet in Indian Territory (present-day Oklahoma), where they purchased a new reservation. The current Otoe-Missouria tribal offices are in Red Rock, Oklahoma.

Cradleboards

The Otoe-Missouria word for cradleboard is *uxuwe*. The only written source I found on the Otoe-Missouria cradle was William Whitman's *The Oto*. According to Whitman, the cradleboard was a Siouan prairie type, which was also seen among the Kaws, Poncas, Osages, Ioways, and Winnebagos: "The Oto cradle board is similar to the Osage board, and many Oto cradle boards are now made by Osage."[1] The board would be carved and painted above the baby's head in designs similar to those painted on parfleches.

Jimm GoodTracks remembered seeing an Otoe cradleboard in 1971 at the Ioway, Sac and Fox Mission museum in Highland, Kansas. It was a plain board free of decoration, identified on a card as "Hokwawe." Unfortunately, the cradleboard is no longer in the museum. The Kansas State Historical Society collections manager revealed that a cradleboard with

Ioway tribal affiliation was taken off display in 1980 and repatriated in 1985. With no record or history for the cradleboard, however, it could not be identified as Otoe. Considering the close relationship between Otoe-Missourias and Ioways, Otoe-Missourias might have also used a flat board, a bent bow, and a moveable footrest, features found in Ioway cradleboards.

Whitman notes that cradleboards "were made in expectation of birth, and were considered to influence the health of the child. Certain men 'knew how' to make cradles. They were given a present for them, a horse or a blanket." The Otoe-Missourias also reused cradleboards: "If the baby thrived, the cradle was saved for the next child."[3] Otoe-Missouria women usually took their babies off their cradleboards to nurse them, and after about six months, babies were no longer tied to the board. When the tribe traveled, mothers carried the cradleboards on their backs. A baby too old for the cradleboard was still carried on the mother's back but in a makeshift carrier she created by tying a blanket around her waist and shoulders.[4]

A 1998 photograph at the Oklahoma Historical Museum shows Hilda Harris, Otoe, holding the newest generation in a cradleboard in her arms (plate 8). The child is swaddled and lying on a folded blanket, bound to the cradleboard. The board appears to be plain with a broad circular head bow. Trinkets are tied across the front of the bow. Four thongs are attached to each side of the board below the head board, creating loops through which a narrow woven belt is threaded and tied at the bottom loop.

I met an Otoe artist, a granddaughter of Hilda Harris, at Red Earth in 2008 and questioned her about the Otoe cradleboard. She described the carved, painted headboard, which was similar in style to that of the Kaw. The board was divided into halves, with a large X shape carved in each side and triangles outlined with metal brads. Shapes were painted red, blue, yellow, and green.

Birth Customs

Otoe-Missourias erected a separate tipi for a pending birth, where the expecting woman had a bed for the delivery and her own cookware, since she was not allowed to eat with the family. She was attended by only women unless she had a difficult labor, when a medicine man might be called in. During her labor, as Whitman describes, "the father of the child was supposed to walk around as if he were hunting. And for the purification of the mother, he had to provide game and food for the head chiefs."[5]

After the delivery, the umbilical cord was cut by the practiced hands of one of the older women, and "the baby was wiped off, rubbed with tallow, wrapped in rags and tied to a cradle board." The mother remained in her isolated tipi for a month after giving birth to a boy, or for half that time if she'd had a girl. Both boys and girls had their ears pierced in two places on each ear soon after they were born, and their first moccasins were also pierced with several holes in the bottom.[6]

The child was named four days after birth in a ceremony. A highly esteemed male elder gave the family four names from which to choose, each associated with the clan in which the child was born; the names might include, for example, family names and the names of plants or animals related in some way to the clan. According to Whitman, the naming ceremony "was the child's initiation into his gens [clan], and the name given at this time was in the nature of a blessing for a long and fruitful life and for the extension of the family through the individual." First- and second-born children, and sometimes subsequent children, usually received sacred names. Sacred names were based on the origin story of the father's clan (or gens), and each had a song that the bearer of the name would "own."[7]

Following the family ceremony, others were invited to a feast, where gifts were dispensed to honor the child. All who took part in the work and rituals surrounding the child's birth received gifts, including the man who pierced the baby's ears and even, according to Whitman, "the man who wiped away the blood" during the piercing ceremony.[8] Gift giving brought honor to the giver and to the baby who occasioned the generosity. The esteemed man who had provided the names received many gifts. He also offered prayers to the spirits, songs relating the story of the name chosen, and a prophecy for the child.

CHAPTER 9

OSAGE

Culturally and linguistically, the Osage (Wazhazhi) tribe was closely related to the Quapaw, Kaw, Omaha, and Ponca tribes of the Dhegiha branch of the Siouan language family. Before European contact, the Osage migrated westward from the present-day Ohio Valley, separated in what is now Missouri, and settled along the tributaries of the Missouri River. The Osage tribe's original name, Wazhazhi, means the Children of the Middle Waters or the Little Ones of the Middle Waters. They lived in permanent villages of wigwams covered in mats or bark. Their subsistence was mixed, combining hunting, gathering, horticulture, and trade. The Osage were typical of the Prairie tribes. They followed the annual buffalo hunt for meat on the western plains, although they never adopted the tipi for hunting camps.

Osage life was regulated by tribal custom. They were divided into the Sky People and the Earth People. Each of these divisions had numerous clans, with clan membership and ancestry traced through the father. Osages attached spiritual significance to all aspects of life and had ceremonies and rituals to accompany everyday tasks. Every event in their lives had to have meaning and purpose. The Osage had been a relatively wealthy people, one of the few tribes that never had a major war with Europeans or Americans.

The Osages suffered geographical displacement in the nineteenth century, ceding their traditional lands to the United States and migrating to Kansas by 1825. In 1870, the Osage tribe relocated again to a reservation in Indian Territory. Osage Nation headquarters are located in Pawhuska, Oklahoma.

Cradleboards

Osage cradleboards were of the Siouan prairie type, a plank of wood with a face guard, or bow, and no footrest. According to Siouan linguist John Koontz, "Cradleboards were called *odhophe*." John Joseph Mathews, in his book about his people, *The Osages: Children of the Middle Water*, calls the cradleboard *o-lo-psha* (follow trail of animals). Most of the boards I examined were 42 inches long and 10.5 inches wide. The top one-third was usually decorated with a carved and painted panel and frequently highlighted with brass tacks. A row of pierced holes were drilled just below the design section, with each hole flat on the bottom and rounded at the top.

The decorative carved panel on Osage cradleboards had geometric elements and "was usually split into vertical halves, with a common design unit being an hourglass-like element in each half."[2] The geometric designs were frequently outlined with brass tacks. A

Osage child LeeAnn Yarbrough bound to a cradleboard with finger-woven sashes, undated. Courtesy of the Yarbrough family, Pawhuska, Oklahoma.

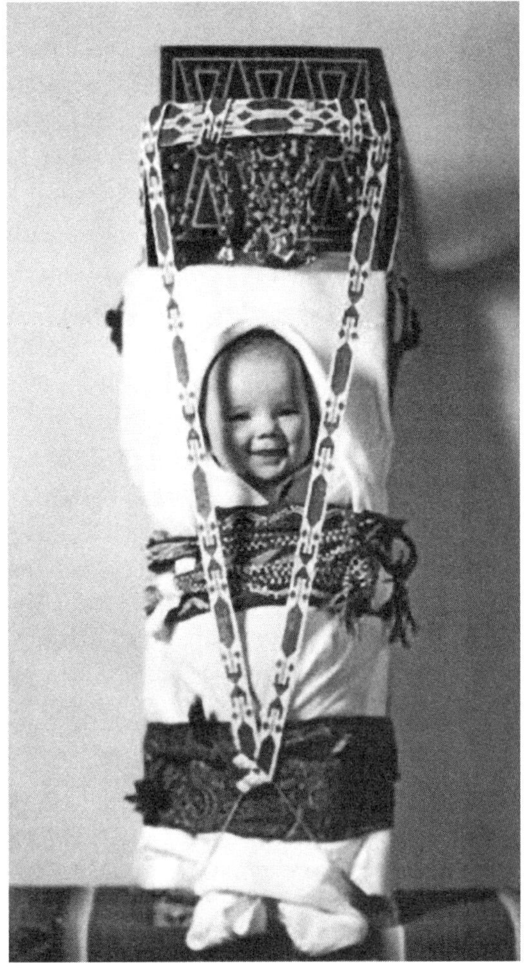

single solid-line border usually completed the panel. The design specifics reflected clan affiliation.

The face guard was tied to the board with thongs just below the row of holes. It could be lowered above the head of the baby. A hole in each side of the board and another hole close to the end of the face guard allowed the two pieces to be tied together. The face guard was usually 2 inches wide, bent in a squared U shape, and made from bois d'arc (Osage orange) wood. The piece of wood would be soaked in water until the wood was pliable; then it would be shaped and dried. Thongs holding this hoop were tied to the board through two holes just below the design area, then folded over the hoop and tied to a short thong at the bottom of the board. A protective cloth or blanket was draped over the wooden bow, and the vertical thongs would prevent the cloth from completely covering the baby's face. The two vertical thongs and the short thong at the bottom of the board secured the bow to the board.

The baby was wrapped in a blanket, then placed on a soft pad or folded blanket on the board. Two small pads were folded and placed under the infant, one behind the neck, and one behind the bent knees. The baby was tied to the board with strips of leather or blanket, or colorful finger-woven belts.[3]

According to legend, weaving came to the Osages from the spider. Finger weaving is unique because no loom is used, and designs are woven from the center to the edge of the piece. Design elements were symbolic and formed patterns with beads interwoven with the design.

Cradleboards were decorated with downy feathers, brass thimbles, hawk bells, beaded strips, ribbon or finger-weaving strips, and yarn tassels. Hanging decorations amused babies and helped them learn to focus their eyes. The face guards were often covered with a piece of navy blue trade wool with colorful stripes at the end, extending beyond the face guard. Red stroud cloth was traditionally reserved for the firstborn son and daughter. The wool would have a beaded band or ribbonwork all along the bent bow. The thongs holding the face guard were often secured with colorful beaded straps.

Osage mothers did not strap the cradleboard to their backs. Instead they carried the board, propped it up, or hung it by the hide loop on the top of the board. According to Mathews, however, Osage mothers did carry the baby boards on their backs in the old days. Infants slept at night with their mothers, wrapped in specially marked buffalo robes. During the day, infants were placed on a cradleboards.[4] Osage cradleboards were made and used long after other tribes discontinued the practice.

Marie Maker, who made cradleboards, explained in her 1968 oral history why the Osages used them. She was eighty years old at the time of her interview in Oklahoma. Maker maintained that babies were put on cradleboards to help them sleep well without moving around in their sleep. The boards kept their backs and legs straight. Also, it was easy to keep the baby warm in the wintertime bundled up on a cradleboard. The board "gives them a good start—I mean, straight, upright person." Maker explained that it was traditional for the relatives on the father's side to give the cradleboard. She described the boards as about a foot wide, three feet long, and three-quarters of an inch thick. The boards were painted, and the designs were outlined with brass tacks. Bells were strung on buckskin strings and tied to the bow. In the summertime, mosquito net or thin cloth kept insects off babies while they slept. Maker described beadwork decorating the bow, with beads also strung on the buckskin strings. When the board was completed, it was traditional for the maker to pray over the board. Maker prayed that the child would grow up to be useful and have a family. She thought good thoughts and wishes for the baby. Later she would be honored with a dinner for making the cradleboard. One time she was given a horse.[5]

Mathews shares the story of the cradleboard in his oral history of his people:

> His parents must have a board fashioned, with a hood of flint buffalo skin to protect his head from the wind. From this hood there must be little things that tinkled in the breeze, or downy feathers that moved with the air's slightest breath. [T]here might have been such *wah'don-skas* as trade thimbles attached to the head of the baby board, and these would be considered wonderful objects of interest to the just focusing eyes of the baby, but of course, there were the long, elegant tail-feathers of the scissortail flycatcher, the tail feathers of the scarlet tanager, or the cardinal.[6]

The baby board would be made of cedar, pine, birch, or poplar according to the father's clan. (In the past one hundred years, cradleboards have been made of commercial lumber.) On the top of board was a loop of hide so that the board could be hung in a tree.[7]

Birth Customs

Nearly all Osage families wanted children, and a birth was an important event. Children were the greatest of Wakonda's blessings and represented the future of the tribe. Mathews told the Osage story of babies as stars from the sky lodge:

The babies were little stars from Spirit-land, and as they grew older and when they become persons, they had to have names, but when they first came to earth they were from the sky and they were nameless and represented an old tribal *ga-ni-tha* before organization, even though their natal cries were not cries of fear of the tragedies and uncertainties of life but the pray-crying to Wah'Kon-Tah in the tribal tradition. They had been taught this prayer before they came to earth. This was the infant chant to the Grandfather the Sun—to his light; if a night birth, a cry to the Moon Woman.[8]

The most basic requirement for survival of the Osage people was their children. According to Mathews, babies were carefully tended until they were named and became a person. The expectant mother was attended by her mother or another female relative in a separate round lodge. A pit was dug between the poles for the afterbirth. Dried moss was used as an absorbent. The newborn was wrapped in rabbit fur, duck skin, or goose skin.[9] Victor Tixier gave an account of an Osage woman giving birth on a journey: "[They] engage in the hardest work until the last stage of the pregnancy. When sharp frequent pains announce that delivery is near, the matrons of the tribe, if the tribe is on its way, hastily build a round hut in which the woman in childbed is placed on skins. In the delivery, nature is generally allowed to take its course and generally labor is terminated without accident."[10] After washing the newborn, the mother strapped the baby on a board and resumed the journey.

Evidence suggests that Osages practiced flattening the skull to some degree, by pressing a newly born baby's head against the board of the cradle. Tixier described Osage heads as small with flat occipitals: "The forehead of the Osage are high and narrow, their temples wide, their eyes small and black, and deeply set but quite bright, their cheek bones prominent."[11] George Catlin wrote about the peculiarity of Osages' heads, produced in infancy by tightly binding the infant head to a cradleboard "as to force in the occipital bone, and create an unnatural elevation of the top of the head." But in comparison to the flattening practices of some other tribes, Catlin wrote, Osages pressed the occipital only "to a moderate degree," causing a "slight . . . departure from the symmetry of nature."[12]

Osage Cradleboard Symbolism

The symbolism of the Osage was complex and sophisticated. During the collapse of traditional religious institutions and practices, in the nineteenth and twentieth centuries, many of the symbolic meanings, forms, and designs were lost. Osage religious ritual and tribal, social, and political organizations were modeled after their concept of the universe. All living things were modeled after their concept of the universe. All living things were manifestations of the mysterious power of Wakonda. Everything was sacred. Every feature of a ritual had meaning and purpose. Life, symbols, and elements were brought together and moved physically in different patterns to focus their composite sacred meaning toward a goal or to meet a particular need. Making a cradleboard was an expression of Osage beliefs.

Parents were expected to have a cradleboard ready, fashioned according to each clan's special life symbols. Cedar was a sacred Osage tribal symbol of long life, but the cradleboard must be made of the wood of the father's clan. Boards without the sacredness of cedar would have a cross in the middle, under the baby's sacrum, as well as the stylized symbol of the father's clan in beads or flattened quills. The cradleboard was a symbol for the path of life, as Mathews explains: "The cradleboard was the beginning of the Road of Life, the true trail such as the animals make to water and food; for the animals have instinct and go straight to water and food."[13]

The sacred robe used to wrap the infant represented the sky, from which all life came, and had to be made by the mother.

> Let the father of your child secure the skin of old male buffalo. You will dress and soften the skin with your own hands. When you have made it soft and pliable, take some red paint and with it draw a straight, narrow line from the head, through the length of the body of the skin, to the tip of the tail. This straight line represents the path of power of day that liveth forever. You will paint all four legs of the robe red, to represent the dawn, the coming of the force of day of the life. Let each child whom you have given birth sleep in the consecrated robe and you will have aid in bringing to maturity your children.[14]

Osage cradleboards were usually painted red, green, and yellow. Red is sacred and symbolic of the red dawn or sun, the source of life. The green and yellow colors suggest the grass and the sun, both important to Osage survival. Green also signifies enduring life. The heart motif found on many Osage cradles refers to the mating of trumpeter swans, which in turn are associated with the union of sky and earth that makes all things possible. The heart is a fertility symbol meant to convey the birth of future generations. It also represents bravery and determination, because the trumpeter swans are known to protect their nest to the death to ensure the survival of the next generation.[15]

Osage Cradleboard

The specimen I studied was at the Sam Noble Oklahoma Museum of Natural History in Norman, Oklahoma (cat. no. E/1952/4/068). The cradleboard was identified as Osage by Kathryn Red Corn of the Osage Tribal Museum. I examined the cradleboard and compared it to a miniature Osage cradle found at the Osage Tribal Museum. Clifford L. Logan collected the cradleboard prior to 1940, and a note attached to the back explains that the cradle was used by Mildred Pitts's baby. She was an Osage from Hominy, Oklahoma.

The board is a plank of commercial pine lumber, 41.1 inches long, 10.5 inches wide, and 0.6 inches thick. The top one-third is carved and painted, with a row of seven holes, 1.5 inches wide, cut out just below the border. The decorative holes are flat at the base and rounded at the top. Four functional holes, two in the middle and one on each side, are twelve inches from the top of the board. Another two holes appear on each side of the board 1 inch from the bottom.

The hoop, or face guard, is 37 by 2 inches, and both ends are notched. Leather thongs tied to the notched ends are also tied through the two holes on each side. The face guard is

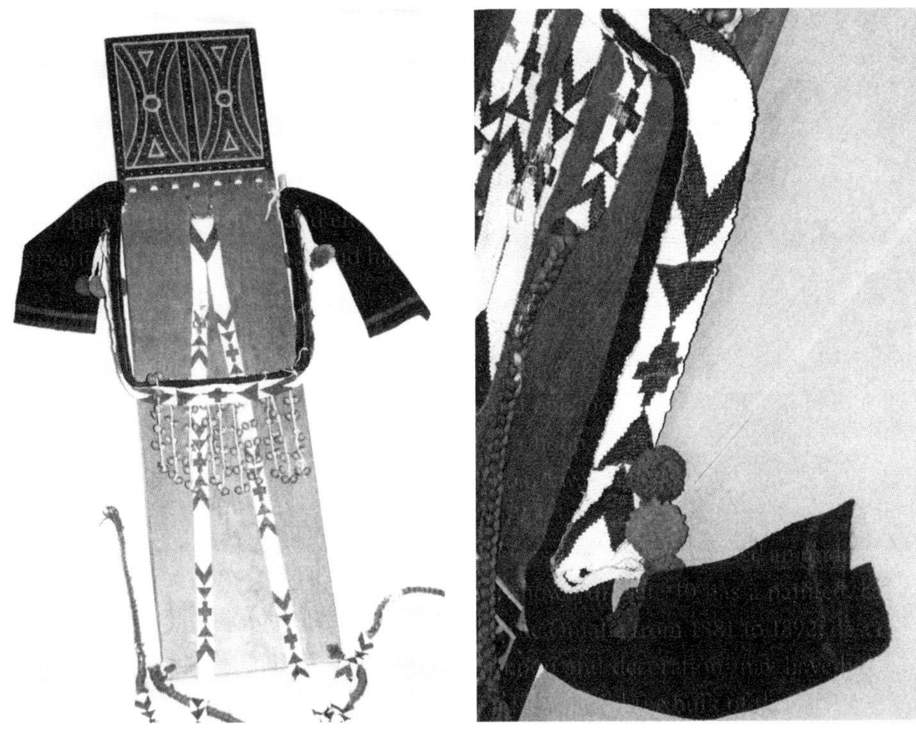

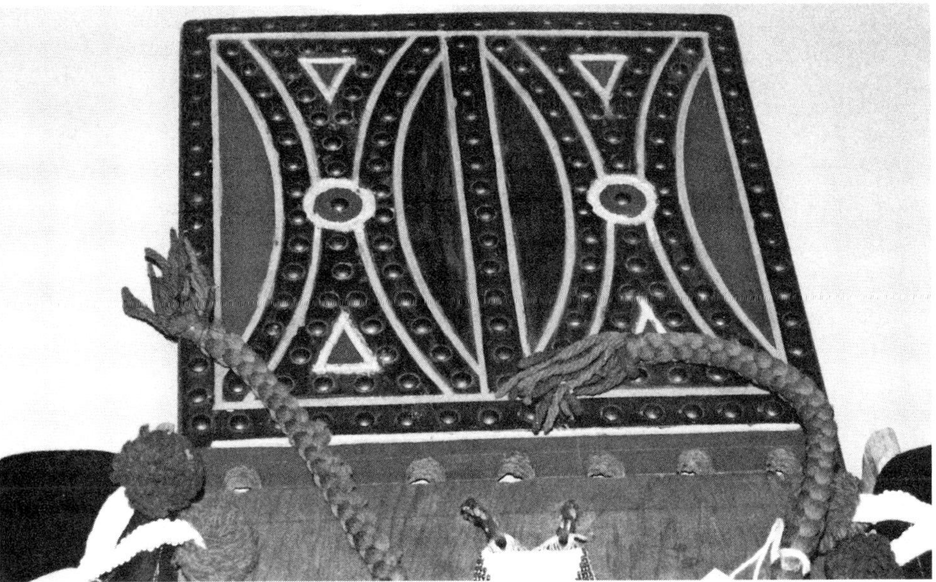

Osage cradleboard, date and measurements unknown: (*top left*) view of the board; (*top right*) loom beadwork stitched on the navy wool strip covering the head bow; and (*bottom*) carved, painted panel with geometric design, outlined with tacks. Photographs by the author. Courtesy of the Sam Noble Oklahoma Museum of Natural History, University of Oklahoma (E/1952/4/068).

covered with navy blue wool cloth that extends 12 inches beyond the board on each side. The cloth was cut to show the red and yellow stripes on the ends. The outer part of the guard is covered with loom-woven beadwork in bands of a geometric design, including triangles, crosses, blocks, rectangles, and diagonal stripes. The pattern repeats three times, alternating dark blue/red/dark blue converging arrows on a white background. The beaded band extends the length of the guard. Attached to the band are four narrow white beaded strips (2.5 inches) with green, yellow, and rose yarn pom-poms. Below the decorated carving, ten 7-inch-long buckskin cords hang from the face guard. Twelve small hawk bells are tied to each cord.

The cradleboard does not have a carrying strap. Osage mothers usually carried their baby boards in their arms or propped them up. Catlin wrote that the infants were lashed to boards and slung on the mother's back.[16]

The board's geometric design is carved and painted, taking up the top 11 inches of the board. The design is split into equal vertical sections, each with the hourglass design, as Feder described of typical Osage designs. The background is painted red. The carved design is green, outlined in yellow and white. The design and border are studded with brass nail heads. The area just below the border of the seven holes is painted red.

A 2-inch-wide beaded band is tied to the board through the two holes just below the carved panel. This band is decorated with two short braided yarn cords, forming the blanket guard. Like the face guard, the blanket guard bead pattern is alternating red and dark blue converging arrows on white background. About 2 inches below the start of the band, it splits into two bands. At the bottom of these bands is tied a 12-inch length of braided yarn in rose and green. A similar yarn rope, 22 inches long, threads through the two holes on each side and is tied to the beaded bands where they fold over the face guard.

The cradleboard is typical Osage boards, including the carving design of mirror-image geometric panels; the red, green, and yellow color scheme of the carving; the brass tack outline; and the row of seven holes below the border of brads.

A cradleboard identified as Osage in the Smithsonian National Museum Natural History (cat. no. 368849) has carved and painted triangles on the panel, highlighted with hot-file burn decorations and outlined with brass tacks. The bow is covered with machine-sewn ribbon work, selvedge trade cloth, and hawk bells. The tie is loom-woven beadwork in white, blue, and red seed beads. The board was collected by V. J. Evans before 1931 in Missouri. A note placed on the back of the board gives its history: "This baby board was the property of Shah-Ke-Wahpe (Bloody Hand) an Osage Indian. The first baby born to them died on this board and as is the custom of the Osage, [the board] could not be used again in the family and he brought it to the present owner to dispose of for him in the year 1883."

CHAPTER 10

KAW

The Kaws, or Kansas (Kanzas), known as the Wind People, spoke a Dhegiha branch of the Siouan language. They shared the traditions with the other Dhegiha tribes: Osage, Omaha, Ponca, and Quapaw. In early times, the tribes lived as one people in the region now known as the lower Ohio Valley, separating when they migrated west to the mouth of the Ohio River. The Kaws settled along a tributary of the Missouri River in what would become Kansas and Nebraska. The French developed trade with the Kaw tribe around 1680. By 1800, the Kaw economy was based on horticulture, buffalo hunting, fur trading, and raiding. During the winter, they scattered into small parties and hunted beaver, deer, elk, turkey, and small game. Kaw women planted corn, beans, pumpkins, melons, and squash, as well as gathered berries, roots, and tubers for food. Kaws established permanent villages of circular bark structures. Their portable hunting lodges were frames covered with painted skins.

Divided by patrilineal clans, each with specific privileges, names, and totemic symbols, Kaws called themselves Kaá^{n}ze (Kanza), the name of one of the clans. The Kaw tribe was settled on reservations in the state of Kansas and ultimately in Indian Territory. In 1902, their land was opened for allotment. Tribal headquarters for the Kaw Nation are currently located at Kaw City, Oklahoma.

Kaw Cradleboards

The Kaw baby board, *oyóphe,* was a long, rectangular flat board with the U-shaped head bow attached one-third of the way down from the top of the board.[1] There was no footrest or step stair. There is also no evidence that Kaw mothers carried babies on their backs or used carrying straps.

The plain narrow bow was attached with leather thongs or beaded straps on each side of the board, enabling the head to be raised or lowered. The upper third of the panel was decorated with carved or painted designs, brass tacks, and usually bright colors—red, yellow, blue, and green—as well as black. The typical design was a double X shape of triangles outlined with metal brads. Five holes were drilled in the board: two holes on each side, 1 inch from the edge, and one in the middle. These holes were for tying the leather thongs or beaded straps that hold the face guard, or bow. The ends of the bent piece were notched on each end to hold the lashing. Strings of hawk bells were tied to the face guard to amuse the baby.

When attending an art show in Tulsa, Oklahoma, I was told by a customer that there was a Kaw cradleboard at the Marland House Museum in Ponca City, Oklahoma. In April that same year, on the way to an art show in Wichita, Kansas, I arranged a visit to the museum. After searching, the board was found stored in a closet. I was able to examine it, take measurements, and sketch the item, but I was unable to photograph the board at that time. Several years later, I arranged a visit to photograph the cradleboard. Staff and I searched for it again and found it in a glass case with another cradle, just below the Kaw headboard, labeled Ponca. The Kaw board had been repainted.

In 2002, while attending a powwow in Tulsa, I met a gentleman who introduced himself as a Kaw. We discussed the miniature Kaw cradleboard I had made. He told me that it was exactly like the one he had been bound to as a baby. He told me I needed to tie strings of bells to the head bow.

The Siouan prairie cradleboard (plate 11) is described as profusely ornamented by Robert H. Lowie in his book *Indians of the Plains*. It is 34.5 inches long and 11.75 inches wide. The head of the board is outlined with brass brads, and the design is exactly like that of the Kaw board I examined in Ponca City, with the two carved X shapes forming triangles "like a parfleche decoration."[2] The board Lowie describes was collected by Alanson Skinner in 1922 in Perkins, Oklahoma, and it was initially identified as an everyday Ioway baby board. Two cradleboards identified as Osage at the American Museum of Natural History and the Smithsonian Cultural Resources Center have identical carving, painting, and brass brad

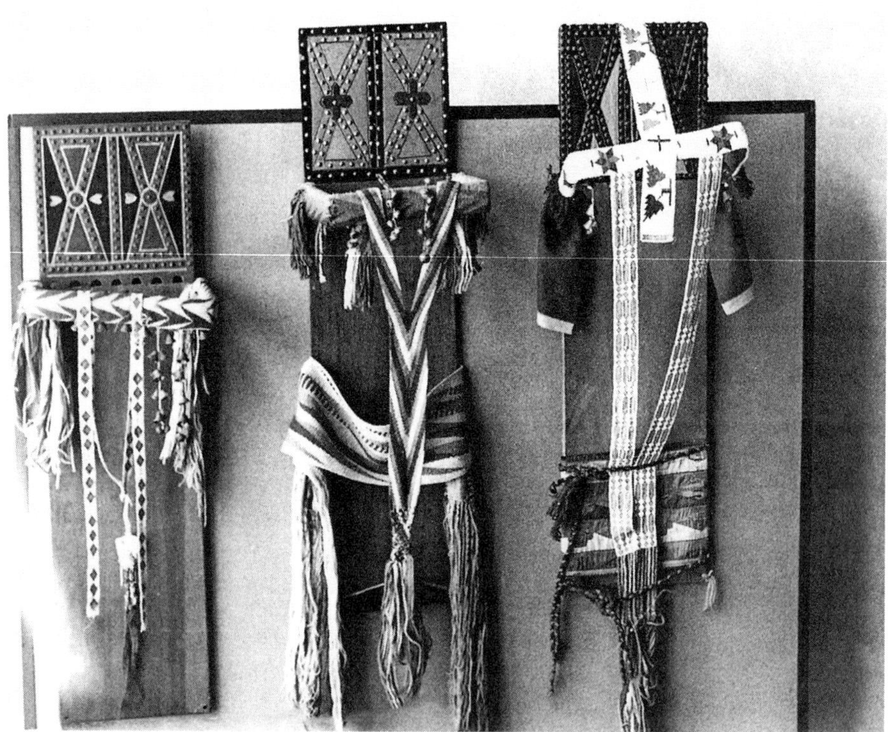

Three Kaw cradleboards. Undated photograph by W. D. Welge. Courtesy of the Oklahoma Historical Society (20682).

decoration, but the boards do not have the row of holes typically found below the carved, painted panel on Osage cradleboards. In late nineteenth century, the Kaw and Osage tribes were closely associated and intermarried to a degree, which makes identification of a Kaw cradleboard difficult without the history of the board.

Edwin James, a botanist and geologist who compiled the notes from the Yellowstone expedition of Major Stephen Long in 1819–20, wrote of the Kaw, "This nation[,] having been at profound peace with the Osages since the year 1806, have intermarried freely with them, so that stature, features, and customs are more and more closely approaching that people."[3] James wrote this account in August 1819, describing a Kaw village, the people, and their customs. He also noted that "the infant is tied down to a board, after the manner of many of the Indian tribes."[4]

Birth Customs

According to William E. Unrau, "Childbirth was a wholly natural and rather uneventful affair" for the Kaw mother. He quotes an unidentified man who traveled with the Yellowstone expedition in 1819 and reported that the Kaw woman in childbirth was not greatly inconvenienced or in need of assistance. "A woman following the roving excursions of her tribe, carrying a bundle on her head or back, will step aside, bring forth her infant, wrap it in a piece of buffalo skin, resume her load, placing the infant on the top of it, and continue her route, without occasioning the least halt or delay to her party. At the first water, she bathes herself and her child."[5]

Kaw Cradleboard

I examined a cradleboard at the Gilcrease Museum in Tulsa, Oklahoma (cat. no. 84.630). The board was identified as possible Kaw or Potawatomi by the museum. No history was available.

The carved, painted board is detailed and outlined with brass brads. The design on the board is typical, with the X design enclosing triangles. The board is 35 inches long, 10.25 inches wide, 1.25 inches thick, and 9.75 inches high

The rectangular frame consists of two pieces of wood: the backboard and curved head bow. Eight holes are drilled in the board: three on each side of the board and two in the middle. Two are close together—11.25 inches from the top, and 1.5 inches from the bottom. The middle holes are in line with the first holes on each side.

The head bow, 24.75 inches long, 10.25 inches wide, 1.25 inches thick, and 9.75 inches above the backboard, is attached to the board with rawhide strips. The ends of the head bow are notched at each end. The leather strips are threaded through two holes, 11.25 inches from the top of the board, on each side of the board, and tied. The two holes in the middle of the board enable the bow to be held in position with leather strips tied to the board. Coverings could be hung from the bow.

The top panel is decorated with paint, incised lines, and brass brads. The background is painted dark green, and the incised design border is light green and yellow. Divided in two sections, the design of two facing isometric triangles is outlined with the brads.

Loom beadwork covers the head bow across the front and around the corners. The beaded background is white with repeated geometric designs in yellow, red, dark blue, and green. Rose, pink, and medium blue tassels are sewn at the end of the beaded head bow piece. Two wide beaded strips, tied in the middle of the board and at the end of the board, hold the head bow in place. The bands are tied together with blue yarn tassels at the end of the board.

A completely beaded panel is attached to the top of the head bow, covering the upper part of where the baby's head would lie. This shade is decorated with brass trade bells sewn on three sides, as well as red and yellow yarn fringe. A separate beaded band attached under the shade, in the middle of the head bow, hangs down from the bow. The color scheme is the same as in the bow beadwork, with red, green, blue, and yellow on white background. Repeated geometric motifs, with an alternating color scheme, complete the beadwork.

The Siouan prairie frame, exemplified by the two decorative zones on the head panel, carved and painted with an X-shaped figure enclosing triangles, has been identified as Osage, Kaw, and Otoe. Osage cradleboards typically have a line of holes, round on top and flat on the bottom, under the painted, incised head panel. The symbolism of the line of seven holes has been lost, and some of the cradleboards without the line of holes that have been identified as Osage in museums and private collections may in fact be Otoe or Kaw.

CHAPTER 11

OMAHA

The Omaha (Umó^{n}ho^{n}) tribe was a Woodland people until migrating westward to what is now known as the lower Ohio River. In the early 1700s Omahas were living near the Missouri River until they ceded their lands to the United States in 1854, settling on a reservation in northeastern Nebraska. They spoke a dialect of the Dhegiha branch of the Siouan language, related to the Ponca, Osage, Quapaw, and Kansa dialects. The Omahas' original name, Umó^{n}ho^{n} (translated by the French as Maha), means Upstream, against the Flow.

The Omahas lived in circular earth lodges in permanent fortified villages. They used bark-covered dwellings in the summer and hide tipis during the buffalo hunts, following a cyclic annual subsistence pattern, alternating between hunting and gardening. Omahas created a complex schedule of substantial gardens, growing maize, beans, and other plants. The Omaha society was structured into moieties, or halves, each composed of five patrilineal clans, usually associated with some symbolic animal. The clans regulated religious and ceremonial functions.

Omahas followed the annual hunting cycle until the buffalo herds were gone in the 1870s. Lands were allotted to families from 1871 to the early twentieth century. Approximately half of the five thousand enrolled members of the Omaha Nation still live on their reservation in Macy, Nebraska, and have a strong interest in Omaha traditions.

Cradleboards

The Omaha cradleboard is similar to the Pawnee, Ponca, Osage, and Kaw boards. The basic form is a wooden plank, about three feet long and one foot wide, often notched near the bottom. Some of the cradleboards have a wooden hoop, or bow, attached. According to Siouan linguist John Koontz, the Omaha cradleboard was called "*udhuhe* (travel in, a tool for traveling). The modern spelling would be *uthu'he*."[1]

According to Alice C. Fletcher and Francis La Flesche, the Omaha used an undecorated cradleboard without a bow, but the cradleboard shown in plate 10 has a painted, carved headboard. James Owen Dorsey, who researched the Omaha from 1881 to 1892, described a decorated board with a hoop. The absence of hoop and decoration may have been the norm in subsequent years, when Fletcher and La Flesche did the bulk of their research on the reservation.[2]

Feder observed babies tied to plain boards on the Omaha Reservation in Nebraska.[3] A Photograph of an Omaha baby in a cradleboard without a hoop is on file at the Denver Public Library.[4] Newer Omaha boards tend to be simple rectangles without the bottom stair step. The stair step was used to keep the lower binding strap from slipping down so that the child could be propped upright:

> There were two broad cloth straps that tapered at each end for securing the swaddled baby to the board. The band was centered across the baby, one tie below the chin across the chest and upper arms, the second tie across the hips and hands. Each band was passed behind the board and brought back to the front and tied snuggly. Binding straps, 4 inches wide, were often topstitched or made of ribbon work to stiffen the band.[5]

Two bands for an Omaha cradleboard at the American Museum of Natural History are of silk and cotton appliqués; one is sewn on with cross stitch, and the other is machine stitched.[6] The cross-stitched band, or *i¢a¢istage*, is 34.4 inches long and 6 inches wide, with two stripes of purple and green, and gold appliqués on the purple and red appliqués on the green. The repeated geometric design is a connected, stepped square with a cut-out block cross. The other band has two pieces, one 21 by 7 inches, and the other 30 by 7 inches. Both pieces of silk are exactly the same, with four stripes of purple, green, red, and blue silk. The appliqués are done in geometric designs of white and pink. Both bands were collected by Margaret Mead in 1930.

Today, Omahas make plain cradleboards boards, approximately 24 inches by 11 inches, without the stair step: "A growing baby was moved to a longer board after the first month or so. After the baby has outgrown the second board, most mothers abandon the board. Many tell stories of the overgrown child sleeping with feet and ankles hanging past the end of the board, waking up and walking around still attached to its board."[7]

In 1896, Dorsey described and illustrated a drawing of a cradleboard with a hoop: "A board of convenient size, usually about a yard long and a foot wide, was selected to form a cradle or *u¢uhe*. No pillow was needed. A soft skin . . . covered with plenty of thick hair was laid on the board, and on it was placed the infant."[8] The cradleboard is long and rectangular, with a narrow bent bow attached to each side of the board, about one-third down from the top. An object similar to a four-pointed star is painted on the board at the end where the infant's head would lie. Two sinew strings strung with beads are attached to the top of the board, drawn taut over the bow, and fastened to the end of the board. The strings keep the face covering in place. The strings were sometimes made of strips of red calico. Dorsey mentioned a woven sinew fan that hung from the bow and was about 6 inches square, strung with beads and sometimes thimbles or other shiny dangling items. The infant would have been held in the cradle by a band of cloth or leather.

During the days of the buffalo on the plains, children were an important part of the Omaha family; they were greatly desired and loved. A baby was the mother's constant companion, although other members of the family would help care for the baby. An uthu'he was used for transport and as a bed. The baby could be laced on its board and hung in the shade of a tree or on the mother's saddle, where the infant would ride safely and comfortably while the mother was on horseback. Cradleboards were often passed down to the next generation.

Birth Customs

An Omaha woman would begin to recognize her pregnancy by the last time she "dwelt alone" (menstruated). She calculated her months with child from the last time she had stayed in a separate lodge from the rest of the family during her menstruation cycle. According to Edwin James's compiled notes on the Omaha's customs, when a woman missed period, she knotted a leather string and tied it to her girdle to indicate her pregnancy. She added a knot each month thereafter until the birth. During her pregnancy, the woman continues her usual duties even in her most advanced stage, and regardless of the weather.

> If, on a march, a pregnant woman feels the pains of parturition, she retires to the bushes, throws the burden from her back, and without any aid, brings her infant into the world. After washing in water, if at hand, or melted snow, both herself and the infant she immediately replaces the burden upon her back, weighing, perhaps, between sixty and one hundred pounds, secures her child upon the top of it, protected from the cold by an envelope of bison robe, and hurries on to overtake her companions."[9]

According to James, Omahas worried about complications only with a woman's first time giving birth. Women assist with the delivery, usually by providing herbs believed to help with childbirth along with the powdered rattle of a rattlesnake mixed with warm water.[10]

Dorsey's informant recounted that sometimes a strong woman "'takes' the child herself but requires assistance subsequently."[11] At the birth, the husband and children leave the lodge, so that no man witnesses a birth unless a medicine man is necessary in a difficult labor. After trying his medicine two or three times without success, he would send for someone else. The outer covering of the root of the Kentucky coffeetree (*Gymnocladus canadensis*) was used to treat hemorrhage during childbirth. The powdered root was mixed with water and administered during protracted labor.[12] Melvin R. Gilmore wrote that the puffball (Lycoperdaceae) was used as a styptic on the newborn's navel by Omaha and Ponca women.[13] According to Dorsey's informant, few Omaha women died in birth.[14]

After delivery, the mother was washed, with the water temperature dependent on the weather. Thereafter, she bathed twice a day. According to Dorsey, she "was bound tightly about the abdomen to reduce the size." The mother was required to bathe twice a day. Strong women were able to resume their duties the next day, but some might require up to three weeks to recover their strength.[15] James wrote, "On the delivery of her first child, the young mother . . . arises almost immediately, and attends to the ordinary house-work; but she does not, in general, undergo any laborious occupation, such as cutting and carrying wood, until the lapse of two or three days." With the second child, if no complications occurred, the mother "ties [the newborn] to a board, after their usual manner, then proceeds with her daily work, as if nothing extraordinary had occurred."[16]

The infant was washed all over and wrapped in cloth. It was bound to a cradleboard in two or three days if not right away, as described above.

> On this [cradleboard] was laid a pillow stuffed with feathers or the hair of the deer, over which were spread layers of soft skins. On this bed the baby was fastened by broad bands of soft skins, which in recent years were replaced by similar bands of calico or flannel. There was no headboard to the Omaha cradle-board but the skins that were laid over the pillow were so arranged as to form a shelter and protection forth top of the baby's head. While the child slept, its arms were bound under cover but as soon as it awoke they were released.[17]

Until the mother's milk came, a wet nurse fed the infant. Omaha and Ponca new mothers drank a tea made from the skeletonweed (*Lygodesmia juncea*) to increase the mother's milk flow.[18] When the father was told that the baby was born, he would announce whether it was a boy or a girl. According to Dorsey, sometimes a father would treat a daughter better because a girl would not be afforded the self-sufficiency of a son.[19] "The birth of twins was a sign that the mother was a kind woman," explained Fletcher and La Flesche. Omahas believed that before birth, "twins walk hand in hand, . . . looking for a kind woman; when they find her, she becomes their mother."[20]

An infant's arrival would be an occasion of great joy and celebration. The Omaha have a moving ritual chant to bless the baby and to petition safe passage and strengthen its journey on the path of life. The chant expresses the love of their offspring and the Omahas' belief in the interdependence of all forms of life. On the eighth day of a newborn's life, a priest would ceremonially announce the birth to the universal entities.

> Ho! Ye Sun, Moon, Stars, all ye that move in the heavens,
> I bid you hear me!
> Into your midst has come a new life,
> Consent ye, I implore!
> Make its path smooth, that it may reach,
> the brow of the first hill!
>
> Ho! Ye Winds, Clouds, Rain, Mist, all ye that move in the air,
> I bid you hear me!
> Into your midst has come a new life.
> Consent ye, I implore!
> Make its path smooth, that it may reach
> the brow of the second hill.
>
> Ho! Ye Hills, Valleys, Rivers, Lakes, Trees, Grasses, all ye of the earth,
> I bid you hear me!
> Into your midst has come a new life.
> Consent ye, I implore!
> Make its path smooth, that it may reach,
> the brow of the third hill.

Ho! Ye Birds, great and small, that fly in the air.
Ho! Ye Animals, great and small, that dwell in the forest.
Ho! Ye Insects that creep among the grasses and burrow in the ground
I bid you hear me!
Make its path smooth, that it may reach
the brow of the fourth hill.

Ho! All ye of the Heavens, all ye of the air, all ye of the earth:
I bid you all to hear me!
Into your midst has come a new life.
Consent ye, consent ye all, I implore!
Make its path smooth then shall it travel beyond the four hills.[21]

One of the baby's first moccasins has a small hole poked into the sole. "If a messenger from the spirit world should come and say to the child, I have come for you, the child could answer, I can not go on a journey[;] my moccasins are worn out!" Likewise, others would comment on the wear of the moccasins from the baby's worldwide travels as a form of wishing the child a long life. The infant received new moccasins, without the hole, at the end of the introduction ceremony, as "an assurance that it is prepared for the journey of life and that the journey would be a long one."[22]

Sex-Specific Cradle Design

No information suggests that Omahas distinguished the sex of the baby in the cradle design. If a woman wanted to know the sex of her expected baby, however, "she took a bow and a burden strap to the tent of a friend who had a child not yet old enough to speak and offered it the articles. If the bow was chosen, the unborn would be a boy; if the burden strap, a girl."[23]

Omaha Cradle Symbolism

The design carved and painted on the head of the cradleboard symbolized the morning star and the evening star, red for day, and blue for night. The sun was masculine, and the moon was feminine. The union of these two forces was regarded as necessary to the perpetuation of all living forms.

The morning star and evening star were also tattooed on women as a mark of honor. The star, emblematic of the night, was the great mother force. Its four points represented the life-giving winds. "It was thought that it was good fortune and an honor to marry a woman bearing the 'mark of honor.' She belonged to a family with a good tribal reputation, and it was believed that she would become the mother of many children."[16] The girl might also have a turtle tattooed on the backs of her hands and a crescent moon on the back of her neck.[24]

Omaha Cradleboard

Norman Feder, during his study of Pawnee cradleboards, found one example of an Omaha cradleboard, collected in 1890, at the National Museum of the American Indian, Heye Center (plate 10).[25] Mark Awakuni-Swetland studied, measured, and photographed the same cradleboard, and then made three such boards patterned from his study. I examined one of the boards Awakuni-Swetland constructed. This cradleboard is currently held in a private collection.

The frame is a flat wood board, 0.75 inches thick and 39.5 inches long. The board is 10 inches wide across the top and 11.5 inches wide at the base. A stair step, about 5.5 inches long, is notched 0.75 inches into each side of the board. A bent wooden strip, approximately 1.5 inches wide and 0.25 inches thick, is attached 10 inches from the top of the board on each side. This hoop rises approximately 19 inches above the surface of the board, with corners at ninety-degree angles. Seven holes are drilled on the board—one in the center of the board at the top, two holes on each side, and two holes at the center of the bottom.

The backboard is painted and decorated within a 10-by-10-inch panel outlined with tacks. The designs are also outlined with the tacks and with four circles, one in each quadrant. A large four-pointed star fills the area, with a triangle at each point; the star is painted red with a blue circle filling its center. The triangles are painted blue.

The hoop has cut-out notches for decoration. Approximately 28 inches in overall length, the hoop is attached to the board with ties through the holes on each side of the board, one hole through the hoop, and the two holes at the center of the base. The hoop is stabilized by two one-inch-wide strips of red trade wool attached to the two outside bends of the hoop and converging at the base of the board.

The 12-by-12-inch sunshade is beaded with size eight pony beads woven on red yarn warp strings and linen wefts. The yarn ends are trimmed as decorative tassels. The beadwork design is four large black diamonds on a white background. The sunshade is tacked to the wool across the front of the hoop and could be flipped upward over the hoop to allow the baby to see.

CHAPTER 12

PONCA

The Ponca (also Pó^{n}ka or Panka) tribe separated from the Omaha in the late seventeenth century or early eighteenth century. Both tribes spoke a single Dhegiha Siouan language and shared common social and cultural characteristics, with inheritance through the father, including the position of chief, and marriage outside the clan. Traditions common to the Omaha, Ponca, Osage, Kaw, and Quapaw tribes state that they were once one people and began migrating westward, eventually splitting. The tribes continued to share similar language, tribal organization, and religious rites.[1]

Of the five tribes, the Ponca and Omaha remained together the longest. The Ponca was a clan of the Omaha before they separated into two tribes. At that point, the Poncas, who referred to themselves as Pó^{n}ka, moved into northern Nebraska.

Hunting, horticulture, and gathering were the foundation of Ponca subsistence. The people lived in fortified towns of round lodges, but they stayed in hide tipis while on a hunt and away from the tribe's permanent village.

In 1870, the government ceded the entire Ponca reservation to the Lakotas. After the Ponca's forced removal from Nebraska in 1877, the main tribe settled in Indian Territory, in present-day Oklahoma, and a small band went back to Nebraska. These two bands are known as the Northern Ponca and Southern Ponca. In 1881, the Ponca tribe was dissolved and legally reconstituted as two separate entities. The Ponca Nation of Nebraska is headquartered in Niobrara, and the Ponca Nation of Oklahoma is headquartered in White Eagle.

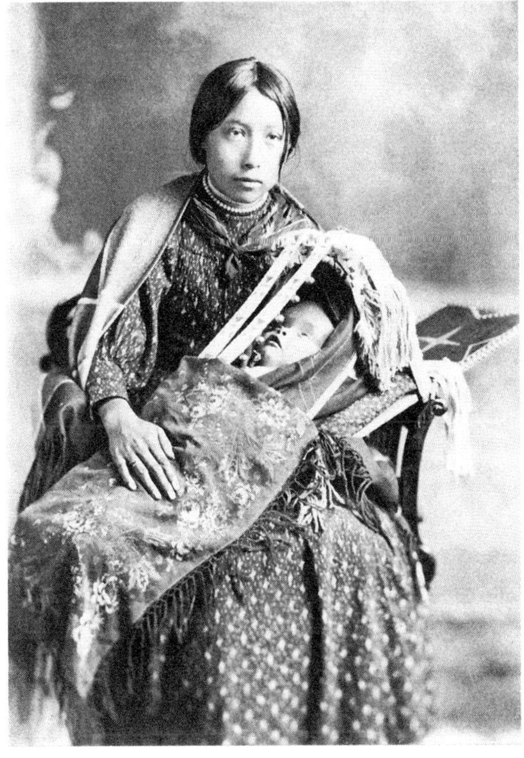

Ponca woman with child in a cradleboard, undated. A four-pointed star is painted in the center panel, with the hoop thong originating at the center of the star. Courtesy of the National Anthropological Archives, Smithsonian Institution (neg. 77-).

Ponca Cradleboards

The Ponca cradleboard is a Siouan prairie type, a thin flat board with an attached hoop, called an *uo*^{n}*he-k*^{h}*e*.[2] James Howard described "well-carved cradleboards of the common Central Algonquian and Southern Siouan type . . . made until about 1915." Wooden "articles were roughed out with an ax or knife, then finished by rubbing with sandstone, scoria, or the scouring rush."[3] The typical Ponca board was slightly wider at the bottom.

The hoop, or bow, was rather wide and bent in a squared U shape, attached at the edge with thongs through holes on each side of the board, one-third down from the top of the board. The thong that secured the hoop originated at the center of the upper third of the board. Two holes were drilled on each side of the board, about one inch from the bottom, through which two more thongs were tied and then attached to the middle of the hoop. These thongs helped secure the baby and keep the scarf or blanket off the infant's face. Often the thongs were replaced with bands of decorative beadwork.

A photograph from the National Anthropological Archives of the Smithsonian Institution shows the cradleboard decorated with a four-pointed star painted on the central panel above where the baby's head lies. The hoop thong originates at the center of the star. A Ponca cradleboard, circa 1870, that I found in the collection of the Wheelwright Museum is a long, thin flat board with a narrow square-shaped bent hoop attached with thongs. The cradleboard is 34 inches long, 10 inches wide, and 11 inches high at the hoop. The wooden hoop is held in position with decorated loom-beaded strips and yarn tassels. The beaded strap is attached below the decorated top panel. A fully beaded sunshade is attached across the front of the hoop.

The upper third of the backboard is decorated with a large white five-pointed star outlined with brads. The board is identified as Ponca or possibly Omaha, because Omahas continued to make this style of cradleboard after the Ponca adopted the Osage-style cradleboard.[4]

The baby was placed on a pad on the board, and then the board and baby were wrapped several times with a long piece of hide or cloth. The Ponca women made soft fabric by weaving the fine wool of buffalo and the hair of wolves and dogs.

The mother would tie the baby on the board and stand it by a tree as she performed her household duties. The restraints kept the baby's body erect, safe, and nearby, while the mother's hands were free to do her work. If it was necessary to walk or to ride a horse, the cradleboard was strapped to her back or tied in her shawl, fastened to her back. Should a baby die, the carrier was filled with moss until she had another baby.[5]

Peter Le Claire, one of James Howard's informants from his study of the Ponca, said that "Ponca children were very carefully brought up in the old days. At first the mother carried the child around on a cradleboard that was fastened to her back. This could be set up against a tree when she was working around the camp. It had a wooden bow in front so that if it fell over the baby wouldn't fall face down in the dirt."[6]

Birth Customs

Le Claire also provided information about childbirth:

> Births came naturally among the Ponca. There was no birth control. In the old days, they tell me, a woman gave birth to a baby in a kneeling position. She was on a hide. Sometimes her female relatives would come and help her. . . . A woman wouldn't have her second child until the first one could walk around and take care of itself. The man and woman stayed away from one another unless they wanted a baby.[7]

Women nursed for an extended period, and the tribe's travel made it difficult to care for more than one infant. No men were allowed at the birth itself, where the laboring woman was attended by older women. Infants were named after an event contemporary to the time of their birth. Poncas could request tribal permission to change their names later, to commemorate bravery, for example, or a memorable event.[8]

Amulet

Poncas preserved the umbilical cord in a small buckskin bag, or amulet. According to Howard, they were made "in the shape of a horned toad for boys and in the shape of a turtle for girls. The horned toad symbolized endurance and longevity, the turtle fertility." Children wore their amulet for varying lengths of time, usually until puberty, not the lifetime wear of some other tribes with an amulet tradition. When the child decides to no longer wear the amulet, the mother will usually hold on to it. The Ponca forged an alliance with the Oglála Lakota and gradually assumed many of their traits, which may account for the use of amulet.[9]

CHAPTER 13

PAWNEE

The Pawnees (Chaticks-si-Chaticks) originally lived in east-central Nebraska and north-central Kansas in four permanent groups of villages. They spoke the Caddoan language and were related to the Arikaras and Wichitas. Pawnee tribal history places them originally in the southwestern United States before slowly migrating north and settling on the Great Plains. Archaeological evidence indicates that Pawnees have roots in central Nebraska and north-central

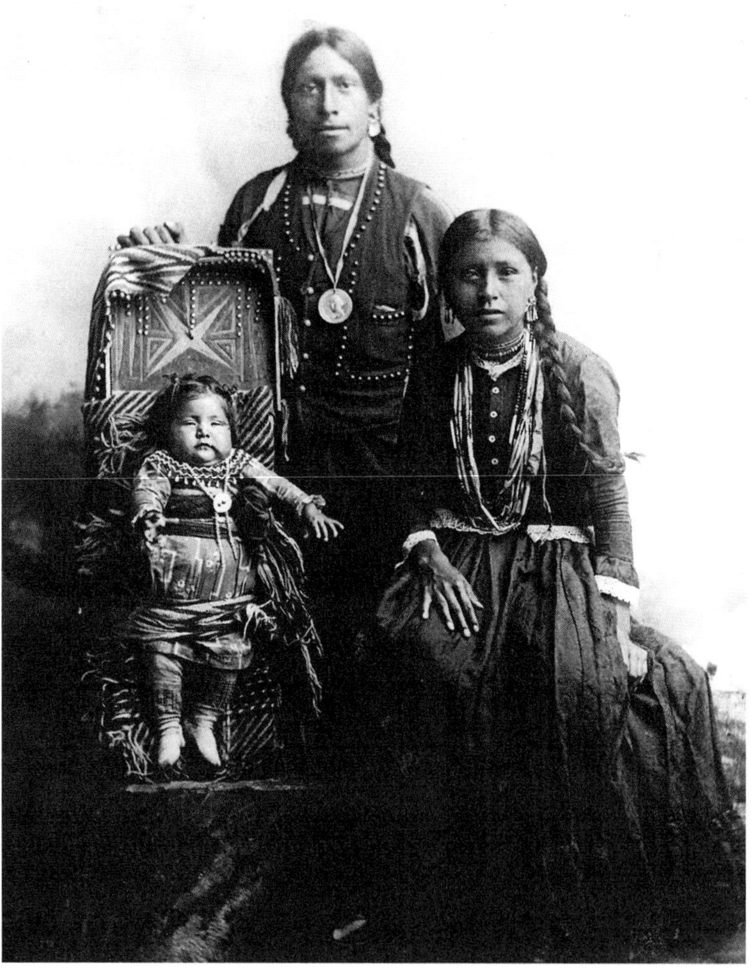

Pawnee family, with baby in a cradleboard, undated. Cunningham-Prettyman Collection, Western History Collections, University of Oklahoma (Prettyman 144).

Kansas, extending back to the sixteenth century, in four permanent groups of villages—Skiris, Chauis, Kitahahkis, and Pitahawiratas—each politically and spiritually independent.

The Pawnees were semisedentary people who alternated between cultivation, hunting, and gathering. They lived in permanent earth lodge villages. The lodges were circular dome-shaped structures from thirty to sixty feet in diameter. The Pawnees used two types of dwellings on their communal buffalo hunts: tipis during the winter and half-bowl-shaped frames of saplings and hides in the summer. Maize was their most important crop.

Pawnee kinship was bilateral, and residence was matriarchal (newly married couples lived in the wife's mother's lodge). Pawnee society was socially stratified into two groups: the upper classes and the commoners. Hereditary rights largely determined the groups, as positions were inherited and sustained by religious sanctions.

In the nineteenth century, their traditional way of life was changed by war and epidemic disease. The remaining Pawnees were relocated to a reservation in Indian Territory in 1873. They formed a single tribal entity from the four historical groups. Pawnee land was allocated to individual farms, and excess land was sold to white settlers in 1889. In 1936, the Pawnees gained tribal government, with a council that consisted of a president, vice president, and five council members. The Pawnee Nation headquarters is in Pawnee, Oklahoma.

Cradleboard

Most Plains Indian tribes, like the Pawnee, considered a birth a special blessing. Infant mortality rates were high, and many Plains tribes tried to protect the baby with sacred powers. The Pawnees had elaborate rituals and ceremonies around the birth and first year of the infant. They developed a distinctive cradleboard, a Siouan prairie type called a *ráci-itu'*, which had designs with symbolic meanings to protect the baby.[1] Infants were placed on cradleboards at birth to keep the baby's legs and back straight.

The Pawnee cradleboard was a single flat cottonwood board, slightly wider at the bottom, with an attached hoop cut from willow. Each side of the bottom had a 7- or 8-inch step cut into it to prevent the straps, which secured the baby in place, from slipping off the bottom of the board. The top one-third of the board was carved and painted. Just below this design panel, a hole in the center of the board and two holes on each side were used for the leather tie thongs that held the hoop in place. The bottom of the board had two holes about 6 inches from the bottom, which were also used for leather thongs to secure the hoop. This kept the blanket above the baby's face when covered.

Waldo Rudolph Wedel recovered several cradleboards, some whole and some nearly complete, from archaeological digs in Nebraska in 1936. They were excavated from thirteen archaeological sites in the hill site described in detail in his journals and records. He wrote that the finest specimen, which may or may not be correctly designated, was found in a grave at the hill site, and it measured 30 inches long and 11 inches wide, with a 0.5-inch border carved with zigzag lightning symbols. An emblem of the sun, 5 inches in diameter, has four long rays and twelve short rays. The upper part of the board was neatly carved and further embellished with brass-headed tacks.

In Norman Feder's article on Pawnee cradleboards, he described two boards found at the Nebraska State Historical Society. One was a carved, painted cottonwood plank, circa 1806, recovered archaeologically from the hill site. It was for a small child, measuring 29.75 inches high and 11.5 inches wide. The other was recovered at the Clark site, circa 1830. It was 35 inches high and 11 inches wide.[2]

In 1915 James Murie from Oklahoma collected three Pitahawirata cradleboards and donated the boards to the American Museum of Natural History. The smallest board was used by Murie's children. The carved, painted cottonwood planks vary in size, with lengths between 33.5 and 36.5 inches, and widths between 10.4 to 13.8 inches. The three head panels are painted black, and each of the centers has a four-pointed red star, with points arrayed to the four corners; decorative designs around the star vary, but all are painted red and yellow. Beaded bow straps originate from the center of the star on at least one board. The decorative panels on two of the boards have three painted borders, alternating red, yellow, red. One board's panel is outlined with metal brads (plate 12). Two boards have a pad of buffalo hide with hair attached to the front. The pad is thick and shaped like a hood, which would cover the baby's head. Two boards are encircled and tied with a wide strip of black material. A woven finger belt is tied to the third board.

Typically, the father and his family made the cradleboard when a grandmother notified them of the pending birth. The board was cut out from a living tree, and protective symbols were carved and painted on the board. According to Feder, "The main feature which distinguishes Pawnee cradleboards from those of other Prairie tribes is the nature of the design carved and painted on the upper third of the board."[3]

George Bird Grinnell wrote of the use of a baby board on a buffalo hunt with the Pawnees in 1872. All their possessions were transported with packhorses on a travois made from lodge poles fastened to the saddles. The hide lodge was folded up and placed on the travois. The riders were usually women, each holding a child or two in her arms or on her back. The cradleboard was often hung over the end of the lodge pole, swinging free.[4]

Garland Blaine, a Pawnee born in 1915 and raised by his grandparents, remembered many childhood experiences and using cradleboards with his own four children. According to Blaine, "The baby boards in our Pitahawirata band were burned out of flat timber. The charred part was scraped off with a rock or knife."[5] The baby would be wrapped in deer skin that had been washed with water and sand or beaten against a rock, then stretched while drying to keep it soft. Blaine recalled the board having "a small pillow and a thin mattress. A little roll of skin or cloth one to two inches thick was placed under the knees. It was almost as wide as the board. The infant's feet were kept together with toes pointed up while the baby was wrapped." The pillow was between 8 by 4 inches and 10 by 5 inches, and a couple inches thick. Blaine's cradleboard was plain, with no decoration, because his grandmother was blind when she made it. According to Blaine, in 1910 Oklahoma, many babies were still carried on cradleboards, but the boards had gotten plainer and were not carved.

Birth Customs

A pregnant Pawnee woman and her husband had to follow certain prohibitions. The woman could not use any sort of cutting tool, like a knife, for fear of causing the umbilical cord to sever, killing the child. She was also not to drink "with a horn spoon or from a small earthenware vessel which was used as a dipper as she would drink in the sound supposed to reside in the utensil," and that would carry though her to the child and cause the baby to be born deaf. At the first sign of labor, the husband wore his hair loose and left the lodge for four days, because being near the birth could cause complications.[6]

An older relative or midwife usually assisted with the birth, and no young women, children, or men were present, unless the woman needed a Pawnee doctor, "who had had a sacred vision in which he received the prayers, songs, and name of herbs, roots, and other things to use as medicines in the birthing process."[7] Women gave birth in a sitting position. The doctor would talk to the expecting mother and relate to her an animal, bird, or plant spirit.

One of Blaine's uncles had been particularly hard to birth, as Effie, Blaine's grandmother, described to him. The doctor sang a special song, talked to Effie, and placed tobacco and medicine from his sacred bundle on hot coals in the room. "Then he started procedures that included talking and putting his hands on vital spots so as to cause childbirth to come about." The doctor told Effie: "Now we are both looking to Tirawahat [the supreme being], and when I doctor you, I have sincere faith that He will bless you, and that you may see yourself again (have your child), and that you will live. So we must think now as one, and put our thoughts in his hands, or give our thoughts to Him."[8]

After the delivery, a wide band was wrapped around the mother's stomach, and she would spend several days lying down unless the tribe was traveling. "A tea was made by ground dried root of the wild four-o'clock (*Mirabilis nytaginea*), to reduce abdominal swelling after childbirth."[9] The father usually buried the afterbirth outside the dwelling, on the east side because a new day and life began in the east.[10]

Pawnee women gathered and used the prairie mushroom, commonly called puff balls (Lycoperdaceae), as a styptic for any wounds, and they applied it to the umbilicus of newborns.[11] The umbilical cord was cut in a special way, and the wrapped cord was kept greased with buffalo tallow: "The midwife wrapped the umbilical cord around her index finger, with the heel of her hand touching the child's stomach, or she would hold the cord and measure it a hand's width from the navel. This gave sufficient length to make the separation. The cord was doubled back and tied next to the stomach with sinew, then the sinew was wrapped around this fold four times and the cord and sinew were cut below the tie."[12]

An adult shaped the newborn's face soon after birth, starting with the infant's nose. "With two fingers on either side of the bridge, the person would press gently down the sides to the base. This was done while holding the baby while it was on its cradleboard. A wetted thumb would be placed in the mouth and pressed against the roof to straighten the ridge and open the nasal passages."[13] People visited the family of a newborn and brought gifts.

The Pawnee thought twins were mystical and had magical powers. They were treated as special "because Tirawahat made them twice." Girls were highly valued because women were associated with life and its reproduction, and they brought wealth at marriage. Pawnee religious beliefs about the importance of Mother Corn and Mother Earth were interwoven. According to Blaine's grandmother, a "boy is lost to the family when he marries and must work to support the girl's family." When his grandmother married, her family received several horses and many other gifts from her new husband's family. It was expected for one child in the family to be the favorite. The other children were taught respect for the chosen sibling, which helped pass authority and responsibility from one generation to the next. Pawnee practiced interfamilial adoptions, which provided for the well-being of children and the adopting tribal members needing assistance. An older couple who needed help would ask a kinsman with several children to let them adopt one. Or parents might offer a child for adoption. The child would be well cared for and loved.[14]

Pawnee Cradleboard Symbolism

Pawnee mythology was rich in symbolism, and their religious system was elaborate and cogent. Their religious ceremonies were connected to cosmic forces. The literature has several references to symbolism on Pawnee cradles. George Dorsey, Alice Fletcher, and Edward Curtis found several references to Pawnee cradleboard symbols in the literature.

Pawnees explain the distinctive designs on their cradleboards in an ancient myth relating to the Morning Star ceremony. Several versions of the myth are recorded in literature.[15] The cradleboard was to be decorated with the emblematic designs that came from the stars. Natalie Curtis Burlin explained,

> Among the Pawnee, the husband brings to his wife the cradle-board. This is ceremonially cut from a tree by the husband's kinsman, and decorated with symbolic emblems. . . . There is a detailed legend of how the Morning Star won the cradle-board, which hung with many other cradle-boards upon posts within a lodge in the heavens. These cradle-boards were decorated with emblematic designs, which the people of earth now use to decorate their cradle-boards. Thus the Pawnee say that their designs came from the stars.[16]

Frances Densmore recorded a different version of the story: "Finally she [Evening Star] insisted that he [Morning Star] make provision for the child that should be born: she even required him to provide perfumed water for bathing the child and a cradle board in which it should be placed. On the hoop, or arch, of the cradle board was painted a morning star and the lightning, this custom being followed by the Pawnee at the present time."[17] Morning Star was also required to plant a tree in front of the lodge so that a mocking bird might nest there and sing to the child. The described decorations were being followed by the Pawnee in 1929. According to the story of Morning Star and Evening Star, after the cradleboard was made, Evening Star requested a mat for the baby to lie on. The mat was to be the softest part of the buffalo hide. Morning Star was instructed to bring sweet fragrant water to bathe the child. The water was rain.

The skin of the wildcat was to be used as a covering, symbolizing the stars. A crooked furrow was cut above the hoop to signify lightning, and the power of lightning was typified by the arrows. Curtis Burlin wrote that the cradleboard should be made of cottonwood, and the hoop should be cut from a willow tree. A child should be bound to the board with strips of otter skin. "All these 'betoken' water or rain: the otter lives in water, rain storms, and the arch is the rainbow. According to the story of Morning Star and Evening Star, after the cradleboard was made, Evening Star requested a mat for the baby to lie on. The mat was to be the softest part of a buffalo hide. Morning Star was also to bring sweet fragrant water [gentle rain] to bathe the infant."[18]

In the story, the number four is symbolic: the four-pointed stars—black star, yellow star, white star, and red star—that hold up the heavens and signify the seasons and weather; four kinds of wood; and four kinds of corn, yellow, red, white, and black. The four-pointed star was usually carved in the center panel. The three cradleboards collected by James Murie have red stars in the center. The colors painted on Pawnee boards are from the four stars: the black star, in the northeast, is autumn; the yellow star, in the northwest, is spring; the white star stands in the south, facing north, the source of winter snow; and the red star, in the southeast, is summer. In the data collected on the Pawnee cradleboard symbolism were frequent references to stars, particularly to the morning star, the sun, lightning, rainbows, arrows, arrowheads, the sky, rain, and water. "A common design was the four-pointed star, but this is often combined with multiple rayed sun symbols. The three basic styles' elaborate borders represent either lightning or rainbows."[19]

PART FOUR

NORTHERN PLAINS FLAT BOARDS

Crow

Blackfoot

CHAPTER 14

CROW

The Crow people, who speak a Siouan language, traditionally call themselves Apsáalooke, Absaroke, or Absaroka (Children of the Large Beaked Bird). Early trappers called the people Crows. They migrated from the Lake Winnipeg region of Canada to the Bighorn and Yellowstone river basins in Montana and Wyoming in the 1600s. Before the historical period, they had separated from their village-dwelling kin, the Hidatsas. Crows retained several elements of their former society, including a matrilineal kinship system, yearly planting and harvesting of sacred tobacco, and a clan system based on thirteen original clans.

Crows had obtained the horse by the 1730s, and they became nomadic buffalo hunters and gatherers on the northern plains, living in hide tipis. The horse became the primary currency for wealth, status, and spouses. The Crows became important intermediaries in trade and were embroiled in constant warfare to preserve their hunting grounds and protect their large horse herds from other tribes. In 1864 Crow leaders realized that white people were their best allies against the Crows' traditional enemies, the Teton Sioux, Arapahos, Cheyennes, and Blackfeet, so the leaders surrendered lands in exchange for help with "civilizing." The Crows moved in 1883–84 to the present Crow agency near Harding, Montana. In 1940s the Crow Sun Dance was revived and held in June or July on the reservation. The Crows wrote their own constitution in 1948.

Cradleboards

A Crow mother used an inverted U-shaped flat cradleboard common in the Northwest groups of the Rocky Mountains and the Plateau culture area. A *băgăt'ĕt-chā* is "something to carry the baby with," and the word *bagate* meant baby.[1] The Crows were the only Siouan tribe to use the plateau/basin-type cradle. The flat board was usually 40 inches long and 12 inches wide, with the ends tapering sharply to the bottom, rounded on each end. "Crow cradles tend to be more narrow and their tops may not be quite so rounded. The beaded area always has a straight bottom edge and Crow cradles always have decorated straps or ties (usually three pairs) and sometimes a small decorated piece at the bottom. Buckskin fringe is always on the top edge of the cradle."[2] The frame was covered with soft buckskin stretched tightly across the back, with a loose pocket in the center of the front. Long buckskin fringe was always sewn on the top edge of the cradle cover. Later, the buckskin was sometimes replaced with canvas.

Three wide pairs of straps attached to each side of the board secured the baby in the pouch. The pairs of bands were tied in the front. "One pair crossed the baby's chest just under the armpits; the middle band crossed his waist and the third band held his ankles in place."[3] These tie straps were a Crow invention and uniquely Crow. The flat surface of the board above the baby's head and straps was covered with beadwork. Often the narrow, curved section of the cradle below the baby's feet was also beaded.

The father's mother or sister usually made the cradleboard. The infant was kept on the board, except for changing, until the baby could sit up. Agnes Deernose related being "laced into my cradleboard with my arms at my side and only my face showing."[4] The board could be stood against the lodge or carried on the mother's back. Infants were wrapped tightly within the buckskin casing of the cradleboard. The board was also tied to the saddle horn on the mother's saddle.

Early Cradleboard

A baby carrier cataloged as Crow, circa 1800, in the Hutter Collection of Harvard's Peabody Museum, is an early example of the U-shaped baby carrier of the Rocky Mountains and plateau regions. It is constructed with a light oval wooden frame encased in hide, with an attached baby bag. Bison hide may have been used, and traces of red ocher pigment cling to the leather, which may have been smoked.[5] Laced flaps were designed to secure the infant. Carrying straps and a collar made of rolled, beaded leather were added to support the baby's head.

The simple geometric design elements are typical of early beadwork. Multiple leather strips covered with beadwork and profuse rows of blue pony beads overlay the surface. The number of blue beads used would have been expensive in the early 1800s. At that time, "they gave a horse for one hundred of them [blue pony beads]."[6] The beaded strips appear to have been used in a hide carrier bag. The beadwork design is asymmetrical. The beaded strips attached on the left side are simple rows of large blue pony beads, with sets of five white beaded lines. In the center of the side is an insert of red wool trade cloth outlined with blue and white bars. Just above the insert are two rows of transparent navy blue beads bordered by partial and whole rows of white beads. A smaller red cloth insert is hidden by one of the hide flaps of the hood opening. Navy-bordered white bead stripes line the foot and the right side of the carrier. Red, white, green, and gray-blue seed beads are lightly sprinkled throughout the navy blue. The beaded row of white isosceles triangles creates a saw-tooth design across the top of the frame.[7]

Beadwork

Crow beadwork styles on cradleboards developed from a common upper Missouri River quillwork tradition of geometric designs. Quillwork and pony beadwork show design concepts and layouts, patterns, and techniques that became more elaborate during the seed bead era. The designs also resemble the painted designs Crow women applied to rawhide parfleche, tipi door flaps, and medicine bundles.[8] In the reservation period (primarily 1867–1887), floral designs were popular. During the 1890s, many elaborately beaded Crow cradles were collected and preserved in museum collections.

In 1854, Edwin T. Denig described a Crow Indian camp on the march: "It is often a strange and barbarous sight to see small children but a few days old tied to a piece of bark or wood and hung to the saddle bow which flies up at each jump of the horse when they gallop, their heads exposed to the hot sun or cold."[9] Denig's description suggests that the elaborately beaded cradle Crows used during the reservation period had evolved from a simpler form.

Crow women took great pains in beading their babies' cradles. A background of light blue was flavored with large angular beaded designs in contrasting colors, with outlines in white beads. They employed a limited number of geometric elements and developed their own separate styles of beading. Barbara Hail describes the Crow style in *Hau, Kóla!*: "[The] Hallmarks of Crow style are the use of long triangles, K-shapes, and a wide variety of colors, especially lavender, light blue, rose, and gray-green; a tendency to fill the entire field with a design; the outlining forms with white or dark blue beads sewn in a different direction than the background; and a combination of lazy stitch, Crow stitch and overlay stitch. Edges were often beaded."[10]

The Crows had limited color options in large pony beads—black, white, blue, red, and amber—until the second half of the nineteenth century. During the reservation period, more colors were available in seed beads. Crow women usually used only seven colors: light blue, dark blue, red, yellow, lavender, white, and green. They seldom used red in the design because the background was often red trade cloth or flannel. Crow beading can be partly characterized by the combination of stitch techniques: the spot stitch; the lazy stitch for narrow borders and small triangles; and a combination of lazy stitch and backstitch for broad backgrounds of solid colors and for filler colors in large designs.[11]

Birth Customs

A pregnant woman prepared for childbirth long before her labor began by engaging in several practices rooted in Crow beliefs. Once a baby was on the way, the expecting woman "put herself under the guidance of her mother," because older women knew what to do. The mother-to-be would walk frequently to keep her weight down, drink plenty of liquids, and rub her abdomen to keep the baby from getting stuck. To have an easy delivery, she would sleep with her feet facing a doorway. Sleeping with her feet toward the wall would make it hard for the baby to come out. To stand or sit with her backside to the fire was dangerous because it would hold back the afterbirth.[12]

A Crow woman delivered her newborn assisted by female relatives, and sometimes with the help of a medicine man or woman. The baby's father and other males were not usually allowed to watch because doing so was believed to delay the birth. The doctor had special medicine received from a dream or vision. The information for the medicine can also be bought by another visionary. Certain herbs and tea were administered to promote the health of the prospective mother and to hasten delivery. Medicine men and women were liberally paid. One of Lowie's informants reported that for assisting with a difficult birth, Grey-bull's wife was paid one horse, a blanket, four comforters, some new calico, and some money. Another medicine woman gained knowledge from a supernatural being in her sleep of using two roots to ease a delivery. The laboring woman was to boil the leaves and drink the infusion to give birth without suffering.

When the woman was in labor, the attendants placed two sturdy stakes in the earth at the end of the tipi where the woman's head lay when sleeping. A fire was built; a bed was prepared of buffalo skin, folded with the hair side out; and soft robes were rolled up and piled against the stakes. The woman knelt down with her legs spread wide apart, rested her elbows on the pillows, and seized the stakes with her hands. When the newborn was delivered, one of the attendants, usually the grandmother, cut the umbilical cord, "which was measured at three fingers in breadth from the navel cord." The medicine woman took the buffalo robe with the afterbirth from the camp. The robe was cleaned and washed four times to make the child grow. The tipi was then purified by the smoke of burning sage.[13]

A new infant was greased with a mixture of red paint, made from chokecherry gum and buffalo hooves, which were boiled until gelled, mixed with colored earths. Dried, powdered buffalo chips and finely pounded clay were used as talc powder, which was dusted on from the hips down to the infant's knees. The infant was laid on a layer of hair from a buffalo, then wrapped in soft buckskin and laid on a piece of stiff buffalo rawhide to keep the head from falling backward. "Each night all the dressing was removed, the baby was washed and again greased, and left to kick up its heels on a soft buffalo robe until the new wrappings were ready for it."[14] Boys were washed in cold water, and girls in warm water when it was available. Mothers did not nurse their infants until their milk appeared.

Pretty-shield, a Crow woman, was around seventy-four years old when Frank Bird Linderman interviewed her in 1932 for the book *Pretty-Shield: Medicine Woman of the Crow*. She described for him her experiences just before the birth of her first child: "One day while playing with some girl friends I felt a little, quick pain, and sat down, laughing about it. One of my friends guessed what was about to happen, and told my mother. But when my mother, and a wise-one, named Left-Hand, came after me I did not wish to go to the lodge with them."[15] Pretty-shield's mother persuaded her to come to the new tipi pitched near her mother's lodge.

> Left-hand's lodge was pitched near my mother's. I noticed now that one of my father's best horses, with several fine robes on his back, was tied there. My father had already paid her to help me, even before I needed help. Old Left-hand wore a buffalo robe with the hair-side out. Her face was painted with mud, her hair was tied in a big lump on her forehead, and in her hand she carried some of the-grass-that-the-buffalo-do-not-eat.[16]

When Pretty-shield entered her new lodge, she saw that her mother had kindled a fire and prepared her bed, "a soft buffalo robe folded with the hair side out." As customary among Plains peoples, a frame had been set up for the childbirth: "Two stakes had been driven into the ground for me to take hold of, and robes had been rolled up and piled against them." Left-Hand then placed four live coals on the ground, in particular places between the door of the tipi and the bed; she instructed Pretty-shield in how to walk over the coals to her bed. "'Walk as though you are busy,' she said, brushing my back with the tail of her buffalo robe, and grunting as a buffalo-cow grunts. I had stepped over the second coal when I saw that I should have to *run* if I reached my bed-robe in time. I *jumped* the third time and the *fourth*, knelt down on the robe, took hold of the two stakes, and my first child, Pine-fire, was there." After Pretty-shield was able to stand, "old Left-Hand wound a strip of tanned buffalo skin around my waist. After this, she greased my baby with grease that had red paint mixed with it, dusting a little powdered buffalo-chips and finely pounded clay from its hips down to its knees."[17]

Agnes Deernose related some of the ways to protect newborn infants in her story *They Call Me Agnes.* Her grandmother always smoked the house every night when she put the baby to bed to drive away evil spirits. People never stepped over a newborn if they wanted it to grow tall. If they "came to a spring where a spirit person lived, a mother would give her infant, or young child, some beads or tobacco to throw in the there so that the infant would grow to manhood or womanhood."[18]

The baby's ears were pierced immediately or within a few days after birth. A heated awl was used and a greased stick stuck through the perforations. Earrings were put in when the holes were healed. Crow people used a name blessing to bring good health and prosperity to the child. Four days after the birth, a father named the baby or invited someone to name the child. This brought the child under the protection of the namer's medicine. The infant's name usually reflected some experience of the person of distinction or a dream. It was customary to lift the baby four times, a little higher each time. The infant's face was painted red and then incense was held toward it.[19]

Amulet

Crow mothers made a triangular amulet of soft hide beaded on the front. When the umbilical cord dropped off, it was wrapped in a piece of soft buckskin and put inside the beaded amulet. If the infant was a girl, the little bag was attached to the cradleboard until she was old enough to wear an elk-tooth dress, when the bag was tied to the back of her dress.[20]

Crow Cradleboard Symbolism

Robert Lowie and William Wildschut found no information on Crow cradleboard symbolism. Wildschut's impression was "that by the 1920s tribal knowledge of the meanings of designs, if they had symbolism was lost."[21] His informants interpreted color symbolism as follows: red represented property and longevity, green represented the earth, white was symbolic of purity, and black was emblematic of revenge accomplishments. Black was rarely employed in Crow beadwork.

Crow Cradleboard

The Crow cradleboard I studied is from the Victor J. Evans Collection in the archives of the Smithsonian Institution's Department of Anthropology (cat. no. E358854-0). The Smithsonian acquired the collection on March 26, 1931.

The cradle is a single piece of wood, 38 inches long, and 11 inches wide, tapering to 4 inches at the bottom. The top and bottom are rounded. The entire board is covered with several thicknesses of muslin, stretched tight across the board. A vertical slit was made 13 inches from the top, ending 4 inches from the bottom. Another slit was made horizontally at the top, leaving 5 inches on each side. The muslin was left full and loose, to bunch around the baby's head for protection. The foot section is stitched together to form a pocket for the

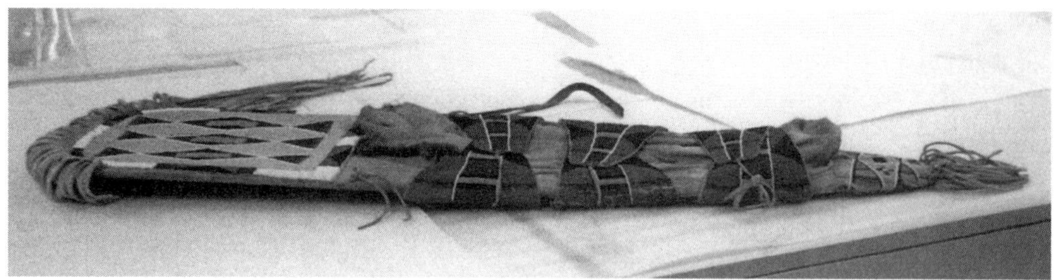

Crow cradleboard, 38 × 11 inches. Donated by Victor J. Evans, March 26, 1931. A beaded geometric design, using multicolored seed beads, on the head panel, with the bottom beaded panel decorated with white buckskin fringe. Photographs by the author. Courtesy of the Department of Anthropology, Smithsonian Institution, Suitland, Maryland (E358854-0).

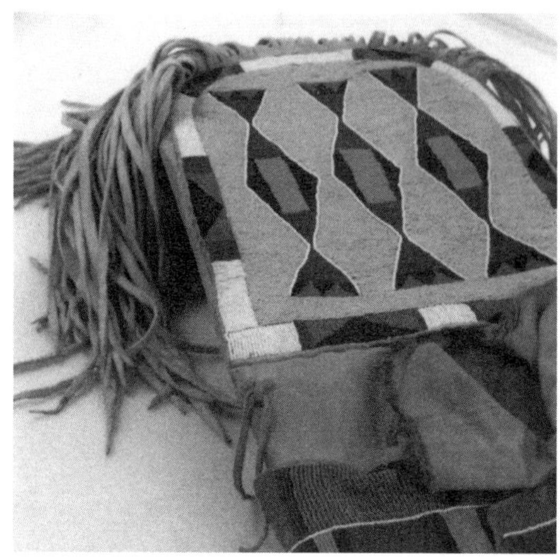

feet. A 12-inch piece of beaded buckskin, shaped like the board, is sewn to the front, covering the top. A strip of 16-inch white leather fringe is stitched across the top of the board. A strip of beaded leather formed like the board is stitched to the last four inches of muslin at the bottom. Five-inch white leather fringe is sewn at the bottom of the board.

Two pairs of three broad beaded leather straps are sewn on each side at 18 inches from the bottom, 11.5 inches, and 6 inches. The two top sets are 8 inches long, 5 inches wide, tapering to 1.75 inches. The bottom set is smaller. A narrow 20-inch strip of leather is stitched to each end of the bands. The strings wrap around the board and tie, and they can be adjusted to the child's size. The carrying strap, a piece of 1-inch-wide heavy rawhide, is attached to the board with two narrow hoops, and then threaded through a hole in the board on each side. Hoops are placed 13 inches from the top of the board.

The design is typical Crow, with a limited number of elements, Crow beadwork techniques, and many colors. The top panel has the light blue background with white outlining preferred by the Crows. The six bands are beaded in the same patterns in colors commonly found on Crow beading with the exception of turquoise and rose. Orange was seldom used. Large areas are set off with narrow white outlines and dark blue on a light blue background. Some of the simpler designs employed on the cradleboard (the narrow solid color bands, outlined rectangles, and the cross) appear to be adopted from earlier quillwork.

CHAPTER 15

BLACKFOOT

The Blackfoot (Piikani) are Algonquian-speaking people and one of the largest groups on the northern plains. The Blackfoot Confederation consist of the Siksikas; Blackfoot proper; Kainahs, or Bloods; Northern Piegans; and Southern Piegans, or Blackfeet. Their prehistory before they were plains dwellers is unknown. Most settled in Canada, but Blackfoot people reached as far south as Montana. Blackfoot territory in the early historical period

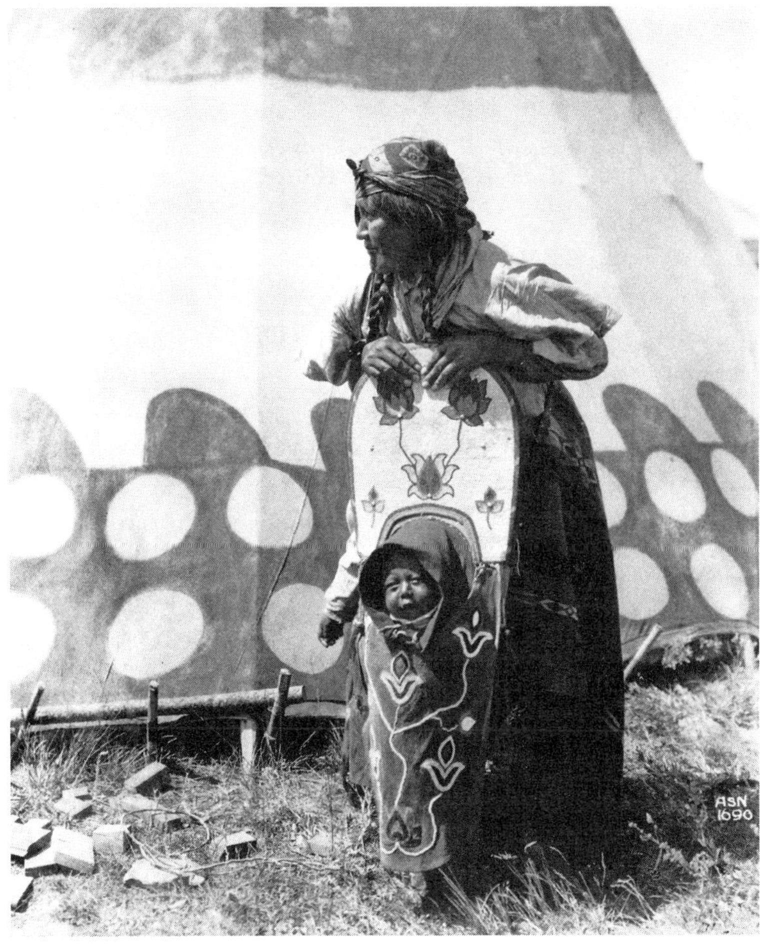

Blood woman holding a cradleboard, ca. 1929. The top third of the cradle is beaded, and a beaded apron is attached. Courtesy of the Glenbow Photograph Archives, Glenbow Museum, Alberta, Canada (NA-1811-66).

extended southward from the North Saskatchewan River to the Missouri River in Montana, bounded by the Rocky Mountains to the west.

The Blackfoot were a nomadic hunting people. They used dogs as pack animals before they began to acquire horses after 1730. Buffalo were the chief source of food and the primary source of raw material. Early on, Blackfoot were known as skilled artists and craftspeople. With horses and firearms, the Blackfoot expanded their concept of wealth and increased their personal possessions. They developed into one of the most powerful tribes on the northern plains.

With the disappearance of the buffalo in the 1870s, the Blackfoot food supply was destroyed, and their economic life collapsed. They became dependent on white society. By 1880 the Blackfoot were split into four locations. The Southern Piegans moved onto a reservation in Montana and became known as the Blackfeet. The Northern Piegans, Bloods, and Blackfoot reside on reserves in Canada.[1]

Cradleboards

Early Blackfoot cradleboard frames were made with willow branches and curved bones, tied together and cross braced. Moss hide bags were tied to the frame. The infants were packed around with dried moss, wrapped with soft buckskin or cloth, and laced in the hide bag or moss bag. When asked about the manufacture and use of cradles in Blackfoot Indian culture, Mollie Kicking Woman stated, "When I was young, I asked my grandmother how the old people made cradleboards before the white man came. She told me that the people used rib bones of buffalo or some other game, rawhide sewn together with sinew for the back and willows covered with buckskin."[2] In 1854, it was reported that Blackfoot women carried their children in their arms or in a robe behind their backs. When traveling, the babies were placed in sacks of skin.[3] John C. Ewers, writing specifically on the Blackfeet, reported that elaborate cradles were a luxury item, uncommon among the tribe in the nineteenth century. "When walking or riding on horseback, women commonly carried their babies on their backs, inside their robes or blankets. The mother stood with her back bent, grasped the infant by both arms, swung it over her shoulders, then quickly drew her robe about her own body and that of the child."[4]

Later, a cradleboard, *kapimáán*, was made of a sturdy board sawed into an oval shape with a narrow flat end.[5] The flat board was cut into a long ellipsoid that was much wider at the curved top than at the bottom. The board was completely covered with buckskin sewn together in several pieces. One piece covered the back of the board. Carefully fitted pieces of buckskin were stitched together and stretched over the board. The covering was tight over the large top section, and the narrow lower two-thirds of the board were made into a shallow bag to hold the baby. The buckskin formed a hood around the face and was laced and tied under the chin. The side of the hood was braced with a piece of stiff rawhide.

Small slits or holes were cut along each side of the bag, starting just below the face. A long narrow thong was tied to the first hole and pulled through each hole, leaving enough of the thong to form a loop. Loops were made down the side and up the other side. A narrow piece of lacing was tied to the last hoop, and the baby was securely laced in the bag. Sometimes another piece of buckskin cut out to fit the area around the head was added to the top one-third of the board. This piece was partly or fully beaded or quilled before sewn to the covering. "Some had decorated aprons that hung down the front and covered the baby bag. Some had long strings of beads and shells hanging down to amuse the baby with their movements and jingling sounds."[6] A piece of cloth or shawl was often tied to the top of the board to help protect the baby's face from the weather and insects. In cold weather, the hide bag would be lined with fur. Often a narrow, smooth circular rod was attached to the board above the child's head.

According to Beverly Hungry Wolf, a Blood Indian born and raised on the Blood Reserve in Canada, a new baby was bundled up most of the time in a moss bag. Infants were wrapped with soft cloth or hide inside the moss bag. The baby bag was laced up the front with only the baby's head exposed. A moss bag was often attached to a cradleboard transporting a baby to keep the baby well protected.[7]

Hammocks

Little hammocks were used for small babies' beds in a tipi or other home. An *awápistaan* (swinging cradle), made with a blanket and two buckskin thongs, was swung from lodge poles.[8] Two parallel cords were tied together, adjoining them, as in a swing. The blanket was folded back and forth between the two cords. A stick across the two sides of the hammock was used to spread it out to be sure there was enough breathing room for the infant. The cords were tied to tipi poles. The baby was placed inside the hammock after being laced in its moss bag.[9]

Quillwork and Beadwork

The work with porcupine quills was a sacred craft with Blackfoot women. A woman who wanted to work with quills had to go through an initiation and be taught by an older woman knowledgeable about the crafts. There were strict rules, such as if a quillworker throws quills in the fire, she will go blind. Quillwork was not to be sold. It could be made for friends or relatives or commissioned by others in the camp. Designs were often the result of dreams and were personal property—not to be copied without permission. A beginner customarily gave her first piece of quillwork as an offering to the sun.[10]

In Hugh Dempsey's article "Religious Significance of Blackfoot Quillwork," he notes that young women were initiated ceremonially into the art of handling the sharp-pointed quills. The religious patterns included symbol-based painting, hand painting, prayers, and wearing a special necklace of porcupine claws and colored quills.[11]

According to William C. Orchard, the Blackfoot employed six traditional methods of applying quills. Narrow bands of quillwork and small angular designs dominated their work. The porcupine is native to Blackfoot country. Quills were used in their natural color or dyed in one of a few different ways: with vegetable dye or aniline dyes from traders, or by boiling pieces of colored blankets with the quills. Early vegetable colors were delicate reds, yellows, blues, and greens. Yellow dye was made from the pine tree lichen, *Evernia vulpina*.

The quills were prepared by breaking off the basal tip. Then they were dyed "by dampening a quantity of the dye plant yielding the desired color in water, placing a number of quills on top of it, wrapping them together in a piece of buckskin, and placing the package under their bed. After the package was pressed by the weight of the woman's body for a couple of nights it was unwrapped and the dyed quills removed."[12]

The beadwork of Blackfoot women was a direct outgrowth of their quillwork. By 1880, beadwork had become popular, and quillwork was almost abandoned. They adapted many of the techniques, forms, and designs from the early craft. Many items were decorated with a combination of quills and beads. Bead embroidery was applied in narrow bands, in the same large, simple geometric designs they had used in quillwork and in painting on rawhide. Early beads were large and expensive, and they were used sparingly. The Blackfoot were able to obtain beads from traders in six colors: light blue, dark blue, dark red, deep yellow, white, and black with white. Light blue was a favorite color. Large geometric areas were compositions of simple units of design: small squares and rectangles in triangles. If the decorative area was large, the patterns covered a small part.

The American Museum of Natural History has a Blackfeet cradleboard in its collection (cat. no. 50/6164), collected by David C. Duvall on the Blackfeet Reservation in Browning, Montana, in 1905. The oval board is completely covered with hide, with a slit in front to form a pouch for the baby. Lacing holds the hide bag together and is reinforced around the head with stiff rawhide. The cradleboard is 36.6 inches long, 15 inches wide, and 7.3 inches deep; the fringe sewn along the top curve is 10.4 inches long. The top third is decorated with rows of white quillwork dyed red and yellow. The design motif is repeated bars and stepped triangles. Metal bells are tied to the fringe, and the pouch is lined with fur.

The cradleboard has a sturdy strap tied to the back. The strap is tied from the left side to the right side. The mother could carry the board on her back with the strap across her shoulders. The cradleboard could be hung on a saddle, sturdy branch, or lodge pole.

From 1870, seed beads supplied by traders in several sizes, colors, and hues were found in Blackfoot beadwork. By then, traditional colors included green, pink, and rose. Entire surfaces of complex floral and leaf designs were covered in several colors. Some beadworkers combined floral designs with traditional geometric designs. Beadwork was produced in the overlay technique, especially to cover large areas. Lazy stitch was used sparingly for edging. Beads were strung on the thread and spot stitched with another thread to secure the embroidery. The overlay stitch resulted in a smooth surface.[13]

Birth Customs

According to Beverly Hungry Wolf, the cradleboard was not made until the baby was one month old and named. When the baby was born, it was bundled up in rags and tied with buckskin cords. The girl's mother would save old rags for her daughter before the birth. "This was a kind of trial period, to make sure everybody would survive the new birth."[14]

A pregnant woman received help with her household chores from a female relative of the father, who stayed with the family until the birth. If the husband could afford a second wife, he would marry at that time. At the time of the birth, the expecting woman was separated from the men in the camp because a man could lose his sacred powers in close contact with a woman at this time. Beverly Hungry Wolf shared her the story her grandmother AnadaAki told of her first time giving birth. After the baby was cleaned up and taken care of, her mother massaged her bones back in place, gave her warm broth, and laid her down to rest. "To bring the mother's body back in shape, in addition to the massages, she was made to wear a 'belt' or girdle of rawhide. This was wide enough to cover her abdomen and tied firmly."[15] The new mother usually stayed with her mother during the time away from her husband. No ill person could stay around the lodge. The confinement was usually thirty days, and the new mother did not do any heavy work during that time. The new mother was bathed and given a cleaning ceremony every four days. "Her mother would wash her and then cover her up with a blanket. She was made to sit by the altar, where incense was made. The incense went up under the blanket and purified her body."[16] She was cared for by a medicine woman and elderly women experienced with midwifery. The mother was given a decoction of roots to drink to ease her pain and facilitate delivery. "While the mother grasped one of the lodge poles an assistant held her around the waist and the midwife attended to the delivery, then laced the mother in her rawhide belt. Sometimes the mother resumed her household chores the next day."[17]

The umbilical cord was cut with an arrow. The newborn was washed and painted red, and prayers were given.[18] The infant was bathed and wrapped in soft skin and diapered with moss or soft punk. A medicine doctor was called for a difficult birth; the mother was given prayers and an herbal brew to drink. He would be given a horse for payment. A Blackfeet woman about to give birth was given tea brewed of the bark scrapings of a cottonwood tree, *Populus deltoides*. They also made a tea from sweet grass, *Hierochloe odorata*, to stop bleeding after birth and to help expel the afterbirth.[19]

A baby was given a name at birth by the mother. Sometimes the name was based on the first thing the new mother saw. Later, the father had the baby officially named by an older relative or important person in the camp. A man or woman of the camp could choose a name honoring sacred animals or holy powers. A man often chose a name that related to his own war experiences. A boy was given his first name in a special sweat lodge ceremony when he was a few weeks old. Several names can be earned through war exploits, hunting prowess, or religious experiences. A girl's name would remain unchanged throughout her life.

According to Hungry Wolf, an expecting mother was not allowed to eat certain foods: heart and innards would discolor the mother's face, eating brains would cause the child to have a snotty nose, and eating leg muscles would give the mother cramps. Standing in an open door, looking outside her home, would cause her to have hard labor.

Hungry Wolf shared the story of her grandfather's birth, in 1877. His mother had had hard luck with her children—all had been born dead or had died shortly after birth. To save this baby's life, he was put through a powerful ceremony after his birth:

> His parents were desperate to have him live, so they went to an old lady named Holy Otter Woman who was a holy woman noted for spiritual powers. The old lady

> prayed for him, then chopped off part of his little finger and gave it to Sun as an offering. This was considered a most powerful form of sacrifice in the ways of my grandmothers.
>
> The old lady also took my grandfather and wrapped him up in a blanket, and tied him up in a tree as if he was dead. His mother stood underneath and mourned for him. The old lady said that she would never have to do that again.[20]

Beverly Hungry Wolf's grandfather lived to be ninety-seven years old.

Amulet

Amulets of small buckskin cases were made for infants. The dried navel cord was preserved in the case, which would later be decorated with quills or beads. Cases for boys were in the form of snakes, and those for girls were shaped like lizards because "the Blackfeet believed that snakes and lizards had long lives and were never sick."[21] Clark Wissler collected three navel amulets, a snake and two lizards, in 1903 for the American Museum of Natural History. The beaded hide lizard bags are the same shape, beaded with three colors. Dimensions varied: 4 inches long, 1.9 inches wide, and 1 inch deep; and 10 inches long, 1.8 inches wide, and 1 inch deep. The smallest one is white and navy, outlined in green beads, with an elongated diamond shape on the back of the lizard shape. Long strips of rawhide sewn on the body represent the legs and tail, with one strip sewn on the back, tied to the cradleboard. The largest amulet is beaded in light blue, outlined in white, with a stripe down the lizard back in navy and white. Six long strips of narrow rawhide are folded in half, tied in a knot, and sewn on for legs and tail. Metal cones are attached on each end of a strip of leather. The amulet shaped like a snake is 6.5 inches long, 2.5 inches wide, and 1 inch deep. It is completely beaded in dark green, light blue, yellow, white, and red glass seed beads, with the snake body in green. Three alternating stripes of yellow, red, and yellow run halfway along the back, with the edges along the body beaded in light blue; the rest of the shape is striped in alternating light blue and green. A piece of narrow rawhide thong is sewn at the end of the tail.

Blackfoot Cradleboard

This Blackfoot cradleboard has a resemblance to collections and pictures in literature. I studied one in a private collection in Idabel, Oklahoma, collected by Quintus H. Herron.

The frame is made of a single board cut in an ellipsoid shape, flat on the bottom part. The curved top is 14 inches wide, tapering to 8 inches at the narrowest part, the bottom of the frame. The cradleboard is 37 inches long.

White buckskin is stretched over the board, completely covering the frame with buckskin. Two pieces are sewn together at the top and bottom. The middle part is sewn to form the hood and the bag to hold the baby. The bag is open from the foot area to the shoulder area. Eleven holes are punched along each side for the lacing. Loops are made with one long narrow strip of buckskin. One end is tied to the first hole, and then threaded through each hole. Loops go down each side. Lacing is tied at the bottom of the bag and laced through the loops to the top.

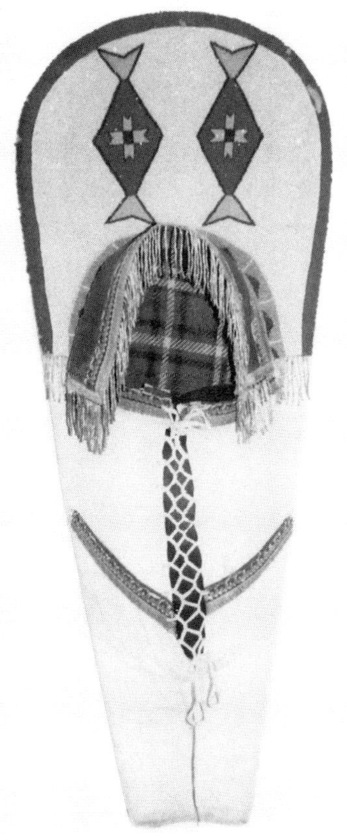

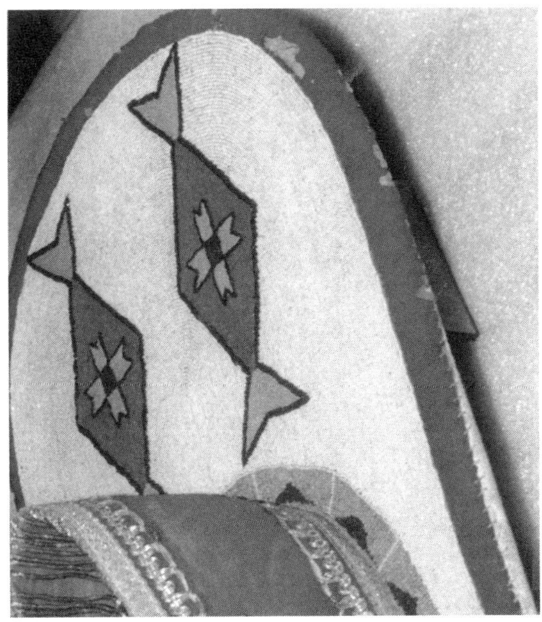

Blackfoot cradleboard, ca. 1885, with a geometric beadwork design on the head panel. Photographs by the author. Private collection, Idabel, Oklahoma.

The hood is made of red velvet and lined with turquoise velvet. The hood is an 18-inch by 4-inch rectangle trimmed with gold military fringe and braid stitched to the buckskin. The back of the hood is lined with red, blue, and white plaid wool. The carrying strap is a length of buckskin tied together with two straps on each side of the frame's back. The original carrying strap appears to be missing.

The top one-third of the cradleboard is overlaid with a beaded covering. The covering is cut to fit the hood and sewn to the skin bag. A 2-inch border of red flannel outlines the bead embroidery. The background is light blue. The design consists of two large red diamonds, a cross with a bar in the middle of the diamond, and two triangles at each end of the diamond. The geometric designs are outlined in dark green beads. The hood area is outlined with a 0.75-inch band of beading. This band is a series of parallel units of rose rectangles with dark blue triangles and light blue bars. The embroidery beads used are red, yellow, dark green, purple, rose, dark blue, and light blue.

An 18-inch strip of gold military braids with 4-inch fringe is stitched on each side of the hood. Gold fringe is sewn on three sides of the hood, with a strip of fringe at the end of the beading. Two pieces of braid backed with red velvet, 7 inches long, is stitched in a V shape on the baby bag. A piece of white buckskin fringe is sewn across the back.

PART FIVE

HURDLE CRADLES

Arapaho

Wichita

Lipan Apache

CHAPTER 16

ARAPAHO

The Arapahos originally called themselves Hiinonon'ei (Our People). The Arapahos of the Algonquian family were early inhabitants of the northern plains, well established there before the eighteenth century. They spoke five different dialects of the Algonquian language in historical times. The northernmost group, Hitúnĕna, broke from the tribe and formed a separate tribe, the Gros Ventre, in the early eighteenth century. The Arapahos are believed to have once lived in the Red River region of what is now Minnesota and North Dakota. Most of the year, they lived in bands that moved together. Kinship was based on bilateral descent. Other individuals were often adopted or absorbed into the kindred. The Arapaho lifestyle was

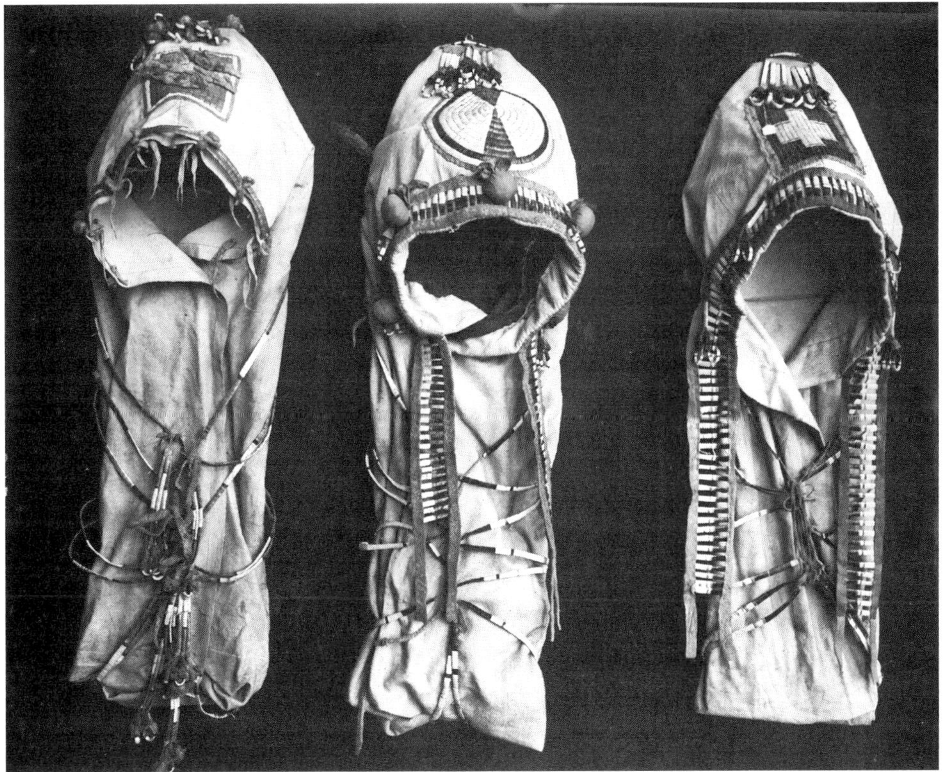

Three Northern Arapaho cradles, late 1800s. Sizes range from 30 to 32 inches long and 9 to 11 inches wide. The ornamentations of the cradle differ from typical examples, particularly in the absence of quillwork around the cradle face and front. Photograph by R. Weber. Courtesy of the Photographic Collection, American Museum of Natural History Library, New York (31211).

similar to that of other Plains tribes. Subsistence was based on the bison for food, clothing, shelter, tools, and other necessities. The diet of game was supplemented with wild plant foods.

Trial government comprised an age-graded series of societies supervised by the elderly custodian of the medicine bundle. These men and their wives performed political duties, kept order in the camp, and supervised the communal hunt.

Eventually the Arapahos claimed territory from the headwaters of the North Platte to the Arkansas River. In the 1800s, the tribe split, and two bands were identified, the Southern and Northern Arapaho. In 1869, the Southern Arapahos were assigned to a reservation in Oklahoma Territory, which they share with the Southern Cheyennes. The Northern Arapahos were sent to the Wind River Reservation in Wyoming in 1878, which they share with the Shoshones. Members of both Arapaho groups consider themselves all one people.

Arapaho Cradles

The Arapahos made two types of cradles called *hectoonohuut*.[1] Jeffrey D. Anderson's *Arapaho Women's Quillwork: Motion, Life, and Creativity*, a comprehensive examination of the ritualized quillwork, expanded work conducted with the Northern Arapaho of early nineteen-century ethnographers, amplifying how quillwork played a central role in religious life within their ancient and sacred traditions. Anderson referred to the types of Arapaho cradles as path, or head-ornament, cradles and lined-path cradles.

The head-ornament cradle is the most recognized as Arapaho and features a central circular or rectangular ornament on the hood. The cradle consisted of a U-shaped wood framework, a cover of tanned buckskin, lashing, and a carrying strap. Decorative elements were traditionally of quillwork. The framework was made by bending a branch of willow, chokecherry, or sumac, about 1 inch in diameter, into an inverted U shape. It was held in place by a cross stick tied to the frame at the open end. The frame was placed inside the cover and tied to it. The cover was originally of tanned deer or antelope hide and later of commercial canvas. Sister M. Inez Hilger studied museum holdings of Arapaho cradleboards and found that "in length the framework museum specimens varied from 27 to 34 inches; the greatest width (near head end) from 9 to 10 inches; the narrowest width (the open end of the U, the foot end) from 3.5 to 5 inches."[2]

The cover of buckskin or canvas was folded lengthwise and stitched together along one of the narrow ends, forming the hood. The depth of the hood varied from 13 to 15 inches. Covers were 10 to 15 inches longer than the framework, allowing the mother to fold the ends up to form a "bag" to hold the baby. A small pillow was placed under the baby's head, and the baby was wrapped in soft fetal or calf hide. In winter the baby was wrapped in a fur-lined wildcat-hide bag, with the baby's head covered with a small cap of the wildcat's head and the legs placed into the sewn-up legs of the animal.[3] Ornaments were prepared separately and sewn to the cover. Both dyed and natural porcupine quills were used to make the decorative elements: a disk, a band, and pendants. A rectangular, oval, or trapezoidal shape was sometimes used instead of the traditional disk. On some cradles, cloth-wrapped bundles of herbs were attached at intervals around the hood opening. A beaded leather case, or amulet, containing the umbilical cord was also attached to the cradle cover at shoulder level.

The disk was sewn over the hood seam on the cover, and the band was sewn to the opening around the face. The pendants were either plain buckskin strips or strips wrapped with flattened quills, with small bells, deer dewclaws, or antelope dewclaws attached with buckskin strings. Lashings were generally quill-wrapped strips of buckskin. The carrying strap was a narrow band of strong leather attached to the frame.

Cradles similar in design to the head-ornament type are the red path cradle, cornered cradle, spotted cradle, lodge cradle, yellow-crossed cradle, ribbed cradle, black cradle, yellow cradle, half-yellow cradle, green cradle, green and yellow cradle, twelfth yellow cradle, the intricate design, yellow lodge cradle variant, yellow oblong, and red oblong cradle.

Alfred L. Kroeber described the meaning of the head-ornament, or path, cradle as follows:

> The round ornament at the top of this cradle, besides denoting the head of the child, represents also a tent-ornament, which it closely resembles. The tent-ornament signifies that the child, when it has grown up, will have a tent. Above the round ornament are pendants having small hoofs and quill-wrapped loops at their ends. These represent the pendants or rattles above the door of the tent. Still higher up than these on the cradle are two quill-wound strips lying parallel to each other. These represent a man and woman, since a man and woman own a tent together. On the ornament representing hair are several pairs of pendants having loops at their ends. These loops represent the holes in the bottom of the tent through which the tent-pegs pass. The whole cradle, owing to its shape and the fact of its being stretched on a framework of sticks, resembles a tent-door, and therefore represents it.[4]

According to Anderson, the overall symbolic meaning of the path cradle head pendant is the sun; the two red triangles are tipis oriented to the sun's path; and the white background is the daylight. All the path ornament styles are connection to the body and the tipi. Most of the head-ornament cradles have the same color scheme: white, red, and black. One that Anderson described had red and white only, and three head-ornament cradles had yellow designs. The ornaments with green added to white, yellow, red, or black are more intricate designs. Two oblong cradles, red and yellow, had a rectangular head-ornament. While visiting the Panhandle–Plains Historical Museum, I photographed a cloth yellow oblong path cradle. The rectangular design consists of yellow and either dark blue or black beads, and the head disk has a white cross on a yellow background. The oblong ornament might represent a tent ornament.[5] The pendants above it are the rattles at the top of the tent. This cradle does not have tufts of wool. The main symbolism for the cradle is of Little Star, "with its brilliancy to the people," thus also associating the child's body and the tipi. See plate 15 for a cradleboard with a geometric rosette design.

An unusual Arapaho cradle housed in the Riverside Metropolitan Museum is made of a flour sack. The sack is mounted on a traditional U-shaped willow frame and is decorated with porcupine quills of red, green, brown, and white. The interior of the cloth has the printed label "U.S. Indian Department . . . flour . . . 100 lbs. J.B. Finney, Contractor, Aimsworth, Nebraska. . . . H & L Chase Bags, St. Louis, Missouri."

Arapaho cradle making was women's work. It was generally made under the guidance of the paternal grandmother or another older female relative of the child's father. She had to sponsor a ceremony for women to work together sewing with porcupine quills on the tanned hide cover. As many as six women might work on the cradle together. Each cradle was made for a specific child before the birth. The completed cradle would be stored until the intended child was born. Only certain sacred designs could be used, appearing in red, yellow, black, green, and white. In the early days, no parts of the cradle were used again for another child.[6]

The cradle maker hosted a ceremony and feast for the new mother and baby. Before the infant was tied to the cradle, it was incensed with a smudge. If the baby was a boy, the smudge was made of sweet-smelling grass; if a girl, a turnip-shaped root found in the mountains. While tying the baby to the cradle, prayers were offered so that everything would go well with the child, so that the baby would grow to be a strong and good person. Only one woman spoke. Holding the baby in an upright position, the cradle maker walked to the door, and then to each of the four directions. Then the cradle was presented to the mother. An outgrown cradle would have been ceremonially dismantled, and the quillwork saved and used again. The cradleboard protected the child from harm, and provided constant warmth. Each part of the cradleboard, and each design had the power to give the child a good mind and strong body.[7]

Hilger interviewed Agnes Yellow Plume and Ann Wolf during her study of the Arapaho people in 1952, and the women shared some of their knowledge about Arapaho cradle making with her:

> The framework of a baby's cradle was made of willow "wrapped around with soft buckskin." It was always placed inside the cover, and never was it attached to the outside. After the framework had been placed in the cover, thongs of buckskin were crisscrossed over the framework. The ends of the thongs were brought out through slits in the cover and left long enough so that they could be brought around the shoulders of the mother when she carried the baby on her back.
>
> In old days the cover of the cradle was buckskin. Its width was a hand-stretch, measured from tip of thumb to tip of long finger, plus the length obtained by holding the tip of the long finger in position and laying the hand backward until the knuckles touched the buckskin. The material was cut where the knuckles rested. The rest of the measurements were based on guess and experience. "If you were in doubt, you went to the old women who knew the measurements, and asked them." A pillow was placed under the baby's head when it was in the cradle.
>
> Cradles were made before the arrival of the baby and each baby had its own. "I had three daughters and each had her own cradle," remarked Yellow Plume. Wolf continued, "When I decided to make a cradle for her daughter, I asked two of my great-grandmothers to show me how to make it. I brought buckskin and rawhide and quills to her. I had to sit for many days working on the quills, my great-grandmother directing me." The disk over the head of the child was always to be 10 successive rings of quillwork, counting the center piece as one. No measurements of diameter or of circumference were followed; only rings were counted. All rings were alike in

width. The band which was attached over the face of the child and reached down the sides of the cradle cover was to have 100 crossbars of quillwork. Some makers made fewer, but bands that contained 100 were prettier. Each crossbar was to be as wide as the maker's thumbnail is long. The length of the crossbar was from the tip of the first finger to just beyond the second knuckle of the same finger. The strips of quillwork that crossed each other over the baby's body were there to hold the baby in the cradle.

Ten pendants were to be attached over the head and toward the back of the child, and to be tipped off with antelope toenails. These were to be rattled for the child's amusement. Four other pendants, two on each side of the cradle, also served as rattles.[8]

Identified Arapaho Line-Path Cradles

The second type of Arapaho cradle carrier, the line-path style, consisted of a soft hood with the traditional T-seam shape but without a wood frame. It was much more related to the Sioux and Cheyenne soft cradle than the Arapaho path cradle in form and decoration. The Arapaho line-path cradle was decorated with closely spaced stripes on both the hood and wrapper. Candace Greene refers to this type of cradle as a "striped cradle" in her article "Soft Cradles of the Central Plains." Arapaho line-path cradles are known from Cleaver Warden's field notes (1903–6), which list and describe in detail the different types of Arapaho cradle styles. His field notes on the striped Arapaho soft cradle include sketches he made of five additional striped cradles. The sketches conform to the basic design of the cradle I examined, but with a different color palette. Warden collected data among the Northern and the Southern Arapahos. According to his notes, the striped style was adopted from the Cheyenne.[9]

The hide cover's decorative elements were ornamented with a series of up to twenty closely spaced horizontal colored stripes, running parallel to the rim of the hood. The symmetrical trapezoid hood, or T-seam pattern, had a triangular decorative field. Red tufts marked transitions along each line. The same number of similar but shorter lines on each side of the body section of the cover ran perpendicular to the baby's body. A pair of triangular beaded fork-like pendants with bells were attached to the peaked hood. The middle part of the hood had a beaded rectangle with one central color and another color for the two other sections.

Greene examined a cradle at the Smithsonian that I later examined, in 2000 (plate 16). James Mooney purchased the cradle for $750 in 1893 from H. R. Voth, along with three boxes of Cheyenne material. One box contained seventy-three items, a "Catalog of Indian Curios, Trinkets, Implements, Clothing," and one Indian cradle (porcupine quilled) among the items. The one-piece hide cradle is twenty-nine inches long and twenty-six inches wide. The hood is fourteen inches long and twenty-nine inches wide. The edges are folded in and sewn together. It is decorated with yellow and orange plant fiber, porcupine quillwork, tufts of red yarn, brass beads, and calico balls at the edges.

Greene described the cradle:

> The hood has a triangular field embroidered with a series of spaced transverse stripes worked in colored plant fiber in a two-thread technique with smaller sections of

> porcupine quills. A convergent band on the top of the hood is formed of colored sections inserted in the stripes and is delineated with yarn tufts which also appear along the outer edges of the triangular field. There are trifurcate pendants from the squared tabless peak of the hood. Stripes of similar embroidery are placed on the body of the wrapper at right angles to the triangular field on hood. A series of loose thongs along the back of the carrier suggest that it was intended to be secured to a frame, probably a U-shaped interior frame of the type used among the Northern Arapaho.[6]

Anderson described the line-path cradles as of smoked hide.

Anderson describes four kinds of line-path cradles: green path, black path, white path, and yellow path. The line-path cradles were identified by the dominant color on the covering. The green path, black path, and yellow cradles were similar in form with different colors of quillwork and beadwork. The hood had twenty horizontal lines; each side of the body also had twenty, with red tufts overlying each color section. Each colored path cradle had five sets of quilled button loops. The white path cradle had only fourteen head rows and fourteen body rows. Each path cradle has a different color scheme, with matching head and body.

Quillwork

Several Plains tribes that practiced quillwork, such as the Blackfeet and the Cheyenne, considered it a sacred art. For the Arapaho and Gros Ventre tribes, quillwork was central to religious life. To Arapahos, counting quillwork achievements was the same as counting men's deeds in wars. Each quillwork project was done by a vow and some sacrifice, including the time commitment, fasting, and giving gifts to the old women involved. Arapahos developed a distinctive sacred system of incorporating symbolic elements and colors into quillwork. An Arapaho women's work guild had seven older women who possessed a sacred workbag, which contained incense, paint, implements for marking and sewing, awls, sinew, and small bones. Quillwork was produced under the guidance of the old women, to be sure that items were done in a consistent, conservative manner. Quills were softened in the mouth and flattened with a bone. A dark fibrous water plant was used to sew in black. Quills were kept in pouches of gut because the sharp quills would not penetrate the bag. These small bags were usually not decorated.[11]

Four colors—red, yellow, white, and black—predominate in quillwork, with the proportions and positions of the different styles part of the sacred techniques and symbolism tied to the core of the Arapaho religion. Green has been found on a few items, a line-path cradle, a robe, and green beadwork, which suggests borrowing from the Cheyennes.[12] Black currants were used for dying quills black, and a root from the swamp for purple. If red was wanted, red trade cloth was wrapped around the quills and boiled. To set the dye, the skin of the beaver tail was added to the dye container. Later, when traders carried artificial dyes, the Arapahos had other colors.

Arapaho mothers carried their babies on their backs in cradles when traveling on foot. A buckskin strap attached to the back of the cradle went across the mother's chest and upper arms. When on horseback, the cradle was often hung on the mother's saddle horn. If the camp was moving, sometimes the baby in its cradle was placed in a basket attached to a travois. A cradle would also be propped against a tree if the mother was busy.[13]

Birth customs

Before an Arapaho baby was born, both parents avoided certain things, including some foods. "A woman must never eat, either while pregnant or at any other time, the two pieces of meat that lie opposite each other on either side of the backbone of a buffalo. They are round and long in shape. She will have twins if she does."[14] Talking about prenatal life was taboo because of the fear of affecting the pregnancy of a relative. Married women who associated with a pregnant woman or borrowed her clothes from her might also expect soon to be pregnant. A difficult birth could be caused by the husband stepping over any part of his pregnant wife's body. A difficult birth could also be caused by sitting too close to fire.[15]

Children were born in the family tipi with the assistance of older women who had knowledge of birth. All medicine bags were removed before the birth. Some fathers assisted their wives, and the mother and father of the expecting woman were present. A medicine man or woman might attend the birth to prepare an herbal drink to facilitate the birth.

The woman in labor knelt and braced herself with a pole crotched into upright posts that had been firmly planted in the ground. The height of the horizontal post was placed where the kneeling woman could reach it with her arms outstretched full length over her head. Her knees were cushioned with hay or grass or canvas. A bed was prepared of a worn hide and later a quilt or canvas. During labor, one of the attendants tickled the woman's throat with a feather until she gagged to help bring about delivery. Myrtle Lincoln, Southern Arapaho, recalled that when the pain of delivery started, no noise was allowed. "They said that if you make noise, it will stop." Sometimes they would put a handkerchief or other object in the woman's mouth. Myrtle assisted her grandson's wife in childbirth. She had the expecting mother stand, then stood behind her, holding both shoulders and pressing on the middle of the mother's back. Myrtle pulled her shoulders back and arched her back, pressing on the side of the pregnant woman's stomach until the baby came. Myrtle was taught how to deliver babies by her grandmother. She said her grandmother was always paid.[16]

The navel cord was cut with a new knife, and the end of the cord near the baby was tightly bound with sinew. "Others placed a generous amount of finely powdered horse or preferably buffalo manure about the navel cord, coiled the cord, placed it on the manure and then placed a thick layer of manure on that. A cloth was then bound around the baby to hold all in place."[17] Immediately after the birth, the mother was gagged again to help expel the placenta. The feather used was to be an eagle wing, hawk, grouse, pheasant, or magpie.

After the baby was cleaned, the midwife warmed a piece of cloth and, using both hands, molded the infant's head into a round ball. When the cord was secured, the newborn was bathed with a handful of cool water dashed on the back. The infant was bathed every day with cold water until the baby could walk. "The baby jumps because of it. Doing this and also trying to hold its head up so as to get its back away from the water makes its body strong. This makes them healthy."[18] After the bath, the baby was entirely greased with an ointment made of red earth mixed with tallow obtained from Cheyennes.

Hilger's informants varied in descriptions of the disposal of the afterbirth. They all agreed that nothing was ever burned. That would cause the child's death. Some thought that birth bundles should be buried, and others thought they should be hung in a tree. A Southern Arapaho informant said that the afterbirth was wrapped and tied. Then one would go straight east as far as possible to place it up high in the fork of a tree.[20]

The infant's ears were pierced soon after birth, usually at one day old. A naming feast and giveaway was given as soon as enough gifts and food could be prepared. The father invited all the old men and women in camp. After the feast, they prayed for the child. One of the old people who had strong medicine was asked to name the child and especially to pray for the child. The name giver sat to the left of the doorway. Then the baby was passed around the circle, and each person touched and prayed for the child. Prayers were given that the child would be blessed to pass through the four stages of life. The old people were always given food to take home. Many families also gave gifts to people who helped with or attended the ceremony. Through ceremonies and gifts, the ties among the relatives were kept strong. Mothers usually returned to work in a few days after birth.[20]

Amulet

When the navel cords of infant boys and girls dropped off, their mothers saved them. "When thoroughly dried, she either rolled it in a ball or into a coil around the tip of a finger, or folded it back and forth to form a little layer about 1.5 inches in length. Then it was packed with either sage or soil tightly around it, and rolled between hands, usually elongating it. Sometimes she made a ball of it."[21] Navel cords were preserved and saved in a small case of tanned buckskin. These amulets were almost always rhomboid in shape, with either fringes of buckskin or strings of beads attached to them. They represented a small animal and had fringes and beads representing limbs and tails of frogs, turtles, lizards, or horned toads. The shapes of the animals carried the power of the animals, giving life and direction. Usually both sides of the amulet were beaded with geometric designs. The shape was no different for boys or girls, but black beads were used on boys' amulets, and red and yellow beads were used on girls'. After Kroeber studied with the Arapahos from 1902 to 1907, he wrote that "the navel-strings of Arapaho girls are preserved and sewed into small pouches stuffed with grass. These pouches are usually diamond-shaped and covered on both sides with beads. The child wears this amulet, which contains its navel-string, on its belt until it is worn out."[22] The child's amulet bag was kept near throughout life to be sure he or she would follow a long, straight road. The amulets were worn on the waist or on shirts. Sometimes the amulet was placed in a porcupine tail and used as a comb. If the navel amulet was lost, "for the rest of his or her life the owner would wander around and snoop into others' belongings looking for it."[23]

An Arapaho woman described to Hilger the making of an amulet:

> A northern woman demonstrated the exact size she usually used in making a diamond-shaped container. Using a dry twig picked from the ground to guide

her pencil in straight lines, she marked off, by eye, on paper, a diamond exactly 5 inches long and exactly 2.5 inches wide. She drew the lower left-hand side first; then moving clockwise, the other three sides. "Here," she noted, pointing to one of the acute angles, "I sew a string of buckskin with which to tie the bag to the belt. Here, and here and here [remaining three angles] I sew fringes of buckskin and strings of beads. This shape of bag may be used for either a boy or a girl."[24]

The amulet case was attached to the outside of the cradle on either side at shoulder level. Two navel amulets in the American Museum of Natural History, collected in Indian Territory in 1899 and 1900, are rhomboid shaped, completely beaded on hide, and sewn with sinew. The length varied from 6 to 11 inches. They are decorated with tin cones or brass beads on the appendages. One is a realistic shape of a lizard sewn with sinew and completely beaded on hide. It was collected in Wyoming in 1900. The amulet lizard body is beaded with yellow glass seed beads with legs of medium blue, eyes, and a stripe down the back with bisecting lines.

Arapaho Cradle Symbolism

Research by Alfred Kroeber, George Dorsey, Cleaver Warden, Inez Hilger, Candace Greene, and Jeffrey Anderson underscores that making and ornamenting the traditional Northern Arapaho cradle was a sacred undertaking, and that the cradle ornaments had symbolic meaning.[25] Kroeber concluded that the various ornaments represented the child in the cradle, as well as parts of the tent. In his extensive study of Arapaho symbolism, Kroeber wrote:

> The round ornament near the top of the cradle, situated over the top of the child's head, represents the head or skull of the child. The long ornament, consisting of two strips of hide connected by red, black, and white quill-wrapped strips represents the child's hair. The smooth, slippery quills denote the greasy hair of the child. At the lower part of the cradle the long quill-covered thongs represent the ribs. The lowest part, however, are the legs. Of the three colors in the embroidery, red represents blood; black, the hair (of the young and middle aged); white (the hair of) old age.
>
> Of the sticks forming the framework inside the cradle, one is unpeeled, the other peeled. The unpeeled one denotes that the child is as yet helpless and dirty in its cradle; the peeled stick represents its subsequent more cleanly condition.[26]

Dorsey gave an interpretation of the symbolism associated with a cradle when he collected one among the Northern Arapaho on the Wind River Reservation in 1900. The Chicago Natural History Museum catalog recorded the information (cat. no. 61470). The cradle is typical of the Northern Arapaho in both form and decoration. The disk over the head symbolizes the sun and the crown of the child's head as well as the baby's intelligence. The red and yellow sectors of the disk form a cross, symbolizing the morning star or a woman. White sectors of the disk represent the four corners of the earth; yellow, the light of the sun; red, its heat; and black, night. The rattles at the top of the cradle symbolize the hearing of the child. The loops on the pendants symbolize the sun. The band of quillwork around the opening of the cradle represent the child's hair. The four pendants attached to the band of quillwork represent the four corners of the world, the Four Old Men important in the mythology of the Arapaho, and the four periods of life. The long strips around the cradle symbolize the child's ribs. The long pendant with the bells represents energy and movements.[27]

The ceremonial, symbolic, and constructive characteristics of the Northern Arapaho cradle set it apart from all others and helped perpetuate it well into the reservation days. Beadwork did not replace the quillwork technique, and the basic cradle structure persisted until the cradles were no longer made.

Colors used on Arapaho cradles and other sacred art forms were white, red, yellow, and black. Green and blue were occasionally used. The four colors had various meanings depending on context and form. White denotes the color of winter, completion, old age, and the moon; red represents humanity, flesh, sacrifice, and the sun; yellow symbolizes youth, dawn, and new beginnings; and black designates a victory, boundary, and transitions.[28]

According to Anderson, Arapaho quillwork is precise and dominated by geometric forms. Geometric shapes tended to have the same meaning across all types and media of quillwork; for example, an isosceles triangle represents a tipi, a circle refers to the sun, and parallel lines denote the paths of humans or animals. Attachments on quillwork also have meanings, such as the four pairs of loop ornaments, which denote the Four Old Men's eyes watching over the child. The lattice formation around the edge of the hood contains eighty to one hundred quill bars, representing the number of years the cradle maker desired for the child to live. The seven pairs of quilled straps around the lower part of the cradle, including the six on each side and one supporting the lower portion, are the ribs, to symbolically mold the infant's body into a straight, upright posture.[29]

Greene wrote that the symbolism of the striped Arapaho cradle followed the sun imagery. The convergent band on the center of the hood was the path of the sun; traverse stripes represented thoughts directed to the sun; alternating colors around the edge of the hood represented the horizon. Those with two sets of colors stood for the earth and heaven, or Father and Mother; those with four sets of colors referred to the Four Old Men. A pair of trifurcated pendants represented the child's instinct, and the five pairs of loops down the front edge represented the pulse points, finger, and toes, or sunbeams shining on the baby.[30]

Porcupine quillwork played a central religious role for Arapaho women creating a cradle in advance of a child's arrival. Each ceremonial quillwork was created with a fixed number of styles and patterns of cradles and had its own name and repeated pattern of colors.

Arapaho Cradle

The cradle I studied is stored at the Smithsonian Museum of Natural History, Department of Anthropology (E200742-0). This cradle was collected by Emile Granier, near the northern border in Montana. His entire collection gathered in Montana was sent to Otis Mason, head curator of the Department of Anthology, in September 1898 and was purchased by the Smithsonian in June 1902.

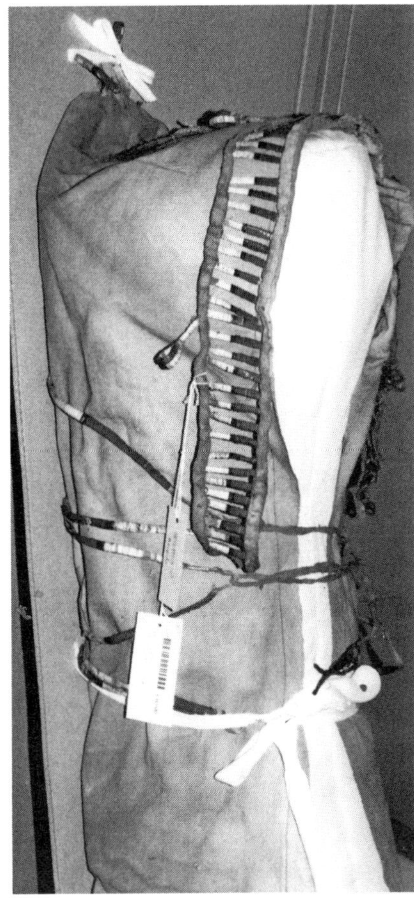

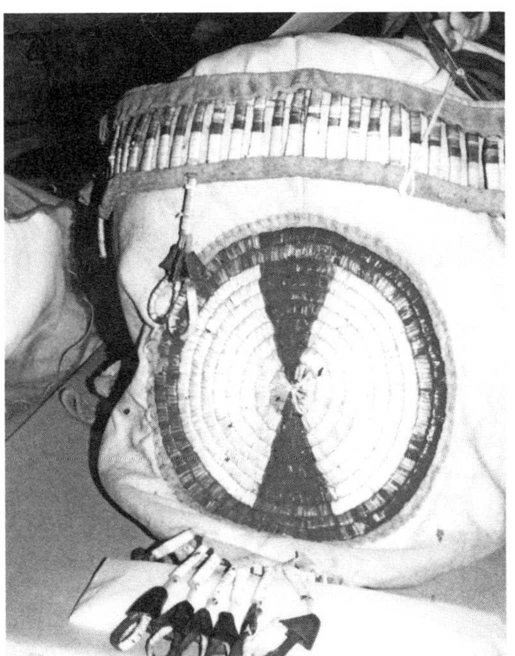

Northern Arapaho red path cradle, 29 × 8 × 12 inches (frame); 36 × 28 × 12 (canvas covering). Collected by Emile Granier, September 14, 1898. Detail of the hood shows placement of the quill rosette directly over the hood seam. The rosette was initially a separate beaded piece. Photographs by the author. Courtesy of Department of Anthropology, Smithsonian Institution, Suitland, Maryland (E200742-0).

The cradleboard's length is 29 inches, and the frame at its widest part is 8 inches; the canvas covering unfolded is 36 inches long, 28 inches wide, and 12 inches wide. The frame is made of two sticks of willow; the longer one is bent into the shape of a narrow U, with notches cut about one inch up from both ends. A short stick is tied to the U frame at the notches. The main stick is 60 inches long, 0.25 inches in diameter on one end, and 0.5 inches at the other. The small cross stick is 8 inches long and 0.25 inches in diameter. Both sticks have been peeled. Cotton rag strips are used to tie the sticks together. Another strip of cotton rag is tied across the frame about midway to help keep its shape.

The hood at the top of the cradle is made by cutting a small V-shaped piece out, about 13 inches long, in the center of the narrow side of the canvas. Horizontally across the point of this V, two small Vs are cut out. The edges of the three Vs are then drawn together to make a T-shaped seam.

The frame is laid on the canvas with the curve of the V just below the short crossbar of the T-shaped seam and tied to the canvas with ten soft thongs. One end is passed through the canvas and fastened to the quilled bands used to hold the child in the cradle. The twelve thongs at the top of the frame are fastened to an ornament on the outside of the canvas. The ornament has two short horizontal quilled strips. After the canvas cover is folded around the child, it is held in place by the straps. The tie bands are strips of quilled rawhide averaging 0.4 inches wide, fastened to the ends of the thongs tying the canvas to the frame. The end of the thong is laid against the end of the rawhide strip, overlapping about 0.25 inches. The thread used to hold the quill wrapping in place is drawn through both the thong and the rawhide. The quills pass around both the thong and the rawhide and hold them firmly together. The rawhide is omitted for about an inch in the middle of each tie band. The quillwork on the ties averages seventeen wraps to the inch. The cradle is carried by the strap of some unidentifiable leather 34 inches long and 1.5 inches wide. The strap is tied to the frame through holes in the canvas about two-thirds of the way up the frame.

To make the ornament at the top of the hood, a piece of soft skin is sewed into the short crossbar of the T-seam. The ends of the thongs pass through the skin fastened to the top of the frame and are attached to two quilled strips. The quilled strips are made of rawhide, 2 inches long and 0.25 inch wide. The lower edge of the piece of skin is cut into a 10-inch fringe, to which is attached a quilled pendant. Each pendant is a strip of quilled rawhide with a thong fastened at both ends. The upper thong ties the pendant to the cradle. The lower end passes through a bell-shaped section of animal hoof and is fastened to a loop of quilled rawhide.

The quilled disk on the hood is made of a thick piece of hide covered with quills. The disk is 5.5 inches wide. The center section of the quilling, 0.13 inches wide, is made of a coil of unflattened quills held down by stitching. In this center are six spirals. The rest of the disk is covered with a series of nine concentric circles of quilled bands 0.25 inches wide. The quills are sewn with a double row of stitching. The two outer circles are dyed red. Around the edges of the hood opening is a lattice of quill-wrapped rawhide strips. Below the opening for the child's face, the lattice hangs free. The lattice is made by fastening a series of quilled strips transversely between two ribbons of soft skin, 0.4 to 0.25 inches wide. The lattice is sewn to the hood around the opening for the face. The lattice is 50 inches long and an average 2.5 inches wide. The color design is red, black, and natural.

There are four quill dewclaw pendants fastened to the part of the lattice that encircles the hood opening. The attaching thong of each pendant is passed through both the upper skin ribbon of the lattice and the canvas of the hood. This holds the lattice flat against the hood. The lattice pendants differ from the hood pendants in that they have two hoof ornaments. Construction is similar.

The design on the disk over the head is of segmented circle patterns of nine circles plus the center, typical of the northern Plains tribes. The color scheme of red, black, and natural color was common among the Arapahos, as was the absence of seed beads for decoration. The quill lattice on the front is found only on the Arapaho cradle. The use of dewclaw pendants is shared with the Cheyennes. The use of buckskin covering is typical of the Plains; but the way it is used as a loose wrapping instead of as a bag is a Southwest trait. The T-seam construction of the Arapaho covering, however, although cut deeper to produce a more peaked hood, is that of the soft cradles of the Cheyennes and Sioux.

CHAPTER 17

WICHITA

The Wichita and Affiliated Tribes speak a Northern Caddoan language, along with the Pawnees, Kitsais, Arikaras, and, of course, Caddos. The Wichita confederacy of tribes includes Waco, Tawakoni, Taovaya, Iscani, and Kitsai. The twentieth-century name the Wichitas use for themselves is Kirikirʔi:s (Raccoon Eyes), a reference to the tattoos around their eyes.

Before the reservation period (primarily 1867–1887), multiple autonomous culturally similar tribes were collectively called the Wichitas. They generally lived in the plains area now known as western Texas, Oklahoma, central Kansas, and Nebraska. In 1541, Coronado encountered a Wichita village, Quivira, in central Kansas. In 1719, the French noted a camp of Wichitas near where they would be 150 years later, but the Wichita people had already started migrating southwest to Texas in the eighteenth century. The tribal tradition places the central homeland of the Wichitas in the southwestern Oklahoma area.

The Wichitas were semisedentary and agricultural, and thus they lived in permanent villages. Their homes were large, solid, and conical, thatched with grass. The buffalo hunt was seasonal, and during that time they became tipi dwellers to supplement the produce of their gardens. The people were extensively tattooed. The Wichitas practiced religious rituals to invoke deities for specific purposes.

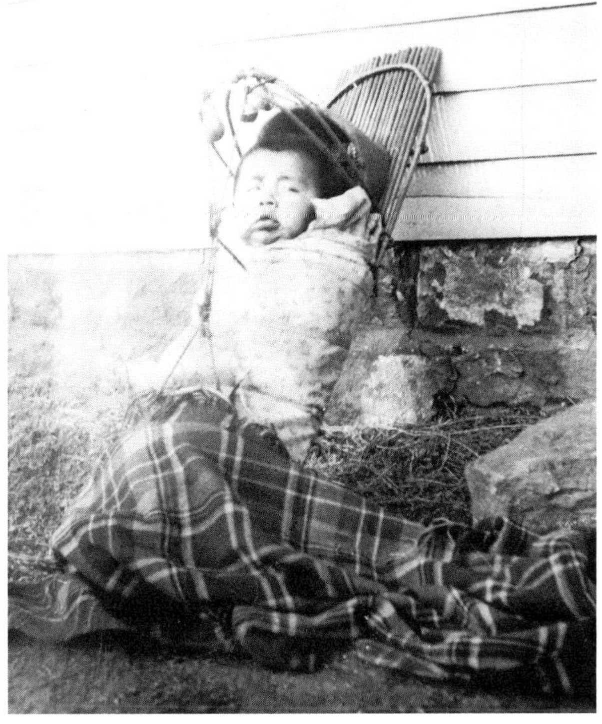

Wichita baby in a cradle, undated. Frank Phillips Photograph Collection, Western History Collections, University of Oklahoma Libraries, Norman, Oklahoma (Phillips 281).

During the U.S. Civil War and Texas's policy to exterminate Indians, the Wichitas fled to Kansas and remained there until 1867. They returned to their old home along the Washita River in Oklahoma in 1872 and were given a reservation in the Washita valley of Caddo County, Oklahoma. The Wichita and Affiliated Tribes was forced to accept allotment for tribal lands.

Cradleboard

The Wichita cradle was different from any other cradleboard on the plains. The light, flat frame was of willow sticks, lashed together with sinew. The board, painted red and yellow, had a hoop, or bow, of bent willow sticks and a footrest. The material for the cradle was prepared by the father and was made ritually by a woman the father selected who had always had good health. The cradle was carried on the mother's back for nine to ten months. It would continue to be used as long as the babies were healthy. If a child died, the cradle would be hung in a willow tree and never used again. "The Wichita word for cradleboard was *ica:c*."[1]

The bark was peeled on the willow, and five sticks were lashed horizontally across the back. The braces were the width of the frame and spaced evenly. One long oblong stick bent into an oval was lashed vertically across the rods to the front to strengthen the frame. The carrier was about 32 inches long and 10 inches wide. Two thin, bent willow sticks forming the bow were attached to the outer rods on each side of the head area. Two holes were drilled in each end for thongs to tie the sticks to the frame. A sunshade was fashioned of stiff rawhide, with a rectangular piece formed like a bonnet. It was tied to the frame by rawhide strings just below the bent rod on the frame. The bonnet was sometimes covered with calico, and extra material was gathered inside for covering the child's head. A small pillow of rolled material was tied to the frame and could be positioned to protect the baby's neck.

The Wichita cradleboard had an unusual footrest. James Mooney collected a cradle in 1891, on the Wichita reservation in Oklahoma Territory, that has a carved wooden footrest (plate 17). The footrest is an oblong shape about 9 inches long and rounded on the ends. Two long cords tied to the bottom of the frame keep the footrest in place. The cords are each looped and tied around the indented, carved ends of the footrest; tied together in a knot about the baby's abdomen; and then tied to the bent hoops above the baby's head. The child's legs were tied together with soft cloth just below the ankles. A cradle at the Southern Plains Indian Museum in Anadarko, Oklahoma, has the same carved footrest. The footrest was moved and raised to ensure that the baby did not develop a rash. The cradle on exhibit was used to carry two babies. Pieces of yarn were still tied to the top of the cradle, used to tie mosquito netting in the summer and wool cloth in the winter. One carrier I found at the Heye Center of the Museum of the American Indian, collected in 1910, did not have the footrest.

Otis Mason called the Wichita type of carrier a hurdle cradle: "These consist of a number of rods or small canes or sticks arranged in a plane or an oblong hoop and held in place by lashing with splints or cords. The Yuman tribes and Wichita so made them."[2] This

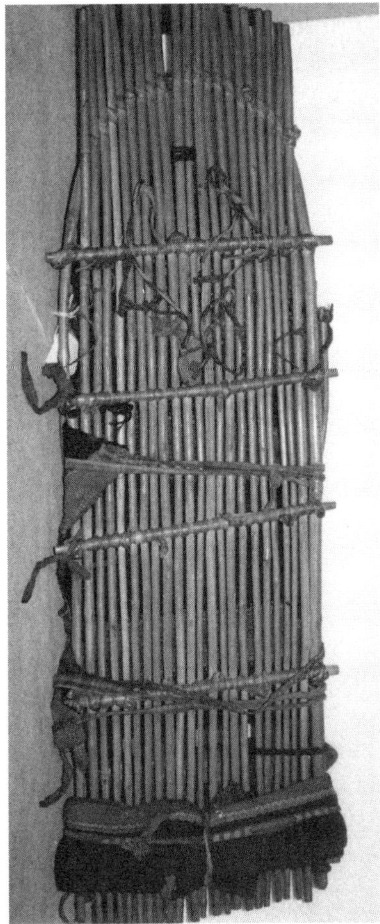
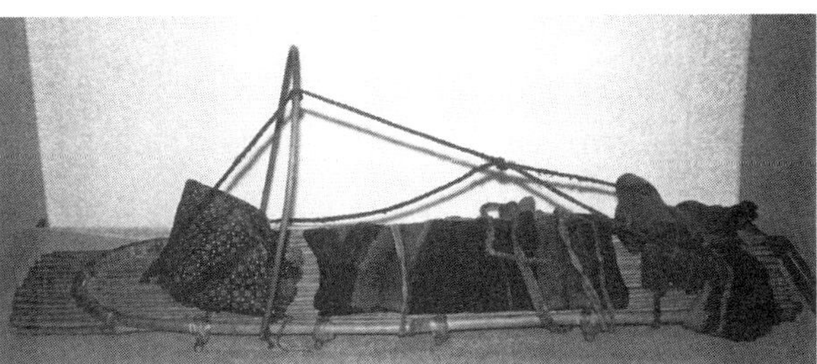
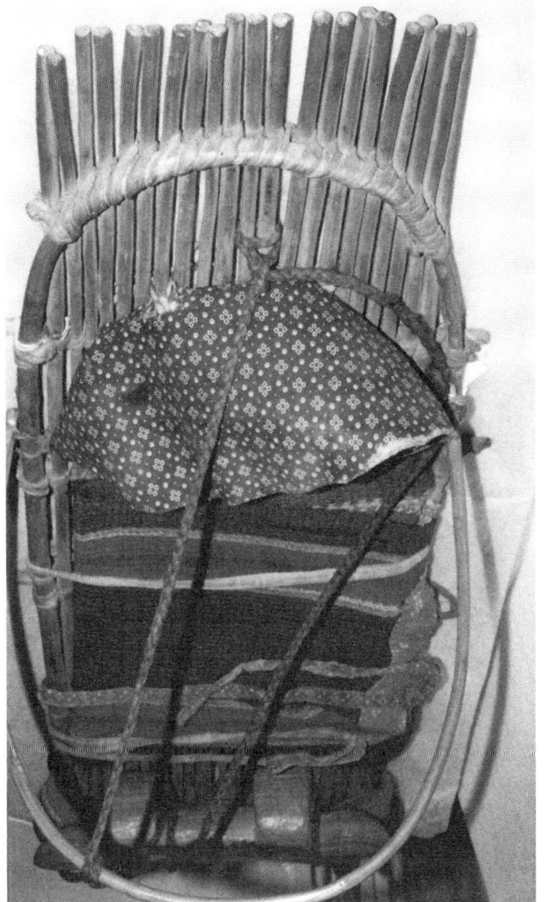

Wichita cradleboard, 33 × 11 inches. Collected by James Mooney in 1891. (*Top left*) Back of frame; (*top right*) head bow and footrest; and (*left*) head bow, head shade, and curved bent brace lashed to peeled willow sticks. Courtesy of the Department of Anthropology, Smithsonian Institution, Suitland, Maryland (E152944-0).

carrier could have been similar to the ancient Caddoan type recorded archaeologically in the Southeast. The elliptical type of cradle is quite old in the Southwest, with the oval frame and longitudinal rods in a medial position, in addition to transverse rods. This type of cradle is found among the Southern Paiutes, the Shivwits, Moapas, and Paviotsos.[3] Samuel C. Dellinger described some prehistoric cradles from Pine Hollow and Cobb Cave as "oval frame[s] set longitudinally with reeds united by open twining found in caves in Arkansas."[4]

Birth Customs

The Wichita were matrilineal, with the family being the most basic unit; children were raised by the mother's extended family. Birth was regarded as a supernatural event, and as the birth approached, the expecting mother put up a tipi by the side of her grass house. The father was prohibited from entering his wife's lodge until four days after the birth to prevent the mother and child from becoming ill. Elderly midwives assisted expectant mothers. One of the women took the infant to a stream for bathing and prayers. The infant was held aloft, and prayers were offered to the moon and the creator god. The infant was immersed in water, and prayers were addressed to the powers of water.[5]

George Dorsey described the ritual for a newborn to be taken to water by one of the midwives. First there were prayers to the moon then to the Woman-Having-Powers-in-the-Water:

> The moon is the special guardian of women for she is a woman and possesses all the powers which women desire. She instructs the women as to the monthly sickness, informs them when they are pregnant, and when the child is to be born, and has told them that after birth the child must be offered to her by passing the hands over the child's body and raising it aloft, offering it to the Moon, at which time she is asked to bestow her blessing upon the child, that he may grow into power rapidly, for she herself has the power to increase rapidly in size.
>
> The infant is taken to water, a stream or river to ask a blessing from the "Woman-Having-Powers-in-the-Water." She is chief of all water potencies and all things living in the water. She not only furnishes drink, but cleanses and heals the people by the action of the water. The child is taken to her at birth and she bestows upon it the power to grow to old age.[6]

Wichita Cradle Symbolism

Like the Pawnees, the Wichitas had a great amount of ceremony developed around the birth of a child. A woman of the village who had always had good health made the cradle ritually. The father cut and prepared the materials for the cradle following a ritual. Twenty-four small slender willow rods were cut, the longest first, to form the sides of the cradle. Before he began, he told the stick, "'I have now come to take your life. You are to be used for a cradle.' Standing on the south, he cut the stick on the east side, then stepping to the west of the stick, he cut it on the south side. He then stepped to the north and cut it on the west side, and then he took hold of the stick and made it fall towards the north."[7] Twenty sticks were to be cut and trimmed the proper length. He took the sticks home, decorated the rods, carefully saving the bark and shavings, and straightened the rods. Then the prepared rods were taken to the woman who had been selected to make the cradle.

The woman took the sticks and shavings and made a cradle according to the proper manner. She hid the bark and shavings toward the north so that the child would not be unhealthy. Praying for help to make the cradle properly, and for the child's fast growth, she made the cradle. "The sticks were then painted red or yellow and were bound together in the form of a flat mat by sinew from the back of the neck of a buffalo. As soon as the cradle was finished, she took it to the parents, and handed it to the mother, telling her that . . . she had prayed to the maker of all things and to the moon; and that the moon would see to it that the child would grow rapidly and be healthy."[8]

Wichita Cradleboards

The cradleboard I studied is found at the Smithsonian Institution, Department of Anthropology (plate 17). The cradleboard is identified as Wichita, collected on the Wichita and Caddo Reservation in Oklahoma, in 1891. The Heye Center, Museum of the American Indian, identified an identical cradle, except without the footrest, as Wichita.

The cradleboard at the Smithsonian is 33 inches long and 11 inches wide. The frame comprises twenty-one peeled willow sticks, about 0.5 inches in diameter, lashed together with sinew, making the frame 9.5 inches wide. Five sticks, 11 inches long, are lashed horizontally to the back, 5 inches apart, to reinforce the frame. One thicker rod, 64 inches long, is bent in an oval shape and lashed to the frame on the front and along the bent part, as well as at several places on the sides. The top of the oval is 3 inches from top of the frame. The only tie straps are strings of calico.

The head bow should have two willow sticks bent in a U shape; however, one of the sticks is missing. The existing stick is 21 inches long; a hole is drilled on each end of the bent stick and tied with thongs to the frame, 10 inches from the top. A rectangular piece of stiff rawhide, 18 inches by 3 inches, is shaped like a bonnet and tied to the frame with strings of calico. The bonnet is tied below the head bow in five places to shape it. The rawhide is covered with calico, and extra material is folded inside the bonnet.

The carved oblong footrest is tied just above the last horizontal stick at the bottom of the frame and at the first horizontal stick at the top. A block of wood carved in the shape of a turtle is tied to a long woven cord at each end of the footrest. The cord to secure the footrest is made of braided strips of wool, 72 inches long. The braided cord is looped twice around the two middle rods just above the rawhide shade, tied into a knot, and then looped along the willow hoop. The separate ends of the cord are looped around the carved ends of the footrest and tied to one side.

The baby cover is a large piece of dark blue worsted wool with red and yellow stripes. The blanket is 18 inches by 12.5 inches, with three long strings of calico sewn to the right side of the coverlet. The strings pass under the frame, loop back over the baby and blanket, and tie on the right side. The long side of the coverlet is trimmed with an inch strip of calico. A piece of the blanket is folded at the bottom of the frame and tied with a string of calico. This piece is used to tie the child's ankles together. A small pillow of rolled calico is tied to the frame with cotton strings. The pillow is 4 inches by 1 inch and can be positioned to fit the baby's neck.

The decorations are several pieces of colorful calico. The calico string ties, the covering on the rawhide bonnet, and the blanket add some color. A small beaded yarn tassel is tied to the footrest on the right side.

CHAPTER 18

LIPAN APACHE

The Lipan Apache people (Ndé) spoke a southern Athabascan language, which they shared with speakers in what is now Alaska, western Canada, and the U.S. Southwest. The Apaches have been separated into Eastern and Western groups, based on language, cultural similarities, and geographic locations. The Lipan were one of last groups to migrate from 1450 to 1650, along with Jicarilla and Kiowa Apache, or Plains Apache. The recorded history of Spanish explorations identified twenty-two Plains Apache buffalo and trader groups that roamed the high plains, in parts of what is now Nebraska, Kansas, Oklahoma, Texas, Colorado, and New Mexico. But only the names Lipan, Mescalero, Chiricahua, Kiowa, and Jicarilla Apache survived into the nineteenth century. The Mescalero, Chiricahua, and Jicarilla Apaches hunted the buffalo on the plains, but they lacked many other traits characteristic of plains life. The Lipan and Kiowa Apaches showed more plains orientation.[1]

The Lipans lived in nomadic bands in Texas. Their first recorded name was Ypandis in 1732. When on a hunt, they lived in bison hide bell-shaped tipis while moving with the buffalo herds. In the high country, they constructed wickiups, a circular framework of saplings lashed together. They established small rancherias, built huts, and planted crops in the spring until harvest; ate fish and bear; counted coup; used sign language; and spoke good Spanish. During the nineteenth century, the Lipans roamed the lower Rio Grande region across Texas to the Gulf Coast. They were allies of the Texans against the Comanches and Wichitas but were driven to Mexico by Texas's policy to exterminate Indian tribes. In 1905, many of the surviving Lipans were taken to reservations in New Mexico with the Mescalero Apaches and in Oklahoma with the Tonkawas. Because of the Lipan people's migration pattern, family pockets survived decades of isolation, avoiding name changes and language restrictions. The Lipan never surrendered as a tribe.

Lipan Apache families were matrilineal and believed in one deity. Bands with lineal descendants who had genealogical ties to the following listed bands were the Lipan Apache of Texas: People of the High Grass and the Big Water People, who did not go to reservations; Tough People of the Desert, Rock Tied to Head People, and People of the Lava Beds, who lived on the Mescalero Indian Reservation; and the Choctaw Apache Tribe of Louisiana, Many Necklaces People, who were taken from central Texas and sold as slaves in Louisiana.[2]

Lipan Cradle

Lipan mothers made and used two different baby carriers. A temporary cradle was made at the time of the baby's birth and a permanent cradle at about three months. The unique

Lipan cradle was made by someone skilled in the trade. The Lipan had customized trades, and only families from the trade could make cradles for all the bands. The cradle was called *istl tsg* (to hold).[3]

A captive of the Lipans who lived with them for several years described the cradle as made of buckskin stretched over a wooden frame, often elaborately beaded. The buckskin covering was laced up the front. The baby was wrapped with cloth, or swaddled, and placed in the cradle. "In cold weather they put the little hands down beside the baby and lace him up tight to keep him warm. In warm weather he was not laced so tight so his hands were left out so he can play."[4] The baby was taken out at night to sleep with the mother but was nursed in the cradle.[5] According to John Upton Terrell, when the baby was three months, a permanent cradle was made of and laced with buckskin. A comfortable bed consisted of "soft bedding of shredded bark or crumbled grass [which] was placed on the face of the carrier. Over this bedding was laid the tanned, spotted hide of a fawn, the hair side up or at times the skins of cottontail rabbits."[6] The baby was placed on the bedding and covered with diapering material, and another fawn hide, hair side in, was laid over the baby. The edges were tucked about the baby's body and up under the feet. Under the baby's head was a pillow of a squirrel pelt or a piece of beaver fur. Beaver fur "was thought to keep all sickness from the baby, for the 'Beaver' had power."[7]

The first carrier was discarded and hung in a tree. It was not to be touched again. The mother would show the baby the tree when the child was old enough, and before the carrier rotted and fell apart. The child would be told, "Here is what you were in when you were a baby."[8] The permanent cradle would be thrown out if a baby was sick in it, but otherwise it would be used for the next one or two babies. When no longer needed, the permanent carrier was hung on the east side of a young tree, a fruit tree if a girl, "so that she would gather much wild plant food when she grew up." As the mother removed the baby and hung the cradle, she would say "Here is the baby-carrier. I put this on you, young and still growing. I want my child to grow up as you do."[9]

I found no photograph of a Lipan cradleboard in the literature. The mural painted by George Nelson at the University of Texas Institute for Texas Cultures, in San Antonio, depicts the Lipan cradle as a hide cover attached to a bent wooden frame with a large wickerwork hood. Three other eastern Apache cradles—Mescalero, Jicarilla, and Chiricahua—are similar in construction. Daniel Castro Romero Jr., general council chairman of the Lipan Apache Tribe of Texas, shared personal photographs of one of only four known Lipan cradles in the world.[10] The cradle was made by the great-granddaughter of Chief Magoosh of the Túntsaõde (Big Water People). Great respect should be shown for the photographs of the cradleboard.

The frame rod is bent into a complete oval, or two rods laced together to form an oval. The upper arch was used as a handle. The frame support is made of a series of carved wooden slats that cross the frame and are lashed to the oval rod with thongs. Slats are carved, thin and flat, about 1.5 inches wide. A board is attached at the end of the slat frame for a footrest.

The hood is made of peeled twigs or willow withes lashed together and laid on top of each stick horizontally. The sticks are bent in a horseshoe shape, and the wickerwork

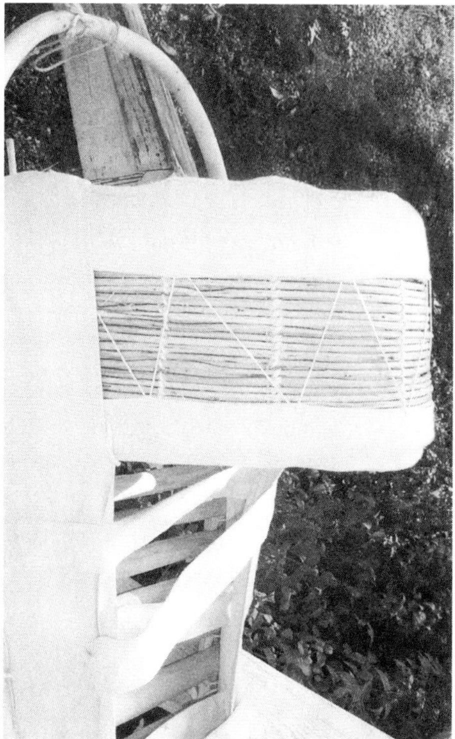
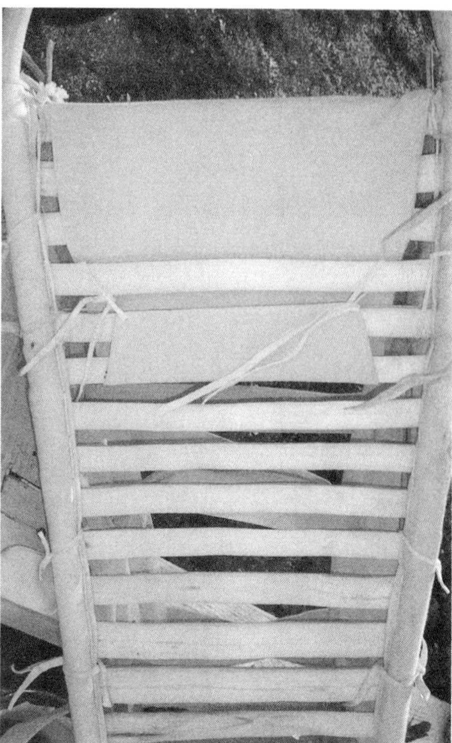

Lipan Apache cradleboard, undated: (*Left*) Cradle hood with wickerwork shade. (*Right*) Back view of the frame. Photographs courtesy of Daniel Castro Romero Jr., Lipan Apache Tribe of Texas.

sharp ends are covered with buckskin or cloth and lashed to the oval rod on each side, at the curve of the oval. A lined shade is stitched across the top of the wickerwork. The back part of the shade hangs down the back of the frame, over three slats, then under the next three before being pulled through and up over two of the slats, where the shade is tied. Two buckskin pieces are stitched on each side of the frame. Slits are cut on each side of the flaps, and the baby would be securely laced in the cradle. A wide strip is sewn to the right side of the buckskin bag, threaded through the slits, and tied on the left side. The carrier has two lacing straps. A buckskin carrying strap is tied on each side of the frame in the middle. Lipan women used a tumpline across the chest to carry the cradleboard.

If a permanent cradleboard was not ready at a birth, a temporary cradle was constructed with a frame of unpeeled wood, lashed together with buckskin or cloth strips, and a hood of wickerwork. The buckskin top was not put on. The buckskin side flaps were stitched to the frame with buckskin thongs, and a carrying strap was tied to the back of the frame. The infant was laced in the cradle with buckskin thongs.

Terrell notes in *Apache Chronicles*,

> Various things designed either to amuse the baby or to act as charms were attached to the hood. Sometimes the beard from the breast of a turkey cock was fastened

> where the baby could watch it swing back and forth, or the turkey beard, the tail of an Abert squirrel, and the striped cones from the western yellow pine (thrown to the ground by these squirrels) were tied together and hung inside the hood of the carrier, near the baby's head. The squirrel tail was to make a baby a good climber, the striped pine cones so that [the child] would not be injured in falling from trees, and the turkey beard merely for ornament . . . Pieces of oriole's nest were likewise used to bring good luck as it was believed they were composed of every known species of tree.

The claw of a bear was especially powerful and kept all sickness away. Other ornaments to prevent illness and injury were stone arrow points and bits of prehistoric shell beads.[11]

Birth Customs

Apaches, including the Lipan, "believed that lightning and a small whirlwind were the mysterious forces that gave breath and warmth to a new body, and that they enter it through the mouth as it emerged from the womb."[12] Childbirth took place within the tipi with female attendants; male members of the family were excluded. The position of a Lipan woman in labor was on her knees with her limbs separated, aided by a female attendant who stood behind and held her shoulders firmly. After the delivery, the placenta was disposed of where no animal could get to it, buried some distance from the birthplace.

The umbilical cord was tied and cut. Nothing was usually applied to the navel unless it became sore, in which case horse excrement was burned and applied. The infant was cleaned with warm water, "brought in the horn of a buffalo."[13] The infant was introduced to its world by the midwife holding the newborn up to the four points of the compass, showing the baby to the sun. After wrapping the newborn with soft cloth, the attendants laid the baby "on a skin or on bedding spread over weeds, known as *tlo-til-spai*." The baby was not nursed for two days. The mother was confined for four days, after which the newborn was placed on a cradleboard. Shortly after birth, the father named the child after some natural object.[14]

A blood relative or medicine man or woman performed a ceremony of song and prayer to protect baby girls from evil, to provide supernatural powers into womanhood, and to ensure their fertility before marriage. The girl's family collected wood for this ceremony, which was used to make her cradle on a clear night, while the cradle song was sung. Pieces of prehistoric shell adorned the outside of the cradle, which was never to touch the land for fear of making the girl infertile. Gifts were given of corn or meal, and the performers of the ceremony were given respect.[15]

A Lipan medicine man sang the tribe's song: "This song had been hidden from view for more than 80 years. The song was recorded by a BIA agent in 1910 in the White Mountains area, just off the Clear Fork River. The name of the Apache Medicine Man [who these] songs . . . belong to is long dead. As is Lipan custom, his name is not allowed to be spoken in public. Permission to use the song was given me [Daniel Castro Romero Jr.] by a modern-day Lipan Medicine Man."

The "Gòjó sí" Song (The Blessing Song for Girls)

'ìs' à' nà yái k' è' gòjó 'àná' hòkùs
  Long life like, good, moves back and forth
t' á ìgaì bìt ' á' éd yùd 'á lzà tc' ìndí
  White water underneath in a circle, it is made, they say.
yò gài sìyùdì 'ìt á' nèz' ágò' 'á lzà tc' ìndí
  White shell curved over, beneath its rest, it is made, they say.
gòdìt' ó' bàsxà' híljìj tc' ìndí
  Lightning alongside dances, they say.
gòdìt' ó' bèbìk' è nà ìst ' ó tc' ìndí
  Lightning by it fastened across, they say.
hí tsát ' ùl bìt' ùl 'á lzà tc' ìndí
  Rainbow its rope it is made, they say.
t' ádì xì bìtc' ìd bìt ' á' sì tsò z
  Black water blanket underneath rests;
t' á ìgaì bìtc' ìd bìt ' á' sì tsò z
  White water blanket underneath rests.
'ìs' à' nà yái k' è' gòjó ts' á 'á lzà tc' ìndí
  Long life like, good, baby-carrier it is made, they say.
djùnà' ái bìnànt' à' bè bìyì' gùdìtní tc' ìndí
  Sun, his chief, by, inside it rumbles, they say.[16]

Amulet

After the newborn infant's navel cord dropped off, it was wrapped in downy turkey feathers in a small buckskin bag tied to the wooden part of the hood, inside, over the baby's head. Later, if the baby was a boy, the mother buried the amulet in the deer track to make him a good hunter.[17]

PART SIX

LATTICE FRAMES AND SOFT HOODS

Comanche

Kiowa

Apache Tribe of Oklahoma

Cheyenne

Tonkawa

Lakota

Assiniboine

Pahn-t ope (Cradle)

"Wah-ho e-pah-shun."
before there was lightning
we felt our way
deep within my ribs
"Wah-ho e-pah-shun."

Nephew, here are my sticks
use them as you please
I will guard you
with my strength

Sister, here is my pelt
use it as you please
I will keep you dry
and laughing

Daughter, here is my sinew
use it as you please
my strength will hold you
and make you strong

"Wah-ho e-pah-shun."
hide your dark eyes
wrapped in glass oak leaves
dream where little ones dream
"Wah-ho e-pah-shun."

Brother, here is my hide
use it as you please
I will protect you
shield you from the cold

Son, here are my songs and prayers
use them as you please
they will watch over you
and keep you happy

Grandchild, here are my decorations
use them as you please
my symbols will protect you
make your journey safe

"Wah-ho e-pah-shun."
nourish the world for me
swallow my milk
nourish the earth
"Wah-ho e-pah-shun."

Ray C. Doyah, *Powwow Chairs*

"Wah-ho" is the singsong lullaby which I [Ray Doyah] heard most often. Mom said that it was sung while rocking the baby, and the five-syllable verse was repeated over and over. I added "e-pah-shun" (little baby) in place of "tah-lee shun" (little boy) and "mab-tawan shun" (little girl).

Ray C. Doyah, quoted in Hail, *Gifts of Pride and Love*, 61

CHAPTER 19

COMANCHE

The Comanche tribe spoke the only Uto-Aztecan language family on the plains. The name Comanche means "enemy" in Ute, or "anyone who wants to fight me all the time," and the Spaniards picked up the word.[1] The original name for the tribe was Nʉmʉnʉʉ (Our People). Their ancestors had lived on the northern plains since the 1500s. When first identified, they were closely associated with the Shoshones culturally and linguistically. They migrated southward in the 1600s and lived near the Rocky Mountain headwaters of the Arkansas River until the early 1700s. Their range came to include what is now Texas, western Oklahoma, southwestern Kansas, southern Colorado, and eastern New Mexico. The Comanches lived the nomadic existence of a warrior society, in temporary villages year round, following the buffalo migrations. Comanches were the first Plains people to adopt the horse-mounted lifestyle.

The bison hunts occurred during the late summer and fall. The Comanche economy included gathering, trade, and raids. They used a unique tipi: a four-pole base, with the rest of the poles set up as in a three-pole tipi covered in skins. The social units were bilaterally extended family.

In 1867, the Comanches agreed to go to a reservation in Indian Territory in what is now southwestern Oklahoma. During the reservation period, their entire way of life changed. The reservation was terminated in 1906,

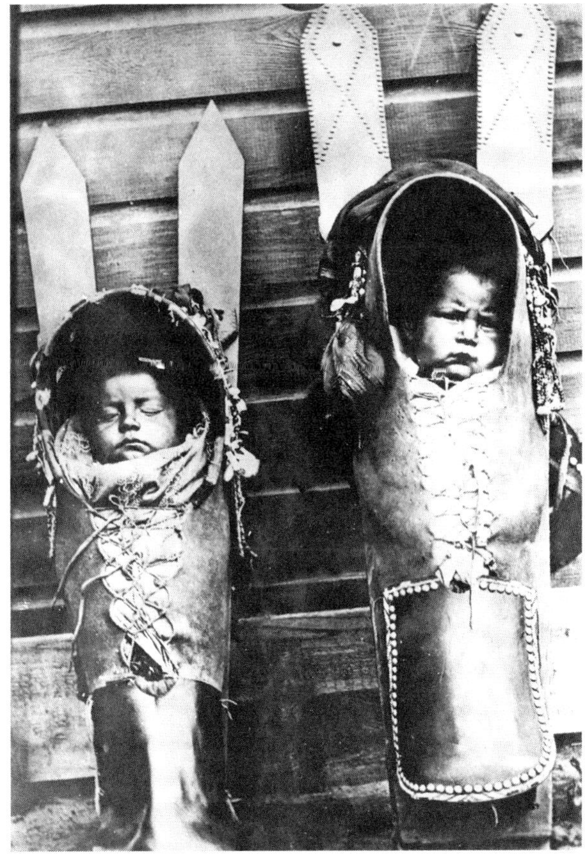

Two Comanche boys in their cradleboards, undated. Courtesy of the Frank Phillips Photograph Collection, Western History Collections, University of Oklahoma Libraries (Phillips 672).

and the people were given allotments in Oklahoma. Most Comanches live in the Lawton, Oklahoma, area.

Cradles

Comanche mothers used three different cradles: wooden board, lattice cradle (in the 1860s), and the night, or lying down, cradle. The night cradle, *haabikuno*, was a tubular case made of heavy rawhide. Solid wood cradles were used in the southern plains in the early 1800s. A French biologist gave us the first written description of cradles used in western Texas in 1828. Jean Louis Berlandier described the cradle as a "lidless case."[2] It was probably the type of board cradle used across North America in the 1800s, with a solid board backing to which the infant was secured with wrapping.

As Barbara Hail describes,

> Comanche cradles are packed on horseback on long journeys and the way they are carried is strange indeed. The Comanches take a plank, a little longer and a little wider than the infant, and build sides onto it so as to form a sort of lidless case. This they line with soft skins and place the baby on them, holding him securely in the cradle by means of straps wrapped around it. Usually the top plank projects a little beyond the infant's head, so that a line can be passed through a hole bored for the purpose. When a rancheria is on the march you may see the women on horseback with the babies swinging from the pommels of their saddles, for all the world like so many pistols. When they reach the day's campsite, the mothers may swing the cradles from the branch of a tree, or prop them against a convenient rock, and so they nurse their babies.[3]

Lattice cradles began to appear in collections and written documentation in the late 1860s. The Comanche lattice cradle was called a *waakohno*, or a cedar carrier.[4] Lattice cradles consisted of a cover, made of hide, wrapped around rawhide supports at the head and foot, with rawhide backing and a frame composed of two narrowly pointed boards and two shorter crosspieces, which formed a V shape.

The origin of the lattice style is unknown because pictorial evidence is absent before the late 1860s. The limited distribution and the simultaneous use of two other types of cradles indicate that the lattice style may have originated as recently as the 1860s. The earliest lattice cradle with firm documentation was collected in 1868. Edward Palmer, a botanist, collected two cradles at the same time from the Comanches in Texas: a cedar carrier and the night cradle.[5] Lattice cradles were made from 1870 to 1900, during the cultural transition to settled reservation life.

Ernest Wallace and E. Adamson Hoebel's informants called the cradle a papoose board, or a day cradle. As soon a new mother resumed her everyday life, she swaddled her baby in its cradle "so that it could be stood out of harm's way or, if the mother was out gathering seeds or roots or on the march with the camp, it could easily be carried along on her back. The cradle-board was either a sort of basket made of rawhide fastened to a flat, angular board or a soft buckskin sheath that laced up the front and was anchored to a back board."[6]

LATTICE CRADLE

Comanche infants were carried in an upright position, tightly wrapped and laced into the cradleboard. Bodily contact was restricted during the early months of life. At night the baby was rolled up in the stiff rawhide tube. Nine or ten months passed before the child was allowed out of the cradle for any length of time. Muscular activity was also restricted during this time. The child slept on the board and was fed on the board. When the tribe was traveling, cradleboards were hung on saddles or travois poles. During the reservation days, the women of the family carried the cradles to public events on their backs. A thick leather strap supported the cradle across the chest, with the weight evenly distributed, as it rested against the hips and shoulders. The carrying strap was attached to the outside of each of the boards about two inches down from the top crosspiece. Cradleboards stood about four feet tall but were relatively lightweight.

The Comanches preferred undecorated covers and elaborate boards of cedar, with the pointed boards decorated with incised, pigment-filled lines, pigment-covered surfaces, and metal studs, buttons, or tacks. The designs appeared above the hood on both sides, and the long boards went in the back, with crosspieces at the head and foot. The designs were painted with red, green, or yellow powdered rock paint. Two pigments used were a red mineral, *equipsia*, found in southcentral Oklahoma, and a purple vegetable dye from a tiny forest berry.[7]

Barbara Hail studied thirty Comanche cradleboards. Average measurements for the boards were 45 inches long, 13.4 inches wide, and 10.9 inches deep. Cradle covers were made of buckskin (or, later, canvas), with rawhide supports at the head, foot, and backing. The supports were tied with narrow buckskin leather thongs to the frame. The rawhide support formed a hood around the face, and a sturdy rawhide at its back protected the infant. The lining was soft buckskin or rabbit fur. Later, calico was used. The rectangular footrest piece at the foot of the cover protruded at a right angle. Loops and laces were made of narrow buckskin thongs. Women made the covers. A sunshield made of cloth or blanket was often tied to the top of the cradle so it could be drawn over the baby's face as needed. Often mothers would drape long strands of pony beads on the head opening, which they tied to each side so the strands would rest over the lower laced front. They also hung strands of seeds, small gourds, metal filigree, and other objects, which dangled in front of the baby's face. The Comanches often used yellow ocher paint on their covers. "In 1970, a Comanche woman was selling yellow-painted cradles in Indian arts and craft shops in Anadarko, Oklahoma."[8]

Cedar was preferred for the frame. Traditionally, men constructed the frame and rawhide supports, as well as decorating the boards. Commercially prepared lumber or lumber from packing cases, discarded furniture, or abandoned wagons might be used. Two pointed boards were attached to two narrow short boards with leather thongs. The upper crosspiece was about one-third the length of the board from the top, and the bottom crosspiece formed the V-shaped frame. The decorations on the support points were arranged in a symmetrical pattern.

Special cradles with beaded covers were called *turokohna* or *tsumo waakohno.*[9] The beads were sewn directly on the buckskin or canvas, covering the tops, sides, and foot at the bottom. A small beaded rectangular buckskin piece was attached to the hide where the crosspieces were attached. Not all babies had fully beaded cradleboards.

Completing construction for the cradleboard took months. Generally, it was made for the firstborn, but all members of the family had access to its use. Often a cradle would be passed down through several generations. When a cradleboard was finished, the baby was placed in the cradle, and both the cradle and the baby were smoked with cedar, while a medicine man prayed over them.

A combination of bead stitches was used. A curvilinear shape was normally executed in an overlay stitch with straight interior rows; raised, outlined geometric designs were sewn in the lazy stitch; and small geometric designs in the netted or flat gourd stitch. Designs were usually geometric shapes made up of small elements asymmetrically placed on the sides. Sometimes a white background with designs outlined in a dark color was used, with predominantly red, blue, and white.

NIGHT CRADLE

The earliest known night cradle collected was a tubular cradle of rawhide with the hair side turned inward, collected by Edward Palmer in 1886. The haabikuna predated the lattice cradle among the Comanches and was used through the mid-twentieth century. It was a single piece of rolled sturdy rawhide with a footrest. The top was rounded or cut straight. It would be laced from the bottom to the top. Otis T. Mason, of the U.S. National Museum, in 1887 described the cradle as "the most primitive cradle in the museum."[10]

The foot piece (almost square shaped) could be sewn at the bottom using an awl and sinew or it could be cut before the rawhide was rolled. The two slits were made in the sides at the foot, where it was to be folded up and sewn in place. The holes for the loops started at the top, where the baby's shoulders would be, and went down to the foot, across the bottom of the foot, and up on the other side. The loops were made of a long narrow strip of buckskin going through each hole. Three narrow strips were cut for the lacing: two long and one shorter. The long strips were attached to the center loop, one above the other. The top strip was laced going upward. The lower one was laced going downward. The smaller strip was attached to the bottom loop and laced upward to meet the lower long strip. The two ties were attached on each side to the top loops.[11]

The night cradle was specially made for sleeping. The haabikuna provided a safe place for the swaddled baby to lie in bed between adults. The tiny infant could be laced in and remain in the rawhide case cradle during the day. At night, the rawhide case provided sturdy protection and support for newborns.[12] Night cradles were used for infants up to four months old. They were accessible, light, and easy to transport. The mother could hold or carry the infant in her arms and nurse the baby when needed.

Birth Customs

A Comanche infant was always welcomed and cherished. Babies were looked at as valuable additions to the tribe. Girls were welcomed, but boys were preferred and received greater care. The new parents sometimes painted a black spot on the door of the tipi if the newborn was a boy, informing the people that the tribe has been strengthened by another warrior.

Comanche women made natal preparations whenever possible. A pregnant woman, to ensure an easy birth, might wear a belt of otter fur decorated with beads. A nineteenth-century Comanche otter belt can be seen on exhibit at the Southern Plains Indian Museum in Anadarko, Oklahoma (cat. no. 72021.6). A separate tipi was constructed of brush about eight feet in diameter and six or seven feet high. Two pits were dug inside the lodge for the afterbirth and to heat water. A four-foot stake or two were driven into the soft ground by the expectant mother's bed. One of the pits was in front of the dry pit. She would grasp the pole as an aid in delivery. A fire was prepared with hot coals, and dried sage was brought in. An older woman knowledgeable about birth was usually the mother's attendant, and additional women gave assistance. Men did not enter the delivery hut. The mother walked around during the labor and squatted over the prepared hole during delivery. Assistants would aid the delivery if necessary by holding the mother's abdomen and exerting pressure and placing hot rocks against the mother's back or giving her a hot drink.

In a difficult birth, a medicine man or woman would be called. Wallace and Hoebel gave accounts of one who had buffalo power, and the other, otter power. "The medicine woman carried the afterbirth to a running stream (the purifier that nullifies power). The baby was bathed and wrapped in soft rabbit skins and placed in its cradleboard."[13] According to Wallace, babies had to put up with being wet and messy until the time to transfer them to their night cradle. After the baby was washed, it was greased and powdered with "pulverized dry root of cottonwood."[14] To change the soiled diapering material, the mother only had to undo the lower section of the lower lacings.

During the new mother's recovery, the grandfather had the right to ask the sex of the child. If it was a boy, the woman would call, "It's your closest friend." But if it was a girl, she would simply say, "It's a girl." Sage was burned over the coals every day to purify the tipi. The first thing the woman did was to bathe in running water. The proud father usually gave away something to the first person who came to see the new baby. The gift would be a horse if the father was wealthy. Twin boys might bring dishonor to the woman who bore the boys. Because the birth was regarded as unnatural, one or both twins might be destroyed, especially if one or both were girls. "The mother would sometimes dispose of one and not tell her husband that she had given birth to twins."[15]

Amulet

The umbilical cord was not dried and saved in a leather bag. "After the umbilical cord had been cut, a medicine woman wrapped it and hung it in a hackberry tree when one was convenient. If it was undisturbed before it rotted, the child was supposed to have a long and fortunate life."[16] Charms or amulets were put on very young children by their mothers to ensure good health and protection from evil influences. "Crow feathers had protective power for babies; tied to cradleboards, to keep away evil spirits. A stuffed bat on the cradle would watch protectively over the baby."[17]

Sex-Specific Cradle Design

Children of either sex were welcomed and loved, but boys brought the greatest joy to a family because boys became warriors that defended the home.[18] The sex of the baby was distinguished for a boy with tiny archery bows on the cradle. "A few days after a son is born, the father makes him little weapons, proportional to his size, and hangs them on so that one can tell at a glance the sex of the child who occupies it."[19] Comanche boys' cradles also had a unique feature called a shield, or *si'wuparru*. A piece of commercial leather was cut, shaped, and attached to the lower half of the cover with thongs. The purpose of the shield was to deflect urine away from the cover. The infant's penis would rest on the leather shield so that he could urinate outside the cradle and not stain the interior of the cradle. Often the shield would be shaped out of harness leather. The si'wuparru could be removed if a female child used the cradle.[20]

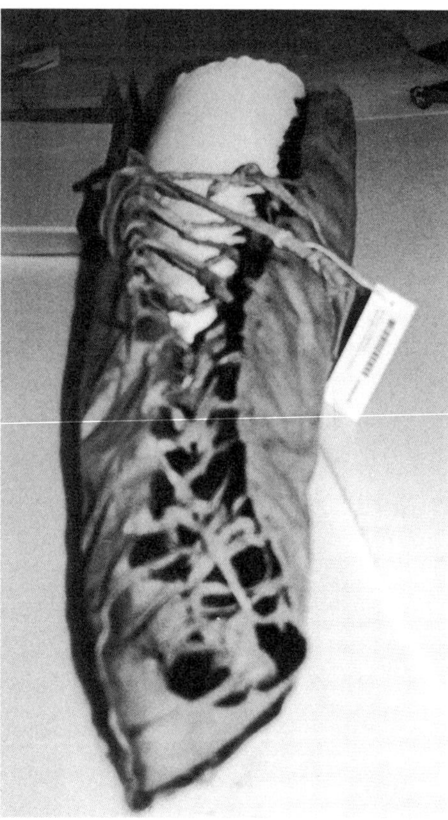

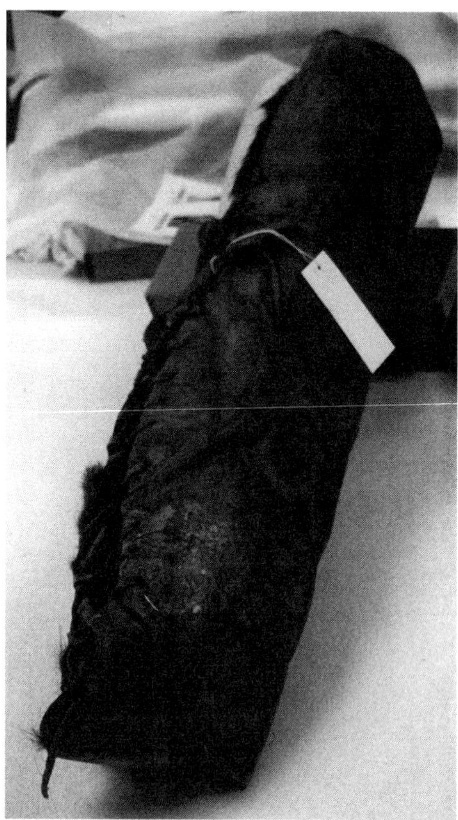

Comanche skin bed (night cradle), 28 × 17 inches (at widest), 11 inches (at narrowest). Collected by Edward Palmer in 1868 in Texas. The cradle is a tubular piece of rawhide, with the fur turned inward, laced up the front. Courtesy of the Department of Anthropology, Smithsonian Institution, Suitland, Maryland (E6970-0).

Comanche Cradles

One cradle I examined, a Comanche night cradle, is found at the Smithsonian Institution, Department of Anthropology (cat. no. E6970-0). Edward Palmer collected the cradle in 1868 in Texas. Otis T. Mason identified the hide as bearskin.[21]

The cradle is made of two pieces of stiff hide with fur inside. A 28-inch piece of rectangular rawhide rolled into a cylinder, tapering from 17 inches wide to 11 inches at the bottom. There are twenty holes along the longer side. The last five holes are for the 8-inch rounded footrest, which is laced to the rolled rawhide. The loops are made of a long narrow strip of buckskin, which is drawn up to form a loop in each hole it passes through. The loops run down from the top, across the bottom of the foot, and up the other side. The narrow buckskin lacings pass through the loops, side to side, much as a shoe is laced. The lacing is tied to one center loop then laced upward and tied to the first loop, closing the cylinder. Another tie strap is tied to a center loop then laced downward.

The other cradle I studied is also in the Smithsonian Department of Anthropology (cat. no. E6918-0), another cradleboard collected in Texas by Palmer in 1868. The V-shape frame is made of Osage orange (bois d'arc) lumber. The two vertical boards are 42 inches by 5 inches, tapering to 2.5 inches wide at the narrow end. Both boards are pointed at the top and rounded at the bottom. Two horizontal rounded boards complete the frame. The top board is 10.5 inches by 2.25 inches, and the bottom board is 5.5 inches by 2.5 inches. These crosspieces, which are laced to the pointed boards, have rawhide thongs and four diamond-shaped holes drilled in each. The first is laced 10.5 inches from the top, and the second is laced two inches from the bottom.

The cradle cover is a piece of tanned deerskin with hair on the tabs at the bottom. The soft deerskin is folded under, stretched over the support, and then laced to the frame. The support is made of three separate pieces of stiff rawhide, which are also laced to the frame. The largest curved piece at the top of the cradle, 23 by 8.5 inches, forms the hood, which is 8.5 inches deep. The curved foot piece is 16 inches by 3 inches. The stiff rawhide rectangle supports the baby's back. The deerskin covers the rawhide pieces. The tanned hide strips measure 4.5 inches by 2 inches.

The rawhide pieces are laced through holes drilled in all the boards. The vertical boards have eight holes along each side of the frame. The crosspieces have four holes on each side that form a diamond shape. The top crosspiece also has a hole in the center. The rawhide and deerskin cover is laced to the frame with narrow leather thongs. Small slits were made along each side of the cover, starting with the edge of the rigid rawhide hood to the small reinforcement for the footrest. The loops are made of one narrow strip of leather going through the holes, starting at where the shoulders would lie. The thongs are tied at the first hole then passed through each hole, leaving part of the thong for a loop. The lacing is done with three thongs. Two are tied in the middle hoop, laced upward, and then tied together. The lower strip is laced downward. The carrying strap, 68 inches long, is made of harness leather and folded red wool. It is attached to the frame on the outside, 2 inches down from the top crosspiece. One end is attached to the frame with a short thong, and one end is buckled to a piece of harness leather with its buckle attached. The carrying strap went across the mother's chest when she carried the cradle on her back.

The cradle is decorated with six pairs of twisted buffalo leather strings, 5.5 inches long. The strings are punched through the skin and tied on each side on the hood. The top fringe has hair on the hide strings. The pointed boards are painted red and decorated with brass brads down to the first crosspiece. Brads outline each board in symmetrical patterns of diamonds and the top half of a diamond. Two large German silver hair plates are laced in the center of each diamond pattern, and two medium-size hair plates are laced to the top crosspiece. Four raised round silver ornaments are attached on each long board.

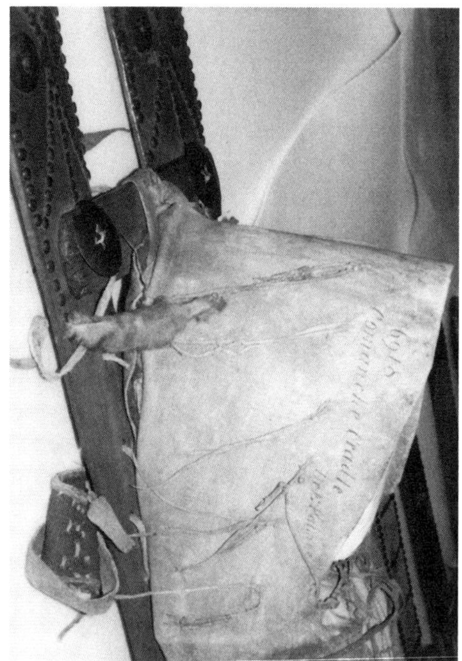

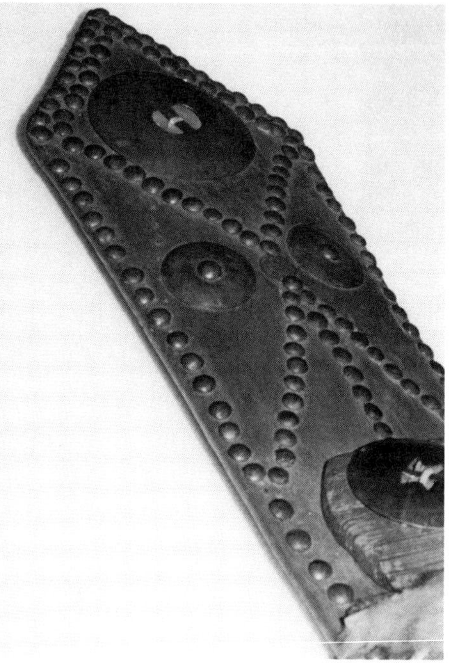

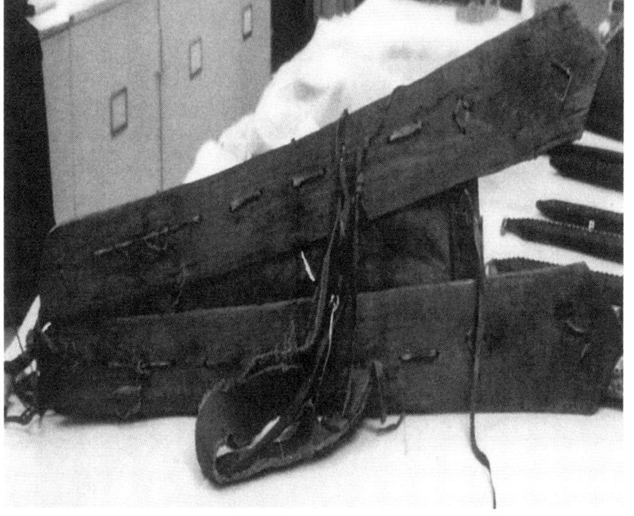

Comanche cradleboard, 42 × 14 inches (width measured at head), narrowing to 10.5 inches. Collected by Edward Palmer in 1868 in Texas. (*Top left*) Tanned deer hide cover stretched over the rawhide hood support and lashed to the wooden frame; (*Top right*) frame detail, showing brass brad and German silver disk design; and (*left*) back view of frame with leather thongs laced to the cover, also showing the red wool and leather carrying strap with pieces of harness leather and buckles attached. Photographs by the author. Courtesy of the Department of Anthropology, Smithsonian Institution, Suitland, Maryland (E6918-0).

CHAPTER 20

KIOWA

The earliest known homeland of the Kiowas (Cáuigú, or Principal People) was in the area now known as Montana before they migrated east and south. The Kiowas and Kiowa Apaches joined together, and after the acquisition of the horse, the tribes shared a nomadic lifestyle on the plains. An alliance between Kiowas and Comanches in 1806 enabled them to share common territory on the southern plains. The Kiowa language is in the Kiowa-Tanoan family, whose other branches were spoken in the Pueblo Southwest.

The tribe's subsistence centered on the buffalo. Men were responsible for providing food and protection, and the women were responsible for the children and maintaining the camp. Kiowas lived in a ranked society, where prestige depended on success in warfare and wealth attained through horses and trade goods. The Kiowas recognized four classes of people, with leaders and warriors of influence and wealth at the top and those with no wealth or fighting experience at the bottom. Cousins were classified as brothers and sisters.

Kiowas practiced the Sun Dance, kept medicine bundles, and organized into secret societies typical of the Plains tribes. The tribe's distinctive clothing showed no evidence of quillwork decoration.

The Kiowas' mobile lifestyle ended with their assigned reservation in southwestern Oklahoma in 1869, although hostilities continued until 1875. Forced allotment in 1906 terminated the reservation. Tribal offices are currently located in Carnegie, Oklahoma. Kiowa people are still involved with intertribal powwows and cultural activity that promotes tribal identity.

Cradleboard

In the late nineteenth century, Kiowa women had more time in their sedentary environment on the reservation, and they started creating colorful, decorated lattice cradleboards, called *paih'dodl*.[1] Documentation on the use of lattice boards began to appear in the 1860s. An early illustration of a lattice cradle appeared in *Harper's Weekly* on May 25, 1867.[2] It showed Theodore R. Davis's sketch of a woman, probably Kiowa or Kiowa Apache, wearing a lattice cradle in a Kansas trading post store. In 1868, a Comanche lattice board was collected in Texas. From 1860 to 1920, Kiowa women produced lattice cradleboards.

The cradle consisted of a wooden frame; a beaded hide covering wrapped around rawhide supports at the head, foot, and back; a decorative bib above the cover; and a carrying strap. Babies were well protected by the rawhide hoods around their faces and rawhide at their backs. The V-shaped construction of the frame enabled the mother to safely lean the cradle against a tree or post. A cloth sunshade was tied to the cover in the head area to protect the child from the weather and insects. Infants were wrapped before they were placed on the cradleboards.

A grandmother or aunt made cradles in the family for a special child, usually the firstborn grandchild. Sometimes a specialist in cradleboard making was commissioned to make them. Cradles were not started until after a baby's birth, and not every baby had a beaded cradle. Creating and giving one was a significant event. A newly made cradle would be smoked with cedar and sage and then blessed. If a baby died, the cradle would be placed in the grave.[3]

The cover was made of a rectangular piece of hide and usually completely beaded; beads were attached with sinew and laced to the framework, starting just above the top crosspiece. Covers were made of two pieces, beaded separately and put together when the beading was complete. Later, the beaded hide covers were replaced with canvas and red wool; steel needles and thread replaced sinew and awls; pieces of linoleum replaced rawhide backs; and soft buckskin linings replaced the cloth. A small strip of leather was sewn on one side of the canvas or wool to hold the hide loops for lacing; another strip of leather was added around the head opening. If the cover was canvas and completely beaded, the cradle looked as if it were made entirely of hide.[4] The decorated rectangular piece was tightly laced to the frame and then sewn together at the ends.

The cover was wrapped around the rawhide supports and tied to the frame. The lining, cut to a length to fit the interior circumference of the cradle, was stitched to the hide cover or strip of buckskin. The rawhide base was a pad the shape of the dimensions of the frame, tied with thongs. The head support was a rectangular piece of heavy rawhide shaped like a hood, tied to the frame below the top crosspiece. This added reinforcement supported the top of the beaded cover, making a firm shaped opening for the baby's head. A shorter piece of rawhide, similarly

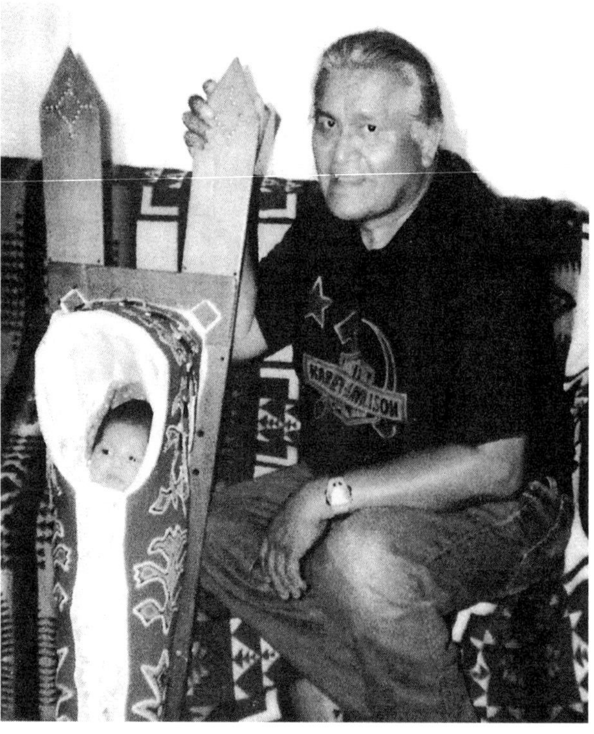

Ray Doyah with grandchild laced in family cradleboard made by Guohaddle, his great-great-grandmother, undated. Private collection of Ray Doyah.

shaped, tied to the lower part of the frame supported the feet. The foot support gave the cradle a rounded bottom.

Decorative rectangular bibs were attached with nails or brass tacks just above the cradle cover, covering the upper crosspiece to the pointed sticks. Bibs were made of hide or cloth and decorated with beads or sequins. Pieces of old leggings were also used for bibs.[5] Other decorative items included a long fringe at the bottom of the cover, beaded or brass beaded thongs hanging on the sides, and beaded hide tabs at the top and bottom of the front lacing.

The loops for lacing were made of two buckskin thongs and started at the shoulders. Two long thongs were threaded through the slits of folded buckskin along each side of the cover and tied at each slit, leaving enough of the thong to form a small loop. Lacing was tied at the top loop, laced to the bottom, and tied together. As the lace was threaded through the loop, it crossed over the previous lacing. There could be fourteen loops or more.

Men usually made the frame, primarily using bois d'arc (Osage orange) wood. Other hardwoods were used, including commercial lumber and even salvaged packing crates or discarded furniture. Vanessa Jennings, a Kiowa cradleboard maker, shows in a video how her husband, Carl, makes and constructs the frame and supports.[6] The frame was composed of four boards: two narrow boards with pointed ends, and two shorter crosspieces laced diagonally together with thongs, forming a modified V shape. The top crosspiece was laced a foot from the top of the pointed ends. The pointed ends were placed at an angle with the length of the two diagonal cross boards, which were cut equal to the width of the board.

In the book *Gifts of Pride and Love*, Jacob Ahtone shared memories of his mother, a cradle maker, and the process his father, a board-making specialist, used to make and prepare the lattice framework:

> In preparing the wood pieces, a hardwood of suitable length was selected. Preference was given to pieces with little or no knots as the wood had to be split with the grain to its approximate length, width and thickness, and subsequently rubbed to a smooth finish. When the boards were complete in size and design, I recall dad placing them on a short distance from an open flame to heat them thoroughly. Following a satisfactory heating period to harden and darken the wood, he used animal fat to give it a pleasing sheen. Sometimes he heated the pieces several times until he was satisfied with the texture, color, and sheen.[7]

Holes for the lacing were originally burned through the planking with sharpened, heated metal rods. Later, hand tools were used. The cover maker determined the placement as well as the number of holes needed to lace the cover to the frame.[8] The pointed sticks were often decorated with silver buttons, brass tacks, and silk ribbon. The carrying strap hole was positioned about one-third of the way from the top. Two holes were drilled on each slat about two inches apart. A piece of buckskin was tied to the board, making a small loop on the back. The strap was tied to the loops. Carrying straps were often made of decorative woven belts, colorful large scarves, or wide leather belts with metal conches.

According to Jennings, before a baby was placed in a cradleboard, the infant was wrapped securely. The baby would be placed on his or her back on the blanket, arms folded across the chest. The first fold of the blanket secured the arms, slightly lifting one of the baby's shoulders and pinning the arms with the corner of the blanket. The back and legs were straightened and fastened with the blanket. With the baby swaddled, the cradleboard afforded warmth and protection.[9]

Barbara Hail examined several Kiowa cradleboards during her study and found them remarkably consistent in total length, width, and depth, an average of 45 inches long, 13.2 inches wide, and 10.9 inches deep. "The Kiowa also made a slightly smaller cradle, newborn size, about 39" long."[10]

Kiowa children's toys were a preparation for life, and the miniature cradleboards made for girls by their mothers and grandmothers taught the domestic skills that would take them to adulthood. Each toy carried a unique legacy of history, traditions, design, and practical technique. The miniature Kiowa cradleboard made in exact detail reflected the culture. Little girls learned the proper construction and use of the cradle from play. A girl would practice lacing the toy cradleboard and rocking her doll to sleep in it.

Early Kiowa beadworkers did not bead completely, except for small items, with narrow edgings and little trim. During the fifty years that cradle making flourished, Kiowa women's bead designs were bold and colorful, with figures outlined in multiple rows of large abstract floral, geometric, and amorphous designs in different colors. Abstract representations of the maple, oak, and sumac leaf were common designs. Each woman created her own designs, and they were never copied or traced without the permission of the creator; each design had its own history. They used a combination of stitches: lazy stitch, overlay stitch, Crow stitch, and netted stitch. The covers' sides were often asymmetrical in color, design, or stitch type. Blue was a common beaded background, and a red wool background with widely spaced beaded designs was popular in the twentieth century.[11]

Birth Customs

Kiowa children were appreciated, well cared for, and loved. Thomas C. Battey, a missionary in Oklahoma Territory, wrote about the Kiowas' affection for their sons: "Parental affection is very strong, and more strongly manifested toward the boys; both parents are proud of a son—a young warrior—who may become a great man in his tribe, while in a daughter they see only the advantage of the servile assistance in the household."[12]

Mary Haumpy, a Kiowa woman born in 1901 and reared in Caddo County, Oklahoma, described Kiowa birth customs in a 1967 oral history: "In the old days, a baby was born in a tent or tipi where the expectant mother lived. Fresh grass was cut and put down for bedding on the ground in the lodge. The mother was attended with a woman knowledgeable about birth to help with the baby. If the birth was not a quick birth, the woman in labor was assisted to walk around the tent or tipi until the delivery."[13]

Mary Buffalo recalled the earlier practice of placing a hide flap filled with buffalo hair or some other material in the cradle to serve as a diaper. To remove the soiled material, the lower section of the front lacing was undone.[14] Other absorbent materials served as diapers: shredded moss and dried pulverized buffalo manure.[15]

Amulet

A navel amulet at the Sam Noble Oklahoma Museum of Natural History is trapezoidal in shape and beaded on the front. Eight beaded thongs are attached to the shape, decorated with large white beads, brass beads, and hawk bells. A string of buckskin is attached at the top to hang the amulet to the hood of the cradle. Mary Jane Schneider described the amulet as a small beaded diamond tied to the hood. It was kept there as long as the cradle was used.[16] Battey noted the use of charms for the young: "The charm is worn by which the individual may be recognized by his protective spirit; nearly every person, old or young, wears something of the kind."[17]

Baby Swing

The Kiowa mothers used a baby swing or hammock for a bed, made with two ropes, two sticks the same size, and a blanket. In the early days, a piece of animal hide would have been used. The two parallel ropes were tied to two poles or trees, and the blanket was folded several times over the ropes. The sticks were placed horizontally between the ropes, inside the blanket, to keep the blanket from the baby's face. A separate piece of rope was often attached to swing the baby. The swing was sometimes attached to the boards on the window or tied in the willow arbor. Willow arbors are still built for the Sun Dance and powwows. The arbor shade, built with willow poles and leaf-covered branches, could lower the temperature twenty degrees. Arbors provided a safe, cool place for baby swings.[18]

Kiowa Cradle Symbolism

The lattice cradle was recognized as a symbol of new life, and today it is a symbol of the continuity of Kiowa life. The four-direction motif was beaded on many cradles as symbolic protection for the child.

Kiowa Cradleboard

The cradleboard I studied is stored at the University of Oklahoma's Sam Noble Museum, in Norman, Oklahoma (cat. no. E/1959/9/001). The Beatrice Ahpeatone Doyah Smith family identified the cradle as Kiowa, made by Beatrice's grandmother prior to the Haffenreffer Museum of Anthropology traveling exhibit on Kiowa and Comanche cradleboards. Guo-haddle (Mesquite Beans), wife of Chief Ahpeahtone, Mountain View, Oklahoma, made the cradle between 1900 and 1912. She was a Kiowa woman, born around 1860, who was known among the Kiowa people as a gifted beadworker.

The cradleboard is 42 inches long, 13.25 inches wide, and 11 inches deep. The frame is four boards of smoothed, polished dark wood with metal tack decorations forming a cross. Two boards, 42 inches long and 3.4 inches wide, are pointed at one end. Another board is 11.5 inches long and 3 inches wide, and the shortest board is 5.25 inches long and 2.5

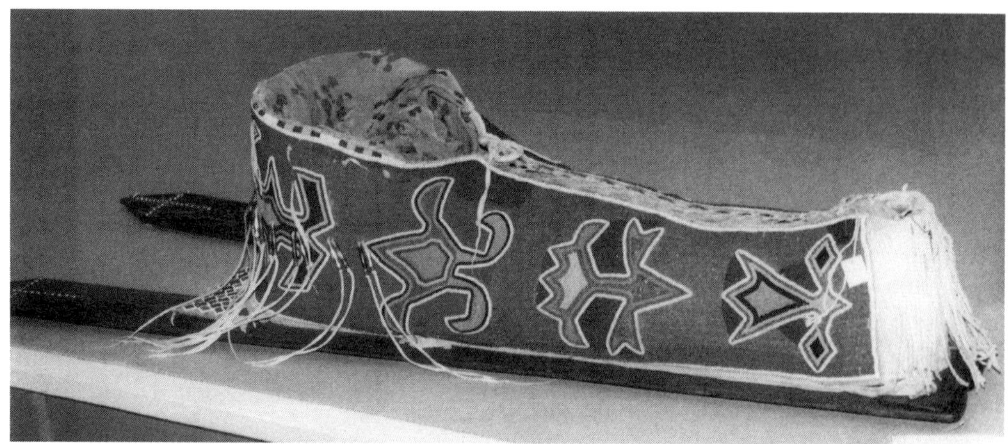

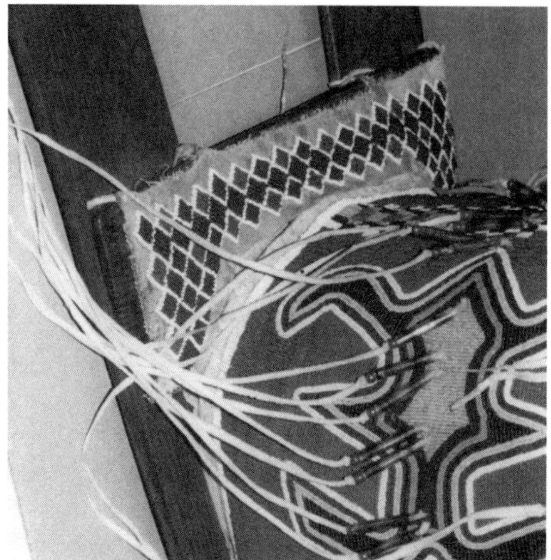

Kiowa beaded cradleboard, with intricate cover lacing, ca. 1900–12, 42.5 × 13.25 × 11 inches. Collected by Hedwig Schaeffer October 23, 1933, and donated to the museum by Gertrude McBride. Photographs taken by the author and museum staff. Courtesy of the Sam Noble Museum, University of Oklahoma, Norman (E/1959/9/001).

inches wide. The four pieces are shaped by hand and laced together with buckskin thongs. Four holes are drilled into the requisite attachment locations, and the boards are lashed together with buckskin thong. The longer crosspiece is attached 11 inches from the top of the pointed ends; the shortest crosspiece is 2.4 inches from the bottom of the vertical boards. The crosspieces are rounded and smoothed. Twelve holes spaced close together were drilled into the center of the two staves. The frame forms a V-shaped lattice construction. The pointed ends are notched.

The cradle base and support is a pad shaped to the dimensions of the frame, which is laid on top of the boards to provide a solid base for the cradle. Holes are punched through the thick, folded canvas pad to match up with the holes drilled into the boards. A rectangular stiff piece of rawhide is shaped like a hood, and a smaller piece forms the footrest support. The pad, the rawhide supports, and the beaded cover are aligned over the holes in the boards, laced in place with buckskin thong and tied to the frame. The beaded cover is sewn together at the bottom of the footrest.

The cover is a rectangular piece of tanned deerskin, 43 by 9 inches, completely beaded except for a band of buckskin where the cover is sewn together at the bottom. The rawhide supports the shape of the cradle. A 1-inch unbeaded strip of leather along each side of the cover is folded back. The folded strip of buckskin is stitched over the rawhide hood and sewn together. This folded strip strengthens the area for the lacing in the front of the cradle. The hood opening is 7 inches across.

The lining is calico cotton with tan and navy print on light green cotton material. It is cut to fit the cover, and one end of the cloth is stitched to the rim under the folded edge of the buckskin all around the top of the cover. The lining is folded into the cradle to cover both the inside and the pad. About an inch of wrap beadwork, all along the rim on the hood, shows on the outside and the interior. Slits are cut on both sides of the cradle. Two long buckskin thongs are tied at the bottom of the cover, threaded through the slits, and tied at each slit, leaving enough slack to make a loop. Buckskin thongs are laced through the loops in a zigzag pattern. The carrying strap is missing. Separate holes are drilled in the frame to hold the thong for the strap. The thong is 2 inches long and tied to the frame.

The beadwork is done in the lazy stitch with seed beads on a blue background. The cover is completely outlined with a white border. The designs are geometric and floral, outlined in various colors, ending with white. The wrap bead around the hood is done with white, navy, light blue, green, light blue, and a navy-striped pattern. Some of the beads are faceted. The design of isolated abstract oak leaves is symmetrical, with four large leaves on each side of the cradle. The bodies of the leaves are rose outlined in navy, yellow, green, red, and white; yellow outlined in light blue, light green, rose, and white; light blue outlined in red, yellow, light green, and white; and rose outlined in navy, light blue, rose, and white. The top of the hood has a wide beaded band of various colored stripes in a checker block pattern. The colors used in the wide band are light green, white, navy, and rose.

A bib of beaded buckskin, 3 inches by 11 inches, is tied to the top crosspiece. The design is a checked diamond pattern in light green, navy, and red, outlined in white, forming an arch across the rectangular buckskin.

Stitched around the footrest is a 6-inch-long twisted white fringe. Buckskin pendant thongs with clear glass beads, tube beads, and one orange bead are held in place with a knot. The white buckskin thongs, 17 inches long, are doubled and sewn to a beaded cover in a line halfway from the opening of the hood. The pendants start at the top of the third leaf and go across the hood, ending at the top of the third leaf on the other side of the cradle. Similar but shorter (5-inch) thongs are stitched around the hood.

The Kiowa cradleboard is made to be used primarily for transporting the baby on the mother's back or hung on the mother's saddle horn. During a period of cultural transition, however, after the Kiowas' nomadic lifestyle had ended, elder women had begun to make a unique beautiful yet functional new art form: the lattice cradleboard. In the words of Ray Doyah:

> My great-grandmother Guo-haddle was a master bead worker whose vision and dexterity enabled her to create intricate patterns using needle and thread.

Guo-haddle's intuition also saw to the needs of her family as tradition guided her hand and heart to produce works of quintessential beauty. She created the baby cradles at the end of her life's journey for the beginning of another life, and without knowing it—Guo-haddle's essence has gone beyond substance to touch many more lives. Each bead was selected for its uniformity and sewn in exact measurements with the naked eye as her only guide. Each pattern she created was her personal statement and signature. Each color marked her essay in beads as hers and hers alone.[19]

Guohaddle's Cradle

Museum cradles
Shunted in subdued light
Temperature regulated
Dew point set
Neat historical data
How they were obtained
. . . Blasphemy to the maker

Lifeless museum cradles
Collecting dust

Mothers give life to cradles
Children give life to cradles
The buckskin breathes
The wood sings
Through threads of sinew
Through beads of perspiration
Of pregnancy, of childbirth
Until a pattern is sewn

Then skin touches skin
Of the newly born
To preserve the living.

Ray C. Doyah, *Powwow Chairs*

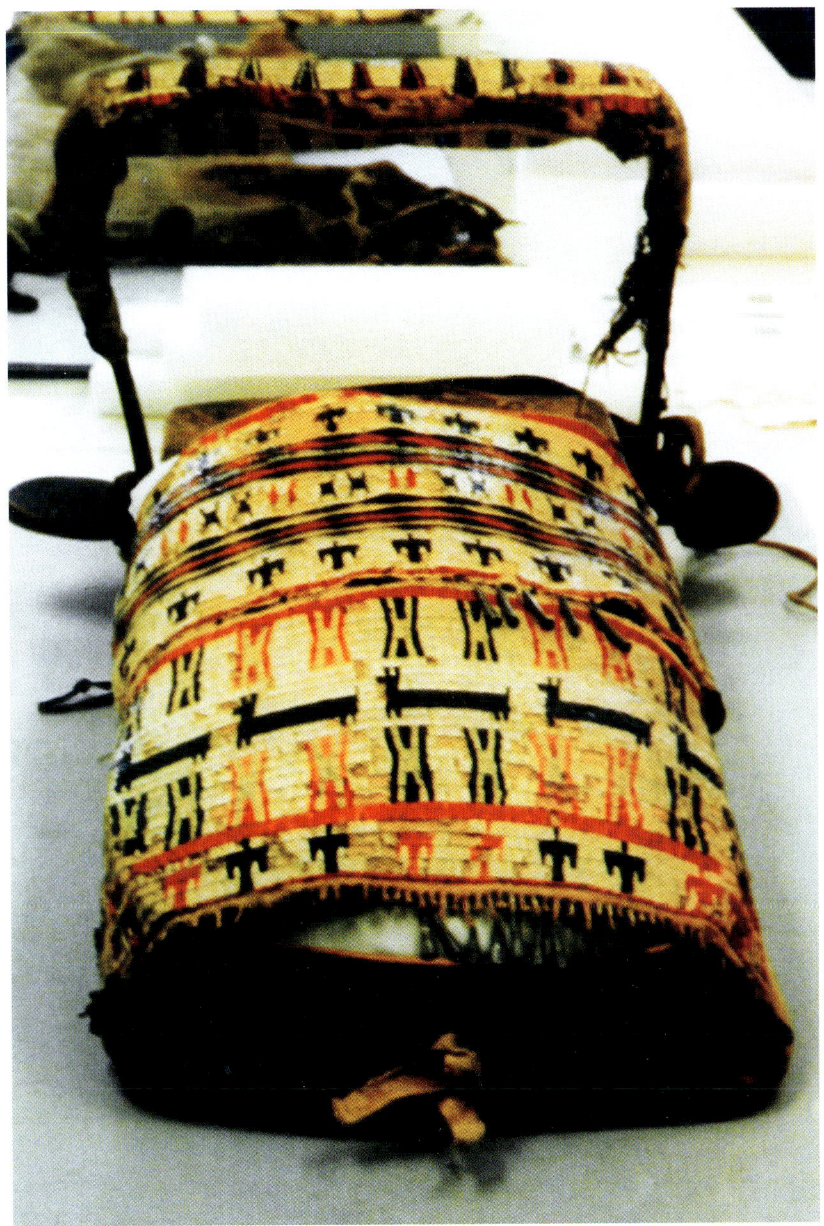

PLATE 1. Santee Dakota cradleboard, 1832, 31.1 × 17.5 × 9.8 inches. With dyed quills, wood, and metal, and a hide burden strap, or tumpline. The Dakotas were known for their fine porcupine quillwork. Courtesy of the Department of Anthropology, Smithsonian Institution, Suitland, Maryland (E73311-0).

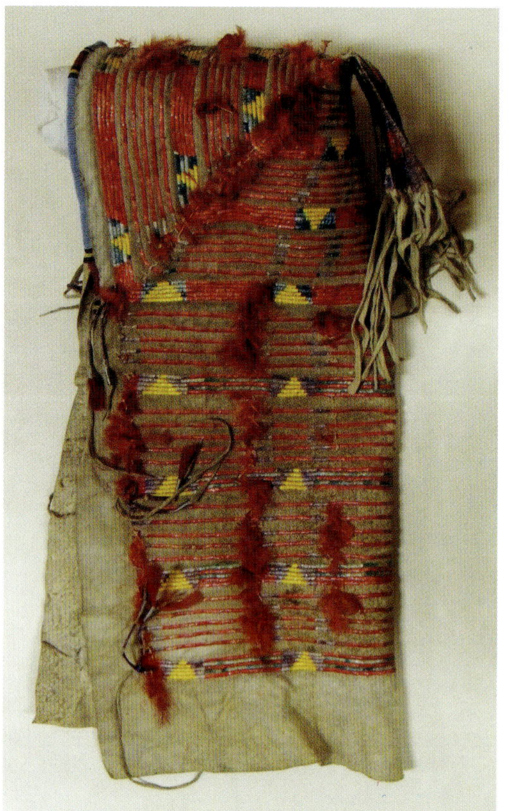

PLATE 2. Dakota baby cradle, ca. 1880, measurements unavailable, made entirely of buckskin, with simple line quillwork. Courtesy of the State Historical Society of North Dakota, Bismarck (SHSND 4369).

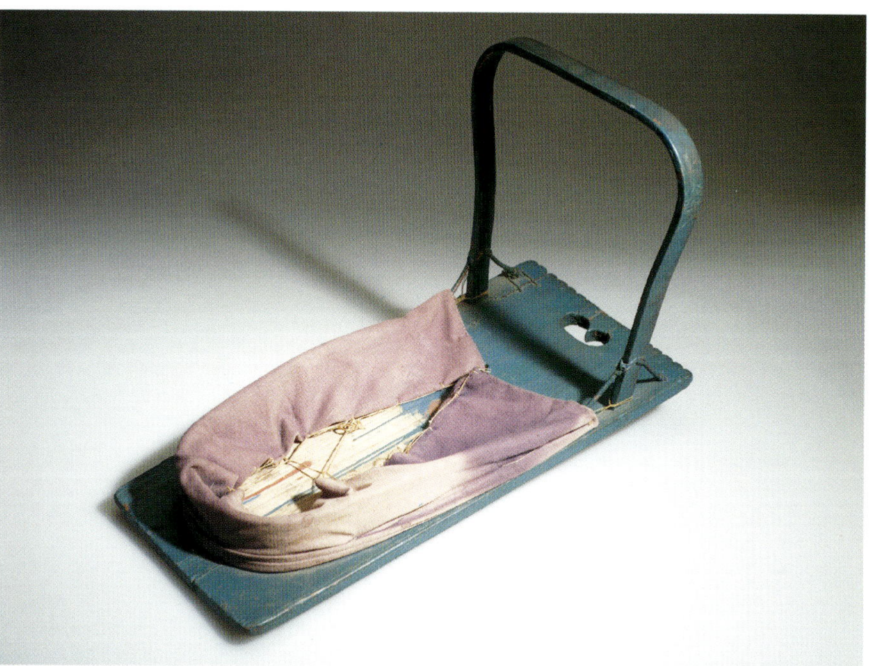

PLATE 3. Eastern Cree cradleboard, 18.5 × 8 × 11 inches. Collected by Alanson Skinner in Moose Factory, Ontario, in 1908. Made of Wood, pigment, cloth, thread, and hide. Courtesy of the Division of Anthropology, American Museum of Natural History, New York, New York (50/6943).

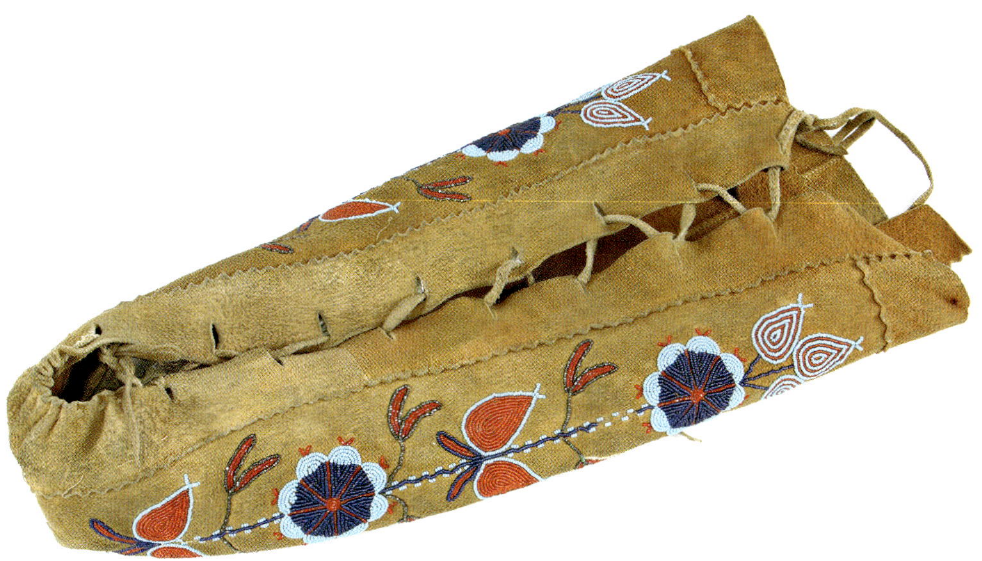

PLATE 4. Plains Cree moss bag, ca. 1865–1925, 11.8 × 28.7 inches. Made of hide, glass beads, and cotton thread. Courtesy of the McCord Museum, Montreal, Quebec (M6011).

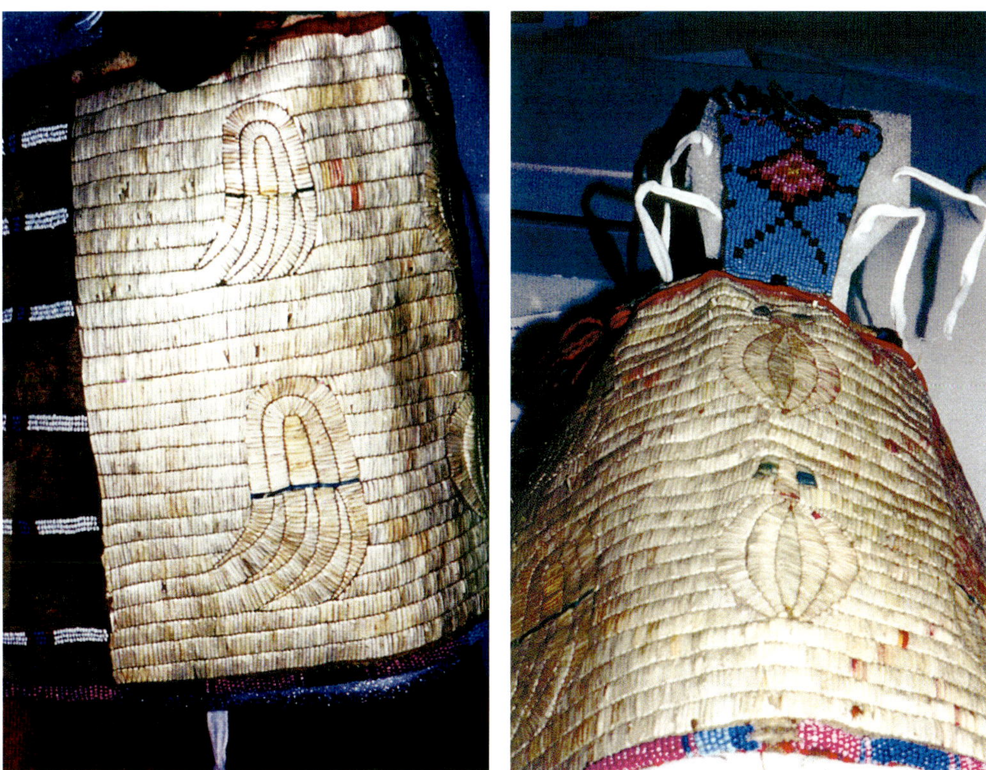

PLATE 5A AND B. Sioux (Yanktonai) soft cradle, side (A) and top (B), with "Lone Wolf" hood done in quills, decorated with seed beads, 36 × 25 inches; tab: 6 × 3 inches. Donated by Lt. H. M. Creel, May 21, 1888. Courtesy of the Department of Anthropology, Smithsonian Institution (E129885-0).

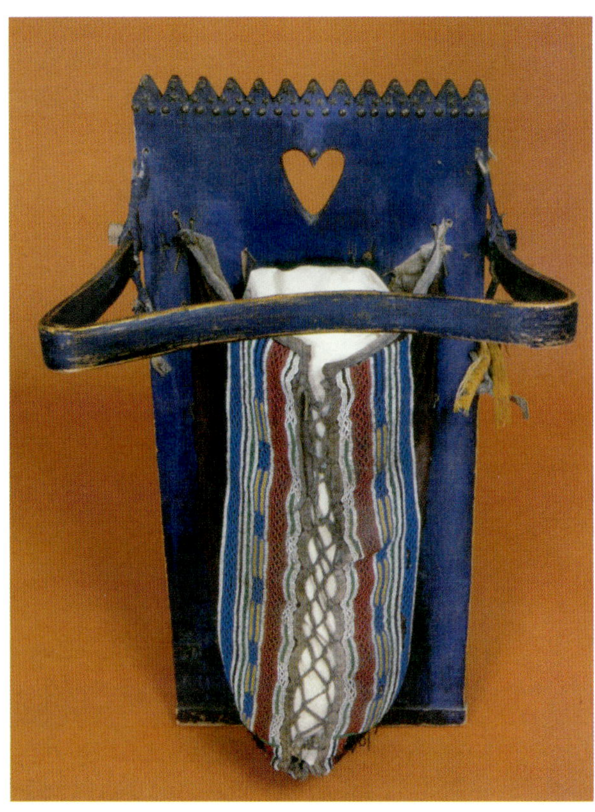

PLATE 6. Plains Ojibwa cradleboard, ca. 1880, baby bag, black wool covered with diamond and otters' tail motifs in blue, red, and green beads attached to wooden cradleboard. Courtesy of the State Historical Society of North Dakota, Bismarck (SHSND 475).

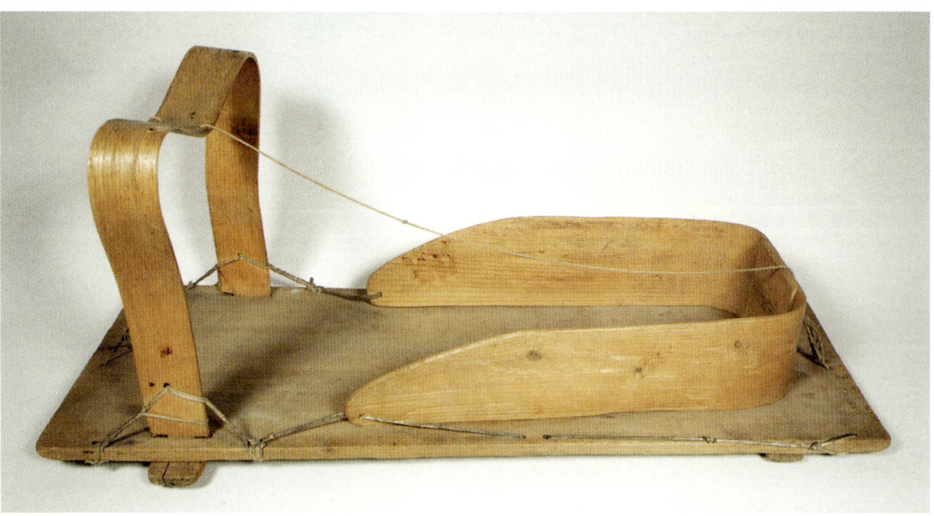

PLATE 7. Ioway cradleboard, 27 × 10 inches. Central Algonquian type, made of wood, cotton string, leather, and nails. Collected by Alanson Skinner, 1922, in Perkins, Oklahoma. Courtesy of the Milwaukee Public Museum, Wisconsin (30159).

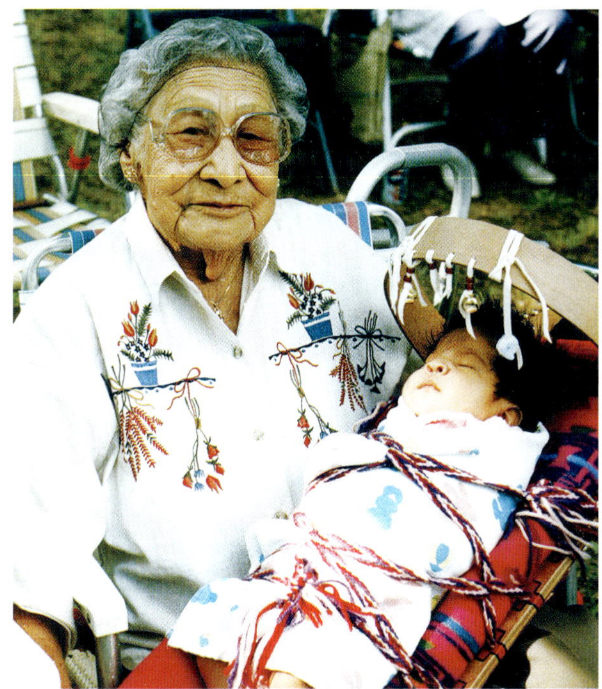

PLATE 8. Otoe grandmother, Hilda Harris, with baby in cradleboard, 1998. Courtesy Oklahoma Historical Society.

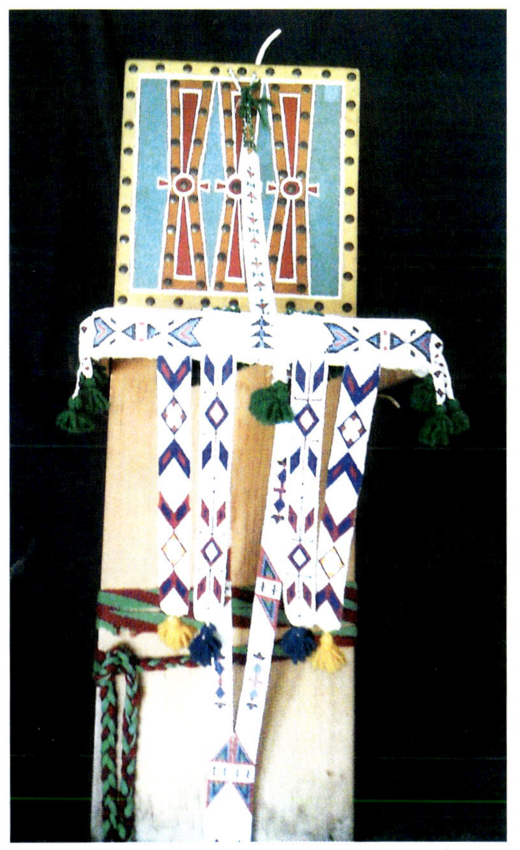

PLATE 9. Osage carved, painted panel, with geometric designs outlined in brass brads that rest on a row of pierced holes, date unknown. Photograph by the author. Courtesy of the Deupree Cradleboard Collection, Red Earth Art Center, Oklahoma City, Oklahoma.

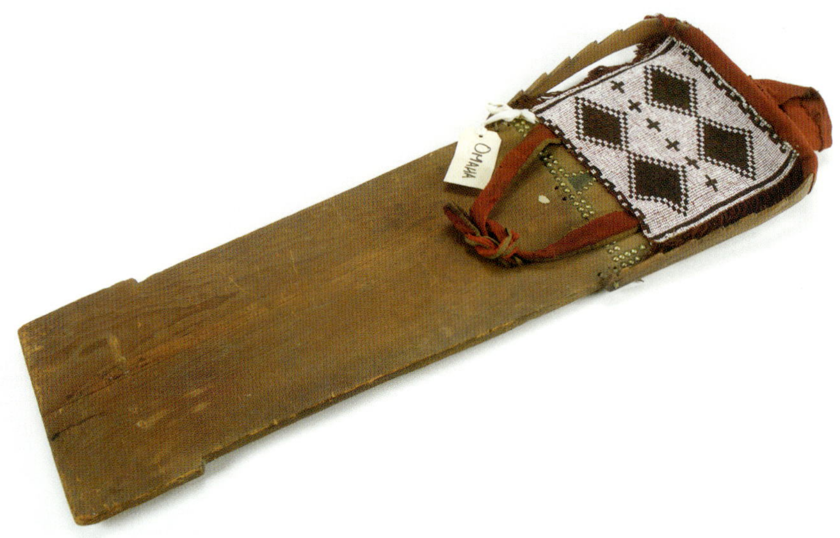

PLATE 10. Omaha cradleboard, ca. 1880, cottonwood plank, 38.5 inches long, with projecting bent hoop, approximately 1.5 inches wide, and beaded sunshade, approximately 12 × 12 inches. Collected in 1890 by artist De Cost Smith on the Omaha Reservation, Macy, Nebraska. Courtesy of the National Museum of the American Indian, Smithsonian Institution, Suitland, Maryland (20/1373).

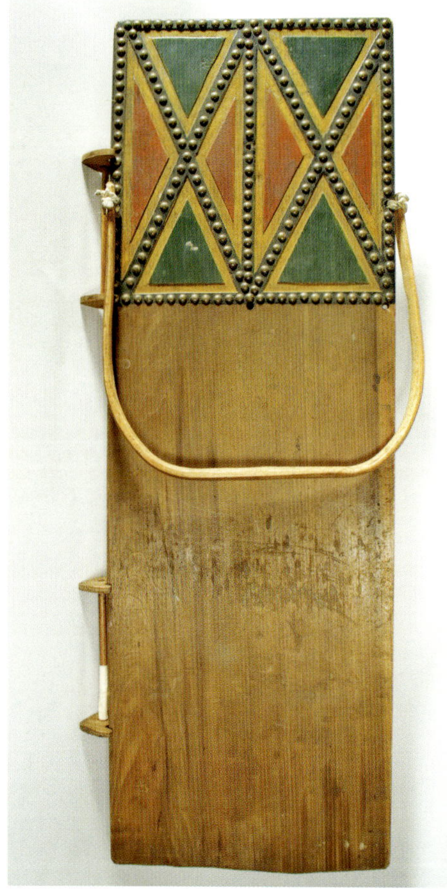

PLATE 11. Kaw prairie cradleboard, 34.5 × 11.75 inches. Collected by Alanson Skinner, 1922, Perkins, Oklahoma. Made of wood and leather, with brass tacks and paint decoration. Courtesy of the Milwaukee Public Museum, Wisconsin (30158).

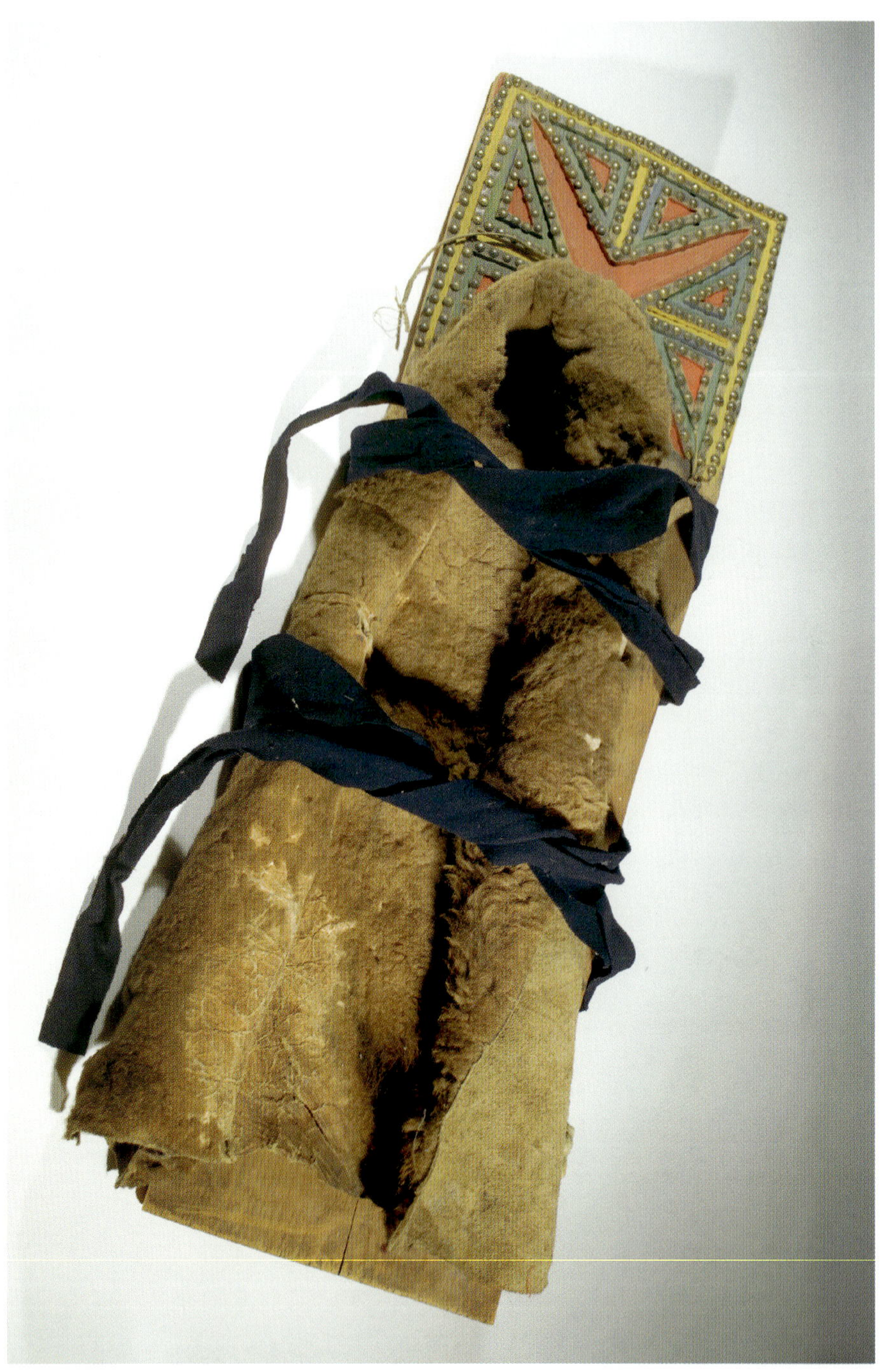

PLATE 12. Pawnee cradleboard, wood, pigment, hide, fur (buffalo), cloth, metal, date unknown, 33.5 × 10.4 × 3.0 inches. Courtesy of the Division of Anthropology, American Museum of Natural History, New York, New York (50.1/9629).

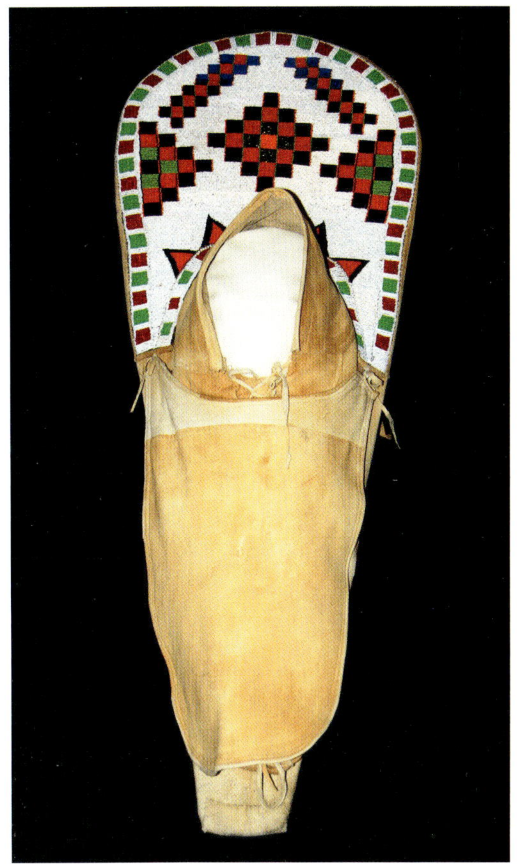

PLATE 13. Blackfeet carrier, ca. 1900, 37 × 14 inches. Smoked buckskin beaded in overlay stitch, with beaded panel detachable from cradle. Louis W. Hill Memorial Collection, Gift of Great Northern Railroad, Museum of the Plains Indian, Browning, Montana (cat. no. 1113). Image courtesy of the U.S. Department of the Interior, Indian Arts and Crafts Board.

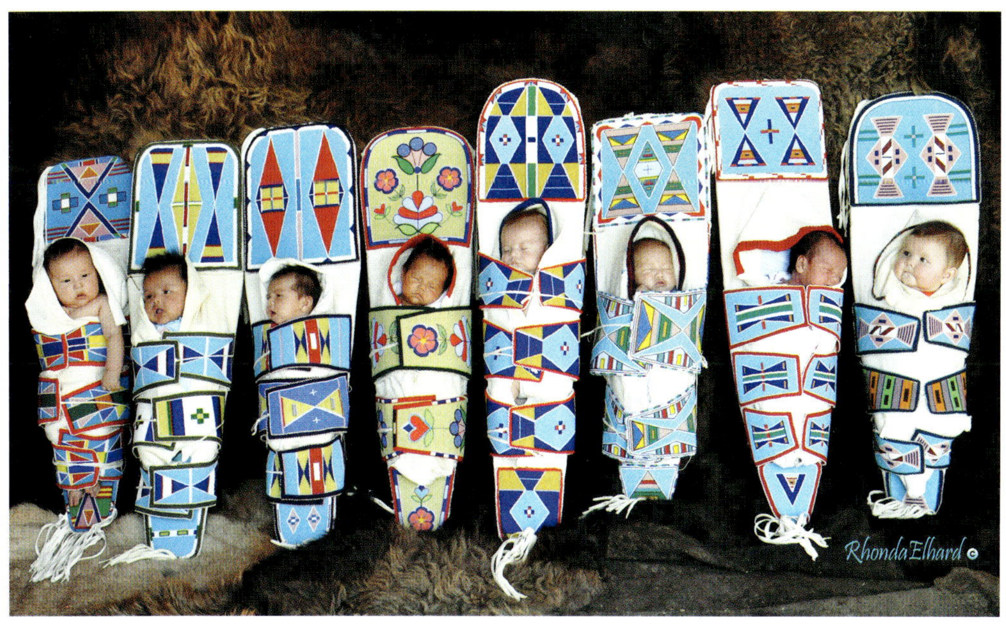

PLATE 14. *Bound in Tradition*, by photographer Rhonda Elhard. Eight Crow babies snug in their beautifully beaded cradleboards. Copyright Rhonda Elhard. Courtesy of the Custer Battlefield Trading Post, Crow Agency, Montana.

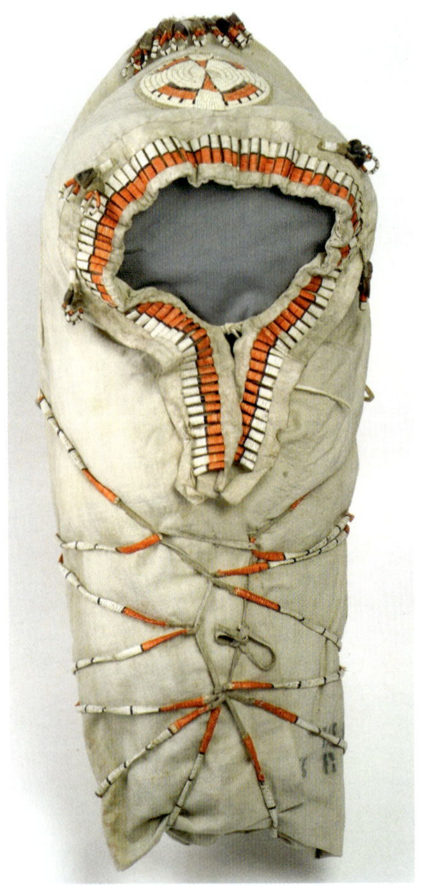

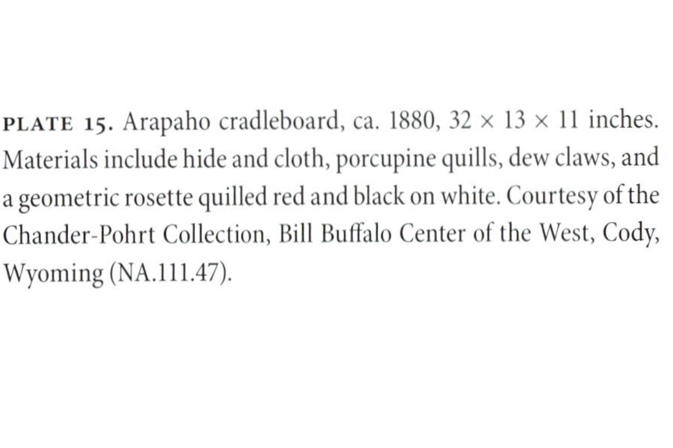

PLATE 15. Arapaho cradleboard, ca. 1880, 32 × 13 × 11 inches. Materials include hide and cloth, porcupine quills, dew claws, and a geometric rosette quilled red and black on white. Courtesy of the Chander-Pohrt Collection, Bill Buffalo Center of the West, Cody, Wyoming (NA.111.47).

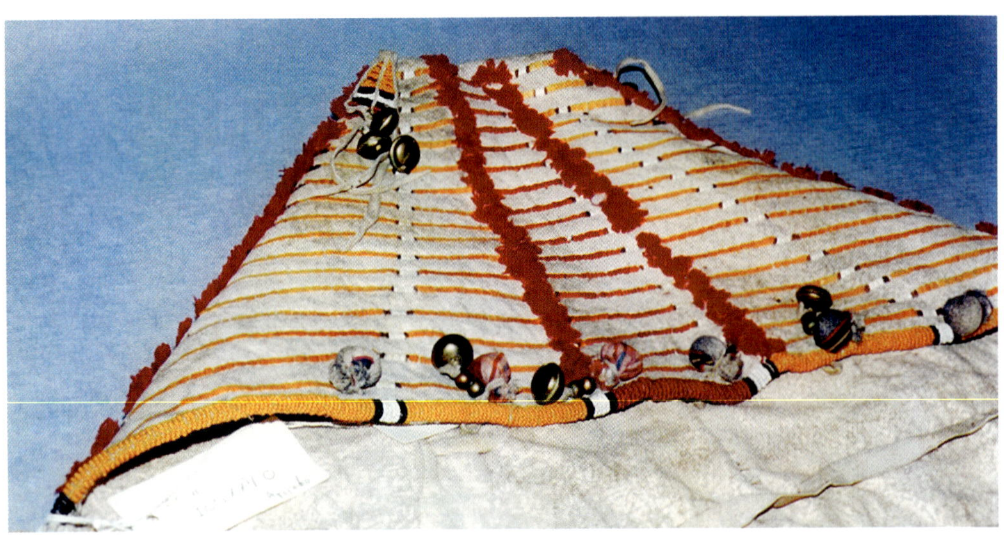

PLATE 16. Arapaho soft hood, 39 inches long. Collected by H. R. Voth, December 25, 1893. Materials include tanned hide, porcupine quills, tufts of red yarn, brass bells, small round bags of calico at the edges of hood, and quill loop ties. Courtesy of the Department of Anthropology, Smithsonian Institution, Suitland, Maryland (E165774-0).

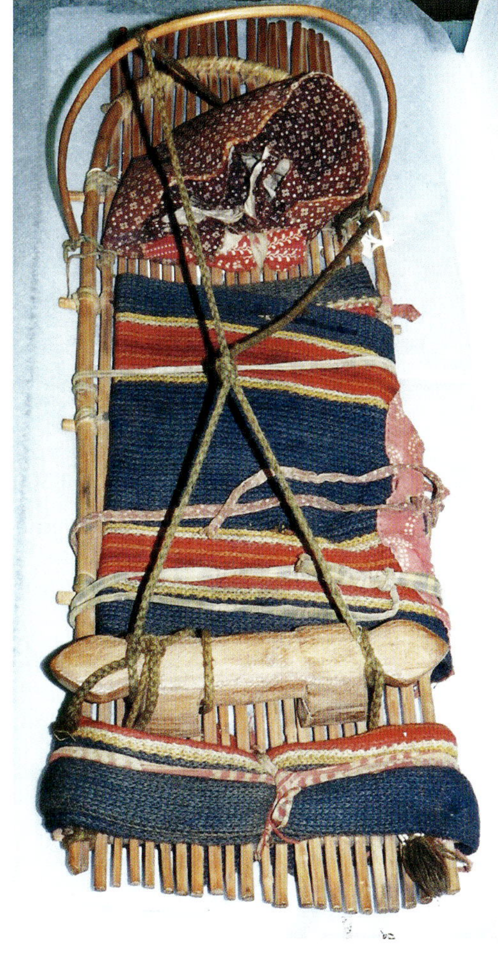

PLATE 17. Wichita cradleboard, 33 × 11 inches. Collected by James Mooney in 1891. Courtesy of the Department of Anthropology, Smithsonian Institution, Suitland, Maryland (E152944-0).

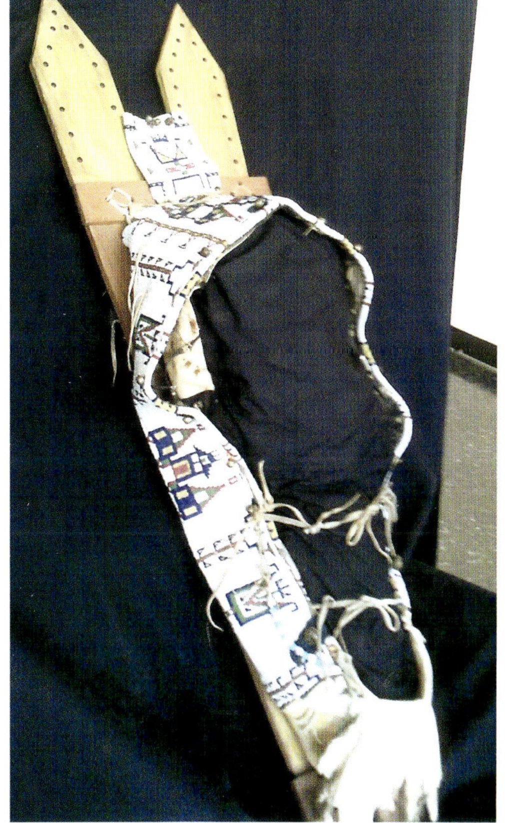

PLATE 18. Northern Cheyenne cradleboard, date and dimensions unknown. Photograph by the author. Deupree Cradleboard Collection, Red Earth Art Center, Oklahoma City, Oklahoma.

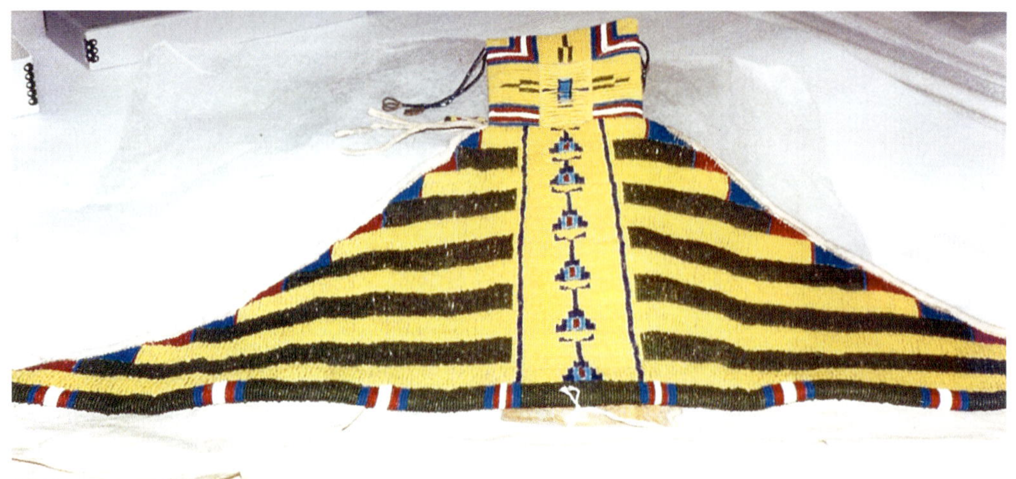

PLATE 19. Old-type, two-color-striped Cheyenne beaded soft hood cradle, 40 × 17 inches. Donated by Victor J. Evans, March 26, 1931. Courtesy of the Department of Anthropology, Smithsonian Institution, Suitland, Maryland (E358013-0).

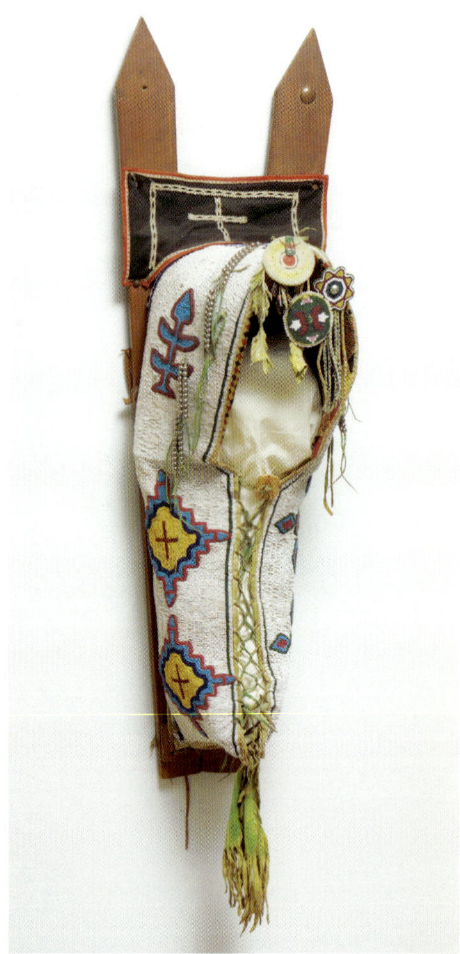

PLATE 20. Kiowa cradleboard, 1890, with yellow, red, dark blue, and aqua designs on a beaded white background, measurements unknown. Different designs appear on each side, with long strings of brass beads and ornaments at the top. Courtesy of the Museum of the Red River, Idabel, Oklahoma.

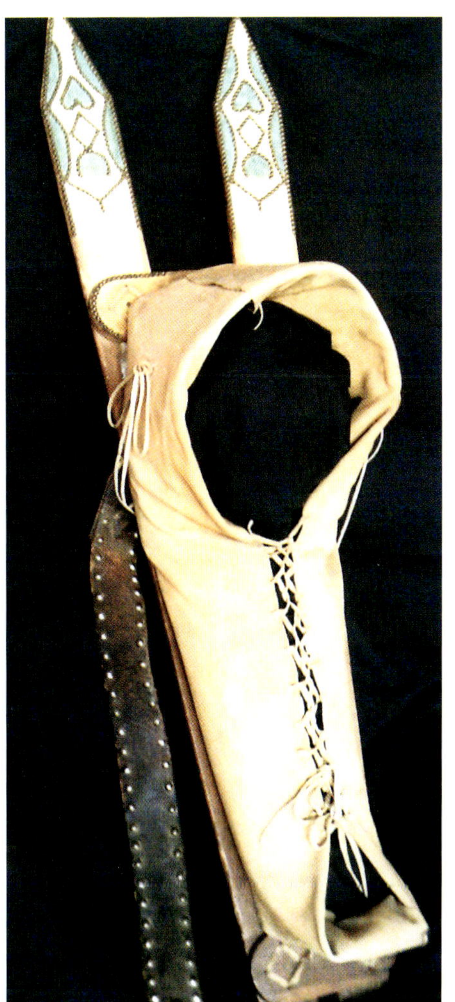

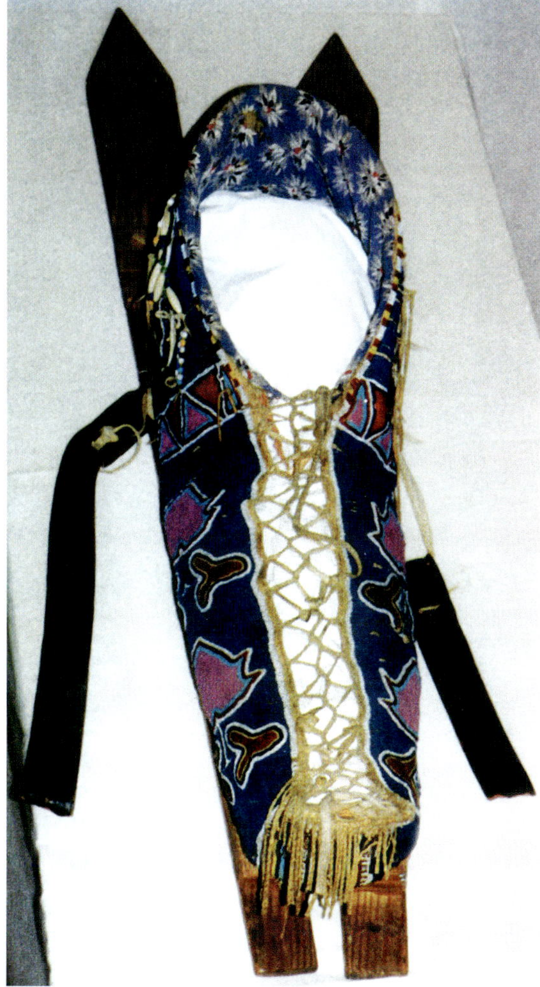

PLATE 21A AND B. Comanche (A, *left*) hide cradleboard and (B, *right*) beaded cradleboard, dates unknown. Prior to the 1880s, Comanche cradleboards were made of hide and adorned simply with painted pouches and brass tack designs on the boards. Photograph by the author. Courtesy of the Deupree Cradleboard Collection, Red Earth Art Center, Oklahoma City, Oklahoma.

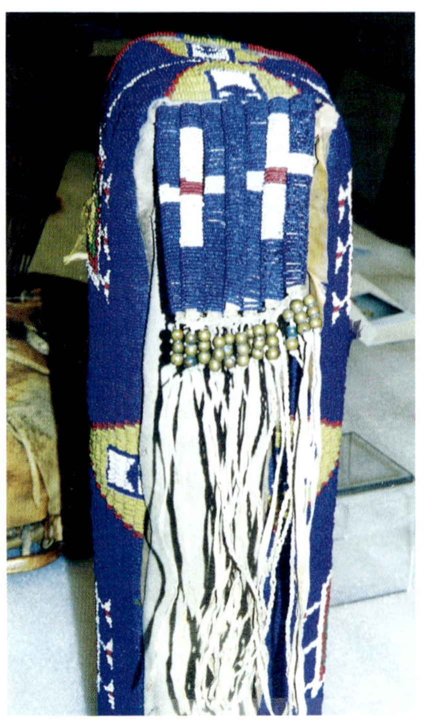

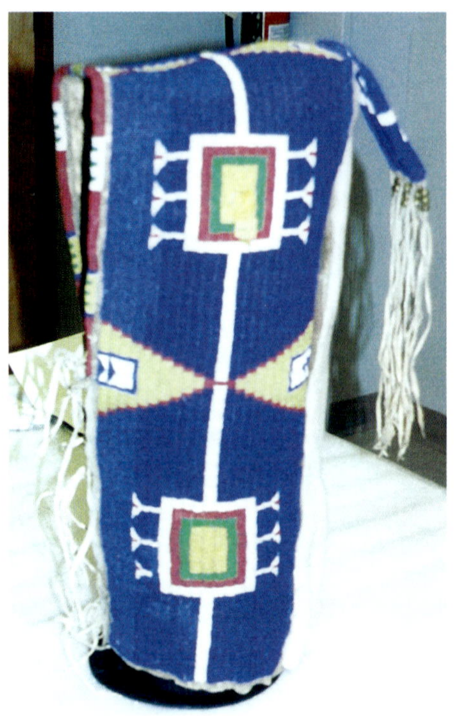

PLATES 22A AND B. Lakota soft cradle, 1890, (A, *left*) front and (B, *right*) side. Fully beaded cradle with an unusual background color for Lakota cradles: bright blue. White backgrounds are the norm, with the occasional sky blue. Courtesy of the Museum of the Red River, Idabel, Oklahoma.

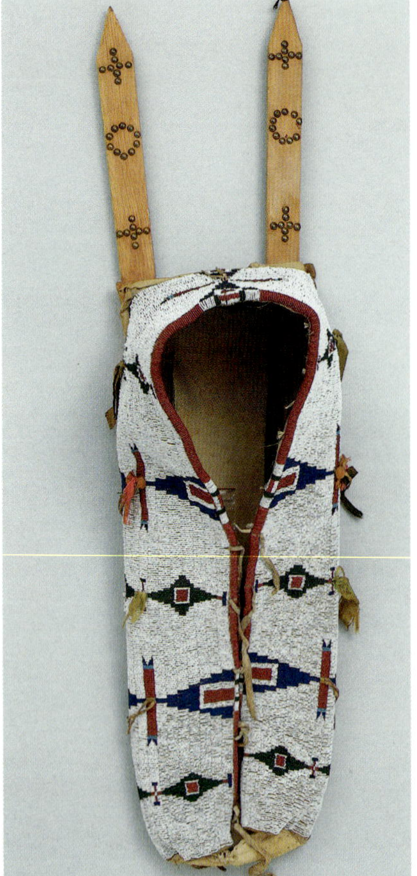

PLATE 23. Oglála lattice cradleboard, 1875, 41.0 × 9.5 inches. Beaded hide, gingham, and canvas cover mounted on wooden frame with crosspieces. Courtesy of the Chander-Pohrt Collection, Buffalo Bill Center of the West (NA.111.33).

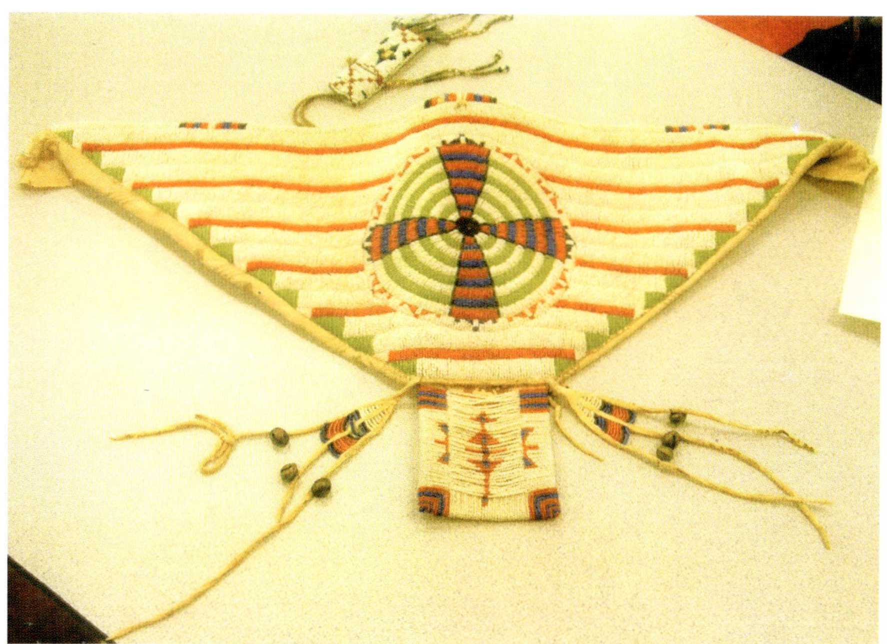

PLATE 24. Tonkawa beaded baby canopy, date and measurements unknown. Soft cradle features a central symbolic design of the circle of life and four sacred directions. Courtesy of the Tonkawa Tribal Museum, Tonkawa, Oklahoma.

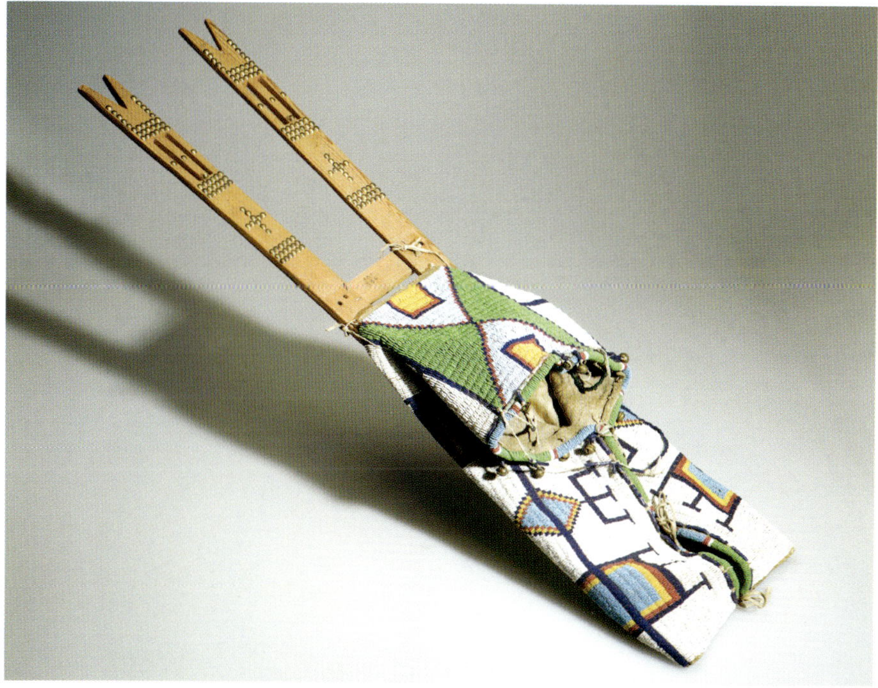

PLATE 25. Assiniboine cradleboard, 39.8 × 10.6 × 2.4. inches. Donated in 1910. Made of hide, beads, wood, metal, thread, sinew, and pigment. Courtesy of the Division of Anthropology, American Museum of Natural History (50.1/754).

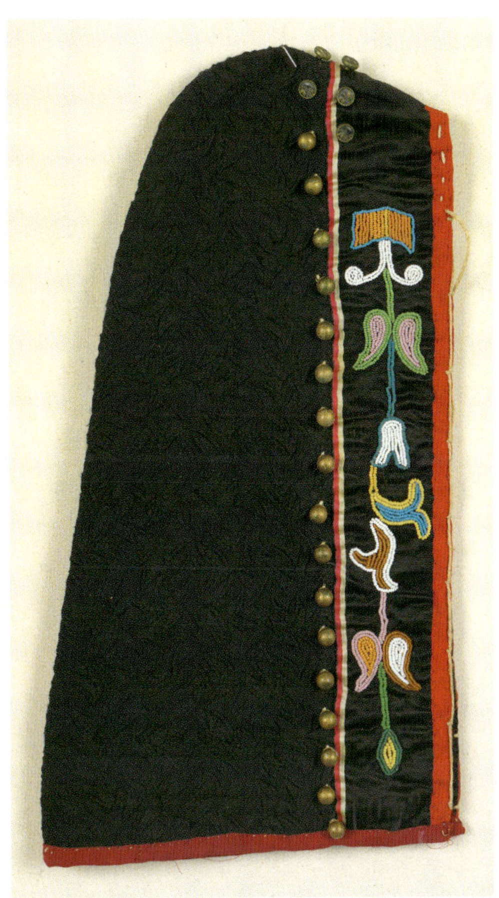

PLATE 26. Sarcee baby wrapper, about 18 inches long. Donated in 1905. The baby bag is made of wool with silk ribbon trim, beadwork embroidery, and brass buttons. Courtesy of the Division of Anthropology, American Museum of Natural History (50/5892).

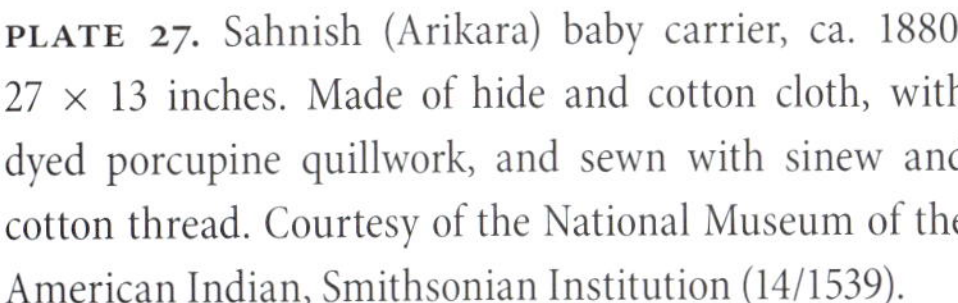

PLATE 27. Sahnish (Arikara) baby carrier, ca. 1880, 27 × 13 inches. Made of hide and cotton cloth, with dyed porcupine quillwork, and sewn with sinew and cotton thread. Courtesy of the National Museum of the American Indian, Smithsonian Institution (14/1539).

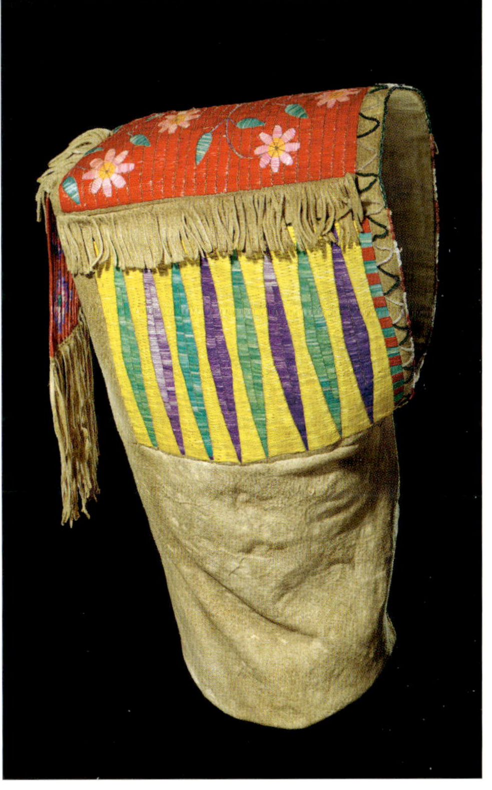

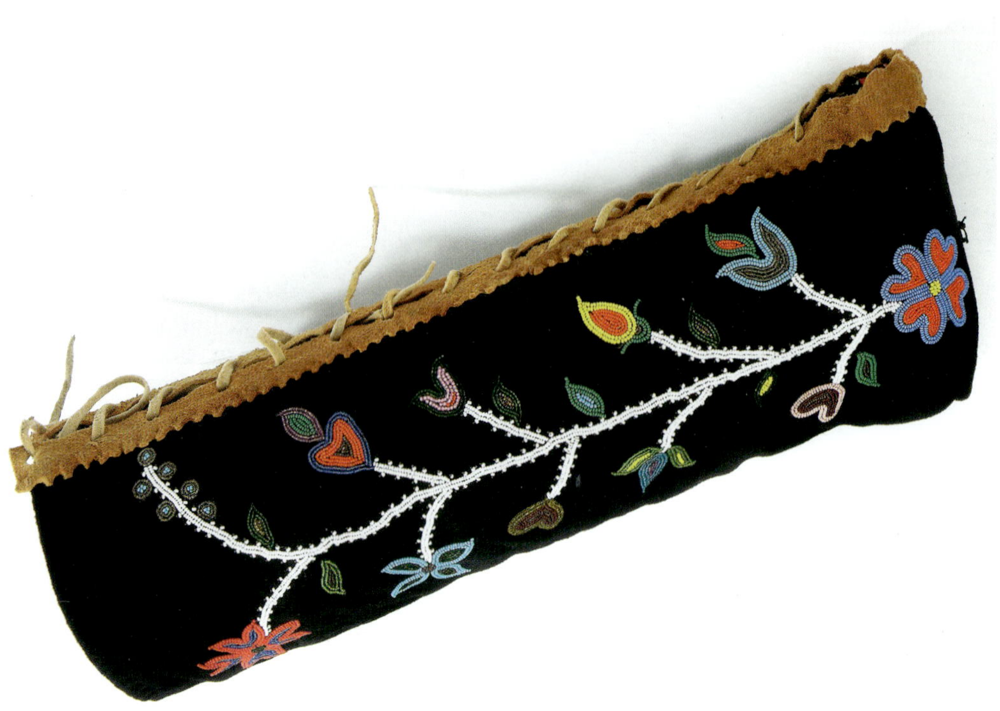

PLATE 28. Plains Métis moss bag, n.d., 25 × 12 × 6.5 inches. Made of wool cloth, smoked hide, and beads. Courtesy of the Glenbow Museum, Calgary, Alberta, Canada (AP 2606).

CHAPTER 21

APACHE TRIBE OF OKLAHOMA

The Apache Tribe of Oklahoma (Na'isha) is a Southern Athabascan band that was at one time called the Gattaka, the Kiowa Apache, and the Plains Apache. The Plains Apaches' oral history records their existence with the Sacree in Canada. First written mention of them was in Robert de La Salle's accounts of exploring the Mississippi River in 1682. After the Plains Apaches formed an alliance with the Kiowas in the seventeenth century, they had no political connection to the Apache proper. In the nineteenth century, they roamed the area of present-day southwestern Oklahoma through the Texas panhandle to Chihuahua, Mexico. They were buffalo-hunting nomads with soldier societies and four medicine bundles. These nomads traded extensively, bartering bison hides for salt, meat, produce, and other goods. War and raiding allowed the men to gain power and prestige in their soldier societies. Women did not hold positions of power. They were in charge of maintaining the family possessions and tipis as well as gathering food. Apache women had their own women's societies. Inhabiting a true plains environment, they represented the easternmost extension of the Southern Athabascan–speaking people of the Southwest.

The Plains Apaches shared a reservation in Oklahoma Territory with the Comanches and Kiowas. In 1972, the Plains Apaches were officially called the Apache Tribe of Oklahoma. The tribal office is located in Anadarko, Oklahoma.

Cradleboard

The Oklahoma Apache made carriers similar to those of other Apache tribes: an oval frame with slats, hide covering, and large basketry hood. The cradleboard was called a *tsis-ts'áál* (*tsis*, "wood"; *ts'áál*, "swaddling clothes") or *číšc'áál* (*číš*, "wood"; *c'áál*, "swaddling clothes").[1] Ethnologists and anthropologists have documented little of the Plains Apache culture. John Upton Terrell's work on the Plains Apache shared information about the prereservation carrier.[2]

Two carriers were made for Apache babies, a temporary one for newborns and a permanent one three months later. The foundation of the permanent cradle was a piece of wood bent and secured in an oval curve at the bottom. A series of flat wooden slats were tied to the oval frame. The cradle frame was covered with soft buckskin and laced up the front. A sunshade of woven willow withes held together with buckskin strips formed an arch over the baby's head. Soft bedding of shredded bark or crumbled grasses often filled the bottom bed of the cradle, covered with soft fur. Dangling objects to amuse or protect the baby hung from the hood. These items also aided in the development of the infant's eyes.

When the baby was walking, the cradle outgrown, the child wore a buckskin jacket, a long loose belt of buckskin attached about the waist hanging down in the back by which the baby could be lifted and slung over a shoulder or the horn of a saddle. Carrying jackets were made of two pieces of buckskin sewn at the shoulders and down the sides, leaving holes open for the arms and for the head at the top. A jacket was often decorated with tassels, charms, and amulets.

Lattice Cradleboard

Lattice cradleboards were made by Plains Apache from prereservation times to about 1920. Alfred Chalepah described the lattice cradleboard as being built the same as "the Kiowa—all beadwork." The cradle was usually made by the paternal grandmother or another relative. Alfred and his sister used the same cradleboard made by his mother's cousin. The baby was bundled up carefully so the arms and legs would not be hurt, then laced "up like a shoe. A big belt was attached to the cradle. You put it over your head and put it on your back."[3] If a baby died, the cradleboard was usually buried with the baby.

In the late nineteenth century, the Kiowas, Comanches, and Apaches living on the reservation in southwestern Oklahoma began to create the lattice cradleboard, a unique art form, both functional and beautiful. In the late 1860s the lattice cradleboard began to appear in collections and documentation. It was the preferred type of baby carrier among the Kiowas, Comanches, and Oklahoma Apaches from 1870 to 1920.[4] The lattice cradle consisted of a beaded hide cover, wrapped around rawhide supports at the head and foot and attached to a V-shaped frame of two narrow pointed boards and two shorter crosspieces. Men usually made the frame.

There are no living active Plains Apache cradleboard makers. The last one was Irene Chalepah Poolaw. Jeanette Berry Mopope was a Plains Apache cradleboard maker from the area of Red Stone, near Anadarko, Oklahoma, and her granddaughter Vanessa Paukeigope Jennings is a well-known, award-winning Kiowa cradleboard maker from Red Stone. Jennings learned beadwork from her Kiowa and Apache grandmothers, who were renowned for their beadwork. Jennings started beadwork with her Plains Apache grandmother sorting beads for her, then began doing her own beadwork by age eleven. She recalled that her grandmother had strict rules about using only the family designs. That kind of respect does not exist anymore. "To copy another family's designs would be disrespectful and dishonest because each design has a life and history of its own. The only time she should use another family's designs is if they were given to her by a family member such as an elderly beadworker with no daughters or granddaughters who wanted to ensure that a design would be preserved for posterity."[5]

Birth Customs

Fred Eggan wrote that the Plains Apaches had no mystical notions about conception. Either a man and woman had children and were fertile or they were not. There were no charms, prayers, or ceremonies that produced children. The pregnant woman or a grandfather kept count of the passage of the moons, so they knew approximately when to expect the child. Menstruation, pregnancy, and birth were closely associated with the phases of the moon. "New moon, that's time woman has her blood, or maybe full moon. Woman says 'I got monthly: next new moon I didn't have no monthly'; she keeps track nine or ten moons that baby comes. It comes with the moon. Great thing when woman see new moon for they say, I come with moon. Another frequent expression was that children are made when the new moon comes up."[6] The Apaches thought that the moon was female and that in the moon, "you could see a woman with a newborn baby on a travois." A man or a woman may pray to the moon for a baby.

Older women, usually female relatives, assisted with a birth. One would be experienced with childbirth. Some old women had special medicines for childbirth, "a herb which they gave to women as a kind of tea in hot water." During a difficult labor, "a medicine man might be called to perform a ceremony which would aid the delivery. The child would be born before the man left the tepee."[7] The Apache child was born with the mother in a kneeling position; midwives would hold her shoulders firmly.

After delivery, the placenta was taken away from the camp and buried. The newborn was greased instead of washed. The umbilical cord was cut and tied close to the child's body, and string was tied on both ends of the cord. Apaches "believed that lightning and a small whirlwind were the mysterious forces that gave breath and warmth to a new body, and that they entered it through the mouth as it emerged from the womb." After being anointed and greased, the newborn was held up to the four directions and displayed to the sun.[8]

Alfred Chalepah related how a mushroom was used to care for the navel. Apaches used toadstools that were small and

> kind of dark-looking. And inside it looks like powder. The navel, it takes a few days for this to come off. And they put some grease on it to keep from getting hard. They used to cut out a piece of cloth and put that over it. They made a little round hole and put that navel—or whatever it is through there. They keep it moist. They put grease on it. And when they do that, they take this stuff I'm talking about [powdery stuff from inside the mushroom] and they kind of sprinkle it on there. It is just like powder.[9]

The baby was bandaged and tied up to prevent it from moving its hands and arms. They were afraid the baby might kick around or move its arm and tear out the cord. The baby was watched carefully for four or five days until the cord dropped off.

The new mother would wear a buckskin belt to regain her figure. She would stay in her tipi for four days or more after the birth, and then she gradually resumed her normal duties. A few days after the birth, a feast was given for the elder women who had assisted and the relatives on both sides of the family. Four presents were given to the woman who was in charge of the birth. The gifts depended on the wealth of the family. Each of the old women would pick up the infant and pray for its welfare, stressing the wish for long life and good health.

During pregnancy, women were to avoid eating beef from the leg because that meat clings to the bone, and the delivery would be difficult; women avoided eating fat because the birth would be a dry birth; they avoid pounding meat forced into the intestine of a cow because it could cause the baby to be born with the navel cord wrapped around the neck. Heart and tongue could be eaten, but only after the tips were cut off. Removing the tip of the tongue before a woman ate it prevented the baby from being tongue-tied or slobbering. According to Ray Blackbear, a woman should pray to the ground and up to the air, asking for good luck, before cutting the top of the heart off. While holding the heart, she would say the word that meant she means to feed the whole earth by throwing out the top of the heart. A woman was told not to sit with her back to the sun because the afterbirth would stick; not to allow a child to sit on her lap because it would cause the baby inside to sit up and cause a difficult birth; to avoid looking at ugly things because the baby could be born ugly; and to avoid animals with undesirable attributes because they might transfer to the child. For instance, if the mother stares at a rabbit, the child might be born with a harelip.[10]

Children were particularly vulnerable to ghosts. One practice to protect a baby from ghosts and anything evil was to place a small stick across the cradle on the baby's chest if the baby was left alone. The Apaches believed that if you lived an evil life you turned into an owl or whirlwind after death. When a whirlwind came up, a child was always covered with a blanket.

Amulet

The umbilical cord was encased in a small beaded buckskin bag, sometimes with turkey feathers, and attached to the cradle. It was kept there until the child began to walk, and then it was tied to the child's garments.[11] Pliny E. Goddard, from the American Museum of Natural History, collected two umbilical stump cases in 1911 that he identified as Kiowa Apache. Both cases are 6 inches long, 2 inches wide, and 0.5 inches deep. They are diamond shaped, made of hide, and beaded with red, blue, and white seed beads and black pony beads. A strip of folded leather is stitched at each diamond point.

CHAPTER 22

CHEYENNE

The Cheyennes (Tsitsistas) are one of the seven Plains tribes that speak a language of the Algonquian family. Cheyenne was the Sioux name for the tribe, meaning People of a Different Speech. The Cheyennes formally lived far to the east of their present range. They moved gradually west and southwest, from what is now Minnesota to the central plains, adopting an equestrian lifestyle as buffalo hunters. They lived in permanent villages and cultivated the soil in addition to hunting and gathering.

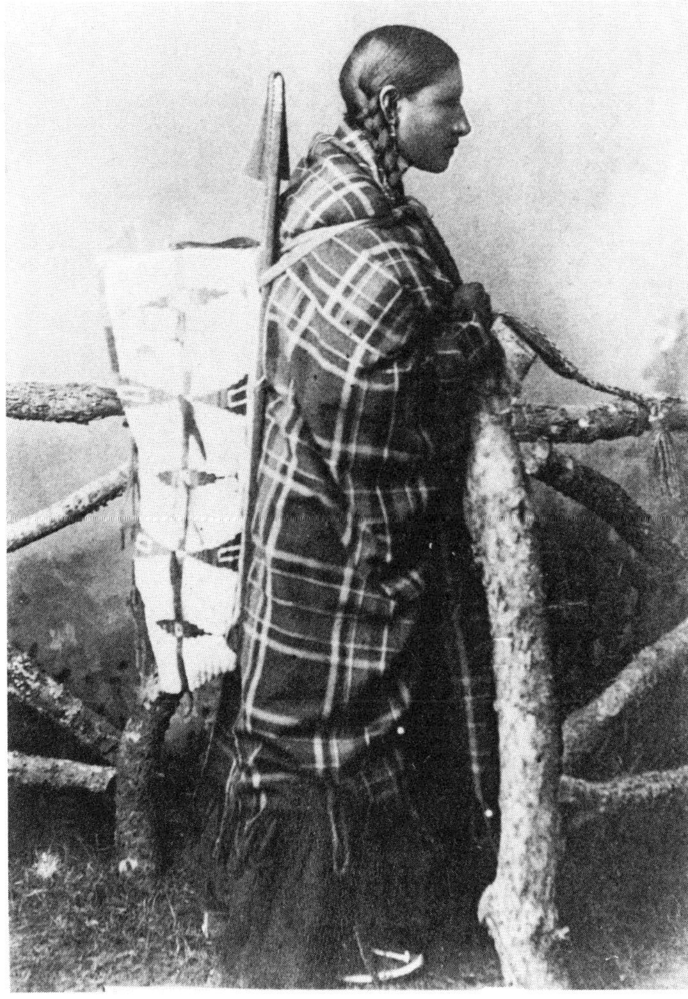

Emma Walters, Cheyenne, with baby in a cradleboard, undated. Courtesy of the Noah H. Rose Photograph Collection, Western History Collections, University of Oklahoma (Rose 1076).

The Cheyenne political system had two subdivisions—war and peace, with a war chief and a peace chief. Trading, supervising trade, adjudicating disputes, and leading the nation's bands were the peace chief's responsibility. When war was threatened, the war chief controlled the nation.

Daily work was done by women, organized into matrilineal lines. Women owned the tipis, furnishings, and horses. Cheyenne women were organized into guilds that honored the women. The Cheyenne society practiced sororal polygyny. If a man died, his brother was required to marry his widow. If a woman died, an unmarried sister was required to marry her widower. If there were no unmarried sisters, a married sister adopted the children to maintain the ties between the families.

Separation of the tribe into northern and southern divisions was forced by the U.S. government in the early nineteenth century. The Northern and Southern Cheyennes regarded themselves as one tribe with ten different bands. In 1867, the Southern Cheyennes were assigned to a reservation in Indian Territory with the Southern Arapahos. During this period, several Cheyenne bands were still fighting for freedom, but eventually all bands were confined to reservations. In 1878, Dull Knife and several different band members fought the U.S. military. The Tongue River Indian Reservation was established, and the U.S. government began to refer to this group as the Northern Cheyenne. Modern-day Northern Cheyennes live on a reservation in eastern Montana, and Southern Cheyennes share federal trust lands with the Southern Arapahos in Oklahoma.

Cradles

Two types of cradle have been identified as Cheyenne: the lattice cradles and soft hoods. The cradleboard was called *pȧhoešestȯtse*, and the soft hood cradle, *hóhkėha'e.*[1] In 1941, Victor F. Lotrich recorded Southern Cheyenne word for cradleboard as *päh-chĭst-to͝ots*, and the Northern Cheyenne word as *pä-šis'-toz*, or *ve-ce-vox-ca* to refer to the soft cradle. The term pä-šis'-toz meant "'cuddle' and was so called because the carrier was well made for the comfort and the protection of the baby. It was generally used in the roaming days of the Cheyenne when the baby was either carried on the horse's back or on the travois."[2] The lattice cradle was a V-shaped frame of pointed sticks, with a deep, straight beaded skin bag attached. Soft cradles were triangular hide hoods with a rectangular piece of hide or cloth sewn to the bottom of the decorated hood. The heavily quilled or beaded hood had a square tab projecting from the top of the back. The lower edges of the decorated section were drawn together to form a hood, and the cloth hung down to wrap the infant's body. The precise origin of the soft carrier is uncertain.

Triangular hooded baby carriers were associated with all the Cheyenne bands. Most soft cradles studied by Candace Greene had been collected among the Cheyennes in Oklahoma Territory. Only two carriers from the reservation period were made entirely of hide, though a smaller piece of hide was required for a hood. The increasing scarcity of hides large enough to make an entire cradle may have motivated the use of cloth for the carriers. Cloth also had the advantage of being more comfortable than hide in the warmer Oklahoma climate of the Southern Cheyennes.[3]

In the second half of the nineteenth century, glass beads became plentiful on the plains; therefore, glass trade beads mostly replaced quills as an embroidery medium. The tradition of quillwork was continued in the formation of beading societies. The work of women's craft societies had all been formerly done with quills, grasses, fine roots, cornstalks, and painting. A piece of work must be done in a prescribed ceremonial fashion and under instruction. Women selected for the societies were usually elderly, those who knew the patterns and understood the meanings of the different designs. The selected ones "had strict rules in their designs and they kept secret the meaning and arrangement of the colors, as well as the relation of the design to each other. The designs were always symbolic and talismanic, representing concrete, organic objects, whereas the colors were more emblematic of the abstract in creatures and creation."[4] Cheyenne women's craft guilds were formalized, and recognition was won for producing various objects as it was for "coup counting" among the men. Membership in a guild was a mark of social prestige for Cheyenne women. They gathered for a certain purpose: either social or religious. Particular standards of membership and workmanship were religiously adhered to. Articles might be made by any woman, but the allocation of certain designs to them was the prerogative of the guild. The work was done in fulfillment of a beneficial vow, such as for an easy delivery in childbirth.[5]

The women in John Sipe's family, of Norman, Oklahoma, all beaded. Cleo Wilson Sipe (Red Feather), John's mother, followed the family tradition of beading passed on by his grandmother Mattie Standing Bird (Living Woman), great-grandmother Measure Woman Standing Bird (Tah-neh), and great-great-grandmother Mochis (Buffalo Calf Woman). Sipe's living room is decorated with aged photographs, a testimony to the pride of his Cheyenne lineage. One of the photographs is of a fully beaded cradleboard with Cleo, or Red Feather, snuggled in and laced to the cradle. Mattie Standing Bird had beaded the cradleboard. The family's beading tools are displayed in a glass case: assorted sizes of awls, beeswax, a roll of sinew, spool of thread, and large scissors. Beeswax was used to keep the thread or sinew from tangling, and the awl was sharpened by sticking it in the dirt.[6]

The Cheyennes embroidered in glass seed beads, using the lazy stitch and sinew sewn to cover large areas of background. Simple geometric units of blue, red, green, and yellow would be beaded on a typically white background. Geometric designs of stepped triangles, rectangles, and bars were popular. Cheyenne stitches lie flat against the hide or cloth, and the rows line up evenly through an entire piece, because of the technique of looping the thread at the end of one lazy-stitch row around the last bead in the previous row, then pulling the current row tight. This technical precision, with care in choosing color and design, has earned Cheyenne craftswomen the reputation of being among the finest Plains beadworkers.

SOFT HOOD CRADLE

The soft cradle of the Cheyennes, as well as the cradle wrappers of other central and southern Plains tribes, was typically used without a board. Cheyenne mothers used these cradles as soft, protective wrapping for their infants. The carriers, which gained shape when wrapped around a baby, were also convenient for carrying a child in the arms. The soft cradles were decorated with beadwork and/or quillwork and were productions of the women's societies.

The carrier would have been made with a rectangular piece of tanned buckskin or canvas and a much smaller rectangle of stiff rawhide. The buckskin was usually made of antelope. Early wrappers were made with a single piece of buckskin. The triangular form hood and the design layout identify particular carriers as Cheyenne.

The soft hood cradle was cut to fit the shape of the triangular hood, or the upper corners may have been folded in to achieve triangular forms. The hood was often lined. The stiff rectangular piece of rawhide was inserted into the seam joining the wrapper and the hood. The tab at the peak of the hood, usually three square inches, would have been held upright by the pressure of the child's head against the portion inside the wrapper. Tabs were always decorated with solid beading, usually with beaded trifurcated pendants at the corners. The tab may have also been decorated with hide fringe, metal bells, ribbons, brass beads, tubular glass beads, tin cones, feathers, cowrie shells, or horsehair.

The stiff hood was arched around to protect the baby's face. The bottom of the carrier was folded up over the baby's lower legs; then the sides were folded in to overlap in front. Finally, a separate thong was used to tie the carrier snugly around the baby.[7]

The Cheyennes used sinew or thread for their lazy-stitch beadwork. The beadwork lanes lay flat on the surface of the hide, executed in wide lanes of alternating colors. Most soft cradles had a series of dark and light transverse stripes, broken at the center by a slightly converging band that extended from rim to tab. Small geometric motifs, such as crosses, diamonds, or stepped triangles, sometimes appeared in the central or side field.[8] In Greene's study of soft cradles, a few hoods were decorated in transverse stripes of cowrie shells, ribbon appliqué, or sequins rather than beads.

Richard Green studied the Cheyenne cradle cover in 1990 and found that the range of bead colors characteristically used in Cheyenne beadwork included "white, transparent dark green, dark blue, rose-inside-white, corn yellow, pink, medium green, light blue, pumpkin orange and black. The Cheyenne employed a relatively small palette of colors on the soft cradles."[9]

LATTICE CRADLEBOARD

The Cheyenne cradleboard consisted of a wooden lattice frame, a beaded cover of soft buckskin, lashing, carrying strap, bed covering, decorative items, and protective amulets. The framework's two pointed wooden staves were vertical and spaced wider at the head, with two short crosspieces at the head and at the foot. The vertical boards were decorated with brass tacks toward the top, and often the boards were painted.

After a thorough study of Cheyenne cradleboards, Mike Kostelnik was able to formulate a conceptual model for a nineteenth-century Cheyenne cradleboard. He created a cradleboard in 1987 that emulated a cradle from the Smithsonian collections, then provided detailed instructions in his article "Nineteenth-Century Cheyenne Cradleboard: One Step at a Time."[10]

Kostelnik found in his study that the beaded cover was a rectangular piece of soft brain-tanned buckskin, buffalo, elk, or deer hide. The cover dimensions were typically 60 to 65 inches long and 10 to 12 inches wide. Portions of the buckskin were left unbeaded, such as the four edges for 3 inches along the bottom, 0.5 to 1 inch along the top, and 3 inches along the short ends. This made the beaded area approximately 57 by 8 inches before assembly of the cradle. The 3-inch unbeaded bottom segment was punched with holes, used to attach the cover to the frame. The 1-inch top edge was folded over after the cover was assembled and was wrap beaded to form the decorative cradle rim. Beadwork on the rim was normally patterned in a contrasting color to the background.

Cheyennes seemed to commonly use nine design elements to cover the background field. The lanes of beadwork consisted of seventeen, nineteen, or twenty-one lanes, varying 0.5 to 0.6 inches wide. "The bead worker used whatever number was required to maintain a relatively constant row width. With an odd number of bead lanes, the design elements could be centered symmetrically on the cradle cover. It is a very common Cheyenne practice to have this center lane beaded in red (white core rose, white-heart) beads the full 63 inches of length, centrally separating the beaded field."[11] The middle design element centered on the baby's head, with four design elements on each side, evenly spaced. The number four and its multiples were sacred to Cheyennes, and a minor emphasis was placed on the number seven.[12]

The typical white background provided a strong color contrast to the dark navy blue, light blue, dark green, rose, and yellow beads that were commonly used. Two design elements traditionally used on Cheyenne cradleboards were the triangle, or "tipi," and the closed rectangle. These elements were usually stepped instead of straight edged, and the elements came out to the edge of the beadwork.

Boards for the frame were 0.4- to 0.6-inch planks made from softwoods or hardwoods. The frame consisted of four boards—two long pointed vertical boards, and two shorter crosspieces. The pointed boards were spaced wider at the head. Cheyenne cradleboards were traditionally decorated with brass brads in geometric patterns. Some were inscribed with patterns and painted or decorated with German silver ornaments or silk ribbon steamers.

The cradle base was a simple pad shaped to the dimensions of the frame. A pad could be folded cloth, rawhide, canvas, or a painted piece of parfleche. Holes were punched through the material to match the holes drilled in the frame. All the holes were aligned on the boards, cover, and pad. Then the cover was laced into place with buckskin thongs.

A rectangular piece of rawhide added reinforcement to the top of the cover, making a firm shaped opening for the baby's head. It was inserted inside the beaded cover, under the lining. Cradles were usually lined with colorful calico cloth. During the nineteenth century, traders carried various colors and patterns. Three or four sets of tie thongs were sewn down on each side of the cover's front, on the rim, 3 or 4 inches apart.[13]

Cheyenne mothers used various materials to decorate the cradles, including elk teeth, dentalium shells, hawk bells, necklace beads, amulets, and silk ribbons. The father's sister usually made the cradle, but another woman relative of the father might make it. When the cradle was brought to the lodge and presented, the father would give the maker a gift. Often the gift would be a horse.[14]

The infant was placed in the cradleboard two or three months after birth. If the weather was cold or bad, the baby was carried in the mother's arms instead of laced on a baby board. "Old people say that in earlier days, when the tribe lived in lodges, and moved about on the prairies a large proportion of the children born in winter died."[15] As soon as an infant was strong enough, he or she was laced in the cradleboard. The mother's arms and hands were free to go about her day while staying near her baby. The baby board could be leaned against the lodge or hung on a lodge pole. If the mother was traveling, the cradleboard was carried on her back, hung on the mother's saddle, or swung on a travois pole.

Birth Customs

As soon as a baby was expected, a Cheyenne mother began to observe certain taboos to protect the new life. She would not stare at any unusual person, animal, or object for fear that her unborn child would be marked at birth. She would walk before sunrise, as Cheyennes believe that babies grew in the early dawn and that walking helped the baby grow. To prevent a hemorrhage following a birth, a woman was not to eat sour foods or meat for four days after she gave birth. Some women would eat soup made with dried, well-pounded meat.[16]

Guild members who had made a sacred vow were advised to put their beadwork aside if they became pregnant. The beadwork was stored in a safe place until after delivery. Sitting for long hours in a stooped, cramped position could injure the expectant mother or the child. The undetermined sex of the expected child was also a problem. Contact with an unborn male would have a serious effect on the work, as would contact with a male adult. Any man who violated the rules of the guild by touching or seeing the uncompleted beadwork or learning anything of the ceremonies might become deaf or be gored by a bull. Longevity and fertility were felt to be the greatest benefits for guild members. They were said to have been longer lived than other Cheyennes and to have had more children. A guild member could secure safe childbirth by a vow of sacred beadwork.[17]

The birth, which took place in a special hut or in the mother's home tipi, was attended by female relatives of the mother. She knelt and grasped a sturdy upright pole planted in front of her. A medicine man or woman might be called in to give the expectant woman *Balsamorhiza sagittata*, or bark medicine, from time to time so that she would have an easy delivery.[18] After delivery, one of the women tickled the mother's throat with a feather to make her expel the placenta. The afterbirth was tied in a bag, and the father took it out of camp and hung it in a tree. To bury it, the Cheyennes believed, might cause the death of the newborn. When the navel cord had been cut and dried, the mother saved the cord in a small leather pouch. Midwives preserved a special flint knife for that purpose. The blood was squeezed out of the umbilical cord, which was wrapped around the midwife's finger and cut off short. The umbilical cord area was dusted with spores of the puffball fungus, or prairie mushroom. The infant was greased and powdered with finely ground, dried buffalo dung or decaying cottonwood pulp. The newborn was washed, wrapped in a soft cloth, and placed in the soft cradle. The husband's mother and female relatives were in charge of the child for the first ten days.[19]

Sipe's mother Cleo Wilson was born in a tent on the Standing Bird allotment on Turtle Creek near Clinton, Oklahoma, in 1931. When she was born, her great-aunts were making bread. They had to stop and attend to Cleo, and she ended up with flour all over her when the great-aunts picked her up and held her.[20]

Babies were cherished by the tribe, and all children were welcomed and loved. The birth of boys was especially celebrated for they represented potential warrior strength. Twins were not desired but accepted. No supernatural power was attached to them. They had to be treated exactly alike to prevent any jealousy. If one twin was less well treated, he or she might become ill and die. According to Fred Eggan, twins were two spirits who traveled together and decided to go into the same mother. The Cheyennes seemed to have a belief in spirit children who enter the mother. The spirits could be long-dead children or old people who wished to return as children. Children belonged to the mother because they came from the mother. The husband "really has no part in the child, but it is his child because he is the husband."[21]

When the infant was strong enough, the father would give away presents. A horse was usually given to every relative that made a cradle. An elderly relative of the father usually named the newborn baby a few days after the birth. It was customary for a paternal relative to declare a name for the child before the birth. A boy was usually named after the father's brother or some older male relative, a girl after her father's sister or grandmother. A boy name might be drawn from an animal or a physical attribute with an added descriptive word or phrase. A girl's name usually included the word "woman" in the name. It was considered an honor to have one's name chosen for a child. The person honored would give the baby a present and usually look after the child until he or she reached maturity.[22]

Amulet

The navel cord was of crucial importance to the Cheyennes. They believed it represented the child's connection to both the family and the tribe, as well as a link between the baby's existence before birth and the child's life after birth. The navel cord was dried, wrapped in herbs, placed inside a small leather bag, and worn throughout childhood. The charm was thought to guide behavior. The Cheyennes often said restless children was looking for their misplaced navel bags. It was said that children who did not have their navel cords prepared in the traditional way would always be searching for their souls.

The little bags were attached to the cradle as the baby's first toy, and then later worn around the child's neck or tied to clothing up to the age of six or seven years. The amulet was kept for a lifetime as a charm to ensure long life. Often two amulets were made for an infant. The "real" amulet containing the dried umbilical cord was placed next to the baby's heart inside the cradleboard. The false amulet was attached to the cradleboard. The false amulet was made to protect the child from spirits.[23]

To make the amulets, two small pieces of soft buckskin were sewn together with one edge open. They were usually quilled or beaded on the top and decorated with fringe, horsehair, and metal cones. A thong strip was stitched on the backside, used for hanging the amulet on the cradleboard and later around the neck of the child. The navel cord was dried and sewn into the little bag, which was stuffed with sweet grass. Often the amulets had the shape of a lizard or turtle, or a trapezoidal shape that represented one of the animals. The lizard, for the girl, typifies activity and swift motion. It is never quiet for long. The lizard can endure heat and goes without water. A boy's amulet was in the shape of the turtle. A turtle's heart will continue to beat after it dies. It was a powerful war charm and gave courage to one who wore its image.[24]

Cheyenne Cradle Symbolism

Cradle symbolism information is limited for the Cheyenne. Designs appeared not to be related to the gender of the child, as cradles were usually made before birth. During Candace Greene's research with the soft cradle, she told of the only published reference, appearing in P. Ehrenreich in 1889, and an English version in Franz Boas's *Primitive Art* (1955). Greene wrote,

> The symbolic interpretation of the cradle appears to be focused on the child and contains anthropomorphic elements as well as references to the course of life. According to Ehrenreich's informants, the convergent central band on the hood represents the path of life of the child, alternating colors on the edge of the hood represents the child's age, and the figure in the center of the front of the tab is the child's heart. The trifurcated pendants on each side of the tab are the child's ears, and the bead fringe in the back was hair.[25]

Sacred colors for the Cheyenne were blue, yellow, red, green, and white. Two especially important colors were red and yellow, representing the life-giving powers of the sun and earth. Red was for warmth, food, blood, and home, and amber yellow for ripeness, perfection, and beauty, as in sunsets.

A child is born and life begins within the circle of the family. The circle represents creation, respect, tradition, and harmony. The Cheyennes follow the path of life at birth, a never-ending circle of life for women from childhood through puberty, womanhood, and old age. The female is at the center of the sacred circle. A woman placed great emphasis on her family; the mother, aunts, sisters, and grandmothers shared in raising the child, and family ties continued to be important throughout life. The birth of a child was a joyous event in a family, and the child was never excluded in the world of adults.[26]

Cheyenne Soft Hood Cradle

A typical Cheyenne cradle hood is found at the Smithsonian Institution, Department of Anthropology (plate 19). The cradle is 40 inches long and 17 inches wide. Embroidered with glass seed beads, the triangular hide hood is lazy stitched in medium green and yellow striping. A rectangular piece of parfleche is inserted under the top, extending outward to form a square back tab. The center has blue, navy, and red on a yellow background; the tab is yellow with blue, red, white, and navy; the hood edge is green with blue, red, and white stripes. The lower section is canvas. The small units of geometric designs are typical of a Cheyenne soft

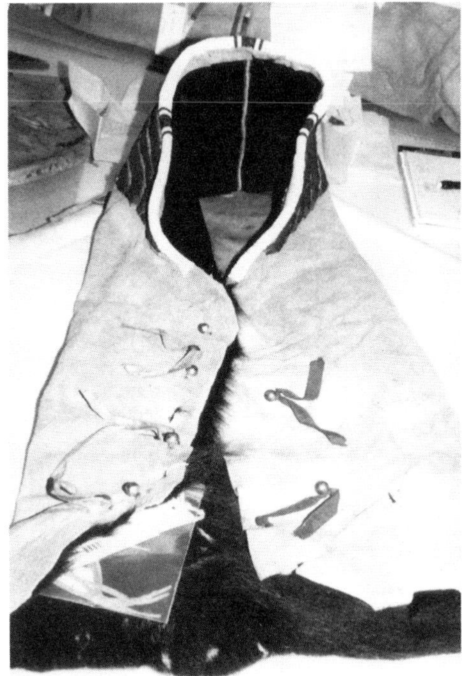

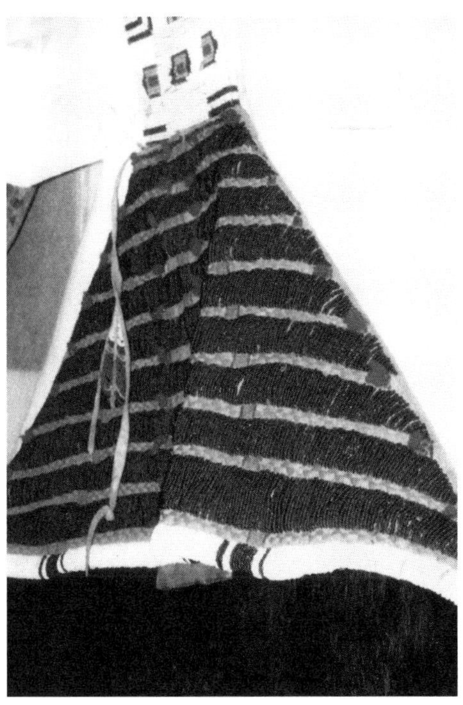

Cheyenne soft cradle, 35 inches long. Collected in 1892 by James Mooney. Photographs by the author. Courtesy of the Department of Anthropology, Smithsonian Institution, Suitland, Maryland (E152804-0).

hood. The four corner squares used on the tab represent the sacred number four.

I examined another soft hood cradle at the Smithsonian (cat. no. E152804-0). James Mooney collected it in 1892 at the Cheyenne-Arapaho Reservation in Oklahoma Territory. The Bureau of Ethnology National Museum, Washington, D.C., purchased it, and it is now stored in the Smithsonian's Department of Anthropology.

The cradle is 35 inches long and 26.5 inches wide (unfolded); the hood is 9.5 inches long; and the beaded tab and the rawhide stripe are each 9.5 inches long and 3.75 inches wide. The soft cradle covering is a rectangular piece of light tan dog hide with black fur turned to the inside. The hood is decorated with rows of glass beads, plant matter (possibly cornhusk), dyed yellow-orange embroidery, and tufts of red wool thread. Narrow strips of silk ribbon are attached to each of six brass buttons laid out in two rows. The plant embroidery quillwork is yellow, orange, red, and black. The triangular hood has beaded lines of dark green glass, with a rounded edge of white and green beads. The tab at the top is beaded in white, dark green, yellow, and red seed beads. There is no rigid frame, and no holes, indicating that the soft cradle was made to hold the infant in the arms or lap.

The rectangular skin is placed flat, then two top corners are folded down, creating the hood. The middle section, 3.5 inches wide, is left open at the top. The triangular fold extends down 9.5 inches. These two pieces are stitched together, forming a triangular hood with a 3.5-inch opening at the top. A stiff rawhide strip, 3.5 inches wide and 9.5 inches long, is placed at the back of the hide, with the strip slipped through the opening and extending 3.75 inches above the hood.

Brass button spacing suggests that two buttons are missing. There should be four buttons on each side. Faded red and blue narrow silk ribbons are used to close the edges together.

The decorations on the hood are the typical Cheyenne design of stripe decorations sewn in beads. Cheyenne women started beading the stripe design in 1870. Nine wide rows of transparent dark green glass beads alternate with ten narrow stripes of hide decorated with a quill pattern.

Nine wide lazy-stitch beadwork lanes lie flat on the surface of the hide. To produce the lazy stitch, two small holes are punched with a needle or awl through the surface of the hide, and then tied with a knot at the end of a strand of sinew. A predetermined number of beads are added to the thread. Then the sinew is secured by punching two more holes in the hide. The predetermined number beads is usually from five to nine, to produce the rows and to secure them. Bands of the beads are continued until the design is produced. The last beaded lane is white with three vertical bands of dark green beads on the rolled edge.

The quillwork is a single-thread sawtooth technique. The pattern is done with an unidentified vegetable fiber dyed yellow-orange, red, and black. The single-thread sawtooth technique has a great deal of visual appeal. The lanes of the quill pattern are interrupted with tufts of wool thread sewn to the end of a vertical design. The interruptions in the quillwork create the central design. The red tufts are sewn at the end of each narrow stripe, forming four vertical rows of red tufts. The sawtooth patterns are interrupted by rectangles of vertical rows alternating black and red. Black quillwork and tufts of wool thread sewn into the narrow strip of hide are similar in design to other Cheyenne covers, in which separate central designs interrupt the stripe design.

The tab of heavy rawhide extends from the top of the triangle. In some cases, the tab may be an extension of the rawhide reinforcement to the cover or a separate insert projecting into the back of the cover. The tab is beaded with narrow bands of lazy stitch running horizontally with seed beads. The rectangular tab has the typical square corner blocks with transparent dark green glass beads. The central design is rectangular with triangles of yellow, red, and green. The corner squares are repeated at the top, left to right. The bottom corners have two green stripes at each corner.

The bottom right of the tab is adorned with a beaded pendant. The pendant is a piece of rawhide split in three parts about halfway down and decorated with dark blue, light blue, red, and white seed beads. Pendants are usually placed on each side at the bottom of the tab; therefore, one pendant was likely lost over the years.

The beadwork and design are typical of the overall design, done in flat lazy-stitch beadwork. The stripe design, usually of two alternating colors, most often transparent dark green and white, is instead alternating one narrow strip of hide embroidered with quills in the sawtooth pattern with a wide lane of lazy stitched dark green. Other beading colors are white, red, light blue, dark blue, and corn yellow. The plant quills are dyed yellow-orange, black, and red. The small palette of color used is typical of Cheyenne designs. The cradle hood is usually done in three sections: the heavily beaded hood, the tab, and then the cloth wrapping.

Cheyenne Lattice Cradleboard

A Northern Cheyenne cradleboard, circa 1890, at the Buffalo Bill Center of the West, in Cody, Wyoming (cat. no. NA.111.2), is a typical lattice board, 47 inches long and 10 inches wide, narrowing to 5.25 inches at the bottom. The cradle is of buckskin, wood, seed beads, trade cloth, brass tacks, and cotton cloth. The tanned hide has a fully beaded geometric design on a white background, done in lazy stitch. It is lined with red trade cloth and has buckskin lacing. The wood frame is decorated with brass tacks.

Another Cheyenne lattice cradleboard is located at the Museum of the Red River, in Idabel, Oklahoma (cat. no. 04 204). The cradleboard is 40 inches long and 10.5 inches wide, made of tanned hide, wood, seed beads, cotton cloth, brass tacks, hawk bells, and silk ribbon. The baby bag is fully beaded in lazy stitch, in stepped geometric designs: a dark blue, red, and green-white background with a red stripe. Lined in red cotton, the bag is laced with buckskin thongs and has a 7-inch-wide band of buckskin at the bottom of the beadwork. There is a beaded tab on top of the hood. A recycled piece of parfleche is used for a pad on the frame. Rawhide thongs on each side of the frame are used to attach a carrying strap. The cradle appears to have been a soft hood cradle, lengthened by a piece of buckskin on the bottom, and laced to a pad and wooden frame.

CHAPTER 23

TONKAWA

Tonkawa (Tickanwatic) Indians were multiple small, independent subtribes that united in the eighteenth century. They lived in a region that extended west from what is currently known as south Texas and western Oklahoma to eastern New Mexico. Evidence suggests that the Tonkawa proper had migrated from the high plains to Texas in the seventeenth century. Little is known of the social and political organization before the consolidation. The name, Tonkawa (Tonkaweya), was a Waco term meaning They Stay Together. The Tonkawas' language belongs to the Tonkawan linguistic family. Their name for themselves is Tickanwatic, meaning Real People.[1]

The Tonkawas had a Plains culture, subsisting on buffalo, small game, fishing, and gathering. Maternal clans were the basic unit in their society, with children becoming members of the mother's clan, and the husband living with his wife's clan, within family groups. Tonkawas lived in small conical hide tipis until the buffalo became scarce, at which point they started living in more permanent structures covered with brush.

The Tonkawas were staunch allies of the English-speaking settlers in Texas, serving as scouts for the Texas Rangers and the U.S. Army. In 1884, the Tonkawa tribe and some Lipan Apaches were moved to the old Nez Perce reservation at Fort Oakland in Indian Territory. In 1891, they were forced to accept allotments of land. The annual powwow now coincides with end of the Tonkawa Trail of Tears, June 30, 1885, when they reached Oakland after a final long and arduous forced relocation from their homelands.

Cradles

Little is known of Tonkawa infancy and training of children. Soon after birth, a baby was placed on a cradleboard, to which the mother tied a thin board over the infant's forehead to flatten it into a slope. Babies stayed in the cradleboard until they were a year and half old, or until the forehead was sufficiently flattened.[2] The Tonkawa term for a cradle or cradleboard is elusive, but a combination of terms conveys the meaning: *t'ca-bxan* (sleeping place) and *wi'xwan* (small one), a term used to refer specifically to a child.[3]

I photographed and examined two cradleboards at the Tonkawa Tribal Museum and the McCarter Museum of Tonkawa History, both in Tonkawa, Oklahoma. Don Patterson, Tonkawa historian, shared information with me on both cradleboards. The cradles are of the newer type: the lattice. One cradle, a miniature, is similar to the Comanche style, and the other is similar to a beaded Cheyenne soft cradle. The miniature cradle is a classic Comanche-type cradle of muslin, lined with velvet, laced to a lattice frame. The McCarter museum had no information on the Comanche-style miniature cradleboard's history. It was possibly a trade item or gift.

Tonkawas began using lattice cradleboards while living on reservations in Oklahoma Territory, around the same time and circumstances in which Cheyennes and Kiowas began using the style. Patterson described the lattice as a wooden frame of four narrow boards, the longest two with sharpened points, and the other two as crosspieces holding the long boards together. The frame was padded with some kind of thick material for the baby's comfort. Buckskin or some other durable material was tacked around the outer edges to the wood. Holes near the edges along both sides of the material were used with thongs to lace the sides together like a shoe. The baby was wrapped in a blanket before being placed in the cradle. The canopy formed a hood around the baby's head. The hood was attached to the horizontal bar at the top of the frame, which formed the hood into a bonnet shape.[4]

The soft cradle (plate 24) has beadwork on the triangular field sewn with seed beads and sinew on heavy, hard rawhide. The back interior of the hood is covered with calico. A 4-inch square is sewn above the peak of the hood. This rawhide tab starts 3 inches below the top seam and is designed to stand up. Twelve wide stripes of white beads cover the front of the hood, divided by six narrow transverse stripes of red. Each white stripe ends with bright green beadwork. A 7-inch central design breaks the transverse stripes with concentric circles in alternating bright green and white, overlaid with a four-directions design in red and blue. The outer circle with red beading on white completes the design.

The tab is beaded in white with red and blue seed beads. Four corners of the tab are done in the traditional Cheyenne style. The bottom corners of the tab are decorated with trifurcated beaded pendants, with hawk bells attached to amuse the baby.

Birth Customs

Tonkawa ritual and social activities connected with childbirth were minimal or not recorded. Parturition lodges were used for the delivery. "Women bore their children alone in a separate special brush hut. A rope hung from the center of the hut where the woman in labor would clutch for support. The new mother bathed in a stream within a day. They also painted their faces with white clay."[5] A few taboos on parental behavior were recorded. Before a child was born, the father was not to touch any bird, nor break open the bones of animals for marrow, or the child might be born with weak legs. The parents of a newborn baby did not smoke or use firearms for four days because Tonkawas believed that smoke would cause the child to have weak eyes.

Tonkawa Cradle Symbolism

The large circle on the canopy of plate 24 represents the circle of life, with the four sacred directions. The symbol on each side of the tab is a talisman often beaded on cradles and on women's items, such as moccasins and leggings: two right-angled triangles standing on the same line, their acute angles facing each other, with a bar on the line between the triangles.

The Tonkawa story of creation can be told with the beaded symbols found on a woman's knife case at the tribal museum, as Patterson explained:

> In Tonkawa mythology, the first humans [Tonkawans] were created at a place in Texas called La Tortuga, the turtle. This symbol represents the red steps going up and down: the Red Mountain. Man was in the blue diamond above the Red Mountain with one white bead within the yellow rectangle. Two dark blue baby symbols were on each side of the bottom point of the star. Completely beaded, the sides were identical and decorated with tin cones on short fringe across the bottom and four buckskin strings.[6]

CHAPTER 24

LAKOTA

The Sioux tribes shares a common language, social organization, and culture. By the early nineteenth century, there were three divisions with distinct dialects: Dakota, Lakota, and Nakota. The Western Council Fire comprises the Lakota (Lakȟóta) tribe, who are also known as the Teton (Thítȟuŋwaŋ) Sioux, including the seven Lakota bands: Oglála, Sicangu (Sičháŋǧu), Brulé, Hunkpapa (Húŋkpapȟa), Miniconjou (Mnikȟówožu), Itázipčho (or Sans Arc), and the Sihásapa. Lakotas were at the forefront of the westward movement of the Sioux, driving the Kiowas and Crows from the Black Hills area. The name Lakota means Friends (or Allies), and Teton means Dwellers on the Prairies. The Lakotas lived primarily along the Missouri River but ranged all over the western plains, from Colorado along the Rockies up to Canada.

The Lakotas evolved to the lifestyle of equestrian nomads living in tipis year round, following the buffalo and its migration. They subsisted by hunting and gathering. Bands were autonomous units, usually related, that separated into small groups in the winter. Each of the seven groups was recognized as a separate tribe, and the bands all came together for communal hunts and religious ceremonies in the summer. The basic unit of Lakota society was the small group of bilaterally related kin led by a headman. Each of the seven bands had societies that together formed a national council. Holy men and medicine men were consulted on important matters.

Attempts by the U.S. government to take the Black Hills, sacred to the Sioux, culminated in the Battle of the Little Bighorn in 1876. With buffalo gone from the region, starvation forced all the Sioux tribes to go to reservations or to southern Canada. The western Sioux were scattered over five reservations in South Dakota, North Dakota, and Montana. Lakotas to this day continue to speak their language and practice their traditions.

Cradles

The Lakota, like the Cheyenne, made and used two types of cradles: lattice cradleboard and soft cradle. The lattice cradleboard was a buckskin bag, decorated with beadwork and attached to a wooden frame. The soft cradle was a buckskin or cloth cover, tied in the front and decorated with quillwork or beadwork, with a tab on the top of the bag. Cradle production was the province of women, a visible symbol of female industry and achievement. Baby carriers and cradleboards, elaborately decorated, were a mark of respect in tribes with formalized women's craft societies, and this respect transferred to the production of various objects. The Lakota word denoting the decorated baby carrier was *pȟóštaŋ*; quilled cradle, *pȟóštaŋ ipátȟapi*; and beaded cradle, *pȟóštaŋ kšúpi*. The term for full-length cradleboards, like the lattice board, was *čhuwíč'iŋpa*, meaning literally "wood fastened one to another."[1]

The ancestral Sioux-style cradleboard of the Dakotas was lost during the migration to the plains area, during the Lakotas' early eighteenth-century separation from the Eastern Sioux. The early baby carriers of the Lakotas might have resembled those of other Siouan groups: a rectangular board type common to all of eastern North America. The rectangular cradleboard was used for an infant wrapped in hide then fastened to the board with a long, wide band of hide. A narrow board, bent into a U shape, was fastened to the top of the main board, forming a hoop, or bow. The bow protected the baby's head in case the cradle fell forward. Nineteenth-century observers of the Eastern Sioux described in writing and depicted in drawings Siouan cradleboards (see the Santee Dakota cradleboards discussed in chapter 3). During the period of separation, however, the wide cradleboard disappeared from use among Lakotas.[2]

The father's sisters, or a female relative, were obligated to make the cradle. Shortly after the birth of the newborn, the maker presented the cradle to the baby's family. Cradleboard making was a symbol of sisterly respect and an opportunity for women to publicly show their abilities and handiwork. Royal Hassrick reported that They-Love-Her, the child of a large prominent family on the Rosebud Reservation in South Dakota, was presented with a total of twenty-two beaded cradles at her birth: "The maker brought acclaim and even wealth since a cradle was equal in value to a horse. The rank of the family was enhanced by such lavish displays of gift giving."[3]

SOFT CRADLE

In 1830 Prince Maximilian noted the use of leather baby bags by the Mandans, Sioux, and Assiniboines during his travels in North America. He observed that the bags were sometimes hung from the beam of an earth lodge and commented, "These cradles of the Mandan are not so elegant and beautifully worked as those we saw among the Sioux and Assiniboins."[4] The Lakota baby bundle was made the same for both sexes, with no distinctions in form or decoration. The soft carrier was not carried on the mother's back. The carriers were folded around the child, much as a blanket is folded when swaddling a baby.

An early baby carrier made of buffalo hide, decorated with porcupine quills and pony beads, was collected by Lieutenant G. K. Warren in 1855 from the site of Little Thunder's village and the Battle at the Blue Water Creek. Lt. Warren donated the cradle, along with a toy cradle he had also collection, to the Smithsonian Institution. The toy cradle is 10 inches long and 5 inches wide, and the full-size cradle is 29 inches long and 32 inches wide.

Candace Greene found that the Sioux soft cradles are based on a rectangular pattern for all the components, including the hood, tab, interior tab extension, and back. In a schematic drawing, Greene represents a carrier made completely of hide, with a separate panel on the back, a tab, and an interior extension. The rectangular carriers "gain shape only when wrapped around a bundled baby[,] and little of their form or beauty can be appreciated when they are flattened and folded."[5] Most Sioux soft carriers have a separate panel in the back, although some have a variant form, joined with a central back seam carriers instead of the panel. Some soft carriers have cloth wrappers at varying lengths, and many have a cloth lining for comfort. Some soft carriers were completely beaded. Completely beaded cradles were usually tied together in the front and bottom with a series of thongs attached in pairs along facing front edges.

Rawhide tabs were usually about 5 inches square. The tabs were variable in form, but all typically terminated with long fringe. "Some tabs are of rawhide designed to stand upright while others are of soft tanned skin and hang pendant[s]. Upright tabs are stitched to a rawhide extension inside the carrier, which provides leverage to help hold them in a vertical position."[6] Some quilled cradles had tabs with quill-wrapped rawhide slats. A few had beaded wrapped slats, some heavily beaded; however, all the tabs terminated in long buckskin fringe.

Quill and Beadwork

Quilled cradles were basically similar in construction to the fully beaded ones. The early quill pieces had geometric designs, with a greater use of quillwork stripes on a tanned background than in later cradles. A red background is by far the most common, but yellow and orange were also used. As Greene noted, "Quilled cradles typically have a series of spaced stripes or narrow bands parallel to the edge of the carrier. The stripes are broken on the top of the hood by the placement of other design motifs or a large section of solid figured quillwork, broader than the central band of its beaded counterpart."[7]

Lakota women developed extensive skills with quill embroidery, which required delicate dexterity. They formed quill societies through older craftswomen and passed down the stitch techniques to younger women. Quilling and painting were Lakotas' primary art expressions. Yet, the porcupine did not live on the plains, so Lakota women must have learned the art of quill embroidery in the East before the Sioux migrated onto the plains, where they obtained quills through trade with other tribes.

Before quills were applied to the embroidery, the quillworker softened them in her mouth to make them more workable. When she needed one, she would pull it out and flatten it with her teeth or fingernails. After the quills were sewn down, the craftswoman would sometimes use a "quill flatter," such as a piece of bone, to smooth out the quills. Enzymes in the saliva probably made the quills more pliable.[8]

Various vegetable substances and minerals were used to obtain dye materials. The quills were soaked or boiled with dye until the desired color was achieved. Aniline dyes were available by about 1880, when they were substituted for native dyes. Only four natural colors were used by the Lakotas before the aniline dyes: red derived from buffalo berry (*Lepargyraea*) and squaw berry (*Viburnum*), with dock root added for brighter color; yellow from wild sunflower or coneflower (*Ratibida columnaris*), boiled with decayed oak bark or cattail roots; black from wild grapes (*Vitis* spp.); brown from hickory nuts (*Hicoria ovata*) or black walnuts (*Juglans nigra*), which were used when wild grapes were not available.[9] After quills were washed, dyed, and sorted by size, they were stored in special containers.

According to Carrie A. Lyford, the Western Sioux women's typical sewing method was to use two or more lines of parallel stitching with quills folded back and forth across them. "The two threads, instead of being stretched taut in the air, are stretched through the buckskin, and the stitching goes on at the same time as the folding of the quills. Its effect is that of broad lines and bands, straight or slightly curving, and this banded appearance is characteristic of western Sioux quillwork." The main unit in Lakota quillwork was a narrow band. The short quills do not permit wide areas of embroidery. Designs were created by varying the color in each band according to a regular formula, or by building up larger designs by placing several bands close together, so that the sections united to form the complete pattern-created designs. Designs made by each woman were considered her personal property and were not to be copied.[10]

The traditional origin of quillwork was explained in the Oglála legend of the mythical Double Woman, or Deer Woman, Anukité, who taught humans the art of working with quills. Anukité came in a vision as a human but disappeared as a deer. The first woman who dreamed of the Double Woman learned the art in her vision, and in turn taught others how to use the quills.[11]

Around 1800, glass beads appeared in embroidery on the hides traders' brought in on their ponies. These pony beads were first used on bands in combination with quillwork. The bands were narrower than 6 inches and were solidly beaded with geometric designs similar to early quillwork designs. A few basic forms were arranged in various combinations, or design units: rectangles, bars, tall triangles, crosses, concentric squares, and diamonds. White and medium sky blue were the two colors most commonly used.

Small seed beads appeared on the plains in quantity around 1840, replacing the larger pony beads for embroidery. Lyford set the "first seed period" as 1840–70. Designs were much the same, with beadwork done in narrow bands to create geometric design elements and units: circles; tall figures; and triangular, K-shaped, and terraced figures in solid colors. Although various colors were available, Lakotas preferred red, blue, green, yellow, and white.[12]

Toward 1870, Lakota beadwork changed style and was marked by a profusion of beads and new design elements: thin lines, terraces, and forks spread out on a solid background. The design usually had a strong central figure, outlined forms, lines created with a straight edge, and ridged stitch work. According to Lyford, Sioux-type beadwork was a combination of the simple geometric forms, tall triangles, and K shapes reminiscent of the parfleche, along with delicate lines. Various design elements and units were combined in patterns and symmetrically doubled to fill the entire space. The white background, careful placement of figures, and colors chosen gave an effect of lightness even with massive forms. Lakota beadwork followed an increasing trend toward elaborate designs and overcrowded patterns. By about 1900, it was popular to bead life forms, such as elk, deer, horses, and men, as well as American flags. The old traditional geometric forms were abandoned.[13]

Common patterns have been given descriptive names by beadworkers, such as star, dragonfly, and tipi. Lyford found no evidence that the names have been standardized.

Individual women named their designs as they wished: a triangle may be a tipi or an arrow point. Designs have been received in dreams, yet naming designs did not always imply symbolism. The design might be for decorative value or for use especially for men or on certain objects. A design might possess symbolic implications just for women. Turtle and spider designs, for example, were used as protective symbols on baby carriers and cradles.

Embroidery with glass beads was done with the overlaid, spot-stitch, or lazy-stitch technique. The most common stitch used by Lakota women was the lazy stitch, which lent itself to geometric patterns. The lazy stitch was an easy method for covering large areas, like a cradle cover. The beads were applied in a series of short parallel rows, with a single thread passing through the material at the ends of the rows only. A given number of beads, from six to twelve, was strung on a thread of sinew, which was fastened to the buckskin by threading it through a perforation, made by an awl or needle, that does not go through to the underside of the skin, so no stitches show. Another hole was made to admit the sinew at the end of the row of beads. The same number of beads was again strung on the sinew, carried back to the starting point, and passed through another hole close to the first one. The pattern was made up of beads sewn down only at the ends at each row.

Rosemary Lessard, through her twenty-five-year association with the Sioux on the Rosebud Reservation, analyzed the decoration on a Lakota beaded soft cradle and helped readers visualize how the maker did it. The disassembled cradle spread out flat was one main piece: a long, wide beaded strip that forms the top and the sides. The beaded panel generally had seven designs. The central design, which would be at the top of the assembled cradle, frequently differed from the designs on the sides. "The whole pattern of designs on the beaded cradle is an ABA/B/ABA or ABA/C/ABA arrangement reading from one end of the beaded panel to the other. The next most frequent arrangement is that of the five designs per main panel in an AB/C/BA, an AB/A/BA or an AA/B/AA pattern. Use of only one repeated design is also found, leading to AAA/A/AAA and AA/A/AA arrangements."[14]

The design on the tab was different from the designs on the body of the cradle. The tab often had a border around three or four sides. One long edge of the beaded rectangle might have a line of beadwork going over the edge, for example, giving the front edge of the cradle a rounded look. Other decorative items found on soft cradles were trade bells, silk ribbons, and tufts of fluffy feather—usually red.

Turtle Lung woman told a story about some of the small ways a Lakota mother was always ensuring that her baby would be safe:

> The Lakota mother wrapped the infant in a soft deerskin blanket to keep it warm and covered its head in a small, soft tight-fitting cap similar to a baby bonnet. She did everything in her power to ensure the well-being of the *wakh'ayezala* (baby). . . . When the wakh'ayezala was a few weeks old, the mother put her into this soft deerskin pouch, no different from the soft womb that had been the baby's home for nine months. It gave the wakh'ayezala a sense of security, being swaddled and laced into the soft pouch.[15]

Lattice Cradleboard

Lakotas made and used lattice cradleboards with fully beaded baby bags on a wooden framework. I recorded lattice cradleboards at the Smithsonian Institution, the Buffalo Bill Center of the West (plate 23), and the Museum of the Plains Indians. The cradleboard has a V-shaped wooden frame consisting of two pointed boards, which are held in place vertically at the head and foot by two shorter crosspieces. Holes are drilled in the four pieces of wood for lacing the frame together and attaching the cover with buckskin thongs. The tops of the vertical (pointed) slats are usually decorated, such as with geometric patterns done with brass tacks, German silver disks, silk and ribbon streamers, sets of bead streamers and cowrie shells, and paint on the boards.

The cradle base is a pad of rawhide, cloth, or other material cut to fit the dimensions of the frame. The pad and beaded cover are laced to the frame. A hood support of shaped thick rawhide is inserted between the beaded cover and cloth lining to form a firm head opening and to provide protection for the baby's head. A row of wrapped beading hides the seams of the cover and lining. This beadwork was normally patterned in a contrasting color to the background. Three or four sets of thongs are attached down the front. The carrying strap, often a sturdy, wide, and long piece of leather, is attached to the upper crosspiece. The soft cover, often fully beaded, is attached to the frame, sometimes at just the top and bottom, making the cover easy to remove and use as a soft cradle. A thong is often laced through small slits near the end of the strip of unbeaded leather at the bottom and tied together to close the cover. Greene noted that "of all tabbed cradles, only eight examples of the Sioux-type found were attached to wooden frames. Four were on lattice frames constructed similarly to Sioux and Cheyenne cradleboard frames, but of narrower, lightweight slats with forked, rather than pointed tips. They also differ in method of attachment. While cradleboard sacks are usually tightly lashed to the frames along their length, these tabbed cradles are tied only at the top and bottom and could be easily removed."[16]

Birth Customs

According to Lakota belief, the White Buffalo Calf Maiden's charge was to be fruitful. The birth of a child was the fulfillment of a woman's role in Lakota society, for the birth of a child was the greatest gift.[17] The Lakota term for being pregnant is *iglúš'aka*, meaning that the expecting woman is "growing strong" or "strengthening herself."[18] A midwife or medicine woman assisted the mother in her tipi. Preparations for the birth included driving a sturdy wooden stake firmly into the ground at the rear of the tipi until the top of the stake was waist high. A clean square of deerskin was readied to catch the baby. During labor, the woman squatted at the stake, holding at the top, and pressed her knees against it. If the pain was too intense, she knelt on the ground. After the delivery, the new mother's abdomen was wrapped with a strip of deerskin, and she rested on her bed.[19] The afterbirth was wrapped with a piece of hide, taken far from camp, and placed high in a tree. It was never buried in the ground for that would invite death to the newborn.

The umbilical cord was severed about three inches from the newborn's stomach with a sharp knife, then tied off in several places with deer tendons. Buffalo grease was applied to the cord, which was then dusted with dry spores from the fungus powder of the prairie mushroom, or puffball. A strip of soft, clean deerskin was securely wrapped around the infant's stomach to hold the navel in place.

The infant was cleaned with sweet grass soaked in warm water or sage water and wiped with soft deerskin, then greased with buffalo fat. Sometimes the baby was symbolically painted with red ocher to signify that the child was from the Buffalo Calf People. The ocher kept the baby's skin soft.[20] After the bath, a relative of the same sex as the infant, a "good person" chosen for her or his outstanding character, breathed into the baby's mouth. It was believed that the person's touch would transfer his or her character to the newborn. The baby was named shortly after birth. Children were nursed for up to five years, and women believed it was a natural form of birth control, spacing their children.[21]

Midwives and medicine women had a special calling among the Lakotas, and some women were able to practice midwifery and doctoring with herbs and spirits. A shaman pierced the baby's ears in a public ceremony. This ritual was essential for proper upbringing. Small rawhide thongs were inserted to keep the holes open for earrings. Symbolically, it "opened a child's ears," making him or her capable of understanding and establishing the baby as a member of society.[22]

The birth of twins was a mysterious event, particularly sacred to the Oglálas. Twins were thought to wander the land seeking suitable parents to give birth to them. A woman who dreamed of twins or bore twins would be a good quillworker because Anukité, the Double Woman, had the power to influence artists. Lakotas believed that twins had to be treated in exactly the same way or one might return to the hills and die. According to Hassrick, the Sioux believed that sometimes the babies argued over who would be born first. "The stronger of the two always won the right to be eldest, but the other, being weaker, pouted after birth, was generally sickly, and frequently died." The Lakotas believed that a twin who dies will be born again in a different family, but that the twins would still recognize each other after rebirth.[23]

Amulet

During pregnancy, a woman's mother or grandmother made two small pouches: effigies of a lizard and of a turtle. Both animals were revered because they were difficult to kill and had long lives. Their protective power was enlisted as guardians and to guarantee the child's long life. Made of soft tanned skin sewn together and stuffed, these amulets were decorated with beadwork, quillwork, metal cones, or dyed horsehair. A slit was made on the underside for a thong, and then the slit was sewn together around the cord, which would be used to hang the amulet from the cradle. After the baby was born, the dried umbilical cord was placed inside the turtle, while the lizard served as a decoy to lure away malevolent forces. According to Turtle Lung Woman, the turtle amulet was the one that ensured long life. "The other was made in the shape of the lizard to ward off the dreaded Anúg Iité, who delighted in making newborns miserable with stomach and bowel ailments. The umbilical cord was kept in the turtle-shaped pouch. The lizard-shaped pouch was kept as a decoy for certain bad spirits that could harm the *Wakh'ayezala*, the small sacred being."[24] The effigy was a potent charm against the malevolence of the Woman of Two Faces (a.k.a. Double Woman), a mythical character who was responsible for the suffering of women.

Another reason for the little bags was to remind children that life is a precious gift from their parents, and that when children grow up, they have a responsibility to marry and pass on the gift of life to their own offspring. The bag was attached to the baby's cradle as a first toy and later worn around the child's neck or tied to clothing. The small pouch was known as a "carry your navel." Later, the little bag was put away, kept by the mother. Sometimes it was hung from a tipi wall. Turtle Lung Woman said the amulet was kept "by the person for whom it was made for. They did this for the children they cherished. If this was not done properly the child would spend his life searching for his umbilical cord."[25]

Lakota Cradle Symbolism

According to John Fire Lame Deer, from birth to death "we Indians are enfolded in symbols as in a blanket. An infant's cradle board is covered with designs to ensure a happy, healthy life for the child."[26] The red stripe on articles associated with women and cradles symbolized a life span. When Clark Wissler collected a quilled soft cover at the Pine Ridge Reservation in 1902, he attached a tag in his own handwriting reading "red quilled line span life."[27] Lattice cradleboards and soft cradles, for boys as well as girls, often had one red line running the length of the beaded cover. "The red line was also known as the 'trail on which woman travels' and was regarded as symbolic of that portion of a woman's life during which children may be born. Red lines or stripes on an article used by women were often associated with women's functions and virtues and symbolized the good life."[28]

Colors were significant in other ways as well. Lame Deer explained the importance, symbolism, and power of colors: "Black represents the west; red the north; yellow the east; white the south. Black is night, darkness, mystery, the sun that has gone. Red is the earth, the pipestone, the blood of the people. Yellow is the sun as it rises in the east to light the world. White is the snow. White is the glare of the sun in its zenith. Red, white, black, yellow—these are the true colors."[29]

The four cardinal directions were symbolically important for Lakotas, who shared the magic of numbers with many tribes. The significant symbol was often depicted as squares or rectangles with straight or concave sides and a line extending from each corner. The sacred number four also stands for the four winds, whose symbol was the cross. When used on a cradle, those designs were powerful symbols for an infant.[30]

The turtle was a common zoomorphic motif for the Lakota women's dresses and baby carriers. Many Plains groups share a creation story in which the first human life was carried safely through the water-covered world on the back of the turtle, on which dry land mass was subsequently created. "The turtle shared a close relationship to 'mother earth.' It was thought to exercise a beneficent influence on human reproduction, offering protection against the danger of child-bearing and of infancy."[31] The turtle design had power over disease, birth, and babies. Turtle amulets and turtle motifs are common protective ornamentation. The design representing the turtle was "a diamond with forked designs or two small right-angled triangles facing one another at the opposite ends, lengthwise of the diamond."[32]

Another powerful zoomorphic motif was the spider web, a symbol for the future good of the wearer. The Oglálas associated the web with the power to protect people from harm, as the spider web cannot be destroyed by bullets or arrows, which merely pass through it, leaving a hole. It represented the heavens, the four directions, the home of the winds and the thunder. Thunder was considered a friend of the spider, and thus the spider web symbol helped to protect the wearer from danger. Lines radiating from the four corners of a web are often lightning symbols.[33]

Sicangu Soft Cradle

I studied a soft cradle at the Gilcrease Museum (cat. no. 8426.739) that had been collected by Mrs. Garner on the Rosebud Sioux Reservation in the 1890s. The cradle is 31.25 inches long and 25.75 inches wide, a sinew-sewn rectangular animal hide with a red patterned calico lining. A 5-square-inch stiff rawhide tab is inserted between the front and back section at the top of the carrier. The hood fastens in front with three sets of thong ties and one tie anchored at the bottom middle of the back panel.

The soft cradle is completely beaded, front, back, and around the edges, in glass seed beads—red, green, yellow, and three shades of blue on a white background. Connected with thin red lines, the design elements are geometric: triangles, squares, bars, cut-out stepped triangles, and stepped diamonds. All colors are used in the main design. The tab design has four corner boxes and a central square inside the larger square, outlined with two contrasting colors. Within the middle square are small bars and rectangles, and outside that square, against a white background, small triangles and squares fill the space. The tab design differs slightly on the back. A strip of white fringe is stitched across the top of the tab. Seven pairs of red and yellow ribbons are attached across the front of the cradle. Trade bells are sewn to some of the ribbon sets. Some of the bells are missing

Oglála Cradleboard

I examined an Oglála lattice cradleboard with an AB/A/BA design, located in the Smithsonian's Anthropology Department (cat. no. E75472-0). Originally collected by Mrs. Anderson in the Black Hills of North Dakota, the cradle was sold to the Smithsonian on March 2, 1885, for six dollars.

The cradleboard is 45 inches long and 10 inches wide, with a V-shaped frame of four narrow boards, 0.5 inches thick, two long major boards, and two shorter crosspieces. The two longer boards are 43 inches long by 2.5 inches wide, tapering to 2 inches at the bottom. One end of each long board is carved to a point, with the other ends slightly rounded. The four pieces are laced firmly together with buckskin thongs, forming a rectangular frame. Four holes are drilled through each board so that holes line up when the crosspieces are

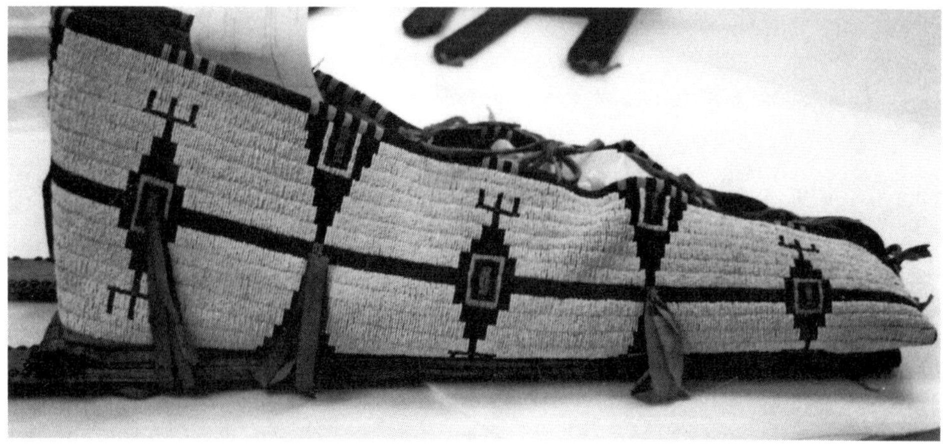

Oglála lattice cradle with an AB/A/BA design, 45 × 10 inches. Collected in the Black Hills and sold to the Smithsonian for six dollars on March 2, 1885. The sides, top, and tab are beaded with lazy stitch in geometric designs on white background. The designs elements are combinations typical of the late 1870s. Photograph by the author. Courtesy of the Department of Anthropology, Smithsonian Institution, Suitland, Maryland (E75472-0).

placed horizontally on the vertical pointed slats; buckskin thongs tie the board together. Ten evenly spaced holes are drilled in the center of the boards for attaching the cover.

The beaded cover is a rectangular tanned hide, 61 inches by 10 inches, with wrap beadwork along the rim. A strip of leather approximately 2 inches wide along the bottom is not beaded. This part is attached to the frame. A cover maker would usually leave about 1 inch unbeaded on the top edge of the cover, folding that section over after the cover is assembled.

The base is a pad of cloths several folds thick to fit the dimensions of the frame. The pad is laid on top of the frame, and holes are punched through the material to match the holes in the frame. The cover is laced in place with a buckskin thong, which is pulled through the cover, pad, and board, and then tightly tied to the frame.

A U-shaped piece of thick rawhide is inserted inside the beaded cover. The rawhide reinforces the cover and makes a firm shaped opening for the baby's head. The rawhide is 36 inches by 12 inches. The strip of buckskin at the top of the cover would have been folded over the rawhide hood. The lining is brown and tan plaid calico. The folded strip is sewn over one edge of the lining and the rawhide under the rim. During the nineteenth century, the calico used for cradles was available in a wide variety of colors and patterns, usually in pieces 25 to 27 inches wide. After the length of cloth is sewn to the cover, the bottom of the cloth is folded into the cradle to cover both the inside and bottom pad. Wrap beading runs the length of the cover from one end to the other. Five short thongs are stitched to the folded buckskin at the bottom of the cover. When tied, they form the footrest, which has a squared-off appearance. Four pairs of thong ties are attached, evenly spaced, down both sides of the cradle cover.

The carrying strap is missing. In *The Indian Tipi*, Reginald Laubin and Gladys Laubin illustrate what a Sioux carrying strap looks like and how it is attached. A length of leather long enough to go across the woman's shoulders and chest, just a little wider than the width of the top cross board, is attached before the frame is assembled. A slit the width of the crosspiece is made just before each end of the leather. The crosspiece is threaded through the two slits and laced to the frame.

The cradleboard was probably made in the period when Lakotas were making a profusion of completely beaded pieces. The beadwork follows the color scheme and designs attributed to Lakotas. A white background was almost universally used by Lakota beadworkers, although some cradles had sky blue backgrounds. Of five full-sized fully beaded cradles attributed to the Sioux that I examined at the Smithsonian, four are similar in construction, color scheme, and design. Only one (cat. no. E358409-0) had a sky blue background, wider color pattern, and different design.

The usual Lakota color palette was white, sky blue, dark blue, red, and yellow. The Oglála cradleboard cover is fully embroidered in glass seed beads, sinew sewn with the lazy stitch in seventeen lanes of beadwork, with the ninth being the red lane. The wrap bead lane is dark green with a yellow and dark blue stripe pattern at each motif.

The design motifs are units of simple forms: triangles, rectangles, squares, and simple forks with little elaboration. The pattern is strong and simple, giving an impression of openness, although the figures are quite large. The design elements are centered symmetrically on the cradle. Stepped triangles with filled elongated rectangles are outlined in two contrasting colors, with a fork on each end. There are five large pairs of triangles and six smaller diamonds. The first design motif is a diamond, followed by the triangles. This repeats, ending and starting with the diamonds. The third large triangle motif is in the middle of the hood. The red line interrupts the design.

Silk ribbon strips, 6 inches long and 0.75 inches wide, are attached together along each side of the cradle at the first, second, and fourth design. Red, yellow, and green ribbon streamers are affixed in the sky blue square on the red lane. The design at the top of the cradle also has ribbon streamers, but they are 9 inches long and folded in half. The pointed slats of the frame are painted yellow, with tacks outlining the boards. Two horizontal lines complete the design.

Comment on the Lakota Lattice Cradleboards

Rosemary and Dennis Lessard, after a twenty-five-year residence among the Lakotas on the Rosebud Reservation, tend to believe that the traditional Lakota-manufactured cradle, fully beaded or quilled with the small tab at the top, did not include the lattice-type wooden frame. Sioux attributions for wooden frame cradles constructed before the 1900s could have been the result of intermarriage and the blending of tribal preferences, rather than traditional Sioux manufacture. Fully beaded covers have often been mounted on a lattice frame by request of the buyer. This practice of mounting covers on a frame has enhanced some old soft cradles.

CHAPTER 25

ASSINIBOINE

The Assiniboines, Siouan people of the northern plains, call themselves the Nakota. Assiniboines in Canada, called the Stoneys, lived in and around the Morley Reserve west of Calgary, Alberta. Assiniboines separated from the Dakotas in the eighteenth century and spoke a distinct dialect. They inhabited an area from what is now the White Earth, Minnesota, to west of Sweet Grass, Montana, as well as roaming and living north of the U.S.-Canada border from the Hudson Bay to the Rocky Mountains. Their wintering grounds were the woodlands in Canada.

Assiniboine society was organized into autonomous bands, all subsisting primarily on buffalo. A clear division of labor between men and women was observed. In the late eighteenth century, the Sioux tribe separated, and the majority migrated south into the Missouri Valley, out of the woodlands and onto the prairie. Plains Crees and Ojibwas were close allies of the Assiniboines and provided protection against other Sioux, Arikaras, Cheyennes, Blackfeet, and Gros Ventres. The demand for buffalo hides and the expanding Métis and Sioux populations began to diminish the buffalo herds. By 1883, the buffalo were gone. The Assiniboines were settled on reservations at Fort Peck and Fort Belknap in Montana, and on four reserves in southern Saskatchewan.

Cradle Types

Assiniboine mothers used the moss bags, or baby bags, commonly found in the Northwest. Dry moss was packed around the baby, who was then wrapped with blankets or furs with only the face showing. The baby was tightly laced into a baby bag. "The buckskin cradle looked like miniature sleeping bags."[1] Like the soft cradles of other tribes, the Assiniboine baby bag was a rectangular piece of hide folded lengthwise, sewn together at the bottom, and then laced together at the sides. Holes were punched along each side, and one narrow thong was laced through the holes. Many baby bags were elaborately decorated with porcupine quills or beads. Prince Maximilian noted the use of baby bags in 1830 during his travel in North America. The leather bags hung from the house beams with leather straps. He commented that the Sioux and Assiniboine cradles were more "elegant and beautifully worked" than those of the Mandan. The cradle was an *iyók'iba*. "The word means 'to tuck in,' and not merely 'to tuck in' but 'to tuck in tightly.' The purpose is to make a tight neat bundle. When a baby was tucked into a cradle, his hands were also tucked in and only its face was exposed. In bad weather the face was also covered with a large shawl that was attached to the upper part of the cradle."[2] Edward Curtis's vocabulary for the Assiniboine baby bag was *yo-k'i-ba*.[3]

Edwin Denig commented on the Assiniboines' use of a moss bag:

> These Indians made a kind of sack with eyed holes in front of a sack of scarlet or blue cloth ornamented with beads and the child being is placed well wrapped all except the head, it is placed in the sack and strapped up. It is no doubt but this is the cause of their feet being straight, although they are not intoed, as one would judge by their manner of walking. We can offer no objection to this mode of caring for children. Their natural growth is not affected thereby. At least it is the only method they could adopt to answer in extremes of cold, heat and rain with infants on their backs.[4]

Cradleboards were often obtained through trade with the Plains Crees and Plains Ojibwas. Denig described the cradleboard used as "a flat board with a bow across the front where the head of the child is placed. A rim runs along the inside the size of the child, cloths were attached inside this rim to the boards or back, and the whole ornamented in various ways. The child is then bundled up, enclosed in the rim, and the covers strapped over it. This is carried on their back."[5] The cradleboard described is like the one the Ojibwas used, a carved flat board, narrower at the bottom, with a bent bow and a U-shaped footrest.

A baby carrier at the American Museum of Natural History (plate 25) is of the lattice, or slat, construction, with a wood frame and hide bag, completely beaded, similar to the Lakota soft cradle. The cradleboard is 39.8 inches long, 10.6 inches wide, and 2.4 inches deep. The frame is decorated with metal tacks and deeply carved Vs at the top of the slats. The beaded baby bag is tied to the frame with rawhide thongs.

Baby Swing

Assiniboine mothers used baby swings for beds. The swing was made with two ropes and a blanket or a large hide. The ropes were tied to two small trees or tipi poles. The hide or blanket was folded over the ropes, letting it sag, and the baby was laid on it. To be sure there was enough breathing room for the baby, a stick across the ends of the two sides of the swing kept it open. The baby was usually wrapped up and tied in a moss bag before being placed in the swing. Karl Bodmer sketched a baby in a hammock during his trip with Prince Maximilian in 1830.[6]

BIRTH CUSTOMS

When a birth was approaching, the husband and children left the lodge; if the husband remained within, the child would not be born. A midwife and several women assisted the mother, who gave birth on her knees, aided with the support of a crosspiece on two poles firmly planted in the ground of the lodge. The supporting pole was just below the woman's abdomen, which she would press on the crosspiece. The newborn was washed with a tea made of medicinal roots. The placenta was wrapped and "put in a high tree; some people are afraid that if it was put in the ground it be might touched by some animal, [and] the child would be taken ill."[7] A medicine man or woman was called for a difficult birth to administer herbs or pulverized rattles of the rattlesnake. If the doctor was a man, he would then leave; but a female doctor would stay.[8] Sometimes the medicine man or woman had to resort to magic, but no assistance was given. "When told that the child had come, he smilingly remarked to the nurses, 'I told a tortoise to chase the baby out.'"[9]

One of women assisting with the birth cleaned out the newborn's mouth, wrapped the baby up, and put her or him in a cradle. By these acts, the child inherited the good qualities of that woman. Because of that belief, women tried to have a woman with a kind disposition and an industrious nature to sponsor the infant. In an emergency, any woman could serve as sponsor regardless of her traits. A woman took great pride in telling people that she was responsible for the good traits of a good child.[10]

Gifts were placed in the lodge of the expecting parents before the birth and were not to be touched until after delivery. Only one cradleboard was prepared beforehand. If two were prepared, twins would be born, and only one would be allowed to live. If the twins were a boy and a girl, the boy would be allowed to live. The mother could not care for two infants.[11] Male babies were desired because a male was of greater value. Sons were a source of profit and support for a good portion of their lives.

Assiniboine parents showed their love for their children. Their families were usually small, with one to three offspring. Grandparents cared for the children. After the birth of the first grandchild, one of the grandmothers would give a feast to announce the birth. During the ceremony, one old woman or man would receive a special invitation to the feast and be given a horse or other large gift.[12]

Amulet

When the navel cord broke off, it was wrapped with some tobacco, enclosed in a small decorated buckskin bag, and hung from the cradleboard. The small bag was usually shaped like a diamond. Later it was attached to the child's clothing. The bag was also decorated with beaver claws, which were sewn to the two side points and the bottom point. If a medicine man or woman had been called before the birth of the child and had used magic, the amulet was decorated with a small design representing a tortoise.[13]

Six Assiniboine navel amulets at the American Museum of Natural History are of various shapes and sizes. The length varies from 2.8 to 11 inches, the width, 1 to 3.4 inches, and the depth, 0.4 to 0.6 inches. All are completely beaded except one with quillwork on the back. The amulets are decorated with fringe, beads, cowrie shells, and thimbles.

PART SEVEN

HIDE BABY BAGS, SWINGS, AND HAMMOCKS

Hidatsa
Mandan
Arikara
Gros Ventre
Sarcee
Stoney
Plains Métis
Quapaw

CHAPTER 26

HIDATSA

The Hidatsas (Nuxbaaga) were part of the large Siouan language family. They lived on the west-central plains of North Dakota, high on the Missouri River. The Hidatsa tribe consisted of three divisions, each of which spoke a distinct dialect: Hidatsa proper, Awatixa, and Awaxawi. The three villages were further divided into moieties. The Awatixas claim that they have always lived on the Missouri River, that Hidatsa proper and Awaxawis arrived later and adopted many Awatixa customs. These sedentary horticultural communities were essentially endogamous, matrilineal villages of large round earth lodges on the Knife River. They had pottery ware made by specialists, who would purchase the rights to certain designs and patterns. The Crows broke away from the Awatixas and Hidatsa proper in late prehistoric times and moved west.

The first written accounts of the peoples that occupied the upper Missouri River valley were by the French around 1738. In the early eighteenth century, the three tribes lived in fortified villages of permanent lodges overlooking the river and their gardens. The villages were important trading centers, where many of the nomadic tribes of the northern plains met annually to trade for corn and other agricultural products. They hunted to supplement their agriculture; the most important animal hunted was the buffalo. According to the *Encyclopedia of the Great Plains*, "Clans and societies incorporated each Hidatsa person and bound them together in mutual obligation while also providing care, identity, and community. Membership in the seven or eight clans active in the historic era was matrilineal. . . . Likewise, religious observation and devotion were woven throughout daily life."[1]

Epidemic disease and enemy tribes decimated the Hidatsas in 1846, and they moved to Like-a-Fishhook Village with the remaining Mandans and Arikaras. The three tribes were similar and shared common horticultural and cultural features but retained their original traditions and identities.

Fort Berthold Indian Reservation was established in 1866 for the remaining Hidatsa, Arikara, and Mandan people. The General Allotment Act of 1887 separated their lands into 160 lots and divided the nation. Garrison reservoir took a fourth of the reservation in 1947, and the new reservation seat is in New Town, North Dakota. The Mandans, Arikaras, and Hidatsas, collectively known as the Three Affiliated Tribes, have retained their own culture and heritage.

Cradle Types

The Hidatsas used a sack bag, a tanned hide container without a backboard, and a swinging cradle. The word for cradle was *i si-da i-za wu-ze*, but the term describes "a stiff piece of leather . . . to which the baby was tied with cloth or similar material. This was used for a week as a back straightener."[2] Prince Maximilian wrote about a time some Minnetarees (what he called Hidatsas) came to see the steamboat. As some chiefs came aboard for a short time, a distressed woman left on the bank "carried a little child wrapped in a piece of leather, fastened with straps."[3] Alfred W. Bowers wrote that a baby was wrapped in soft tanned hide and placed in a cradle made of buffalo hide. The women of the house made the cradle by cutting and sewing the parts together.[4]

Buffalo Bird Woman, a Hidatsa mother, described her baby carrier as a baby bundle made of tanned buffalo calf hide, with the fur inside, tied around the baby:

> A finely dressed buffalo calf skin was first laid down on the floor fur up. The skin was so laid that the head of the skin would be at the babe's feet. Over this first skin would be laid a second, of like size but older or less valuable skin than the first one; it also lay fur up. Warmed sand was then placed in the bottom of another skin that had been folded and sewn to form a sack.
>
> He was dropped into the sack with his feet resting on a small skin that covered the warm sand. The sack, enclosing the babe, was then laid on the two calf robes or skins and folded. Last of all the binding thong was passed around the bundle.[5]

Skins were arranged as a hood over the child's head, turned fur side in to keep the child warm. The wrapping was tied with a single strip of buckskin. When the village was on the march, two wildcat skins and a calfskin were kept for a baby's use like a robe. The wildcat skin was a soft and warm wrapping that folded over the child's head. The mother wore a belt outside her buffalo robe and put the baby inside the robe on her left side, with the baby's feet pointing

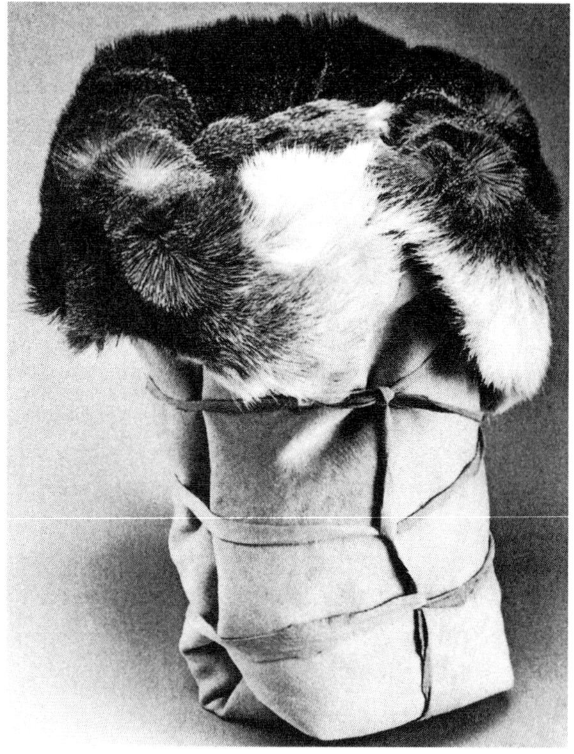

Hidatsa baby swing used as cradle, date and measurements unknown. The hide bag was hung from a rafter. A long rope was usually attached to the swing to enable the busy mother to pull the swing. Courtesy of the Minnesota Historical Society Press.

downward. If she rode on a horse travois, the baby would be tucked inside her robe but not belted. The mother was always with her baby. The cradle bundles with babies in them were not put on dog travois because the dogs would lie down every time they stopped.

Baby Swing

From ten days old to the time a child could walk, a mother kept the baby in a swing, *ma í dăk u dsi*. The swing took the place of the cradleboard for the sedentary Hidatsas. It was made from a buffalo skin pouch and hung from a rafter of the earth lodge. A swinging cradle made with ropes and blanket was called a *ma ka dĭ'šta i dăk u dsi*.[6] A mother could go about her household work and be near her baby. A rope tied to the bottom of the pouch "trailed to the fire where the mother could pull the rope and swing the child."[7]

Birth Customs

Birth was serious to Hidatsas; an expectant mother would ask a sacred society to pray for the child to be all right. Either a men's or a women's society could be approached to pray. If the birth was a successful event, a reward was given.

> A Hidatsa had certain beliefs that a pregnant woman would follow during her pregnancy: if she ate a pancreas, or killed snakes or any animal she would have a difficult delivery; if she ate eggs the child would awaken early in the morning and keep people awake; if she quarreled and became angry, the child might come early and soon die; if she ate or looked at a rabbit, the child would have a split lip; and if she braided grass and made a ring of it, the male child might be deformed.[8]

Hidatsas also believed that working in a cornfield was good for a pregnant woman because it made the baby strong.[9]

It was customary for the first baby to be born at the lodge of the expecting woman's mother, assisted by her clanswomen. Two posts were driven into the earth floor, where the bed was to be, about three feet high and two feet apart. The bed of hay was 4 to 6 inches thick and covered by a buffalo robe. The pregnant woman knelt on the bed and grasped the posts for support during labor. Everything was kept as quiet as possible during the birth, and for ten days after. All present talked in whispers. The maternal grandmother disposed of the placenta and took care of the newborn infant. A Hidatsa midwife purchased both the right to practice and knowledge of the medicines from another midwife. When labor began, a midwife was called and a medicine man might be sent for to sing a sacred mystery song to influence a normal birth. There were several ceremonies that aided a woman in labor.[10]

The Hidatsas believed that human beings exist in physical and spirit form. Every infant was a spirit that entered the mother's body, and these little spirits inhabited hills in tribal territory. "Women would put toys at the foot of these hills if they wanted children."[11] The maternal grandfather named the baby, and a ceremony introduced the child to his or her father's clan. The name giver was associated with his personal power bundle and would pray to the spirit associated with the bundle to bless the child.[12]

CHAPTER 27

MANDAN

The Mandans (Neuídia) were Siouan-speaking people who lived on the northern plains of North Dakota along the Missouri River. They referred to themselves as Numangkake, or People of the First Man, a name that reflected their own creation by First Man.

Blending the Eastern Woodland and Plains culture, Mandans were a settled agricultural civilization, living in permanent villages of round lodges made of earth. The Mandans hunted buffalo, which was also central to their ceremonies and trade. In the early 1700s, the Mandan were well established in permanent villages along both sides of the Missouri River, combining bison hunting with growing agricultural crops like beans, squash, corn, and sunflowers. Their vast gardens were on the river terraces. When hunting buffalo, they lived in tipis.

Family relationships were organized by maternal clans. All the women and children were members of the same clan. All members of a clan were cared for, disciplined its children, assisted its members in acquiring membership in military and religious societies, and helped obtain sacred bundles.

After a smallpox epidemic in 1781, the number of villages was reduced to two. Unable to defend themselves from hostile tribes, the surviving Mandans moved north to settle near the Hidatsas. Another smallpox epidemic occurred in 1837, decimating the tribe again. In 1845, the last independent Mandan village joined the Hidatsas at Like-a-Fishhook Village. In the early 1880s some Mandan families established kinship-based communities along the river. In 1934, they joined the Hidatsas and Arikaras at the Fort Berthold Reservation.

Mandan Cradle

A Mandan child was placed in a leather bag shortly after birth. The cradle, *nä-he i-su-suk-he-nuk*, was "a leather bag suspended by a strap to a crossbeam in the hut."[1] For additional warmth, the hide was cured with hair, and the baby was wrapped with the fur on the inside. At night the infant was taken out of the bag, cleaned, and greased. The mother slept with her baby at night. In 1830, when Prince Maximilian visited the Mandans, he wrote about the leather baby bags hanging from the beams of the earth lodges. The baby bags were not as decorated as those of the Sioux and Assiniboines.[2]

Birth Customs

An expecting woman preferred to give birth in her mother's lodge, attended by her mother. The lodge was prepared by being darkened, with everyone except the older women leaving.

A bed of buffalo robe was made near the bed post, which the woman could reach up and hold for support. If labor was prolonged, the expecting father's sister was called, and she prepared a ceremonial drink containing plants from her brother's medicine bundle, to which she held rights. In some cases, a sacred rite was employed or, to expedite the delivery, a drink of desiccated rattlesnake was administered. Doctoring rights were sold with tribal hereditary bundles. "Rights could be acquired through supernatural instructions or purchased from one who had secured the right through visions. Both men and women doctored."[3]

The women assisting with the birth disposed of the afterbirth. The newborn was greased and painted with red ocher, under the arms, around the neck, between the legs, and at the top of the head to prevent chafing. Dried buffalo chips were pounded into fine powder, and the powder was warmed with hot stones, then rubbed on the baby's bottom, under the arms, between the legs, under the toes, and between the fingers. The infant was wrapped in a piece of tanned hide taken from a tipi smoke hole, since this leather did not harden when it got wet.[4]

On the tenth day after the birth, a feast and ceremony was held for the child, and a name given. Until the baby received a name, the child was not considered a part of the family and clan. Gifts were distributed to members of the family in exchange for prayers for the success of the child. A girl usually kept her name, but if she became sickly, her parents could give her another feast and a new name.

A child who died before being named was wrapped in hide and placed in a tree with no rites. The Mandans believed that baby spirits lived in a hill in Mandan territory and were cared for by an old man. An unnamed child's spirit returned to the Baby Hill. Mothers were chosen by babies. A mother who desired to have a baby could go to the hills and pray for a child. If a mother wanted a daughter, she would bring a ball or girl's clothing; for a baby son, she brought a small bow and arrow.[5]

A newborn was laid on a bed of buffalo hair. Gray sage was burned to charcoal, then the infant was put over the smoke. Raising the baby up and down in the smoke would help the child grow.[6]

CHAPTER 28

ARIKARA

The Arikaras (Sahnish, meaning The People) were an aggregate of autonomous bands, each with its own dialect of the Caddoan language family. Arikaras were from central Kansas and Nebraska. Around the fifteenth century, they moved northward and merged with the Middle Missouri Village people in the region of the modern-day Dakotas.[1] They lived primarily in dome-shaped earth lodges, creating tipis as temporary shelter for seasonal summer and late fall bison hunts. To supplement the buffalo, the Arikaras grew corn, bean, and squash crops in the rich soil of the Missouri River valley. They also grew sunflowers and tobacco.

Arikara women were responsible for the crops and for basket weaving and pottery, including making and designing cooking vessels. Women also built and owned the lodges, which were large enough to house multiple generations. Each Arikara village was organized by rank. Leaders also had religious duties. Arikara religious practices revolved around the Creator and Mother Corn, who had taught humans how to live on the earth. Each man had to seek a spirit guardian, who helped him create his own sacred bundle.

Arikaras, like Hidatsas and Mandans, were decimated by enemy tribes and epidemic disease, and they joined those tribes to become the Three Affiliated Tribes, at Fort Berthold Reservation. The three tribes were similar and shared common horticultural and cultural features, but they held on to their own identities and traditions.

Arikara Cradle

Melvin R. Gilmore and Edward Curtis gathered information on the Arikara cradle. Curtis wrote that Arikara babies were not strapped to a board but wrapped "securely and tied in a calf-skin then in a heavier piece of buffalo-skin. They were stood upright in a deep sack which was suspended from a roof timber."[2] Gilmore recorded his notes in 1926 from an eighty-six-year-old Arikara midwife, Stesta-kata, and her interpreter, Julia Red-Bear. Arikara babies were swaddled and wrapped in a buffalo hide, tanned with the hair on, which came up on the baby's head like a hood. The cradle, or baby bag, was called a *be-ra-ka-kuth-o͞o*. "The cradle was made up with the rawhide of a buffalo, covered over with tanned deer skin, with a layer of plucked catnip for padding and a deer skin string for lacing the baby in the cradle."[3]

Birth Customs

Prenatal preparations began as soon as a woman knew she was pregnant. Older women advised her on diet and exercise. She was told to eat sparingly as her delivery time neared, to get plenty of exercise, and to keep herself in good condition. She was to do her ordinary household duties: cutting wood, carrying water from the river, and working in the garden. Walking up and down banks carrying a load on her back made her delivery seem comparatively easy.

A small willow lodge was built for the expecting mother to give birth. She was assisted by female relatives and a midwife. The bed was prepared with the head and shoulders sloping down to the feet. A vertical pole firmly set in the ground was placed near the head of the bed, convenient for the expecting woman to grasp with both hands. The woman was to lie on her left side with her feet toward the east or southeast, "because that is the direction of the Wonderful River, or Holy River which is the Arikara name of the river which a white person calls the Missouri. Since the Missouri River and all its tributaries deliver their waters toward southeast or east[,] delivery in childbirth should be in accordance to nature."[4] A folded buffalo robe or pillow was placed between the knees, and the woman was given some material to put between her teeth to bite on in case of a paroxysm of pain.

Before the delivery, the midwife manipulated the woman's abdomen to be sure the baby was in the right position to deliver. Any malposition of the baby was corrected by gentle pressure on the abdomen, sometimes with a move in the woman's position as well. For a delayed or difficult birth, an infusion of the roots of the red baneberry (*Actaea rubra*) was put on the woman's head. The midwife forcibly gave her a drink of the infusion to "scare the baby," and it would be delivered quickly. She took a sprig of wild sage (*Artemisia gnaphalodes*) and brushed downward on the woman's body—front, back, and both sides—with sweeping motions. "It is said that when all this is done[,] the delivery is no longer delayed, and the baby comes quickly."[5] After delivery, the mother would rest for two to five days. She would also wear an abdominal band for several days.

After the infant's birth, the midwife cut the umbilical cord, leaving a length to the newborn's knees. She took the cord between her thumb and the finger close to the navel, pressed the blood downward and out, twisted the cord, and coiled it in a spiral, leaving the end turned upward. A ripe puffball was applied and bound with a soft tanned buffalo hide bandage. The dried cord dropped off in three or four days. The placenta was wrapped in calico and tied in a bundle. Stesta-kata said, "In ancient times before the coming of the traders, with white men's manufactured goods, this wrapping was of fine deerskin."[6] A small bit of Arikara tobacco as an offering acceptable to all the mysterious powers was placed in the bundle. The sage that was used to brush the mother at the time the baby was born was securely tied to the bundle, which was then carried to an out-of-the-way place and fastened to a thorny shrub or tree. After the bundle was secured, a pipe was lit, and a smoke offering was made with the prayer that the child would be well. Any disease would be confined within the bundle.

The infant was bathed with warm water and dried, and the mouth, nostrils, and eyes were washed with an infusion of the root of the red baneberry. Swaddling was made of a piece of old tent cover because the tanned buffalo hide would become soft and pliable from long use, weathering, and washing. Down of the cattail was placed against the infant's skin and packed inside the swaddling. The wrapping was done in a cylindrical bandage, and the outside covering was of buffalo skin.

New young mothers gave extra care to their breasts to prevent the nipples from becoming too large and misshapen. The midwife would moisten the mother's nipples with saliva. If the mother did not have enough milk, the breast was bathed with an infusion of red baneberry to cause a good flow. A wet nurse might be employed for the baby or a broth given made from flint corn and buffalo meat. Babies were usually nursed until three years old.[7]

Amulet

Arikaras did not have an amulet case for the dried navel cord. After a son's cord dropped off, the father carried it away and buried it on the top of a distant hill. He then lit his pipe and made a smoke offering and prayer "to the Wind that this man-child be healthy and vigorous and grow up to be a man strong, brave and courageous." If the baby was a girl, the mother took the dried cord out to her cornfield, where she buried it and prayed that "this woman-child may grow to maturity and be quiet, kind, helpful to others, virtuous, and hospitable, and thus fulfill the Arikara idea of useful and happy womanhood."[8]

Arikara Baby Bag

The baby carrier I examined is identified as a Sahnish (Arikara) cradleboard cover, constructed around 1880 (plate 27). The hood is 27 inches long and 13 inches wide; the tab is 5 inches long. The hood cover is made with two pieces: the hood and the tab sewn along the back edge. Rawhide was cut in a rectangular piece, 27 inches by 13 inches, and folded in half to form the hood. It is not lined. A piece of cotton cloth, pink flowers and green leaves on a red background, covers the top of the hood. The side seams are covered with fringed leather. The tab sewn on the back edge is also covered with a row of fringe.

The decoration is quillwork and beadwork. The quillwork was done in a wide band across the front two sides of the hood. Eight long narrow green and purple bands, which get wider in the middle, filled the band against a yellow background. The quills are lane stitched and flat-wrapped. The Edges of the front of the hood are decorated with beadwork.

CHAPTER 29

GROS VENTRE

The Gros Ventre (Atsina) was an Algonquian-speaking tribe and division of the Arapaho. Gros Ventre is a French name, and the people referred to themselves as the A'aninin, the White Clay People, or Clay People, referring to the white clay of the river from which they believed their people had been made. A'aninin and Arapaho peoples' oral tradition told that they were one people living on the Canadian plains. When they parted is unknown. The earliest known document of the tribe's contact with white traders dates from 1754.[1] After 1795, bands of Gros Ventres began moving south into Montana.

Little is known about the Gros Ventres. Social organization, work activity, hunting, and technology varied with the season. During the summer the bands separated from time to time, and in the fall, they came together for hunting buffalo. Bands separated into smaller groups in the winter. Before the Gros Ventres had a large number of horses, they hunted buffalo by impounding, and then, with trained "buffalo horses," shooting with bow and arrow. Subsistence was supplemented by foraging and hunting small game. Women's activities varied seasonally also. They collected plant food, prepared food, and stored it. Gros Ventre women moved camps, made clothing, and prepared buffalo skins. Special clothing was decorated with quillwork, paint, polished deer hooves, elk teeth, and hair from slain enemies worn as fringe.

As the buffalo diminished in northern Montana, the tribe began going to Fort Belknap for food and supplies. The Gros Ventre share the Fort Belknap Indian Reservation with the Assiniboine in north-central Montana. The Fort Belknap Reservation, established in 1888, encompasses 675,147 acres in Montana, forty miles south of the Canadian border. Most of the tribe members live on or near the reservation.[2]

Cradle

Gros Ventres did not use a traditional cradle. They used a baby bag (baby, *wɔɔnité'iyɔɔnéh*, plus bed, *'ɔɔɔw'u*).[3] A newborn infant was called a "sack baby."[4] Soon after birth, the infant was laced in a hide bag, made of fine, soft buckskin or buffalo calfskin with the fur left on, laced up the front. The baby sacks were often elaborately decorated. Little deer hooves that rattled were often sewn on the sack. A piece of rawhide, the size of the bag, was placed inside to stiffen it. The rawhide was rectangular and rounded at the top, and it reached only to the baby's neck. Rags were padded around the baby's body to prevent any chafing. Small rounded caps were tied under the chin. The caps were made of soft calfskin with little fur earmuffs.

Mothers were careful in placing the baby in the sack. The feet and legs needed to be properly placed to ensure that the baby's legs stayed straight. Traditionally, the father's sister was expected to make the infant's baby bag at the child's birth. If the aunt failed to provide the hide bag, the mother wrapped the baby in soft skin and tied it with leather straps.

Infants were kept in their sacks day and night. When old enough, their arms were left free of wrapping. When not being carried, babies in their bags were hung from lodge poles. Infants slept in their baby bags alongside their mothers. Babies and small children were washed and powdered every morning. In wintertime, children were rubbed with snow.

When the powder in the sack was changed, the baby would be free to crawl and play around. If babies showed any inclination to walk, they were encouraged by adults holding them up and helping them. Mothers watched their babies closely and never left them alone.

According to one informant, Coming Daylight, cradleboards, probably of the Arapaho style, were used before her time, and babies were carried on a travois if the family had to move household items. The cradleboard was often hung on a travois pole. Coming Daylight recounted that if a mother did not have a cradleboard, she might have used "a piece of stiffened leather hooked over horse saddle horn."[5]

Birth Customs

Prenatal care was important to ensure an easy delivery and a healthy baby. According to Regina Flannery's informants, in the old days, pregnant women were well cared for. A man usually had two wives so that the pregnant one was looked after by the other. The pregnant one was to cook only what was necessary and to wear a heavy leather apron to protect the baby because the afterbirth was believed to stick from the heat. She was not to pack heavy loads and or work too hard.

A woman kept track of her pregnancy by counting the moons. When she ceased menstruating, she marked with charcoal on a piece of wood or notched a stick, and then did so again each successive time the moon was in the phase it had been in when she started marking. Childbirth usually took place in the woman's own lodge, and a midwife assisted. A male doctor would not touch a woman in labor but would dispense medicine to alleviate the pains. Different practitioners used different ways to dispense medicine. One doctor might have received his power to relieve women in labor from some supernatural agent. A doctor was not necessary if the midwife knew medicines for childbirth. Both expected to be paid with gifts for their services, such as a horse, lengths of cloth, or blankets.

Women assumed a kneeling position and grasped a crossbar for support during delivery. The crosspiece was supported in a horizontal position by two upright forked stakes set in the ground.[6] The midwife would massage the woman in labor gently and talk to her softly, telling her to think of pleasant things and that she would not have a hard time.

The mother would try to remain quiet during labor because if she cried out, she would drive the baby back. If she twisted and turned in pain, the cord tangled around the child in delivery.

Anyone assisting the birth could cut the umbilical cord. "They usually cut the cord long, say four to six inches, because they would be afraid the infant would bleed to death if they cut it too short. You kind of drained it and get it cleaned out and tie it once. Apply a powered root and then put a band around the body. It usually takes four days before it drops off."[7] The woman that severed the cord received the knife as a gift. The bowl used to bathe the newborn was given to the woman who washed the infant. The afterbirth was quickly disposed of secretly, hung in the branches of a tree; if it was not disposed of properly, and "left lying to be handled[,] the child would be afflicted with sores."[8]

The new mother was to rest after her child was born, resuming her duties in ten days. It was believed that if a woman worked a great deal immediately after a birth, the child would not grow up to be healthy. Working hard would make a new mother sweat, hurting her milk. The infant was not nursed until the milk was "the right color" and the colostrum had been drawn off.

The midwife usually stayed in the new mother's lodge for a few days to attend to the infant. The mother would wear a belt of rawhide about a foot wide after the delivery. The belt would be laced up immediately, and then laced up tighter every day. Wearing the belt would help the new mother regain her figure. Gros Ventre women were strict about this practice.

Gros Ventre mothers' first duty was to care for their babies. They were cautioned not to leave infants alone. If a mother had to leave the baby "even a minute," she would take a small stick, blacken the tip with nicotine, and leave it on the swing alongside where the baby lay. This would keep the spirits away. If the mother of an infant was going on a short trip, sometimes to pick berries, she always invited the baby's *btă'tao* (shadow, spirit, soul), to come too: "Come on with us or we might leave you. We are going now."[9] Failed to do this was like leaving part of the baby behind, and the baby would be cranky.

Powder made with buffalo chips pounded on rawhide was heated with hot rocks that sterilized the powder. The baby was laid in the powder, which was also rubbed on the baby wherever he or she might chafe—under the arms, between the legs, under the toes, and between the fingers. Horse manure was sometimes used in the same way. Fresh powder was applied every day and heated in the winter time.

Amulet

The dried navel cord was kept in a small decorated leather bag filled with sweet grass or tobacco. The small bag was usually sewn into a turtle shape with a realistic head. The amulet was attached to the child's clothing and kept until adulthood. Girls' amulets were pinned to the clothing right at the back of the neck. Sometimes the boy's amulet was tied at the wrist. Gros Ventre amulets at the American Museum of Natural History are rhomboid shapes with the upper end a small rhomboid, forming the head of the animal represented. They have ornamental strings hanging from the corners, representing limbs and tail. Three navel amulets are illustrated in Alfred Kroeber's report "Ethnology of the Gros Ventre":

> Figure 3 was to represent a horn toad, and figure 2, a person. It will be seen that the mouth in the former is near the end of the head; in the latter, in the lower part of the face. Both these specimens have quilled or beaded appendages at the two side corners and at the lower end. Fig. 1 had a distinct tail as well as head, a cross instead of an attempt at representative ornamentation in the bead-work on the head, and unornamented yellow thongs as sole attachments.[10]

One of the amulets (cat. no. 50/1928) is unbeaded on the lower side, with a quartered, asymmetrical design on the top side and hide pendants. Another (cat. no. 50/1921) is entirely beaded on both sides, showing on the reverse a simple quartering design in yellow and blue. Beaded appendages are decorated with metal cones. The third amulet (cat. no. 50/1756) has curvilinear leaf ornaments on the lower side and tassels, as well as wrapped quill thongs in various colored quills. The attached tassels are also wrapped with various colored quills. The final amulet (cat. no. 50/4278) has beadwork on the upper surface that is quartered in red and white, and there is a distinct attempt to represent eyes. The attachments are short unpainted thongs with tin cones at their ends. The lower side is not beaded.

CHAPTER 30

SARCEE

The Sarcees (Sarsis) were a small Athabascan-speaking group of the Beaver Indians from the woodland subarctic, who hunted on the plains and wintered in woodlands. They call themselves Tsuu T'ina, meaning Many People. The Sarcees separated from the Beavers before European contact. Early in the eighteenth century, the Sarcees adopted the Plains lifestyle and remained in the region, ranging from the Missouri River to the Rocky Mountains and up into Saskatchewan. They were closely associated with Blackfeet and adopted many material and religious customs of the Blackfeet Confederacy. The Sarcees successfully maintained a balance between independence and reliance on their allies.

Buffalo hunting formed the basis of their economy. Eagle trapping was a highly developed religious ritual. The people divided into small bands and roamed apart until the summer ceremonial season. Sarsees lived in skin-covered tipis among their clan group, and individuals were free to move from clan to clan. Five clans were recognized.

After the disappearance of the buffalo, the Sarcees were settled on a reserve in 1881, west of Calgary, Alberta. An elected council and one chief manage affairs for the tribe.

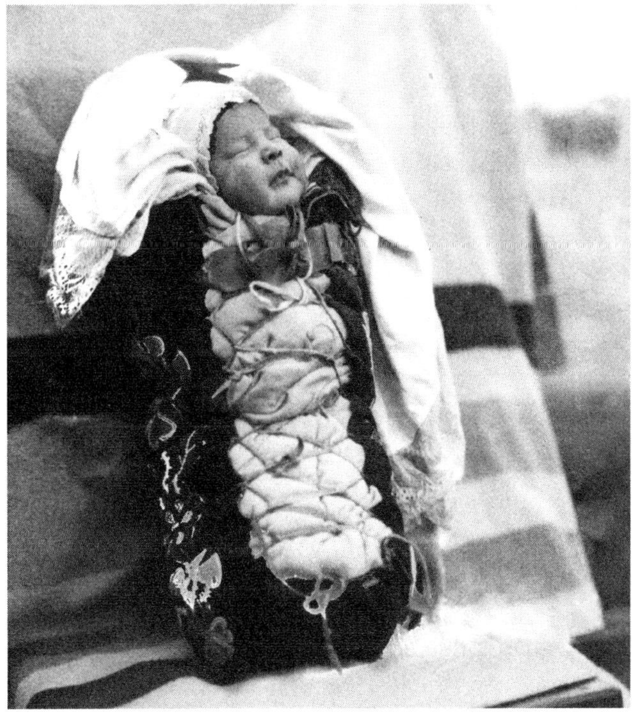

Sarcee baby Elsie Bull, ca. 1920. Elsie is tied in a decorated moss bag, a distinctive northern style of child's cradle linked with the Sarcee subarctic heritage. This view shows the decoration on the side of the bag. Photograph by Arnold Lupson. Courtesy of the Glenbow Museum, Calgary, Alberta (NA-667-419).

Cradle

Sarcee mothers used a baby bag, called a *t͡s!al.*[1] There appears to be no evidence that the Sarcee mothers used a cradleboard. The infant was put in the bag at birth. The baby was taken out in the morning, washed, powdered, and wrapped in a blanket. The early bag was of tanned leather. A rectangular piece of leather was folded lengthwise and laced together. Seams were sewn by perforating the edges with a small pointed bone, often the buffalo's foreleg, making small holes, and pushing in the twisted ends of sinew through the holes. Small slits were cut along each side in the front, creating eyelets for lacing.[2]

Birth Customs

Sarcee birth customs were explained to Edward Curtis by a middle-aged woman who narrated her personal experience. Her labor started in the middle of the night, and unable to wake her husband, she bit him on the toe. Several women were called in, and they put up a small tipi by the side of her log lodge and lit a fire. Just as she got there to the small tipi, her labor started. She clung to the lodge pole, and an old woman pressed on her back. By the time her mother got there, the baby was delivered. The newborn was washed in warm water. The assistants tied the navel cord in two places close together with a deerskin thong, and then cut it between the two places. The newborn was placed on a cloth spread with powdered, dried buffalo chips. The powder absorbed the urine. The women then laid the infant close to the fire. The afterbirth was wrapped in a cloth and buried in a badger burrow. Attendants wrapped the new mother in a tight, wide belt and pressed her hips to put the bones back in place. While recovering, Sarcee women stayed in bed without moving, with their legs close together. During the mother's ten days in bed, other women turned her. Her husband rubbed the bowl of his pipe on the newborn's closed eyes to give the child good eyesight. "Every morning the baby was taken out of the baby bag, washed and powdered with pulverized charcoal where its skin is creased, so as to avoid chafing. After two or three days charcoal powder mixed with tallow was applied to the umbilicus, and the stump of the navel-cord was placed in a little beaded bag."[3]

Girls were named at birth, and boys remained nameless for a week, or until a medicine man or elderly warrior could choose an appropriate name. A girl's name remained with her throughout life. A boy was given a derogatory name during adolescence until he earned a new name by performing a brave deed. The new name was usually that of a deceased relative.[4]

To the Sarcee people, "the child is considered a precious gift from the 'Great Spirit.' Parents often approached a woman known for her kindness, honesty and warm heartedness to bless the baby."[5] A name was bestowed on the child by someone in high standing: a medicine woman or a successful warrior. A name obtained from a vision was highly valued.

Amulet

The stump of the dried navel cord was placed in a small beaded bag, which was attached to the baby bag or on the back of the child's clothing. After a child outgrew the baby bag, the baby's first moccasins and the amulet bag were thrown in a stream, while the mother prayed for long life and health for her child. A boy's navel bag was made in the shape of a snake. If a pregnant woman saw a snake, she would know that she was going to have a boy. A girl's amulet was a decorated rhomboid shape that represented a lizard. Leather strings were sewn at the corners as limbs and a tail.[6]

Sarcee Baby Bag

The baby carrier I studied is in the at the North American Ethnographic Collection at the American Museum of Natural History (plate 26). It was donated by Pliny E. Goddard in 1905.

The bag is eighteen inches long, folded in half. Loops along the edge of the red wool were formed by a thong laced through perforations; the loops are about 3 inches long, stopping where the child's neck would be. A knot is tied and the thong threaded along the face and head, enabling the mother to keep the bonnet area tight. A separate thong is used for lacing.

The highly decorated bag is black silk (trade cloth) damask with a raised pattern. Red wool along the edges is about 1 inch wide, and red and white silk ribbon trim the length of the wrapper on each side. Realistic floral embroidery beadwork along the front is done in symmetrical patterns. Thirty-five round brass buttons with incised designs are sewn along the outside of the ribbon trim. There is a double row of nine brass buttons sewn in the curve of the top of the hood.

CHAPTER 31

STONEY

Stoneys (Nakodas) were known originally as the People of the Mountains, or in their language, the Iyarhe Nakoda, from the original Iyethkabi. They reside in western Canada but lived originally in the United States. The Stoneys speak the northern dialect of the Dakota language, in the Siouan language family. Culturally and linguistically, they are allied to the Assiniboines. Often called the Rocky Mountain Sioux, Stoneys have differences in language and culture from the Assiniboines. Stoney oral traditions assert that the Stoney and Assiniboine tribes separated with the Dakota and Lakota Nations sometime around 1640, migrating westward, then separating again after 1754.

Commonly composed of patrilineal extended families, the Stoneys lived along the Alberta Rocky Mountain foothills and hunted buffalo and other large animals; they were a hunting, fishing, and gathering people. Unlike with most Plains tribes, fish were important to the Stoney diet. They caught fish using three-tined spears, hooks, lines, and fish traps. They were composed of two groups: the Mountain Stoneys, subdivided further into Alexis' Band and Paul's Band, and the Wood Stoneys, which had three bands, Bearpaw's, Chiniki's, and Wesley's. The Stoneys are the only Siouan groups living entirely in Canada. Northern bands, which were primary nomadic, would gather and fish during the warmer part of the year, then disperse into protected areas in the winter. Stoneys were located in the northwestern portion of

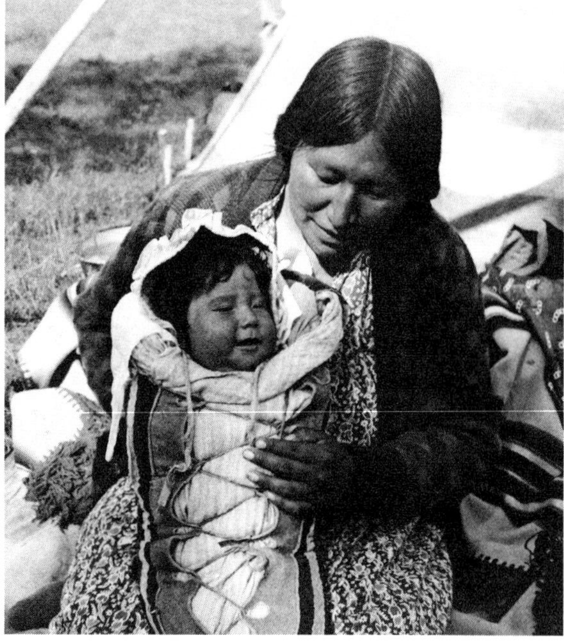

Stoney woman and baby in moss bag, possibly Mrs. Thomas Lefthand and her daughter, Violet, ca. 1941. Photograph by F. Gulley. Courtesy of the Glenbow Museum, Calgary, Alberta (NA-1241-707).

the Great Plains and settled in 1877 on a small reserve at Morley on the Bow River in Alberta, Canada. Today, the tribal council at the reserve regulates the affairs of the entire tribe.

Cradle

Chief John Snow related in his book *These Mountains Are Our Sacred Places* that the first bed for a Stoney child was a traditional moss bag of buckskin with beadwork. Chief Snow described a moss bag as a cradle that a baby was laced in, with the moss serving as a disposable diaper. All his family members were reared in moss bags.[1]

A small cradleboard was sometimes used. The board was a U-shaped piece of board or bark, with the infant lashed to the mother's back, allowing her to continue her work. Older babies were wrapped in a small blanket and carried on the mother's back.

Birth Customs

A newborn (*na-an fu bi n*) was laced into a buckskin bag shortly after birth. The bag was filled with ripe dried cattails or dried moss. A paternal great-grandfather named the new infant. A Stoney baby was brought into the world with the help of women who made a practice of assisting with births.

A tipi or hut was erected specifically for the birth process. The husband had to leave the lodge or else the baby would not be born. Three women assisted the mother through her labor and after, such as cutting the umbilical cord. The afterbirth was wrapped in a piece of hide and buried under a young tree that would grow up strong and healthy like the Stoney child. Stoney women drank an infusion of medical root after giving birth, and another root was boiled as a tea to wash the newborn. Sometimes, the new father gave away a horse.[2]

Baby Bags

A hide bag at the Peace River Museum in Alberta, Canada, is made of rawhide and completely lined with fur. The bag is a rectangular piece of hide folded lengthwise and laced together at the sides. The rectangular rawhide is long enough to support the baby's head and neck. Small slits are cut along each side in the front, creating eyelets for lacing; one narrow thong is laced through the holes in a zigzag pattern, drawn through holes tied on each side.

Baby bags were also made of blanket pieces. A wide strip of leather was stitched on each side to protect the material from tearing at the holes punched along each side.

I found one Stoney moss bag highly decorated with beadwork on the web page "The Plains People" of the Canada's First Peoples website.[3] The rectangular hide is completely beaded on the front with bright blue beads and decorated with geometric shapes in red, yellow, and dark green beadwork. A strip of long leather fringe is attached to each side of the leather back.

The Canadian Museum of History has a Stoney moss bag (V-C-217). The bag, 26.8 inches long and 8.4 inches wide, is black velvet, decorated with a long line of colorful flower motifs on each side. There is a large red rose at the top and a green line along the side, with two small leaves in the middle, another red rose with petals at the bottom, and a large cream-color rose at the top.

CHAPTER 32

PLAINS MÉTIS

The Métis homeland was from the lakes and rivers of present-day Ontario to British Columbia and into the northern territories of what would become the United States, across Montana, North Dakota, Minnesota, Wisconsin, and Michigan. During the seventeenth-century French and English fur trade, intermarriage between Europeans and Native people produced children of mixed ancestry, who would become known as Métis, from the French, meaning "mixed." The Métis have maintained a distinct personal identity and communities in upper North America, including western Canada. Their culture has a distinct composite language called Michif. The Plains Métis, also called the Red River Métis, also have their own culture and traditions.

The Métis society that emerged on the plains in the early nineteenth century reflected the cultural traits of both Native and European ancestors. The Plains Métis had a strong sense of national identity. Their society was patriarchal and had a migratory lifeway. They continued to act as brokers in the fur trade, practicing a mixed economy, with the seasonal buffalo hunt, fishing, gathering, and growing some grain crops. They did not see themselves as under the control of either the fur trade or tribal government. But by the late 1870s, the buffalo were gone, and within the next couple of decades, the fur trade had collapsed. The Métis lost much of their influence, and bands migrated separately to the West and to the North.

Cradle Types

Métis mothers used the well-known child-rearing device the moss bag, called a *waspison*, as well as the northeastern cradleboard, tikinagan.[1] The cradleboard, a flat board with a wooden hoop and a traditional hide or cloth bag attached with leather thongs, provided the infant with a warm, secure, and portable resting place. The board was similar to that of the Plains Crees and Plains Ojibwas. The three peoples often purchased the same type of cradleboard from traders. Lovingly wrapped and bound to decorated cradleboards, their children were initiated into the cultural life of their families and communities.

Moss bags were usually highly embroidered and made with various materials, such as leather, blankets, velvet, and wool, held together with leather bands on each side of the opening (see plate 28). The moss bags were stuffed with moss gathered in the fall. "Little spruce trees were cut in half way, about two feet from the ground, the upper part pushed down, and we put our moss on top of this sort of rack, where it would dry before winter set in. It was hauled in as needed. Moss was a household necessity. We raised our babies with it. We stuffed it in moss bags in which our babies were laced up."[2] Dried moss kept a baby dry and warm.

Ida Bella Tremblay gave an account of how the function of a canvas bag filled with moss was used to protect a swaddled baby. Tremblay's great-grandmother told her how a mother had to stop and check her crying baby's moss bag while her family formed a close circle around her to shield her from a blinding snowstorm. The mother unlaced the bag from the bottom upward and removed a pine needle stuck in the baby's foot. She comforted the baby, laced the bag up, and the family continued their journey. Tremblay, an artist, wrote that a moss bag, a functional part of survival and daily life, can also be a work of art, with beautiful designs on the outside of the bag in beadwork, silk embroidery, quillwork, and moose-hair tufting on canvas or leather.[3]

Birth Customs

Birth was a sacred event in Métis culture. Children were seen as gifts from the Creator to be cherished. Both sexes in the extended families and close-knit communities gave young children much attention. They were held and played with, taking part in all family activities. A baby was kept in the center of the household activity, which was in the cooking and eating area. Infants were swaddled when put to bed in cribs or hammocks over parents' beds. Raising children, while primarily the task of the mother, tended to be a communal effort. Child rearing was loosely structured, and other women and female kin helped look after all the children.

Men were also always around the baby in Métis extended families and close-knit communities. "Pregnant women were considered medicinal women because of the new life they carried and were honoured as a bridge between the spirit life and life on earth. . . . The baby's spirit was thought to choose its parents and would wait sometimes for many lifetimes before entering into the world."[4] The Métis believed that babies in the womb were affected by everything that affected the mother, so pregnant women were encouraged to eat well and stay active, but they were also kept away from anything disagreeable or sad, including injuries and funerals.

One important part of childbirth was establishing a bond between the new mother and infant, so immediately after birth, the newborn was laid on the mother, who massaged the baby. "The placenta was considered sacred and carried life while the umbilical cord signified the connection between the child, her relations and the earth."[5] Newborns were welcomed with much celebration within the family and community. "Some traditional Métis ceremonial practices used during birth and labour included having a drummer, holding a smudging ceremony before and after the birth, and giving the new baby a cedar bath."[6] Others offered welcoming prayers. Elders of the tribe were viewed as important connections to the spirit world that newborns had just emerged from, because elders were closest to reentering. They were therefore responsible for giving infants a spirit name.[7]

Many Métis new mothers followed the ancient Chippewa tradition of the dream net, or dreamcatcher, made of woven sinew or willow and hung above the cradleboard to catch bad dreams, while good dreams slipped through the hole in the center. Dreamcatchers usually don't last beyond childhood.

Quillwork and Beadwork

Métis were known for their intricate, colorful designs on everyday objects. They earned the name Flower Beadwork People for their floral designs. Native women taught their mixed-blood children the centuries-old techniques and methods of harvesting natural media from animal, earth, and plant sources. This required time, skill, and knowledge.

Quillwork was done by both women and men, who fashioned the porcupine quills into intricate geometric and floral designs. Quills were dyed vibrant colors. Red, blue, and yellow were the favorite colors for dyed quills. Métis quillworkers were able to use quills by wrapping, weaving, braiding, and sewing quills into complex, patterned geometric and representational designs. One porcupine can supply about thirty to forty thousand quills. After plucking the quills, quillworkers sort them into sizes and dye them. Natural dyes included roots, mosses, minerals, berries, and flower petals. The stiff hollow quills were soaked to soften them and make them flexible. Quillworkers would pull the quills repeatedly through their teeth or fingernails to flatten them and make them easier to work with. To attach quills to a piece of leather or cloth, the Métis first used an awl to punch small holes in the material. Awls were made of a piece of bone.

Métis women were able to manipulate the long stiff quills into delicate floral designs and motifs. The floral designs originated from their contact with the Roman Catholic missions, when trade beads became common. The craftswomen in the mid- to late nineteenth century produced designs with beadwork and silk embroidery. Early Catholic mission schools introduced silk embroidery around the Great Lakes. Nuns instructed Métis girls in embroidery and beadwork, and the Métis adapted European materials and techniques to the materials they had available, such as using moose hair instead of silk thread, creating the appliqué technique called moose hair tufting.[8] The trailing flower designs became an indicator of Métis handicraft. Their beadwork emphasized symmetry, balance, and harmony in patterns taken from nature and from the models of European lacework and church decoration.[9]

Finger weaving was another ancient Indigenous technique used by the Métis. Women unraveled wool blankets and garters to make the colorful sashes used as tumplines for cradleboards. The woven sash became the most distinctive part of Métis dress and a symbol of their people.

CHAPTER 33

QUAPAW

The Quapaws (Okáxpa or O-Gah-Pah), speakers of the Dhegiha branch of the Siouan language family, historically resided on the west side of the Mississippi River in what is now the state of Arkansas. They share language roots with the Omahas, Poncas, Osages, and Kaws. According to tradition, one group of the ancestral Dhegiha who lived near the mouth of the Ohio moved up the Mississippi and Missouri Rivers and became the Omahas (Upstream People). A second group moved down the river and became the Quapaws (Downstream People). The name Quapaw, derived from Okáxpa, or O-Gah-Pah, is interpreted as going downstream or with the current.

The first recorded contact between Quapaws and Europeans occurred in 1673, and the Quapaws had an alliance with France until the latter ceded Louisiana to Spain. When the United States took control of Louisiana territory in 1804, the Quapaws were residing in three villages on the Arkansas River and in one village on the Mississippi, at the mouth of the Arkansas.

The tribe was divided into large moieties—the Earth People and Sky People—and into twenty-one clans. Quapaw people lived in permanent longhouses covered in cypress bark. They developed a culture carefully tuned to the natural environment sustaining them. Using spears and nets, they took food from rivers, including fish and turtles, and from the forest, such as nuts, roots, and fruit. More important was the abundant meat available. The buffalo were an important part of Quapaw subsistence until the end of the nineteenth century.

In September 1834 the Quapaws moved to a reservation on northeastern Indian Territory. Within two years the tribe was divided and disrupted again by the U.S. Civil War. In a bold move to save their land, the Quapaws voted to allot their land themselves before the government did. Today, the Quapaw Nation headquarters are in Quapaw, Oklahoma, in the northeastern part of the state.

Cradle Types

I found no written evidence that the Quapaws used a cradleboard. A baby bed was called a *shi-zhi-kaazho*. Although Quapaw women wove baskets, they apparently never used them for baby beds. Ethnologists Alice C. Fletcher and Francis La Flesche, while assembling information for their study of the Omahas, encountered difficulty securing relative facts on a cognate tribe, the Quapaws. The two ethnologists were told sadly by their Quapaw informants, "All is gone; gone long ago."[1]

According to Ardina Moore, member of the Quapaw Nation and Quapaw language instructor, a hammock was used as a bed (*azho*) for a baby (*shizhika*).[2] To make the bed, a blanket was triple folded over a long rope tied to a structure like a lodge pole or a tree, and two sticks, the same length (about a foot long) were placed horizontally inside the blanket to separate it at the head and foot, keeping the blanket from the baby's face. The baby's weight held the folded blanket securely in place. The two sticks kept the blanket open. In earlier times, especially precontact, a large piece of hide would have been used instead of a blanket. Another piece of rope was attached to swing the hammock.

Babies were often carried on the mother's back using a blanket or sling. A wide belt or piece of cloth or leather was placed over the mother's shoulders and fastened in the front. The sling was placed under the baby's buttocks, giving the child a secure seat on the mother's back. In cold weather, the infant was placed in the sling on the mother's back wrapped under a blanket.

Birth Customs

Quapaw society was patrilineal. Individual family units were grouped in clans based on the line of descent on the father's side. The clans were named after animals or cosmic phenomenon. "Upon the birth of a child, during a sunrise ritual, he received a personal name from a tribal elder. Not only did this identify him with a specific social unit, but it insured him of a full and lengthy life."[3] With the death of Tallchief in 1918, the last hereditary chief, his daughter, Maude Supernaw, was to bestow on children their Indian names. She stopped giving names, however, because there were no more pure blood Quapaws.

CONCLUSION

Leather Shall Breathe and Wood Shall Sing Again

The functional cradle became a valuable, esteemed collectible artifact, cultural icon, and object of art. N. Scott Momaday wrote that the cradles were utilitarian and their function clear: "And beyond that, they are familiar; and the fact that we are talking about love—the love of people for their children—that is a wonderful universal thing. I can't think of any better way of expressing that familial love than a cradle."[1] To make a cradle and give it to a child was a sacred act. At the time of contact with non-Indians, all Native peoples on the plains used some type of cradle. Many of the cradles had unique regional developments. During the nineteenth century, cradle makers made use of introduced materials in their manufacture, along with their indigenous materials. This often resulted in time-saving devices for the women who made cradles, which gave them increased opportunities for artistic experimentation, such as with cloth, yarn, or glass beads.

Before the Europeans arrived, many Native peoples traded for a product called wampum. Wampum was a bead made by hand from the quahog, a hard-shell clam. The dentalium and the cowrie shell were traded to decorate clothing and cradles. To deal with the Native populations, the Europeans adopted the barter system. Glass beads became the standard for trade in North America. Value was assigned to beads according to particular colors and to beaver pelts. A cleaned, scraped, and stretched beaver hide (a plew) was a prime trade good, and its value was used as a common rate of exchange. One plew was worth six green beads with white centers; two plews were worth one opaque blue bead. William Wildschut and John Ewers wrote that the Crows were so fond of the small blue glass beads that they would trade a horse for one hundred of them.[2]

With tremendous changes and rapid acculturation in the late nineteenth century, many people abandoned the use of cradles, making them highly collectible items.

Europeans collected American Indian material beginning with their first contact. The classic period of collecting Plains art was from 1860 to 1910, when a tremendous amount of art was produced, and with substantial photographic and graphic documentation of tribal characteristics.[3] During this period, many Plains cradles made their way to museum collections. Several items were still not well documented, of course, especially if they had changed hands several times before reaching a museum. Some objects accompanied by histories were collected during the Indian Wars of the 1860s through the 1880s by soldiers, who often turned out to be reliable collectors. The Milwaukee Public Museum has a beaded Sioux cradle cover with good documentation, for example. The cradle was obtained from a scaffold burial by a person in government service. A note is attached stating, "The blue beaded papoose hood Papa stole from an Indian cemetery. The poor little baby having been placed in a tree[,] and [Papa] crawled a quarter of a mile past the encampment at night for his 'dirty work.'"[4]

Plains cradles of the late nineteenth century show distinct regional and tribal characteristics but are not always well identified. This problem, Barbara Hail explains, often stems from the manner in which pieces were collected. "The difference between 'collected from' and 'made by' must be considered in making attributions, since native customs lead to an intermix of material goods."[5] Hail points out that widespread intertribal trade existed, especially within linguistically related tribes. The Plains Crees and the Assiniboines often obtained their cradleboards from the Plains Ojibwa. And most tribes would rather sell the craft of another group than their own to an outsider. Intertribal marriages and wars, especially the spoils system, were also causes of the style confusion that exists today. A woman leaving her tribe for her husband's, for example, would often adapt her people's versions of quillwork and beadwork, blending the two styles. Inaccurate collection data, once recorded in museum files, are difficult to correct.[6]

Collectors often sold and obtained cradles for only a few dollars, such as the Oglála cradleboard (plate 23) that the collector sold to the Smithsonian for six dollars in 1885. Many cradles were sold to obtain food for the family. According to Barbara Hail, many of the Kiowa and Comanche cradles made during the period of cultural transition and economic hardship had "gotten away." It was difficult for Kiowa families to turn down a good offer in the hard years of the Depression. Some were pawned by their owners, and many were given away as gifts. One woman sold a cradleboard that had been made for her as a baby to pay for her college education in the 1930s.[7] With reservation life and forced assimilation, the creation and use of cradles declined. Many cradle-making traditions were lost. Photographs and descriptions in diaries, journals, and oral life histories housed in libraries have prevented the loss of much knowledge.

As an object of art today, a beaded cradle can sell for $25,000. A fully beaded Cheyenne hide and tacked wood cradle, 44.25 inches long, sold for $144,000 at a Bonhams and Butterfields auction in San Francisco on June 4, 2007. A Kiowa beaded canvas and tacked wood cradle, 42 inches long, went for $96,000 at the same sale. At Cowan's in Cincinnati, Ohio, in September 2007, a Sioux beaded hide cradle cover, 23.5 inches long, sold for $21,850. The autumn 2008 issue of *American Indian Art* listed several doll cradles to be sold during an April sale, including a Comanche beaded doll cradle, $15,525; a Comanche hide cradle, $13,800; an Arapaho hide cradle with doll, $9,200; and a Cheyenne beaded hide cradle, $8,625. Vanessa Jennings shared with me that a fully beaded Kiowa cradleboard would cost from $25,000 to $75,000 today, and it would take about nine months to complete.[8]

With the recent emphasis on traditional ways has come a resurgence of interest in cradles. "Old has become new" with baby care. Swaddling, for example, is an age-old practice from around the globe, from ancient Egyptians to migrating Central Asians in 4000 BC, who carried cradleboards on their backs. Swaddling an infant before settling the baby in its cradle was also a widespread practice among Plains mothers. According to

Vanessa Jennings, a Kiowa baby is still swaddled before being placed in the cradleboard. Today, swaddling is standard newborn care practice in many hospitals. Specially designed blankets, called swaddling blankets, can be purchased to secure and help an infant adjust to a new environment.

Cradle making for some Plains tribes is not a lost art, as evidenced by the work of Vanessa P. Jennings, Kiowa/Gila River Pima; Mike Kostelnik, Cheyenne; Susan Webber, Blackfeet; Thomas Haukaas, Sicangu Lakota; William Tall Bear, Cheyenne; and Jimmy Arterberry, Comanche.

Several cradle makers have achieved national acclaim with their skills. Vanessa P. Jennings has been named a Living National Treasure by the United States and Honored One by the Red Earth Festival in Oklahoma City, as well as consistently winning awards at the Santa Fe Indian Market. Her cradles can be found in the Buffalo Bill Center of the West in Cody, Wyoming; the National Cowboy Hall of Fame in Oklahoma City; the Heard Museum in Phoenix; and the National Museum of the American Indian in Washington, D.C. Thomas Haukaas has works in the collections of the Denver Art Museum, the Carnegie Museum of Art in Pittsburgh, and the Peabody Essex Museum in Salem, Massachusetts.

Jimmy Arterberry made a Comanche cradleboard in 1999 for the Haffenreffer Museum of Anthropology.[9] Mark Awakuni-Swetland and Mike Kostelnik examined and studied cradleboards at the Museum of the American Indian's Heye Center and at the Smithsonian Institution's National Museum of Natural History. Kostelnik made a personal fully beaded cradleboard and has published an article with detailed directions for making a Cheyenne cradle. William Tall Bear, from Tulsa, Oklahoma, continues to make fully beaded full-size Cheyenne cradles to compete in art shows. Susan Webber, Blackfoot from Browning, Montana, makes traditional Blackfoot cradleboards. She also serves in Montana's House of Representatives.

Despite a century and a half of political, economic, social, and religious upheaval, and the ongoing process of assimilation, the cradle has been able to adapt and keep its significance in the midst of a changing multicultural society. A child can still be found wrapped up as if in a cocoon, watching, eyes wide, from a baby board, hide, or canvas soft cradle or laced up tightly on a cradleboard. To photograph one's child in a cradle—in a family heirloom—establishes an important link with family history and tribal history. Instead of a "lifeless museum cradle collecting dust," a new cradle will be made to preserve a living child, and "the buckskin will breathe again and the wood will sing," as the cradle becomes a tangible link to a child's cultural heritage.[10]

APPENDIX A
Tribes Historically on the Plains

Apache Tribe of Oklahoma
Arikara
Arapaho
Assiniboine
Blackfoot
Cheyenne
Comanche
Crow
Gros Ventre
Hidatsa
Ioway
Kaw
Kiowa
Lakota
Lipan Apache
Mandan
Omaha
Osage
Otoe-Missouria
Pawnee
Plains Cree
Plains Métis
Plains Ojibwa
Ponca
Quapaw
Santee Dakota
Sarcee
Stoney
Tonkawa
Wichita and Affiliated Tribes (Kitsai, Waco, Taovaya, Iscani, and Tawakoni)
Yankton and Yanktonai

APPENDIX B
Plains Indian Terms for Cradles

Apache (Na'isha)	tsis-ts'áál or číšc'áál (cradleboard)
Arapaho (Hiinono'ei)	hectoonohuut (cradleboard)
Arikara (Sahnish)	be-ra-ka-kuth-oo (baby bag)
Assiniboine (Nakota)	iyók'iba (cradleboard) yo-k'i-ba (hide bag)
Blackfoot (Piikani)	kapimáán(cradleboard)
Cheyenne (Tsistsistas)	páhoešestótse (cradleboard) hóhkėha'e (soft cradle)
Comanche (Nʉmʉnʉʉ)	waakohno (cradleboard) haabikuno (night cradle)
Crow (Apsáalooke, Absaroke, or Absaroka)	bägät'ēt-chā (cradleboard)
Gros Ventre (A'aninin)	?a'hchii (baby bag)
Hidatsa (Nuxbaaga)	ma í dăk u dsi (swinging cradle) i si-da i-za wu-ze (cradle)
Ioway (Báxoje or Bah Kho-je)	hoxwawe (cradleboard)
Kaw (Kansa or Kanza)	oyóphe (cradleboard)
Kiowa (Cáuigú)	paih'dodl (cradleboard)
Lakota (Lakȟóta)	pȟóštaŋ (cradle) čhuwíč'iŋpa (lattice board)
Lipan Apache (Ndé)	istl tsg (cradleboard)
Mandan (Neuídia)	nä-he i-su-suk-he-nuk (baby bag)

Plains Métis	waspison (moss bag) tikinagan (cradleboard)
Omaha (Umó^{n}ho^{n})	udhuhe or uthu'he (cradleboard)
Osage (Wazhazhi)	odhophe or o-lo-psha (cradleboard)
Otoe-Missouria (Jiwere-Nut'achi)	uxuwe (cradleboard)
Pawnee (Chaticks-si-Chaticks)	ráciitu' (cradleboard)
Plains Cree (Paskwâwiyiniwak)	tihkinâkan (cradleboard) wâspison (moss bag)
Plains Ojibwa (Nahkawininiwak)	a'dikina'gûn (cradleboard)
Ponca (Pó^{n}ka or Panka)	uo'^{n}he-k^{h}e (cradleboard)
Quapaw (Okáxpa or O-Gah-Pah)	shi-zhi-kaazho (baby bed)
Santee Dakota (Isanti)	iyoḳopa (cradleboard) pȟóštaŋ (cradle)
Sarcee (T'suu T'ina)	t͡s!al (baby bag)
Tonkawa (Tickanwatic)	t'ca-bxan (sleeping place) wi'xwan (small one)
Wichita (KiriKirʔi:s)	ica:c (cradleboard)

APPENDIX C
List of Museums

The following museums have or have had Plains Indian cradles in their collections.

United States

ARKANSAS

Arkansas State University Museum, Jonesboro

University Museum, Fulbright College, University of Arkansas, Fayetteville

ARIZONA

Arizona Museum of Natural History

Heard Museum, Phoenix

CALIFORNIA

Phoebe A. Hearst Museum of Anthropology, Berkeley

Riverside Metropolitan Museum, Riverside

Southwest Museum of the American Indian, Los Angeles

COLORADO

Center for the Study of Indigenous Languages of the West, University of Colorado, Boulder

Colorado Historical Society Museum, Denver

Colorado Springs Fine Art Center, Colorado Springs

Denver Art Museum, Denver

Western History Collection, Photos, Denver Public Library, Denver

CONNECTICUT

Mashantucket Pequot Museum and Research Center, Mashantucket

Peabody Museum of Natural History, Yale University, New Haven

DISTRICT OF COLUMBIA

George Catlin's Indian Gallery, Smithsonian American Art Museum

Indian Arts and Crafts Board, Department of the Interior

National Museum of the American Indian

ILLINOIS

Field Museum of Natural History, Chicago

Illinois State Museum, Springfield

Schingoethe Center, Aurora

INDIANA

American Indian Studies Research Institute, Indiana University, Bloomington

Eiteljorg Museum of American Indians and Western Art, Indianapolis

Mathers Museum of World Cultures, Indiana University, Bloomington

Wanamaker Collection of American Indian Photographs, Mathers Museum of World Cultures, Indiana University, Bloomington

KANSAS

Iowa and Sac and Fox Mission, Highland

Kansas Historical Society, Topeka

Kansas Museum of History, Topeka

Kaw Mission State Historic Site, Council Grove

Mid-American All-Indian Center Museum, Wichita

Pawnee Indian Museum State Historic Site, Republic

MARYLAND

Cultural Resources Center, National Museum of the American Indian, Suitland

MASSACHUSETTS

Peabody Essex Museum, Salem

Peabody Museum of Archaeology and Ethnology, Harvard University, Cambridge

MICHIGAN

Cultural Heritage Center, Brimley

MINNESOTA

Minneapolis American Indian Center, Minneapolis

Minnesota Historical Society, St. Paul

Southwest Minnesota State University Museum, Marshall

MISSOURI

Museum of Anthropology, University of Missouri, Columbia

MONTANA

Blaine County Museum, Chinook

Carter County Museum, Ekalaka

Cheyenne Indian Museum, Ashland

Cheyenne Indian Museum, Lame Deer

Fort Peck Tribal Museum, Poplar

H. Earl Clack Memorial Museum, Havre

High Plains Heritage Center, Great Falls

Little Bighorn Battlefield National Monument, Crow Agency

Montana Historical Society Museum, Helena

Museum of the Plains Indian, Browning

Museum of the Rockies, Bozeman

Old Trail Museum, Choteau

Peigan Institute, Browning

Western Heritage Center, Billings

William P. Sherman Library Archives, Great Falls

Wolf Point Area Museum, Wolf Point

NEBRASKA

Indian Center, Lincoln

Nebraska History Museum, Lincoln

Omaha Public Library, Omaha

University of Nebraska State Museum, Lincoln

NEW MEXICO

Wheelwright Museum of the American Indian, Santa Fe

NEW YORK

American Museum of Natural History, New York City

Brooklyn Museum, Brooklyn

Fenimore Art Museum, Cooperstown

Heye Foundation Records, National Museum of the American Indian, New York City

NORTH DAKOTA

North Dakota Heritage Center and State Museum, Bismarck

Three Affiliated Tribes Museum, New Town

Turtle Mountain Chippewa Heritage Center, Belcourt

OKLAHOMA

American Indian Cultural Center and Museum, Oklahoma City

Ataloa Lodge Museum, Muskogee

Cheyenne Cultural Center, Clinton

Comanche National Museum and Cultural Center, Lawton

Gilcrease Museum, Thomas Gilcrease Institute of American History and Art, Tulsa

Kanza Museum, Kaw City

Kiowa Museum, Carnegie

Mabee-Gerrer Museum of Art, Shawnee

Marland Grand Home, Ponca City

Museum of the Great Plains, Lawton

Museum of the Red River, Idabel

Oklahoma History Center, Oklahoma City

Osage Nation Museum, Pawhuska

Philbrook Museum of Art, Tulsa

Quapaw Tribal Museum, Quapaw

Red Earth Art Center, Oklahoma City

Sam Noble Oklahoma Museum of Natural History, Norman

Southern Plains Indian Museum, Anadarko

Tonkawa Tribal Museum, Tonkawa

Wichita Tribal History Center, Anadarko

Woolaroc Museum and Wildlife Preserve, Bartlesville

PENNSYLVANIA

North Museum of Nature and Science, Lancaster

University of Pennsylvania Museum of Archaeology and Anthropology, Philadelphia

RHODE ISLAND

Haffenreffer Museum of Anthropology, Brown University, Bristol

SOUTH DAKOTA

Akta Lakota Museum and Cultural Center, Chamberlain

Buechel Memorial Lakota Museum, St. Francis

Heritage Center at Red Cloud Indian School, Pine Ridge

HVJ Lakota Cultural Center, Eagle Butte

Indian Museum of North America and Crazy Horse Memorial, Crazy Horse

Museum of the South Dakota Historical Society, Pierre

Oglala Lakota College Historical Center, Kyle

Sicangu Heritage Center, Mission

Sioux Indian Museum, Rapid City

TEXAS

Panhandle–Plains Historical Museum, Canyon

Texas Memorial Museum, University of Texas, Austin

Texas State Historical Association, Austin

WISCONSIN

Milwaukee Public Museum, Milwaukee

WYOMING

Arapaho Cultural Museum, Ethete

Buffalo Bill Center of the West, Cody

Colter Bay Visitor Center and Indian Arts Museum, Grand Teton National Park, Moose

Hot Springs Historical Museum, Thermopolis

Wyoming State Historical Society, Cheyenne

Canada

Canadian Museum of History (formerly Canadian Museum of Civilization), Gatineau, Quebec

Glenbow Museum, Calgary, Alberta

Nakoda Institute, Morely, Alberta

Whyte Museum of the Canadian Rockies, Banff, Alberta

Peace River Museum, Archives and Mackenzie Centre, Peace River, Alberta

Virtual Museum of Métis History and Culture, Gabriel Dumont Institute, Saskatoon, Saskatchewan

Michif Métis Museum, Vavenby, British Columbia

NOTES

INTRODUCTION

1. Based on a story told by a Crow woman in Frank Bird Linderman's *Pretty-Shield*, 33–36.
2. McQuiston and McQuiston, *Dolls and Toys of Native America.*
3. Quoted in Hail, *Gifts of Pride and Love*, 17.
4. Feder, "Pawnee Cradleboards."
5. Schneider, "Kiowa and Comanche Baby Carriers," 305.
6. Hail, *Gifts of Pride and Love.*
7. DeMallie, *Plains.*

CHAPTER 1. THE WOMAN'S PLACE

1. Mails, *Mystic Warriors of the Plains*, 212.
2. Niethammer, *Daughters of the Earth.*
3. Hyman, *Dakota Women's Work.*
4. Greene, "Art until 1900," 1045.
5. Ibid.; Orchard, *Technique of Porcupine-Quill Decoration.*
6. Greene "Art Until 1900"; Lyford, *Quill and Beadwork.*
7. Fitzgerald and Fitzgerald, *Spirit of Indian Women*, 2.
8. M. Gilmore, *Notes on the Gynecology*, 73.
9. Lowie, *Crow Indians*, 33. A special form of vision can create a *bātsira'pe*, "a mysterious animal or part of an animal or inanimate object that dwells within a person's body and emerges on some definite stimulus" (264). In Muskrat's vision, a weasel stepped on her neck before entering her stomach. It gave her control over weasels but cautioned her that if ever struck in the kidneys, she would go into a trance.
10. St. Pierre and Long Soldier, *Walking in the Sacred Manner*, 82.
11. Ibid., 83.
12. Ibid.
13. Ibid., 74–75. Joseph Rocky Boy was born in 1900 on the Yankton Sioux Reservation in South Dakota. Early in his life, he was active in the Native American church and was a practicing Presbyterian and follower of the older Canku Luta religion of his people.
14. Ewers, *Blackfeet: Raiders*, 101.
15. DeMallie, *Plains.*
16. Wilson, "Horse and the Dog in Hidatsa Culture."
17. Linderman, *Pretty-Shield.*
18. Red Shirt, *Turtle Lung Woman's Granddaughter*, 115.
19. St. Pierre and Long Soldier, *Walking in the Sacred Manner.*
20. Grinnell, *Cheyenne Indians*, 2:174.
21. Hilger, "Notes on Cheyenne Child Life."
22. Hassrick, *The Sioux*; Red Shirt, *Turtle Lung Woman's Granddaughter*; and St. Pierre and Long Soldier, *Walking in the Sacred Manner*

23. Red Shirt, *Turtle Lung Woman's Granddaughter*, 116.
24. Voget, *They Call Me Agnes*, 38.
25. M. Gilmore, *Uses of Plants by the Indians*, 12.
26. Gilman and Schneider, *Way to Independence*, 127; and Gilbert Wilson's field notes, 1916, vol. 20, Gilbert L. and Frederick N. Wilson Papers, Minnesota Historical Society, St. Paul.
27. Hassrick, *The Sioux*; and Powers, *Oglala Women*.
28. Walters, *Spirit of Native America*, 36.
29. Ibid.

CHAPTER 2. PLAINS CRADLES

1. Henry, *All About Horses*.
2. Mason, "Cradles," 358.
3. Ibid.
4. Hail, *Hau, Kóla!*
5. Mason, "Cradles," 358.

CHAPTER 3. SANTEE DAKOTA

1. DeMallie, *Plains*.
2. John Koontz, Siouan linguist, Department of Linguistics, University of Colorado Boulder, email to the author, April 17, 2006; Riggs, *Dakota Grammar*, 207.
3. Riggs, *Dakota Grammar*, 207–8.
4. Pond, *Dakotas or Sioux in Minnesota*, 41.
5. Catlin, *Letters and Notes*, vol. 2; and Pond, *Dakotas or Sioux in Minnesota*.
6. Pond, *Dakotas or Sioux in Minnesota*, 41.
7. Catlin, *Letters and Notes*, vol. 2, plate 232; Kramer, "Intersections."
8. Kramer, "Intersections," 166.
9. Catlin, *Letters and Notes*, 2:132.
10. Quoted in Feest and Kasprycki, *Peoples of the Twilight*, 190.
11. Pond, *Dakotas or Sioux in Minnesota*.
12. Bushnell, *Burials of the Algonquian, Siouan, and Caddoan*; and Wallis, "Canadian Dakota."
13. Hassrick, *The Sioux*; and R. Lessard, "Lakota Cradles."
14. Greene, "Soft Cradles of the Central Plains," 96.
15. Wissler, "Some Protective Designs of the Dakota."
16. Halvorson, *Sacred Beauty*.
17. Ibid.
18. Wallis, "Canadian Dakota," 27.
19. Cited in Diedrich, *Old Betsey*, 19.
20. M. Gilmore, *Uses of the Plants by the Indians*, 62.
21. Wallis, "Canadian Dakota," 27.
22. Ibid.; and Diedrich, *Old Betsey*.
23. Pond, *Dakotas or Sioux in Minnesota*; Wallis, "Canadian Dakota"; and Diedrich, *Old Betsey*.
24. Catlin, *Letters and Notes*, 2:133–34.
25. Hyman, *Dakota Women's Work*.
26. Quoted in Feest and Kasprycki, *Peoples of the Twilight*, 190.
27. Kramer, "Intersections," 166. Petroglyphs of the thunderbird have been found across the plains. Keyser and Klassen, *Plains Indian Rock Art*.

28. My measurements differ from Mason's measurements in the book *Cradles of the American Aborigines*. He measured the cradle as a whole (29.5 × 12.0 inches) but also provided measurements for various parts: a side board 2.5 inches long and 4.5 inches high, and an "awning-frame" 16.5 inches wide and 14.5 inches high (201). Magee, "Anthropology Conservation Laboratory Treatment Report," reported the measurements as 135 cm long, 45.5 cm wide, 0.64 cm thick, and 22.9 cm high.
29. Lyford, *Quill and Beadwork*.
30. Hyman, *Dakota Women's Work*, 18.

CHAPTER 4. YANKTON AND YANKTONAI

1. F. D. Lessard, "Defining the Central Plains Art Area," 43; and R. Lessard, "Lakota Cradles," 45–53.
2. R. Lessard, "Lakota Cradles," 45–46; and F. D. Lessard, "Defining the Central Plains Art Area," 43.

CHAPTER 5. IOWAY

1. Although the words Ioway and Iowa are often used interchangeably, Iowa is the name for tribal entities (the Iowa Tribe of Oklahoma and the Iowa Tribe of Kansas and Nebraska), and Ioway is used for the people themselves and the language. To minimize potential confusion, I use Ioway throughout this book except in formal tribe names and similar contexts.
2. Lance M. Foster, email to the author, March 6, 2007.
3. Jimm GoodTracks, Ioway linguistic specialist, email to the author, March 6, 2007.
4. Blaine, *Ioway Indians*, 178.
5. Ibid., 230–31.
6. Skinner, "Ethnology of the Ioway Indians," 280.
7. Ibid., 281
8. Ibid. See also chapter 9 in this volume.
9. Koch, *Dress Clothing of the Plains Indians*.

CHAPTER 6. PLAINS CREE

1. Curtis, *North American Indian*, 18:207.
2. Dorion, "Opikinawasowin."
3. Mandelbaum, *Plains Cree*, 140. Mandelbaum cites Paget, *People of the Plains*, 122.
4. Denig, *Five Indian Tribes of the Upper Missouri*, 129.
5. Lotrich, "Indian Terms for the Cradle," 85.
6. Skinner, "Notes on the Plains Cree."
7. Hail, *Hau, Kóla!*; and Denig, *Five Indian Tribes of the Upper Missouri*, 129.
8. Hail, *Hau, Kóla!*, 65.
9. Greene, "Art Until 1900."
10. Curtis, *North American Indian*, 18:67–68.
11. Ibid., 18:23.
12. Mandelbaum, *Plains Cree*, 139.
13. Dorion, "Opikinawasowin."
14. Curtis, *North American Indian*, vol. 18; Dusenberry, *Montana Cree*; Mandelbaum, *Plains Cree*; and Dorion, "Opikinawasowin."
15. Dorion, "Opikinawasowin," 52.
16. Mandelbaum, *Plains Cree*.
17. Curtis, *North American Indian*, 18:67–68; and Mandelbaum, *Plains Cree*, 139.

CHAPTER 7. PLAINS OJIBWA

1. Howard, *Plains-Ojibwa*.
2. "Ojibwe Cradle Basket," accession no. 1977.28.1, Artifacts, Collections Online, Minnesota Historical Society, accessed June 27, 2018, http://collections.mnhs.org/cms/display.php?irn=10404335.
3. "Ojibwe Cradleboard Blanket," accession no. 10000.92, Jeannette O. and Harry D. Ayer Ojibwe Collection, Collections Online, Minnesota Historical Society, accessed June 27, 2018, http://collections.mnhs.org/cms/display.php?irn=10257470.
4. Densmore, *Chippewa Customs*, 13.
5. Lotrich, "Indian Terms for the Cradle," 87–88.
6. Toni Jo Atchison, Little Shell Chippewa, Montana, email to the author, September 4, 2007, citing an Ojibwa dictionary.
7. Ritzenthaler and Ritzenthaler, *Woodland Indians*, 30.
8. Howard, *Plains-Ojibwa*, 220.
9. Catlin, *Letters and Notes*, 139.
10. Densmore, *Chippewa Customs*.
11. Ibid., 48.
12. Ibid., 48–49.
13. Pond, *Dakota or Sioux in Minnesota*, 164–65.
14. McKenney and Hall, *History of the Indian Tribes of North America*; and Densmore, *Chippewa Customs*.
15. Densmore, *Chippewa Customs*, 172.
16. Ibid., 173.
17. Ibid.; and Howard, *Plains-Ojibwa*.
18. Howard, *Plains-Ojibwa*.
19. Densmore, *Chippewa Customs*, 51.

CHAPTER 8. OTOE-MISSOURIA

1. Whitman, *Oto*, 65–66. I describe a typical Siouan Prairie cradleboard, collected by Alanson Skinner in 1922 in Perkins, Oklahoma, in chapter 4, "Ioway."
2. Jimm GoodTracks, email to the author, April 16, 2006.
3. Whitman, *Oto*, 65.
4. Ibid., 66.
5. Ibid.
6. Ibid.
7. Ibid., 67.
8. Ibid., 66

CHAPTER 9. OSAGE

1. Koontz email, April 17, 2006.
2. Feder, "Pawnee Cradleboards," 48.
3. Kathryn Red Corn, Osage Tribal Museum, interview by the author, June 27, 2005.
4. Mathews, *Osages*; Bailey and Swan, *Art of the Osage*.
5. Marie Maker, "Indian Doctoring, Baby Beds, Religion and Some Life History Material," Osage Oral History, 1968, vol. 47, Western History Collections, University of Oklahoma Libraries, Norman.
6. Mathews, *Osages*, 329.
7. Ibid.
8. Ibid., 327.

9. Ibid.
10. Tixier, *Travels on the Osage Prairies*, 255.
11. Ibid., 136.
12. Catlin, *Letters and Notes*, 41.
13. Mathews, *Osages*, 329.
14. La Flesche, *Osage and the Invisible World*, 177.
15. Bailey and Swan, *Art of the Osage*.
16. Catlin, *Letters and Notes*.

CHAPTER 10. KAW

1. Kanza Language Project, Kaw Nation, email to the author, April 2006.
2. Lowie, *Indians of the Plains*, 43.
3. James, *Account of an Expedition*, 1:126.
4. Ibid., 1:128.
5. Unrau, *The Kansa Indians*, 35, quoting from "Notes on the Missouri River," 308.

CHAPTER 11. OMAHA

1. Koontz email, April 17, 2006.
2. Fletcher and La Flesche, *Omaha Tribe*.
3. Feder, "Pawnee Cradleboards"; and J. Dorsey, "Omaha Sociology."
4. See *Omaha Papoose*, ca. 1880–1900, photoprint, Digital Collections, Denver Public Library, http://digital.denverlibrary.org/cdm/singleitem/collection/p15330coll22/id/35572/rec/2.
5. Mark Awakuni-Swetland, emails to the author, February 19 and February 27, 2007.
6. Cross stitched cradleboard band, Omaha, collected in 1930, North American Ethnographic Collection, American Museum of Natural History, cat. no. 50.2/3083, https://anthro.amnh.org/anthropology/databases/common/image_dup.cfm?catno=50%2E2%2F%203083%20A; and machine-stitched cradleboard band, Omaha, collected in 1930, North American Ethnographic Collection, American Museum of Natural History, cat. no. 50.2/3084, https://anthro.amnh.org/anthropology/databases/common/image_dup.cfm?catno=50%2E2%2F%203084%20A.
7. Mark Awakuni-Swetland, emails to the author, February 19 and February 27, 2007.
8. J. Dorsey, "Omaha Dwellings," 276.
9. James, *Account of an Expedition*, 1:215.
10. Ibid.
11. J. Dorsey, "Omaha Sociology," 263.
12. Fletcher and La Flesche, *Omaha Tribe*, 584.
13. M. Gilmore, *Uses of Plants by the Indians*, 62.
14. J. Dorsey, "Omaha Sociology."
15. Ibid., 264.
16. James, *Account of an Expedition*, 1:216.
17. Fletcher and La Flesche, *Omaha Tribe*, 327.
18. Kindscher, *Medicinal Wild Plants of the Prairie*, 262.
19. J. Dorsey, "Omaha Sociology."
20. Fletcher and La Flesche, *Omaha Tribe*, 328.
21. Ibid., 114–16.
22. Ibid., 117.
23. Fletcher and La Flesche, *Omaha Tribe*, 329.
24. Awakuni-Swetland email, February 27, 2007.
25. Ibid., February 19 and February 27, 2007; Fletcher and La Flesche, *Omaha Tribe*, 506.

CHAPTER 12. PONCA

1. Fletcher and La Flesche, *Omaha Tribe.*
2. Koontz email, April 17, 2006.
3. Howard, *Ponca Tribe*, 51.
4. Mary Catherine Ellis, collections manager, Wheelwright Museum of the American Indian, Santa Fe, New Mexico, personal communication, February 14, 2007.
5. Zimmerman, *White Eagle.*
6. Howard, *Ponca Tribe*, 144.
7. Ibid., 143.
8. Zimmerman, *White Eagle.*
9. Howard, *Ponca Tribe.*

CHAPTER 13. PAWNEE

1. American Indian Studies Research Institute, *Skiri Pawnee Multimedia Dictionary.*
2. Feder, "Pawnee Cradleboards."
3. Ibid., 41.
4. Grinnell, *Pawnee, Blackfoot, and Cheyenne*, n.p.
5. Blaine, *Some Things Are Not Forgotten*, 126.
6. Dorsey and Murie, *Notes on Skidi Pawnee Society*, 88 and 89; DeMallie, *Plains.*
7. Blaine, *Some Things Are Not Forgotten*, 118.
8. Ibid., 119.
9. Kindscher, *Medicinal Wild Plants of the Prairie*, 264.
10. Blaine, *Some Things Are Not Forgotten*, 120.
11. M. Gilmore, *Uses of Plants by the Indians*, 10.
12. Blaine, *Some Things Are Not Forgotten*, 120.
13. Ibid., 121.
14. Ibid.
15. Densmore, *Pawnee Music*; and Curtis, *North American Indian*, vol. 1.
16. Curtis Burlin, *Indians' Book*, 101–2.
17. Densmore, *Pawnee Music*, 21.
18. Curtis Burlin, *Indians' Book*, 101–2.
19. Feder, "Pawnee Cradleboards," 45.

CHAPTER 14. CROW

1. Lotrich, "Indian Terms for the Cradle," 99.
2. Lessard, "Crow Indian Art," 9.
3. Wildschut and Ewers, *Crow Indian Beadwork*, 34.
4. Voget, *They Call Me Agnes*, 44.
5. McLaughlin, *Arts of Diplomacy.*
6. Wildschut and Ewers, *Crow Indian Beadwork*, 45.
7. McLaughlin, *Arts of Diplomacy.*
8. Wildschut and Ewers, *Crow Indian Beadwork.*
9. Denig, *Five Indian Tribes of the Upper Missouri*, 37. Lessard, "Crow Indian Art," 57.
10. Hail, *Hau, Kóla!* 59–60.
11. Wildschut and Ewers, *Crow Indian Beadwork.*
12. Voget, *They Call Me Agnes.*
13. Ibid., 36; Lowie, "Social Life of the Crow Indians"; and Linderman, *Pretty-Shield.*

14. Voget, *They Call Me Agnes*, 36.
15. Linderman, *Pretty-Shield*, 146.
16. Ibid., 146–47.
17. Ibid., 147–48.
18. Voget, *They Call Me Agnes*, 41.
19. Lowie, "Social Life of the Crow Indians."
20. Lowie, *Crow Indians*.
21. Wildschut and Ewers, *Crow Indian Beadwork*, 47.

CHAPTER 15. BLACKFOOT

1. DeMallie, *Plains*.
2. Museum of the Plains Indian and Craft Center, *Historic and Contemporary Plateau and Plains Cradles*, 3.
3. Mason, *Cradles of the American Aborigines*.
4. Ewers, *Blackfeet: Raiders*, 102.
5. Lotrich, "Indian Terms for the Cradle," 84.
6. Hungry Wolf, *Ways of My Grandmothers*, 248.
7. Ibid.
8. Lotrich, "Indian Terms for the Cradle," 84.
9. Hungry Wolf, *Ways of My Grandmothers*; and McClintock, *Old North Trail*.
10. Ewers, *Blackfeet Crafts* and *Blackfeet: Raiders*.
11. Dempsey, "Religious Significance of Blackfoot Quillwork," 52–53.
12. Ewers, *Blackfeet: Raiders*, 119.
13. Ibid., 120.
14. Hungry Wolf, *Ways of My Grandmothers*, 192.
15. Ibid., 194.
16. Kindscher, *Medicinal Wild Plants of the Prairie*, 256.
17. Hungry Wolf, *Ways of My Grandmothers*, 194.
18. DeMallie, *Plains*.
19. Ewers, *Blackfeet: Raiders*, 101.
20. Hungry Wolf, *Ways of My Grandmothers*, 194.
21. Ewers, *Blackfeet: Raiders*, 101.

CHAPTER 16. ARAPAHO

1. Hartwell Francis, Department of Linguistics, University of Colorado Boulder, email to the author, March 29, 2006.
2. Hilger, *Arapaho Child Life*, 30.
3. Ibid.
4. Kroeber, *Arapaho*, 67–68.
5. Ibid., 68–69.
6. J. Anderson, *One Hundred Years of Old Sage*; M. Gilmore, *Notes on the Gynecology*; and Kroeber, *Arapaho*.
7. J. Anderson, *One Hundred Years of Old Sage*; and Hilger, *Arapaho Child Life*.
8. Hilger, *Arapaho Child Life*, 35–36.
9. Cleaver Warden field notes (1903–6), Dorsey-Warden Collection, Field Museum of Natural History, Chicago, Illinois.
10. Greene, "Soft Cradles of the Central Plains," 106.
11. Kroeber, *Arapaho*.

12. J. Anderson, *Arapaho Women's Quillwork.*
13. Hilger, *Arapaho Child Life*; and R. Gilmore, "Northern Arapaho Cradle."
14. Myrtle Lincoln, "Life History Material: Childbirth and Child Care," 1970, Arapaho Oral History, 1970, vol. 3, p. 14, Western History Collections, University of Oklahoma Libraries, Norman. Myrtle Lincoln was born in 1888 Oklahoma Territory. Her uncle arranged her marriage to Howard Howling Buffalo, a.k.a. Howard Lincoln. Myrtle and Howard had seven children.
15. Ibid.; and Hilger, *Arapaho Child Life.*
16. Myrtle Lincoln, "Childbirth," Arapaho Oral History, 1971, vol. 1.
17. Hilger, *Arapaho Child Life*, 17.
18. Ibid., 21.
19. Ibid.; J. Anderson, *One Hundred Years of Old Sage*; and Sutter, *Tell Me, Grandmother.*
20. Lincoln, "Childbirth"; and J. Anderson, *One Hundred Years of Old Sage.*
21. Hilger, *Arapaho Child Life*, 22.
22. Kroeber, *Arapaho*, 16.
23. Hilger, *Arapaho Child Life*, 23.
24. Ibid.
25. Kroeber, *Arapaho*; G. Dorsey, *Mythology of the Wichita*, *Pawnee*, and *Traditions of the Arikara*; Hilger, *Arapaho Child Life*; Greene, "Soft Cradles of the Central Plains"; and J. Anderson, *Arapaho Women's Quillwork*
26. Kroeber, *Arapaho*, 67–68; J. Anderson, *Arapaho Women's Quillwork*, 44; and Curtis Burlin, *Indians' Book*, 201.
27. George Dorsey, "The Arapaho," undated manuscript, A.1, 2/8, Archives of the Department of Anthropology, Field Museum of Natural History, Chicago.
28. J. Anderson, *Arapaho Women's Quillwork.*
29. Ibid.
30. Greene, "Soft Cradles of the Central Plains."

CHAPTER 17. WICHITA

1. David Roods, linguist, Wichita Language Project, Department of Linguistics, University of Colorado Boulder, email to the author, April 27, 2006.
2. Mason, *Cradles of the American Aborigines*, 358.
3. Spier, "Havasupai Ethnography."
4. Dellinger, "Baby Cradles of the Ozark Bluff-Dwellers," 214.
5. Newcomb, *Indians of Texas.*
6. G. Dorsey, *Mythology of the Wichita*, 19–20.
7. Ibid., 11–12.
8. Ibid., 12.

CHAPTER 18. LIPAN APACHE

1. Terrell, *Plains Apache.*
2. Daniel Castro Romero Jr., general council chairman, Lipan Apache Tribe of Texas, email to the author, January 31, 2007.
3. Terrell, *Apache Chronicle*; Romero, email to the author, September 5, 2007.
4. Buckelew, Dennis, and Dennis, *Life of F. M. Buckelew*, 92.
5. Ibid.
6. Terrell, *Apache Chronicles*, 93.
7. Ibid.
8. Ibid., 94.

9. Ibid.
10. Romero, email to the author, April 6, 2007.
11. Terrell, *Apache Chronicles*, 93.
12. Terrell, *Plains Apache*, 36; and Newcomb, *Indians of Texas.*
13. Hrdlička, *Physiological and Medical Observations*, 74.
14. Ibid.; Newcomb, *Indians of Texas.*
15. Daniel Castro Romero Jr., "Three Lipan Apache Songs," Indians.org, accessed November 30, 2006, www.indians.org/welker/lipsong.htm.
16. Ibid.
17. Terrell, *Plains Apache.*

CHAPTER 19. COMANCHE

1. Wallace and Hoebel, *Comanches.*
2. Berlandier, *Indians of Texas in 1830*, 87–88. During Berlandier's travels in 1825, he wrote an account of birth among some tribes of south Texas—Huecos, Tahuacanos, Comanches, and Lipan Apaches. He did not specifically say which tribe he was writing about. A century later, Wallace and Hoebel obtained a similar description of birth customs from their aged Comanche informants. Wallace and Hoebel, *Comanches.*
3. Hail, *Gifts of Pride and Love*, 24.
4. Ibid., 25.
5. Ibid., 26
6. Wallace and Hoebel, *Comanches*, 120–21.
7. Hail, *Gifts of Pride and Love*, 26.
8. Schneider, "Kiowa and Comanche Baby Carriers," 307.
9. Hail, *Gifts of Pride and Love*, 103.
10. Wallace and Hoebel, *Comanches*, 144.
11. Ibid., 120.
12. Ibid., 119.
13. Berlandier, *Indians of Texas in 1830*, 87.
14. Wallace and Hoebel, *Comanches*, 144.
15. Newcomb, *Indians of Texas.*
16. Wallace and Hoebel, *Comanches*, 161.
17. Ibid.; Schneider, "Kiowa and Comanche Baby Carriers"; and Hail, *Gifts of Pride and Love*; Berlandier, *Indians of Texas in 1830*, 33.
18. Mason, *Cradles of the American Aborigines*, 198.
19. Hail, *Gifts of Pride and Love*, 108.
20. Wallace and Hoebel, *Comanches.*
21. Mason, *Cradles of the American Aborigines*, 199.

CHAPTER 20. KIOWA

1. Hail, *Gifts of Pride and Love*, 23.
2. *Harper's Weekly*, May 25, 1867, 329.
3. Hail, *Gifts of Pride and Love*, 61.
4. Ibid.
5. Ray C. Doyah, interview by the author, February 2007.
6. Jennings, *Kiowa Cradleboard Maker.*
7. Hail, *Gifts of Pride and Love*, 85.
8. Ibid.

9. Vanessa Jennings, interview by the author, August 2008.
10. Hail, *Gifts of Pride and Love*, 26.
11. Ibid.
12. Battey, *Life and Adventures of a Quaker*, 329–30.
13. Mary Haumpy, "Allotment; Land Leasing; Some Life History Material," Kiowa Oral History, 1967, vol. 36, Western History Collections, University of Oklahoma Libraries, Norman, Oklahoma.
14. Hail, *Gifts of Pride and Love.*
15. Schneider, "Kiowa and Comanche Baby Carriers," 313.
16. Ibid.
17. Battey, *Life and Adventures of a Quaker*, 331.
18. Hail, *Gifts of Pride and Love*; and Doyah, personal communication with the author, June 2006.
19. Ray C. Doyah, "Timeless Treasures: The Legacy of Guohaddle's Cradle," unpublished essay, private collection.

CHAPTER 21. APACHE TRIBE OF OKLAHOMA

1. Alfred Chalepah, "Child Care," August 9, 1967, interview, p. 5, Kiowa Apache Oral History, vol. 40, Western History Collections, University of Oklahoma Libraries, Norman; and J. Morgan, "Classificatory Verbs in Plains Apache," 36.
2. Terrell, *Apache Chronicle.*
3. Chalepah, "Child Care"; Eggan, *Social Anthropology*, 137.
4. Hail, *Gifts of Pride and Love.*
5. Ibid.; Hansen, "Paukeigope"; and Jennings interview.
6. Eggan, *Social Anthropology*, 138.
7. Chalepah, "Child Care," 4.
8. Terrell, *Plains Apache*, 36.
9. Chalepah, "Child Care," 7.
10. Eggan, *Social Anthropology*; and Schweinfurth, *Prayer on Top of the Earth.*
11. Schweinfurth, *Prayer on Top of the Earth*, 121–22.

CHAPTER 22. CHEYENNE

1. Chief Dull Knife College, Cheyenne Dictionary, last updated August 23, 2017, http://cdkc.edu/cheyennedictionary/index.html.
2. Lotrich, "Indian Terms for the Cradle," 84–85.
3. Greene, "Soft Cradles of the Central Plains."
4. Grinnell, *Cheyenne Indians*, 1:168.
5. Marriott, "Trade Guild."
6. John Sipe Jr., Northern Cheyenne chief, historian, and consultant, interview by the author, February 3, 2007.
7. Greene, "Soft Cradles of the Central Plains."
8. Ibid.
9. Green, "Cheyenne Soft Cradle Covers," 7.
10. Kostelnik, "Nineteenth-Century Cheyenne Cradleboard."
11. Ibid., 11.
12. Marriot, "Trade Guild."
13. Kostelnik, "Nineteenth-Century Cheyenne Cradleboard."
14. Grinnell, *Cheyenne Indians.*
15. Ibid., 104.

16. Hilger, "Notes on Cheyenne Child Life."
17. Marriot, "Trade Guild," 24.
18. Grinnell, "Cheyenne Woman Customs," 145.
19. Ibid.
20. Sipe interview.
21. Eggan, *Social Anthropology*, 63.
22. Ibid.
23. "Cheyenne Cradleboards," *Cheyenne Visions II*, Denver Art Museum, accessed March 23, 2006, http://exhibits.denverartmuseum.org/cheyennevisions2/CVII_cradleBoards.htm.
24. Grinnell, *Cheyenne Indians*; Sipe interview.
25. Ehrenreich, "Zur Ornamentik"; Greene, "Soft Cradles of the Central Plains," 109.
26. Sipe interview.

CHAPTER 23. TONKAWA

1. Hasskarl, "Culture and History of the Tonkawa Indians."
2. Newcomb, *Indians of Texas*.
3. Hoijer, *Tonkawa*, 131, 139.
4. Don Patterson, Tonkawa tribal historian, interview by the author, February 1, 2007.
5. Newcomb, *Indians of Texas*, 145–46.
6. Patterson interview.

CHAPTER 24. LAKOTA

1. R. Lessard, "Lakota Cradles," 45; and Koontz email, April 17, 2006.
2. R. Lessard, "Lakota Cradles," 46.
3. Hassrick, *The Sioux*, 272.
4. Maximilian, *People of the First Man*, 245.
5. Greene, "Soft Cradles of the Central Plains," 96, 98. Greene systematically examined more than 150 baby carriers in museum collections along with the associated notes and photographs, to define the soft cradles of the central plains.
6. Ibid.
7. Ibid., 101.
8. Lyford, *Quill and Beadwork*; and Orchard, *Technique of Porcupine-Quill Decoration*.
9. Lyford, *Quill and Beadwork*, 42.
10. Ibid., 51.
11. Hassrick, *The Sioux*, 191. Women who dreamed of the Double Woman, or Deer Woman, were said to be famous for their ability to do porcupine quillwork.
12. Lyford, *Quill and Beadwork*.
13. Ibid.
14. R. Lessard, "Lakota Cradles," 51.
15. Red Shirt, *Turtle Lung Woman's Granddaughter*, 116.
16. Greene, "Soft Cradles of the Central Plains," 97.
17. Hassrick, *The Sioux*; and Lame Deer and Erodes, *Lame Deer*.
18. Greene, "Soft Cradles of the Central Plains," 111–12.
19. Hassrick, *The Sioux*; and Lame Deer and Erodes, *Lame Deer*.
20. Hassrick, *The Sioux*.
21. Ibid.; St. Pierre and Long Soldier, *Walking in the Sacred Manner*; and Red Shirt, *Turtle Lung Woman's Granddaughter*.
22. DeMallie, *Plains*, 808.

23. Hassrick, *The Sioux*, 312; Powers, *Oglala Women*; and St. Pierre and Long Soldier, *Walking in the Sacred Manner.*
24. Red Shirt, *Turtle Lung Woman's Granddaughter*, 114.
25. Ibid.
26. Lame Deer and Erodes, *Lame Deer*, 113.
27. Wissler, "Some Protective Designs of the Dakota," 243.
28. Lyford, *Quill and Beadwork*, 86.
29. Lame Deer and Erodes, *Lame Deer*, 116.
30. Ibid.
31. Hail, *Hau, Kóla!* 155.
32. Lyford, *Quill and Beadwork*, 76.
33. Wissler, "Some Protective Designs of the Dakota."

CHAPTER 25. ASSINIBOINE

1. Kennedy, *Assiniboines*, 43.
2. Lotrich, "Indian Terms for the Cradle," 98–99.
3. Curtis, *North American Indian*, 18:216.
4. Denig, "Indian Tribes of the Upper Missouri," 519–20.
5. Ibid., 519.
6. Bodmer, *Karl Bodmer's America*, 321. Karl Bodmer was an artist who accompanied Prince Maximilian on his travels to North America in 1830. The cradle at the bottom of Bodmer's plate 332 corresponds in appearance to Maximilian's description of Mandan cradles: leather bags hung from the house beams with leather straps. Maximilian, *Travels in the Interior of North America.*
7. Lowie, "Assiniboine," 38.
8. Kennedy, *Assiniboines*; and Denig, "Indian Tribes of the Upper Missouri."
9. Kennedy, *Assiniboines*, 33.
10. Ibid.
11. Lowie, "Assiniboine."
12. Kennedy, *Assiniboines*; and Denig, "Indian Tribes of the Upper Missouri."
13. Kennedy, *Assiniboines.*

CHAPTER 26. HIDATSA

1. Cox, "Hidatsas," n.p.
2. Lotrich, "Indian Terms for the Cradle," 99.
3. Cowell, *English-Gros Ventre*; Maximilian, *People of the First Man*, 37, and *Travels in the Interior of North America.* Maximilian called the Hidatsa Minnetarees in 1839–41.
4. Bowers, *Hidatsa Social and Ceremonial Organizations*, 128.
5. Wilson, "Horse and the Dog in Hidatsa Culture," 250–53.
6. Lotrich, "Indian Terms for the Cradle," 99.
7. Gilman and Schneider, *Way to Independence*, 127; and Wilson field notes, 145, Wilson Papers.
8. Bowers, *Hidatsa Social and Ceremonial Organizations*, 126.
9. Ibid.
10. Ibid.
11. Ibid.
12. DeMallie, *Plains.*

CHAPTER 27. MANDAN

1. Lotrich, "Indian Terms for the Cradle," 99.
2. Maximilian, *People of the First Man*, 245.
3. Bowers, *Mandan Social and Ceremonial Organizations*, 174.
4. Ibid.
5. Ibid.
6. Ibid.

CHAPTER 28. ARIKARA

1. DeMallie, *Plains*.
2. Curtis, *North American Indian*, 5:149.
3. Lotrich, "Indian Terms for the Cradle," 90; M. Gilmore, *Notes on the Gynecology*. Lotrich received his information from Peter Beauchamp, Fort Berthold Indian Agency.
4. M. Gilmore, *Notes on the Gynecology*, 72.
5. Ibid., 73.
6. Ibid., 75.
7. Ibid.
8. Ibid., 75.

CHAPTER 29. GROS VENTRE

1. DeMallie, *Plains*.
2. Fort Belknap Indian Community, accessed June 9, 2018, www.ftbelknap.org.
3. John Koontz, email to the author, January 29, 2007.
4. Flannery, *Gros Ventre*, 140.
5. Ibid., 141.
6. Kroeber, "Ethnology of the Gros Ventre"; and Flannery, *Gros Ventre*.
7. Flannery, *Gros Ventre*, 137.
8. Kroeber, "Ethnology of the Gros Ventre," 181.
9. Flannery, *Gros Ventre*, 143.
10. Kroeber, "Ethnology of the Gros Ventre," 166.

CHAPTER 30. SARCEE

1. Curtis, *North American Indian*, 18:212.
2. Ibid.
3. Ibid., 105.
4. Ibid.; and Jenness, *Sarcee Indians of Alberta*.
5. Taylor and Dempsey, *With Eagle Tail*, 41.
6. Curtis, *North American Indian*, 18:105.

CHAPTER 31. STONEY

1. Snow, *These Mountains Are Our Sacred Places*, 108.
2. Lowie, "Assiniboine."
3. "The Plains People," Canada's First Peoples, Goldi Productions, 2007, http://firstpeoplesofcanada.com/fp_groups/fp_plains1.html.

CHAPTER 32. PLAINS MÉTIS

1. Laverdure and Allard, *Michif Dictionary.*
2. Callihoo, "Early Life in Lac St. Anne," 10.
3. Robertson and Racette, *Clearing a Path.*
4. National Collaborating Centre for Aboriginal Health, *Sacred Space of Womanhood*, 6.
5. Ibid., 9.
6. Ibid., 8.
7. K. Anderson, "New Life Stirring."
8. Young, "Métis Embroidery."
9. Peterson and Brown, *New Peoples.*

CHAPTER 33. QUAPAW

1. Fletcher and La Flesche, *Omaha Tribe*, 68.
2. Ardina Moore, discussion at Oklahoma City art show, n.d.; "Quapaw Language," Quapaw Tribe of Oklahoma, accessed June 9, 2018, www.quapawtribe.com/index.aspx?nid=89.
3. Baird, *Quapaw Indians*, 12.

CONCLUSION

1. Momaday quoted in Hail, *Gifts of Pride and Love*, 42.
2. Wildschut and Ewers, *Crow Indian Beadwork.*
3. F. D. Lessard, "Crow Indian Art."
4. Dean, *Beading in the Native American Tradition*, 3.
5. Hail, *Hau, Kóla!*, 29.
6. Ibid.
7. Hail, *Gifts of Pride and Love.*
8. Jennings interview.
9. Hail, *Gifts of Pride and Love.*
10. Doyah, *Powwow Chairs*, 34.

GLOSSARY

amulet: A charm worn as a protection against injury or evil. Many tribes of the plains dried and kept a baby's navel cord in a small buckskin bag and attached it to the cradle or the child's clothing.

aniline dye: Commercial dye produced synthetically from coal-tar products.

appliqué: Technique of embroidery in which pieces of one material are applied to another, as in quillwork or ribbon work.

baby carrier: A device for carrying a child.

band: Subdivision or subtribe of an Indian tribe, often made up of an extended family living, traveling, and hunting and gathering together.

beadwork: Decorative work done in beads strung on a thread and stitched to a piece of hide or cloth. Native beads were made of shell, stone, bones, deer toenails, teeth, quills, and seeds. After the Europeans brought glass beads to the Americas, the glass beads replaced quillwork and other Native materials.

buckskin: A softened and smoke-treated rawhide. Soft and pliable, it can be easily cut and sewn, washes like cloth, and never becomes hard.

bullboat: Circular shallow boat made of buffalo skin, which is stretched over a willow frame and sealed with animal fat and ashes. Formerly used by Plains Indians on the Missouri River.

calendar stick: A wooden stick with cuts and notches representing days or events. Some Plains women tracked their pregnancy with calendar sticks.

clan: Multigenerational social group within a tribe, made up of several families who trace descent in either the male or female line from a common ancestor. Clan members consider themselves related; marriage within the clan is prohibited.

cradle: The term refers to a small bed for a baby. In North American ethnology, a cradle refers to any device in which the infant was bound during the first months of life.

cradleboard: A baby carrier with the cradle enclosed within a frame and/or attached to a solid board, sometimes covered with hide. The child was laced or strapped to the frame or put inside the pouch attached to the board.

dentalium (*Dentalium pretiosum*): A slender univalve shellfish found on the west coast of Vancouver. Dentalia were strung on strings as money or decoration on clothing and cradleboards.

earth lodge: A large dwelling, usually dome shaped, with a log frame covered in smaller branches, mats, bark, or sod.

First Nations: A term that has come to refer to Indian tribes in Canada.

hammock cradle: A bed made of a piece of hide or blanket, suspended by ropes at both ends.

hide: The skin of animals used to produce clothing, housing, utilitarian goods, and storage items. Hides can be scraped of fur and left wet in the form of rawhide or tanned by smoking.

hurdle cradle: A cradle that consists of several rods, small canes, or sticks arranged in a plane on an oblong hoop and lashed in place with cords.

Indian nation: Federally recognized Native group that is a corporate entity and has the right of self-determination.

Indian Territory: A tract of land west of the Mississippi River set aside as permanent homeland for Indians in the 1830s, then diminished over subsequent years until it became part of the state of Oklahoma in 1907.

lattice cradle: A cradle made of dressed skin lashed to a lattice frame of flat sticks. The baby was wrapped and laced in the skin bag attached to the frame. The hide was often decorated entirely with beadwork. The frame was supported and carried on the mother's back or swung on the pommel of the saddle by means of bands attached to the frame in the rear.

matrilineal: A term used to describe a social organization in which descent and property are traced through the female members.

medicine bundle: A collection of various materials, often wrapped in leather or cloth, to which spiritual power and tribal meaning are assigned.

moiety: A social group within a tribe with two primary subdivisions. The word means "half."

motif: A motif is an individual design element. Motifs are repeated and combined to create patterns.

nomadic: A way of life in which people frequently moved from one location to another in search of food.

parfleche: A folded container or storage bag made of rawhide with the hair removed; often incised and painted.

patrilineal: A type of social organization in which descent and property are passed through the male line.

pony beads: A large opaque irregular china bead, which came into use on the plains in the early 1800s. These beads were known as pony beads because they were brought on by pony pack trains. They were made in Venice and about 1/8 inch in diameter. White and medium blue were commonly used among Plains tribes.

Prairie Indians: Tribes that inhabited the vast fertile plains that extended from western Ohio and southern Michigan across the states of Indiana, Illinois, Missouri, Arkansas, Iowa, Kansas, Nebraska, and North and South Dakota, including the southern portions of Wisconsin and Minnesota.

puffball: Fungi with a globe shape that discharge ripe spores in a smokelike cloud when pressed or struck.

quillwork: Embroidery done with porcupine or bird quills to add ornamentation on skins. Quills are dyed and flattened before being sewn on as decorative elements. Quillwork predates beadwork.

rawhide: Untanned animal hide made into leather.

relocation: The forced or encouraged removal of a tribe from one location to another. This was a common governmental practice in the nineteenth century.

removal: A federal policy of relocation formalized with the Indian Removal Act of 1830. The government forced eastern tribes to leave their ancestral homelands and move west of the Mississippi River to Indian Territory.

reservation: A tract of land set aside historically by the federal government for occupation by and use of American Indians, based on treaty negotiations.

reserve: The Canadian equivalent of a reservation.

ribbon work: A kind of patchwork or appliqué in which silk ribbons are sewn in strips.

sinew: Animal fiber used as thread for embroidery or stitching things together. A tendon was stripped out and dried, softened, and shredded into the thickness desired.

stroud: Wool cloth made in England in the 1700s and used in trade with early American Indians.

swaddling: The practice of tightly wrapping an infant in cloth.

thunderbird: Mythical bird in the belief systems of some North American tribes. Thunder and wind are believed to be caused by its beating wings.

tipi: A conical dwelling with a pole frame covered in hides. The covering was made of fifteen or more dressed buffalo hides, cut and sewn together in a semicircular shape. Also spelled tepee.

tradition: Tradition is an ancestral knowledge that guides Indigenous artists' personal and creative development.

travois: A device for transporting possessions or people behind dogs or horses. A travois consists of a wooden frame shaped in a V, the closed end over the animal's shoulders and the open end dragging on the ground, with hide, plank, or webbing serving as a litter in the middle.

tribe: A general term applied to different kinds and degrees of social organization. Tribes usually have language, culture, kinship, territory, and history in common, resulting in a common purpose.

tumpline: A band of animal skin or cloth slung across the forehead or chest to support a load on the back.

BIBLIOGRAPHY

ARCHIVAL SOURCES

Arapaho Oral History. Western History Collections. University of Oklahoma Libraries, Norman, Oklahoma.

Ayer, Jeannette O. and Harry D., Ojibwe Collection. Minnesota Historical Society, St. Paul, Minnesota.

Dorsey, George A., and Cleaver Warden Collection. Department of Anthropology Archives, Field Museum of Natural History, Chicago, Illinois.

Dorsey, James Owen. Papers. National Anthropological Archives, Smithsonian Institution, Washington, D.C.

Kiowa Apache Oral History. Western History Collections. University of Oklahoma Libraries, Norman, Oklahoma.

Osage Oral History. Western History Collections. University of Oklahoma Libraries, Norman, Oklahoma.

Wilson, Gilbert L. and Frederick N., Papers. Minnesota Historical Society, St. Paul, Minnesota.

BOOKS AND ARTICLES

Aadland, Dan. *Women and Warriors of the Plains.* Missoula, Mont.: Mountain Press, 2000.

Ahenakew, Edward. *Voices of the Plains Cree.* Regina, SK: Canadian Plains Research Center, University of Regina, 1978.

Ahler, Stanley A., Thomas D. Thiessen, and Michael K. Trimble. *People of the Willows.* Grand Forks: University of North Dakota Press, 1991.

Albright, Peggy. *Richard Throssel: Crow Indian Photographer.* Albuquerque: University of New Mexico Press, 1997.

Alden, Jill. *Contemporary American Indian Beadwork: The Exquisite Art.* New York: Dolph, 1999.

American Indian Studies Research Institute. *Skiri Pawnee Multimedia Dictionary.* Pawnee Language Program. Bloomington: AISRI, Indiana University, 2008. CD-ROM.

Anderson, Caroline J. "American Indian Cradle Boards." *Field Museum of Natural History Bulletin* 51, no. 2 (1980): 16–21.

Anderson, Jeffrey D. *Arapaho Women's Quillwork: Motion, Life, and Creativity.* Norman: University of Oklahoma Press, 2013.

———. *One Hundred Years of Old Sage: An Arapaho Life.* Lincoln: University of Nebraska Press, 2003.

———. "The Sacred Art of the Arapaho Quillwork." *American Indian Art Magazine*, Spring 2013, 60–71.

Anderson, Kim. "New Life Stirring: Mothering, Transformation, and Aboriginal Womanhood." In *"Until Our Hearts Are on the Ground": Aboriginal Mothering, Oppression, Resistance and Rebirth*, edited by D. Memee Lavell-Harvard and Jeanette Corbiere Lavell, 13–24. Toronto: Demeter Press, 2006.

Bailey, Garrick Alan, and Daniel C. Swan. *Art of the Osage.* Seattle: University of Washington Press, 2004.

Baird, W. David. *The Quapaw Indians: A History of the Downstream People.* Norman: University of Oklahoma Press, 1980.

Bancroft-Hunt, Norman. *The Indians of the Great Plains.* New York: William Morrow, 1981.

Battey, Thomas C. *The Life and Adventures of a Quaker among the Indians.* Boston: Lee and Sheppard, 1875; Norman: University of Oklahoma Press, 1968.

Berlandier, Jean Louis. *The Indians of Texas in 1830.* Edited and introduced by John C. Ewers. Washington, D.C.: Smithsonian Institution Press, 1969.

Berthrong, Donald J. *The Southern Cheyennes.* Norman: University of Oklahoma Press, 1963.

Bittle, William E. "Kiowa- Apache." In *Studies in the Athapaskan Languages*, edited by Harry Hoijer, 76–101. Berkeley: University of California Press, 1963.

Blaine, Martha Royce. *The Ioway Indians.* Norman: University of Oklahoma Press, 1979.

———. *Some Things Are Not Forgotten.* Lincoln: University of Nebraska Press, 1997.

Bodmer, Karl. *Karl Bodmer's America.* Lincoln: Joslyn Art Museum and University of Nebraska Press, 1984.

Boehme, Sarah, Gerald Contay, Clifford Crane Bear, Emma Hensen, Mike Leslie, and James Nottage. *Powerful Images: Portrayals of Native America.* Seattle: Museums West, 1998.

Bowers, Alfred W. *Hidatsa Social and Ceremonial Organizations.* Bureau of American Ethnology Bulletin 194, Smithsonian Institution. Washington, D.C.: GPO, 1965; reprint, Lincoln: University of Nebraska Press, 1992.

———. *Mandan Social and Ceremonial Organizations.* Chicago: University of Chicago Press, 1950.

Boyd, Maurice. *Kiowa Voice.* Vol. 1. Fort Worth: Texas Christian University Press. 1981.

"The Buffalo Culture of the Plains Indian." *Wind Rendezvous* 13, no. 3 (1983): 1–19.

Brokenleg, Martin, and Herbert T. Hoover. *Yanktonai Sioux Watercolors: Cultural Remembrances of John Saul.* Sioux Falls, S.Dak.: Center of Western Studies, 1993.

Buckelew, F. M., Thomas S. Dennis, and Lucy S. Rea Dennis. *Life of F. M. Buckelew: The Indian Captive.* Bandera, Tex.: Hunter Printing House, 1925.

Burns, Louis F. *Osage Indian Customs and Myths.* Fallbrook, Calif.: Ciga Press, 1984; Tuscaloosa: University of Alabama Press, 2005.

Bushnell, David I. *Burials of the Algonquian, Siouan, and Caddoan Indian West of the Mississippi.* Bureau of American Ethnology Bulletin 83, Smithsonian Institution. Washington, D.C.: GPO, 1927.

———. *Villages of the Algonquian, Siouan, and Caddoan Tribes West of the Mississippi.* Bureau of American Ethnology Bulletin 77, Smithsonian Institution. Washington, D.C.: GPO, 1922.

Callihoo, Victoria. "Early Life in Lac St. Anne and St. Albert in the 1870." *Alberta Historical Review* 1, no. 3 (1953): 10.

Calloway, Colin G. *One Vast Winter Count.* Lincoln: University of Nebraska Press, 2003.

Capps, Benjamin. *The Indians.* The Old West. Alexandra, Va.: Time-Life Books, 1973.

Cash, Joseph H., and Gerald W. Wolff. *The Ponca People.* Phoenix: Indian Tribal Series, 1975.

———. *The Three Affiliated Tribes.* Phoenix: Indian Tribal Series, 1974.

Catlin, George. *Letters and Notes on the Manners, Customs, and Conditions of the North American Indians.* 2 vols. 1841; New York City: Dover, 1973.

Center of the American Indian. *Children of Early America.* Oklahoma City: Oklahoma Foundation for the Humanities, 1987.

Chamberlain, Von Del. *When Stars Came Down to Earth: Cosmology of the Skidi Pawnee Indians of North America.* Los Alto, Calif.: Ballena Press, 1982.

Chapman, Carl H. *The Origins of the Tribe of the Osage Indian Tribe.* Vol. 3 of *Osage Indians.* New York: Garland, 1974.

Chisholm, James S. *Navajo Infancy: An Ethnological Study of Child Development.* New York: Aldine, 1983.

Cole, Kristen. "Repair of Cradleboards Is a Labor of Love." *George Street Journal* 23 (July 1999): n.p.

Cooper, John M. *The Gros Ventre of Montana, Part 2: Religion and Ritual.* Edited by Regina Flannery. Washington, D.C.: Catholic University of American Press, 1957.

Corwin, H. D. *The Kiowa.* Norman: University of Oklahoma Press, 1958.

Cowell, Andrew, comp. *English–Gros Ventre/White Clay Student Dictionary.* Boulder, Colo.: Center for the Study of Indigenous Languages of the West, 2012.

Cox, J. Wendel. "Hidatsas." In *Encyclopedia of the Great Plains,* edited by David J. Wishart. Center for Great Plains Studies, University of Nebraska, Lincoln. Last revised August 1, 2003. http://plainshumanities.unl.edu/encyclopedia/.

Curtis, Edward S. *Heart of the Circle.* San Francisco: Pomegranate Art Books, 1997.

———. *The North American Indian.* 20 vols. Cambridge, Mass.: Cambridge University Press, 1907–30.

———. *The Plains Indians Photographs of Edward S. Curtis.* Lincoln: University of Nebraska Press, 2001.

Curtis Burlin, Natalie, ed. *The Indians' Book.* New York: Harper, 1907; reprint, New York: Outlet Book, 1987.

Dean, David. *Beading in the Native American Tradition.* Loveland, Co.: Interweave Press, 2002.

Dellinger, Samuel C. "Baby Cradles of the Ozark Bluff-Dwellers." *American Antiquity* 1, no. 3 (1936): 197–214.

Deloria, Ella Cara. *Waterlily.* Lincoln: University of Nebraska Press, 1988.

DeMallie, Raymond J., ed. *Plains.* Vol. 13 of *Handbook of North American Indians,* edited by William Sturtevant. Washington, D.C.: Smithsonian Institution Press, 2001.

Dempsey, Hugh. "Religious Significance of Blackfoot Quillwork." *Plains Anthropologist* 8, no. 19 (1963): 52–53.

Denig, Edwin T. *Five Indian Tribes of the Upper Missouri: Sioux, Arikaras, Assiniboines, Crees, Crows.* Edited and introduced by John C. Ewers. Norman: University of Oklahoma Press, 1985.

———. "Indian Tribes of the Upper Missouri." In *Forty-sixth Annual Report of the Bureau of American Ethnology,* Smithsonian Institution, edited by J. N. B. Hewitt, 377–628. Washington, D.C.: GPO, 1930.

Densmore, Frances. *Chippewa Customs.* Bureau of American Ethnology Bulletin 86, Smithsonian Institution. Washington, D.C.: GPO, 1929.

———. *Pawnee Music.* Bureau of American Ethnology Bulletin 93, Smithsonian Institution. Washington, D.C.: GPO, 1929.

———. *Teton Sioux Music.* Bureau of American Ethnology Bulletin 38, Smithsonian Institution. Washington, D.C.: GPO, 1918.

Deupree Cradleboard Collection. Red Earth Art Center brochure. Oklahoma City: State Arts Council of Oklahoma, n.d.

Diedrich, Mark. *Old Betsey: The Life and Times of a Famous Dakota Woman and Her Family.* Rochester, Minn.: Coyote Books, 1995.

Dorion, Leah Marie. "Opikinawasowin: The Life Long Process of Growing Cree and Metis Children." Master's thesis, Athabasca University, Alberta, 2010.

Dorsey, George. *The Mythology of the Wichita.* Carnegie Institution of Washington Publication 21. Washington, D.C.: Carnegie Institution, 1904; reprint, Norman; University of Oklahoma Press, 1995.

———. *The Pawnee: Mythology (Part 1).* Carnegie Institution of Washington Publication 59. Washington, D.C.: Carnegie Institution, 1906.

———. *Traditions of the Arikara.* Carnegie Institution of Washington Publication 17. Washington, D.C.: Carnegie Institution, 1904.

Dorsey, George A., and Alfred L. Kroeber. *Traditions of the Arapaho*. Field Columbian Museum Publication 81, Anthropological Series 5. Chicago: Field Museum of Natural History, 1903; reprint, Lincoln: University of Nebraska Press, 1997.

Dorsey, George A., and James Murie. *Notes on Skidi Pawnee Society*. Chicago: Field Museum Press, 1940.

Dorsey, James Owen. "Iowa." In *Handbook of American Indians North of Mexico*. Vol. 1, edited by Frederick W. Hodge, 612–14. Washington, D.C.: Smithsonian Institution, 1905.

———. "Omaha Dwellings, Furniture, and Implements." In *Thirteenth Annual Report of the Bureau of American Ethnology, 1881–1892*, Smithsonian Institution, 263–88. Washington, D.C.: GPO, 1896.

———. "Omaha Sociology." In *Third Annual Report of the Bureau of American Ethnology, 1881–82*, Smithsonian Institution, 205–307. Washington, D.C.: GPO, 1884.

Douglas, Frederic H. *Main Types of Indian Cradles*. Denver, Colo.: Denver Museum of Art, 1952.

———. *Material Cultural Notes: A Northern Arapaho Quilled Cradle*. Denver, Colo.: Denver Art Museum, 1941.

Downs, Aimée J. "Cradleboards." *Oklahoma Today* 48, no. 4 (1998): 56–57.

Doyah, Ray C. *Powwow Chairs*. Anadarko: Zo'dle-toh Press, 2003.

Dudley, Joseph Iron Eye. *Choteau Creek: A Sioux Reminiscence*. Lincoln: University of Nebraska Press, 1992.

Dusenberry, Verne. *The Montana Cree: A Study in Religious Persistence*. 1962; Norman: University of Oklahoma Press, 1998.

Eggan, Fred, ed. *Social Anthropology of North American Tribes*. Chicago: University of Chicago Press, 1937.

Ehrenreich, P. "Zur Ornamentik der Nordamerikanischen Indianer." *Ethnologisches Notizblatt* 2, no. 1 (1889): 27–29.

Ewers, John C. *Blackfeet Crafts*. 1945; Stevens Point, Wisc.: Schneider, 1986.

———. *The Blackfeet: Raiders on the Northwestern Plains*. Norman: University of Oklahoma Press, 1958.

———. *The Story of the Blackfeet*. Indian Life and Customs 6, Bureau of Indian Affairs, Department of the Interior. Lawrence, Kans.: Haskell Institute, 1952.

Ewing, Douglas C. *Pleasing the Spirits, A Catalogue of a Collection of American Indian Art*. New York: Ghylen Press, 1982.

Farabee, William C. "Indian Cradles." *Museum Journal* 11, no. 4 (December 1920): 185–211.

Feder, Norman. "Pawnee Cradleboards." *American Indian Art Magazine* 3, no. 4 (1978): 40–50.

Feest, Christian F., and Sylvia S. Kasprycki. *Peoples of the Twilight: European Views of Native Minnesota, 1823–1862*. Afton, Minn.: Afton Historical Society, 1998.

Fehrenbach, T. R. *Comanches: The Destruction of a People*. New York: Knopf, 1983.

Feraca, Stephen E., and James H. Howard. "The Identity and Demography of the Dakota or Sioux Tribe." *Plains Anthropologist* 8 no. 20 (1963): 80–84.

Fitzgerald, Judith, and Michael Oren Fitzgerald. *The Spirit of Indian Women*. Bloomington, Ind.: World Wisdom, 2005.

Flannery, Regina, ed. *The Gros Ventre of Montana, Part 1: Social Life*. Washington, D.C.: Catholic University of America Press, 1953.

Fletcher, Alice C. *Camping with the Sioux: Fieldwork Diary of Alice Cunningham*. Washington, D.C.: Smithsonian Institution, 2001.

———."Star Cult among the Pawnee." *American Anthropologist* 4, no. 4 (1902): 730–36.

Fletcher, Alice C., and Francis La Flesche. *The Omaha Tribe*. Washington, D.C.: GPO, 1911; reprint, Lincoln: University of Nebraska Press, 1992.

Foster, Morris W. *Being Comanche: A Social History of an American Indian Community.* Tucson: University of Arizona Press, 1991.
Flood, Renée S. *Remember Your Relatives: Yankton Sioux Images, 1851–1904.* Marty, S.Dak.: Marty Indian School, 1985.
Fowler, Loretta. *The Arapaho.* New York: Chelsea House Publishers. 1989.
———. *Shared Symbols, Contested Meanings: Gros Ventre Culture and History, 1778–1984.* Ithaca, N.Y.: Cornell University Press, 1987.
Frey, Rodney. *The World of the Crow Indians: As Driftwood Lodges.* Norman: University of Oklahoma Press, 1987.
Gilman, Carolyn, and Mary Jane Schneider. *The Way to Independence: Memories of a Hidatsa Indian Family, 1840–1920.* St. Paul: Minnesota Historical Society Press, 1987.
Gilmore, Melvin R. *Notes on the Gynecology and Obstetrics of the Arikara Tribe.* Ann Arbor: Michigan Academy of Sciences, 1930; reprint, Pomona, Calif.: Acoma Books, 1980.
———. *Uses of Plants by the Indians of the Missouri River Region.* Washington, D.C.: GPO, 1919; reprint, Lincoln: University of Nebraska Press, 1977.
Gilmore, Robert. "The Northern Arapaho Cradle." *American Indian Art Magazine* 16, no. 1 (Winter 1990): 64–71.
Goodbird, Edward. *Goodbird the Indian: His Story as told by Himself to Gilbert L. Wilson.* New York: Revell, 1914.
Green, Richard. "Cheyenne Soft Cradle Covers." In *Crafts, American Indian Past and Present* Annual 6, 4–12. Folsom, La.: Written Heritage, 1995.
———. "Sioux Fully Beaded Yoke Dresses." *Whispering Wind* 28, no. 4 (January–February 2007): 5–25.
Greene, Candace. "Art until 1900." In *Handbook of the North American Indians,* vol. 13, *Plains,* part 2, edited by Raymond J. DeMallie, 1039–54. Washington. D.C.: Smithsonian Institution, 2001.
———. "Soft Cradles of the Central Plains." *Plains Anthropologist* 37, no. 139 (1992): 95–113.
———. "The Use of Plant Fibers in Plains Indian Embroidery." *American Indian Art Magazine* 40, no. 2 (Spring 2015): 58–71.
Grinnell, George Bird. *The Cheyenne Indians: Their History and Ways of Life.* 2 vols. New Haven, Conn.: Yale University Press, 1923; reprint, Lincoln: University of Nebraska Press, 1972.
———. "Cheyenne Woman Customs." *American Anthropologist* 4, no. 1 (January–March 1902): 13–16.
———. *Pawnee, Blackfoot, and Cheyenne: History and Folklore of the Plains.* New York: Scribner, 1961.
Hail, Barbara A. "Gifts of Pride and Love: Kiowa and Comanche Cradles." *American Indian Art* 25, no. 1 (1999): 42–55.
———, ed. *Gifts of Pride and Love: Kiowa and Comanche Cradles.* Bristol, R.I.: Haffenreffer Museum of Anthropology, Brown University, 2000.
———. *Hau, Kóla! The Plains Indian Collection of the Haffenreffer Museum of Anthropology.* Bristol, R.I.: Haffenreffer Museum of Anthropology, Brown University, 1993.
Halvorson, Mark J. *Sacred Beauty: Quillwork of Plains Women.* Bismarck: State Historical Society of North Dakota, 1998.
Hämäläinen, Pekka. *The Comanche Empire.* New Haven, Conn.: Yale University Press, 2008.
Hansen, Emma. "Paukeigope: An Artist of the Southern Plains." *Points West* (Summer 2004): 29–31.
Hartman, Sheryl. *Indian Clothing of the Great Lakes, 1740–1840.* Liberty, Utah: Eagle's View, 1988.
Harrod, Howard L. *Mission among the Blackfeet.* Norman: University of Oklahoma Press, 1971.
Hasskarl, Robert A., Jr. "The Culture and History of the Tonkawa Indians." *Plains Anthropologist* 7, no. 18 (November 1962): 217–31.

Hassrick, Royal B. *The George Catlin Book of American Indians.* New York: Promontory Press, 1988.

———. *The Sioux: Life and Customs of a Warrior Society.* Norman: University of Oklahoma, 1964.

Hays, Joe S. "Enduring Kiowa Cradles." *Whispering Wind* 27, no. 6 (October 1995): 22.

Heinbuch, Jean. *A Quillwork Companion: An Illustrated Guide to Techniques of Porcupine Quill Embroidery.* Liberty, Utah: Eagle's View, 1990.

Helm, June, ed. *Handbook of North American Indians*, vol. 6, *Subarctic.* Washington, D.C.: Smithsonian Institution, 1984.

Henry, Marguerite. *All About Horses.* New York: Random House, 1962.

Henry, Peggy Sue. *Beads to Buckskins.* Vol. 8. Hill City, Kans.: Beads to Buckskin, 1993.

Hilger, M. Inez. *Arapaho Child Life and Its Cultural Background.* Bureau of American Ethnology Bulletin 148, Smithsonian Institution. Washington, D.C.: GPO, 1952.

———. "Notes on Cheyenne Child Life." *American Anthropologist* 48, no. 1 (January–March 1946): 60–69.

Himmell, Kelly F. *The Conquest of the Karankawas and the Tonkawas, 1821–1859.* College Station: Texas A&M University Press, 1999.

Historical and Contemporary Plateau and Plains Cradles. Brochure. Browning, Mont.: Museum of the Plains Indian and Craft Center, 1995.

Hoebel, Edward Adamson. *The Cheyennes: Indians of the Great Plains.* New York: Holt Rinehart and Winston, 1960.

———. *The Political Organizations and Law—Ways of the Comanche Indians.* Memoirs of the American Anthropological Association 54. Menasha, Wisc.: American Anthropological Association, 1940.

Hoijer, Harry. *Tonkawa: An Indian Language of Texas.* New York: Columbia University Press, 1933.

Howard, James H. *The Plains-Ojibwa or Bungi: Hunters and Warriors of the Northern Prairies.* Reprints in Anthropology 7. 1965; reprint, Lincoln, Neb.: J. and L., 1977.

———. *The Ponca Tribe.* Bureau of American Ethnology Bulletin 195, Smithsonian Institution. Washington, D.C.: GPO, 1965; reprint, Lincoln: University of Nebraska Press, 1995.

Hrdlička, Aleš. *Physiological and Medical Observations among the Indians of Southwestern United States and Northern Mexico.* Bureau of American Ethnology Bulletin 34, Smithsonian Institution. Washington, D.C.: GPO, 1908.

Hungry Wolf, Adolf, and Beverly Hungry Wolf. *Children of the Sun: Stories by and about Indian Kids.* New York: William Morrow, 1987.

———. *Blackfoot Craftworker's Book.* Summertown, Tenn.: Book, 1991.

Hungry Wolf, Beverly. *The Ways of My Grandmothers.* New York: William Morrow, 1982.

Hyde, George E. *The Pawnee Indians.* Denver, Colo.: University of Denver Press, 1951.

Hyman, Colette. *Dakota Women's Work: Creativity, Culture, and Exile.* St. Paul: Minnesota Historical Society Press.

Irving, Washington. *A Tour on the Prairies.* Oklahoma City: Harlow, 1955.

Jablow, Joseph. *Ethnohistory of the Ponca Indians.* New York: Garland, 1974.

James, Edwin. *Account of an Expedition from Pittsburg to the Rocky Mountains.* 2 vols. 1823; Ann Arbor, Mich.: University Microfilms, 1966.

Janulewicz, Richard. *Brave Hearts and Their Cradles.* Centennial, Colo.: Lifevest, 2006.

Jenness, Diamond. *The Sarcee Indians of Alberta.* Anthropological Series 23. Ottawa: National Museum of Canada, 1938.

Jennings, Vanessa. *Kiowa Cradleboard Maker.* Native American Master Artist Video Series. Tulsa, Okla.: Full Circle Communications, 1999. VHS.

Johnson, Judi. *Native American Dolls and Cradleboards.* Springfield: Illinois State Museum, 1983.

Johnson, Michael G., and Richard Hook. *American Woodland Indians*. Men-at-Arms Series 228. New York: Osprey, 1990.

Jones, David E. *Sanapia: Comanche Medicine Woman*. New York: Holt, Rinehart and Winston, 1972.

Jones, Rex L., and Catherine Whitmore-Ostlund. "Cradles of Life: Infant Carriers of Native North Americans." *American Indian Art* 5, no. 4 (1980): 37–40.

Jones, William Kirkland. "Notes on the History and Material Culture of the Tonkawa Indians." In *Smithsonian Contributions to Anthropology*, vol. 2, no. 5, 65–81. Washington, D.C.: Smithsonian Institution Press, 1969.

Kavasch, E. Barrie, and Karen Baar. *American Indian Healing Arts*. New York: Bantam Books, 1999.

Kennedy, Michael S., ed. *The Assiniboines: From the Accounts of the Old Ones Told to First Boy (James Larpenteur Long)*. Norman: University of Oklahoma Press, 1961.

———. *The Red Man's West*. New York: Hasting House, 1965.

Keyser, James D., and Michael A. Klassen. *Plains Indian Rock Art*. Seattle: University of Washington Press, 2001.

Kindscher, Kelly. *Medicinal Wild Plants of the Prairie*. Lawrence: University Press of Kansas, 1992.

Koch, Ronald P. *Dress Clothing of the Plains Indians*. Norman: University of Oklahoma Press, 1990.

Kostelnik, Mike. "Nineteenth-Century Cheyenne Cradleboard: 'One Step at a Time.'" *Whispering Wind* 23, no. 6 (1995): 5–16.

Kozlov, Alexander. "Lakota Baby Cradle." *Whispering Wind* 29 no. 3 (1998): 8–9.

Kramer, Karen. "Intersections: Native American Art in a New Light." *Antiques and Fine Art*, August–September 2006, 164–68.

Kroeber, Alfred L. *The Arapaho*. Bulletin of the American Museum of Natural History 18. Originally published in three parts in 1902, 1904, and 1907. University of Nebraska Press, Lincoln, 1983.

———. "Ethnology of the Gros Ventre." *Anthropological Papers of the American Museum of Natural History* 1, pt. 4 (1908): 141–281.

LaDuke, Winona. *Recovering the Sacred: The Power Naming and Claiming*. Cambridge, Mass.: South End Press, 2005.

La Flesche, Francis. *Dictionary of the Osage Language*. Bureau of American Ethnology Bulletin 109, Smithsonian Institution. Washington, D.C.: GPO, 1932.

———. *The Osage and the Invisible World: From the Works of Francis La Flesche*. Edited by Garrick Alan Bailey. Norman: University of Oklahoma Press, 1995.

———. "The Osage Tribe: Two Versions of the Child-Naming Rite." In *Forty-third Annual Report of the Bureau of American Ethnology*, Smithsonian Institution, 23–164. Washington, D.C.: GPO, 1928.

———. *War Ceremony and Peace Ceremony of the Osage Indians*. Bureau of American Ethnology Bulletin 101, Smithsonian Institution. Washington, D.C.: GPO, 1932.

Lame Deer, John Fire, and Richard Erdoes. *Lame Deer, Seeker of Visions*. New York: Simon and Schuster, 1972.

Lanford, Benson L. "Origins of Central Plains Beadwork." *American Indian Art Magazine* 16, no. 1 (Winter 1990): 72–79.

Larrie, Colleen. *Sioux History and Culture*. Book 2. Spearfish, S.Dak.: Black Hills State College [1978?].

Laubin, Reginald, and Gladys Laubin. *The Indian Tipi: Its History, Construction, and Use*. Norman: University of Oklahoma Press, 1957.

Laverdure, Patline, and Ida Rose Allard. *The Michif Dictionary: Turtle Mountain Chippewa Cree*. Edited by John C. Crawford. Winnipeg: Pemmican, 1983.

Lenssen, Barbara G., Andrew H. Whiteford, and Susan Brown McGreevy. *Lullabies from the Earth: Cradles of Native North America*. Santa Fe, N.Mex.: Wheelwright Museum of the American Indian, 1980.

Lenz, Mary Jane. *The Stuff of Dreams: Native American Dolls*. New York: Museum of the American Indian, 1986.

Lessard, F. Dennis. "Crow Indian Art, the Nez Perce Connection." *American Indian Art Magazine* 6, no. 1 (Winter 1980): 54–63.

———. "Defining the Central Plains Art Area." *American Indian Art Magazine* 16, no. 1 (Winter 1990): 36–43.

Lessard, Rosemary. "Lakota Cradles." *American Indian Art Magazine* 16, no. 1 (Winter 1990): 45–53.

Linderman, Frank Bird. *Pretty-Shield: Medicine Woman of the Crows*. Originally published as *Red Mother* in 1932. New York: John Day, 1972.

Lotrich, Victor F. "Indian Terms for the Cradle and the Cradleboard." *Colorado Magazine* 18, no. 3 (May 1941): 81–120.

Lowie, Robert Harry. "The Assiniboine." *Anthropological Papers of the American Museum of Natural History* 4, pt. 1 (1909): 1–270.

———. "Crow Indian Art." *Anthropological Papers of the American Museum of Natural History* 21, pt. 4 (1922): 272–322.

———. *The Crow Indians*. 1935; reprint, Lincoln: University of Nebraska Press, 2004.

———, ed. *A Crow Text*. Berkeley: University of California Press, 1965.

———. *Indians of the Plains*. Lincoln: University of Nebraska Press, 1954.

———. "The Material Cultural of the Crow Indians." *Anthropological Papers of the American Museum of Natural History* 21, pt. 3 (1922): 201–70.

———. "Notes on the Social Organization and Customs of the Mandan, Hidatsa, and Crow Indians." *Anthropological Papers of the American Museum of Natural History* 21, pt. 1 (1917): 7–99.

———. "Social Life of the Crow Indians." *Anthropological Papers of the American Museum of Natural History* 9, pt. 2 (1912): 179–248.

———. "Societies of the Crow, Hidatsa and Mandan Indians." *Anthropological Papers of the American Museum of Natural History* 11, pt. 3 (1913): 143–358.

Lyford, Carrie A. *Quill and Beadwork of the Western Sioux*. Washington, D.C.: Bureau of Indian Affairs, 1940; Boulder, Colo.: Johnson Books, 1979.

Maestas, Enrique Gilbert-Michael. "Culture and History of Native American Peoples of South Texas." PhD diss., University of Texas at Austin, 2003.Magee, Cathy. "Anthropology Conservation Laboratory Treatment Report, Catalog No. E73311-0." Smithsonian Institution, Department of Anthropology, 2000.

Mails, Thomas E. *The Mystic Warriors of the Plains: The Culture, Arts, Crafts, and Religion of the Plains Indians*. New York: Marlowe, 1995.

Mandelbaum, David. *The Plains Cree*. New York: American Museum of Natural History, 1940; rev. ed., Regina, SK: Canadian Research Center, University of Regina, 1979.

Marriot, Alice. *The Ten Grandmothers*. Norman: University of Oklahoma Press, 1945.

———. "The Trade Guild of the Southern Cheyenne Women." *Bulletin of the Oklahoma Anthropological Society* 2 (1956): 19–27.

Mason, Otis T. "Cradles." In *Handbook of American Indians North of Mexico*, vol. 1, part 1, edited by F. W. Hodge, 357–59. Washington, D.C.: GPO, 1907.

———. *Cradles of the American Aborigines*. Annual Report to the Board of Regents of the Smithsonian Institution. Washington, D.C.: GPO, 1887; reprint, Hummelstorm, Pa.: Tucquan, 1999.

Mather, Christine. *Native America: Arts, Traditions, and Celebrations*. New York: Clarkson Potter, 1990.

Mathews, John Joseph. *The Osages: Children of the Middle Waters*. Norman: University of Oklahoma Press, 1961.

Maurer, Evan M. *Visions of the People: A Pictorial History of Plains Indian Life*. Minneapolis: Minnesota Institute of Art, 1992.

Maximilian, Alexander Philipp. *Maximilian, Prince of Wied's Travels in the Interior of North America, 1832–34.* Translated from German by H. Evans Lloyd. Early Western Travels, 1748–1846, vols. 22–25. Cleveland, Ohio: Arthur H. Clark, 1906.

———. *People of the First Man: Life among the Plains Indians in Their Final Days of Glory; The First Hand Account of Prince Maximilian's Expedition up the Missouri River, 1833–34.* Edited by Davis Thomas and Karin Ronnefeldt. New York: Dutton, 1976.

Maxwell, James A., ed. *America's Fascinating Indian Heritage.* Pleasantville, N.Y.: Reader's Digest Association, 1978.

Mayhall, Mildred P. *The Kiowas.* Norman: University of Oklahoma Press, 1962.

McKenney, Thomas L., and James Hall. *History of the Indian Tribes of North America.* 3 vols. Edinburgh: J. Grant, 1933–34.

McClintock, Walter. *The Old North Trail, or, Life, Legends, and Religion of the Blackfeet Indians.* Lincoln: University of Nebraska Press, 1999.

McLaughlin, Castle. *Arts of Diplomacy: Lewis and Clark's Indian Collection.* Seattle: University of Washington Press, 2003.

McMaster, Gerald, and Clifford E. Trafzer, eds. *Native Universe: Voices of Indian America.* Washington, D.C.: Smithsonian Institution, National Museum of the American Indian, 2004.

McQuiston, Don, and Debra McQuiston. *Dolls and Toys of Native America: A Journey through Childhood.* San Francisco: Chronicle Books, 1995.

Menlove, Becky T. "The Outside Looking In: Photographs of Native America." *Points West* 6 (2000): n.p.

Merrill, William L., Marian Kaulaity Hasson, Candace Greene, and Frederick J. Reuss. *A Guide to the Kiowa Collections at the Smithsonian.* Smithsonian Contributions to Anthropology 40. Washington, D.C.: Smithsonian Institution Press, 1997.

Michelson, Truman. "Narrative of an Arapaho Woman." *American Anthropologist* 35, no. 4 (October–December 1933): 595–610.

Miller, David Reed. "Montana Assiniboine Identity: A Cultural Account of an American Indian Ethnicity." PhD diss., Indiana University, Bloomington, 1987.

Milloy, John S. *The Plains Cree: Trade, Diplomacy and War, 1790–1870.* Winnipeg: University of Manitoba Press, 1988.

Milner, Clyde A. *With Good Intentions: Quaker Work among the Pawnees, Otos, and Omahas in the 1870s.* Lincoln: University of Nebraska Press, 1982.

Momaday, N. Scott. *The Way to Rainy Mountain.* Albuquerque: University of New Mexico Press, 1969.

Mooney, James. "Calendar History of the Kiowa Indians." In *Seventeenth Annual Report of the Bureau of the American Ethnology, 1895–1896*, 128–468. Washington, D.C.: GPO, 1898.

Morgan, Juliet Liane. "Classificatory Verbs in Plains Apache." Master's thesis, University of Oklahoma, Norman, 2012.

Morgan, Lewis Henry. *The Indian Journals, 1859–62.* Edited and introduced by Leslie A. White. Ann Arbor: University of Michigan Press, 1959.

Morrow, Mable. *Indian Rawhide: An American Folk Art.* Norman: University of Oklahoma Press, 1975.

Meyer, Roy W. *History of the Santee Sioux: United States Indian Policy on Trial.* Lincoln: University of Nebraska Press, 1967.

Museum of the Plains Indian and Craft Center. *Historic and Contemporary Plateau and Plains Cradles.* Browning, Mont.: U.S. Department of the Interior, Indian Arts and Craft Board, Museum of the Plains Indian and Craft Center, 1995.

Nance, B. H. "D. A. Nance and the Tonkawa Indians." *Yearbook of the West Texas Historical Association* 28 (1952): 87–95.

National Collaborating Centre for Aboriginal Health. *The Sacred Space of Womanhood: Mothering across the Generations*. Prince George: National Collaborating Centre for Aboriginal Health, 2012.

Newcomb, William W. *The Indians of Texas from Prehistoric to Modern Times*. Austin: University of Texas Press, 1961.

———. *The People Called Wichita*. Phoenix, Ariz.: Indian Tribal Series, 1976.

Newlin, Deborah Lamont. *The Tonkawa People: A Tribal History from Earliest Times to 1893*. Lubbock: West Texas Museum Association, 1982.

Newman, Carl. "19th Century Cheyenne Style Cradle Board." *Whispering Wind* 32 no. 2 (2002): 52–53.

Niethammer, Carolyn J. *Daughters of the Earth: The Lives and Legends of American Indian Women*. New York: Simon and Schuster, 1997.

North Dakota Heritage Center. *A 'nicina 'be manido 'minesikan: Chippewa Beadwork*. Bismarck: State Historical Society of North Dakota, 1996.

"Notes on the Missouri River, and Some of the Native Tribes in its Neighborhood." *Analectic Magazine* 1, nos. 4–5 (1820), 293–313, 347–75.

Nuttall, Thomas. *A Journal of Travels into the Arkansas Territory during the Year 1819*. Edited by Savoie Lottinville. Norman: University of Oklahoma Press, 1980.

Orchard, William C. *The Technique of Porcupine-Quill Decoration among the North American Indians*. 1916; Liberty, Utah: Eagle's View, 1984.

Ortiz, Alfonso, ed. *Handbook of North American Indians*, vol. 10, *Southwest*. Washington, D.C.: Smithsonian Institution, 1983.

Otoe-Missouria Tribe. *The Otoe-Missouria Elders: Centennial Memoirs, 1881–1981*. Red Rock, Okla.: Otoe-Missouria Tribe, 1981.

Paget, Amelia M. *The People of the Plains*. Edited and introduced by Duncan Campbell Scott. Toronto, Ryerson Press, 1909.

Parks, Douglas R., ed. *Traditional Narratives of the Arikara Indians*. Vol. 3. Lincoln: University of Nebraska Press, 1991.

Penman, Sarah. *Honor the Grandmothers: Dakota and Lakota Women Tell Their Stories*. St. Paul: Minnesota Historical Society Press, 2000.

Peterson, Jacqueline, and Jennifer S.H. Brown, eds. *The New Peoples: Being and Becoming Métis in North America*. St. Paul: Minnesota Historical Society, 2001.

Peterson, Larry Len. *L. A. Huffman: Photographer of the American West*. Tucson: Settlers West Galleries, 2003.

Phillips, Ruth B. *Trading Identities: The Souvenir in Native North American Art from the Northeast, 1700–1900*. Seattle: University of Washington Press, 1998.

Pilling, James C. *Bibliography of the Algonquian Languages*. Bureau of Ethnology Bulletin 13, Smithsonian Institution. Washington, D.C.: GPO, 1891.

Plains Indians, special issue, *Faces: The Magazine about People* 9, no. 11 (October 1992).

Pond, Samuel W. *The Dakota or Sioux in Minnesota as They Were in 1834*. 1908; St. Paul: Minnesota Historical Society Press, 1986.

Powell, J. W., ed. *A Dakota-English Dictionary*. Vol. 7 of *Contributions to North American Ethnology*, US Geographical and Geological Survey of Rocky Mountain Region. Washington, D.C.: GPO, 1890.

Powers, Marla N. *Oglala Women: Myth, Ritual, and Reality*. Chicago: University of Chicago Press, 1986.

Red Shirt, Delphine. *Turtle Lung Woman's Granddaughter*. Lincoln: University of Nebraska Press, 2002.

Riggs, Stephen R. *Dakota Grammar, Texts, and Ethnography.* Originally published in *Contributions to North American Ethnology*, vol. 9, 1893, U.S. Geographical and Geological Survey of the Rocky Mountains Region. St. Paul: Minnesota Historical Society, 2004.

Ritzenthaler, Robert E. *Indian Cradles.* Milwaukee, Wisc.: Milwaukee Public Museum [1950?].

Ritzenthaler, Robert E., and Pat Ritzenthaler. *The Woodland Indians of the Western Great Lakes.* Prospect Heights, Ill.: Waveland Press, 1983.

Robertson, Carmen, and Sherry Farrell Racette. *Clearing a Path: New Ways of Seeing Traditional Indigenous Art.* Regina: Saskatchewan Art Board, 2009.

Ronda, James P. *Lewis and Clark among the Indians.* Lincoln: University of Nebraska Press, 1984.

Roper, Donna C., and Elizabeth P. Pauls, eds. *Plains Earthlodges: Ethnographic and Archaeological Perspectives.* Tuscaloosa: University of Alabama Press, 2005.

Russell, Dale R. *Eighteenth-Century Western Cree and Their Neighbors.* Hull, QC: Canadian Museum of Civilization, 1991.

Sager, David. "Tracking Some Characteristics of Assiniboin Quillwork and Beadwork." *American Indian Art Magazine* 28, no. 1 (Winter 2002): 74–83.

Sainte-Marie, Buffy, and Nova Lawson. *Aboriginal Innovations in Arts, Science and Technology.* Thunder Bay, ON: Lakehead University, 2002.

Schilz, Thomas F. "People of the Cross Timbers: A History of the Tonkawa Indians." PhD diss., Texas Christian University, Fort Worth, 1983.

———. *The Lipan Apaches in Texas.* El Paso: Texas Western Press, 1987.

———. "Plight of the Tonkawas 1875–1898." *Chronicles of Oklahoma* 64, no. 4 (1986): 68–87.

Schneider, Mary Jane. "Kiowa and Comanche Baby Carriers." *Plains Anthropologist* 28, no. 102 (1983): 305–14.

———. *North Dakota's Indian Heritage.* Grand Forks: University of North Dakota Press, 1990.

Schultz, James W. *My Life as an Indian: The Story of a Red Woman and a White Man in the Lodges of the Blackfeet.* New York: SkyHorse, 2010.

Schweinfurth, Kay Parker. *Prayer on Top of the Earth.* Boulder: University Press of Colorado, 2002.

Schweitzer, Marjorie M. *American Indian Grandmothers: Traditions and Transitions.* Albuquerque: University of New Mexico Press, 1999.

Seger, John H. "The Tradition of the Cheyenne as Told to John H. Seger." *Chronicles of Oklahoma* 6, no. 3 (September 1928): 260–70.

Shriver, Anne Marie. "'They Cared for Our Corn in Those Days': The Industrious Women of the Upper Missouri River Tribes." *Points West* (Summer 2000): n.p.

Skinner, Alanson. "Ethnology of the Ioway Indians." *Bulletin of the Public Museum of the City of Milwaukee* 5, no. 4 (1926): 189–293.

———. "Notes on the Plains Cree." *American Anthropologist* 16 (1914): 168–87.

———. "Societies of the Iowa, Kansa, and Ponca Indians." *Anthropological Papers of the American Museum of Natural History* 11, pt. 9 (1915): 679–740.

———. "Traditions of the Iowa Indians." *Journal of American Folk-Lore* 38 (1925): 425–506.

Smith, Monte. *The Techniques of North American Indian Beadwork.* Liberty, Utah: Eagle's View, 1993.

Snell, Alma H. *Grandmother's Grandchild: My Crow Indian Life.* Edited by Becky Matthews. Lincoln: University of Nebraska Press, 2000.

Snow, John. *These Mountains Are Our Sacred Places: The Story of the Stoney Indians.* Toronto: Samuel Stevens, 1977.

Southern Plains Indian Museum and Crafts Center. *The Southern Arapaho.* Anadarko, Okla.: U.S. Department of the Interior, Indian Arts and Craft Board, Southern Plains Indian Museum and Crafts Center [197-].

Spector, Janet D. *What This Awl Means: Feminist Archaeology at a Wahpeton Dakota Village*. St. Paul: Minnesota Historical Society Press, 1993.

Spier, Leslie. "Havasupai Ethnography." *Anthropological Papers of the American Museum of Natural History* 29, pt. 3 (1928): 81–392.

St. Pierre, Mark, and Tilda Long Soldier. *Walking in the Sacred Manner: Healers, Dreamers, and Pipe Carriers—Medicine Women of the Plains Indians*. New York: Simon and Schuster, 1995.

Sutter, Virginia J. *Tell Me, Grandmother: Traditions, Stories, and Culture of Arapaho People*. Boulder: University Press of Colorado, 2004.

"Swaddling: An Option to Encourage 'Back to Sleep'?" *Child Health Alert* 20 (November 2000): 4–5.

Taylor, Colin F., and Hugh Dempsey. *With Eagle Tail: Arnold Lupson and 30 Years among the Sarcee, Blackfoot and Stoney Indians on the North American Plains*. New York: Smithmark, 1999.

Terrell, John Upton. *Apache Chronicle*. New York: World, 1972.

———. *The Plains Apache*. New York: Crowell, 1975.

Tixier, Victor. *Tixier's Travels on the Osage Prairies*. Translated from the French by Albert J. Salvan. Edited by John Francis McDermott. 1844; Norman: University of Oklahoma Press, 1940.

Trenholm, Virginia Cole. *The Arapahoes: Our People*. Norman: University of Oklahoma Press, 1986.

Trowbridge, C. C. *Shawnee Traditions*. Edited by Vernon Kinietz and Erminie W. Voegelin. Ann Arbor: University of Michigan Press, 1939.

Tweedie, M. Jean. "Notes on the History and Adaptation of the Apache Tribes." *American Anthropologist* 70, no. 6 (1968): 1132–43.

Unrau, William E. *Indians of Kansas: The Euro-American Invasion and Conquest of Indian Kansas*. Topeka: Kansas State Historical Society, 1991.

———. *The Kansa Indians: A History of the Wind People, 1673–1873*. Norman: University of Oklahoma Press, 1971.

Vincent, Gilbert T. *Masterpieces of American Indian Art: From the Eugene and Clare Thaw Collection*. New York City: Abrams, 1995.

Voget, Fred W. *They Call Me Agnes: A Crow Narrative Based on the Life of Agnes Yellowtail Deernose*. Norman: University of Oklahoma Press, 1995.

Waldman, Carl. *Atlas of the North American Indian*. Rev. ed. New York: Checkmark Books, 2000.

———. *Encyclopedia of Native American Tribes*. Rev. ed. New York: Checkmark Books, 1999.

Walker, James R. *Lakota Society*. Edited by Raymond J. DeMallie. Lincoln: University of Nebraska Press, 1982.

Wallis, Wilson D. "The Canadian Dakota." *Anthropological Papers of the American Museum of Natural History* 41, pt. 1 (1947): 1–223.

Walters, Anna Lee. *The Spirit of Native America: Beauty and Mysticism in American Indian Art*. San Francisco: Chronicle Books, 1989.

———. *Talking Indian: Reflections on Survival and Writing*. Ithaca, N.Y.: Firebrand Books, 1992.

Wallace, Ernest, and E. Adamson Hoebel. *The Comanches: Lords of the South Plains*. Norman: University of Oklahoma Press, 1952.

Warner, John A. *The Life and Art of the North American Indian*. New York City: Crescent Books, 1975.

Wedel, Waldo Rudolph. *An Introduction to Pawnee Archaeology*. Bureau of American Ethnology Bulletin 112, Smithsonian Institution. Washington, D.C.: GPO, 1936.

Weltfish, Gene. *The Lost Universe*. New York: Basic Books, 1965.

Whitewolf, Jim. *The Life of a Kiowa Apache Indian*. Edited and introduced by Charles S. Brant. New York: Dover, 1969.

Whitman, William. "Origin Legends of the Oto." *Journal of American Folklore* 51 (April–June 1938): 173–205.

———. *The Oto*. New York: Columbia University Press, 1937.

Wildschut, William, and John Ewers. *Crow Indian Beadwork: A Descriptive and Historical Study*. New York: Museum of the American Indian, Heye Foundation, 1959; reprint Liberty, Utah: Eagle's View, 1985.

Will, George F. *Notes of the Arikara Indians and Their Ceremonies*. Old West Series 3. Denver: John VanMale, 1934.

Williamson, Ray A. *Living the Sky: The Cosmos of the American Indian*. Boston: Houghton Mifflin, 1984.

Wilson, Gilbert Livingstone. "The Hidatsa Earthlodge." *Anthropological Papers of the American Museum of Natural History* 33, pt. 5 (1934): 341–420.

———. "The Horse and the Dog in Hidatsa Culture." *Anthropological Papers of the American Museum of Natural History* 15, pt. 2 (1924): 127–311.

———. *Waheenee: An Indian Girl's Story*. St. Paul: Webb, 1921; reprint, Lincoln: University of Nebraska Press, 1981.

Wishart, David J., ed. *Encyclopedia of the Great Plains*. Center for Great Plains Studies, University of Nebraska, Lincoln. Last updated 2003. http://plainshumanities.unl.edu/encyclopedia/.

Wissler, Clark. "Material Culture of the Blackfoot Indians." *Anthropological Papers of the American Museum of Natural History* 5, pt. 1 (1910): 1–175.

———. *North American Indian Beadwork Designs*. 1918; Mineola, N.Y.: Dover, 1999.

———. "Some Protective Designs of the Dakota." *Anthropological Papers of the American Museum of Natural History* 1, pt. 2 (1907): 17–53.

Wood, W. Raymond, and Thomas D. Thiessen, eds. *Early Fur Trade on the Northern Plains: Canadian Traders among the Mandan and Hidatsa Indians, 1738–1818*. Norman: University of Oklahoma Press, 1985.

Woodhead, Henry, ed. *Cycles of Life*. The American Indians series. Alexandra, Va.: Time-Life Books, 1994.

———. *The Buffalo Hunters*. The American Indians series. Alexandra, Va.: Time-Life Books, 1995.

———. *Tribes of the Southern Plains*. The American Indians series. Alexandra, Va.: Time-Life Books, 1995.

Wyckoff, Don G., and Jack L. Hofman, eds. *Pathways to Plains Prehistory: Anthropological Perspectives of Plains Natives and Their Past*. Duncan, Okla.: Cross Timbers Press, 1982.

Yarrow, H. C. "A Further Contribution to the Study of the Mortuary Customs of the North American Indians." In *First Annual Report of the Bureau of Ethnology, 1879–1880*, 87–203. Washington, D.C.: GPO, 1881.

Young, Patrick. "Métis Embroidery." Gabriel Dumont Institute. Last updated 2006. www.virtualmuseum.ca/sgc-cms/expositions-exhibitions/batoche/docs/proof_en_metis_embroidery.pdf.

Young Bear, Severt, and R. D. Theisz. *Standing in the Light: A Lakota Way of Seeing*. Lincoln: University of Nebraska Press, 1994.

Zimmerman, Charles L. *White Eagle, Chief of the Poncas*. Harrisburg, Pa.: Telegraph Press, 1941.

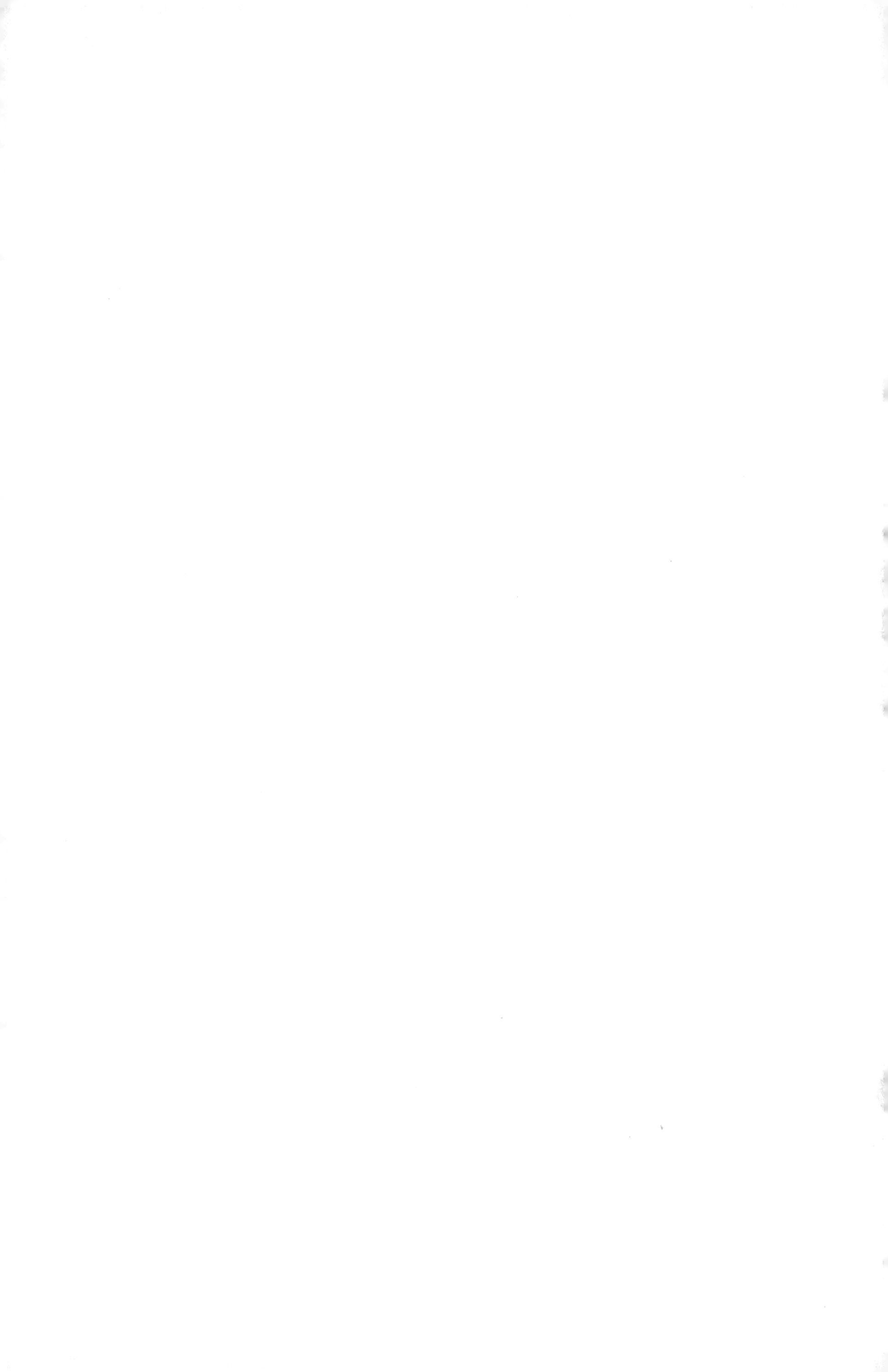